SUFFERING

Its Meaning *for the* Spirit-Filled Life

CRAIG S. KEENER

B
Baker Academic
a division of Baker Publishing Group
Grand Rapids, Michigan

Published by Baker Academic
a division of Baker Publishing Group
Grand Rapids, Michigan
BakerAcademic.com

Printed in the United States of America

Library of Congress Cataloging-in-Publication Data
Names: Keener, Craig S., 1960– author
Title: Suffering : its meaning for the spirit-filled life / Craig S. Keener.
Description: Grand Rapids, Michigan : Baker Academic, a division of Baker Publishing Group,
    [2025] | Includes bibliographical references and index.
Identifiers: LCCN 2025013766 | ISBN 9781540969439 paperback | ISBN 9781540970039 casebound
    | ISBN 9781493453405 ebook | ISBN 9781493453412 pdf
Subjects: LCSH: Suffering—Religious aspects—Christianity | Suffering—Biblical teaching
Classification: LCC BV4909 .K42 2025 | DDC 231/.8—dc23/eng/20250722
LC record available at https://lccn.loc.gov/2025013766

Cover design by Paula Gibson

25   26   27   28   29   30   31   7   6   5   4   3   2   1

To Rolland and Heidi Baker
and Iris Global,
the ministry they founded

CONTENTS

ACKNOWLEDGMENTS

I am grateful to Jim Kinney at Baker Academic for his continual encouragement and support, and to Tim West, one of the best editors in the trade. I am also grateful to those who encouraged this book along the way, including Rolland Baker, R. T. Kendall, Stacey Campbell, and Rob Covell.

A special thanks to Kim Maas. When she was moderating a conference session in Nashville with Jack Deere and me on October 20, 2023, she asked what we believe the church needs for the future. I noted that most of the church in the US isn't ready for suffering and that we need to get ready. Kim then publicly declared, "The church needs a book about suffering, and whenever I pray about it, you come to my mind." She had no idea that I had been discussing such a book with publishers, just waiting for a break in my schedule to write it.

I am grateful to ministries to the persecuted church for their news reports, which supplied many accounts provided in this book. Just as all the author's royalties for *Miracles Today* have gone to compassion ministries, so all those from this book are going to ministries serving the persecuted church.

INTRODUCTION

"Keep on walkin'!" barked the gruff voice from the bench. I was a first-year Bible college student helping at a street mission run by retired Pentecostal church planters. I had come to Christ through others sharing the gospel with me on the street, so I myself would sometimes share Christ with people on the street, including after our evening service and meal for the homeless at the mission.

"I will, sir," I replied, "but first I just wanted to let you know that Jesus loves you."

"I *told* you to keep on walkin'!" the man shouted, bounding from the bench. Within moments, he was pummeling my face with nimble fists. Looking back, I'm pretty sure he was high. I had often shared Christ with people on drugs, but this was the first time one of them responded violently. He was kicking my legs, and I knew that if I fell on the ground—as I had done on other occasions when I was beaten—there would be nothing to stop him from finishing me off. On another occasion someone less angry was present to protest the beating, screaming, "Stop it, John! You're killing him! You're killing him!" and she pulled the aggressor off me as I kept preaching. This time, however, nobody else was even remotely in sight.

"Sir, why are you doing this?" I tried to protest while attempting to back up toward a nearby street corner. "I didn't do anything to you." His rage continued unabated, however. As soon as I reached the corner, I spun around quickly and walked briskly away, feeling that running—if I were still able—would look cowardly. Happily, he did not give chase. "Next time I see you," he shouted after me, "I'll kill you!" Jesus did say to flee from one city to another (Matt. 10:23), and Paul and Barnabas once fled an attempt to stone them (Acts 14:5–6), but I felt ashamed. Should I have just stayed and bravely kept preaching, as I did on earlier occasions when I was beaten? Was I a poor witness to my antagonist?

Certainly that night I could have been more sensitive to the Spirit than I was; I had felt the Spirit's restraint but had assumed that a brief mention of Jesus wouldn't hurt. On another occasion when I was beaten for my witness, my assailant was atop me, slamming my head repeatedly on the floor, tearing out my hair, pounding on my back. I expected death, yet I kept preaching and felt no pain. That was God's grace. This occasion, though, was different. It hurt!

It Could Have Been Worse

Because I escaped when I did, my beating was less severe than what many have experienced. The next day I was sore and had a couple of black eyes, but at the mission we knew of street people who got beaten to death. For example, Pee-wee was on disability, and whenever his check would come some of the other street people would get him drunk and take his money. He became a Christian at the mission and stayed for a while with the Cooks, the retired couple who ran the mission. Eventually, however, he moved to a cheap, roach-infested hotel that was barely a step above living on the street. One day the others beat him close to the point of death. Finding him dying on the street, the police were going to take Pee-wee to the hospital, but he pleaded with them to let him die at the mission instead. The Cooks found him at the door of the mission early that morning, and he died in Sister Cook's arms.

One young man on the street whom I shall here call Dylan used to get high on glue and then beat "Joe," a tall and gentle older man on the street. Dylan had started sniffing glue after his wife left him. One day, Joe's body was found in the bushes outside the Cooks' home. Word on the street was that Dylan was responsible. I didn't yet know Dylan when my much less severe beating took place, but piecing together my snippets of memory I have sometimes wondered whether Dylan was also my own assailant.

My most recent noncommentary book was on miracles, so it is only fitting that this book addresses suffering. Miracles display God's power more directly, but God also provides testimony by sustaining us in hard times. When nonbelievers watch believers suffer the same hardships as nonbelievers, they can witness the eternal hope that sustains those who cling to God. While most stories in *Miracles Today* are encouraging, many stories here are heartbreaking. A balanced Christian spiritual diet, however, includes both kinds of accounts. (Compare the inclusion of both celebration and lament in the Psalms.) In 1950, World Vision founder Bob Pierce cried, "Let my heart be broken with the things that break the heart of God."[1] Just as we "rejoice with those who rejoice," we're also called to "mourn with those who mourn" (Rom. 12:15).

Christians can endure suffering by the power of the Spirit. God often alleviates our suffering, but when he does not, he enables us to go through it (as Paul describes in 2 Cor. 12:9, whatever his debated thorn entailed). I will provide some examples of suffering that perhaps more closely resemble what most of my readers (and I) ordinarily endure, but this book is also meant to stretch us with other examples of greater hardship.

Some stories may sound far removed from where we live, yet we can learn from them. Suffering often comes in unexpected forms. When Médine Moussounga was growing up, her French-speaking country of Congo-Brazzaville was peaceful. She felt sorry for the Ethiopian refugees she saw pouring into her homeland, but she could not imagine that her compatriots would ever experience civil war or famine like Ethiopia had. We don't always give much thought to what others suffer, especially when our hands are full with our own issues. Médine went on to receive her PhD in France and returned to her country hoping to teach in a university. Instead, she landed in the midst of a civil war and eventually became displaced for eighteen months herself. Today Médine is my wife, and I will tell some more of her story later.[2] My point here is just to note that hard times come unbidden and often unexpected.

Merely Samples

Suffering is such a wide topic (including suffering from judgment, war, hunger, and the like) that one could not produce a thorough study on it in Scripture without a volume at least as long as Scripture. Scripture itself spends much more time than I will advising us how to handle suffering. Voice of the Martyrs (VOM), in fact, has produced a devotional using biblical texts meant to encourage those needing to stand firm in their faith—366 passages, one for each day of the year (including the extra day for a leap year).[3] (Because of the accessibility of VOM's material, it is the source of many of the vignettes in this book.)

I therefore don't intend this small book to be comprehensive; I write it in my preaching mode rather than my academic mode.[4] It gives examples of a few kinds of suffering, with a particular but not exclusive focus on suffering for Christ. I am following here the same pattern I used for *Miracles Today*. That book focused more on healing, with just a few nature miracles. Miracle accounts are too numerous to begin trying to recount them all, just as suffering accounts are too numerous to try to recount all of them. Most of the miracles in that book were preceded by suffering, which was why the miracles were needed. In this book I supply examples from both the Bible and elsewhere; I appeal to Scripture as authoritative for us as Christians and use the other examples as illustrations of biblical principles.[5]

Others have contributed far more complete volumes on the subject of suffering in the Christian life, especially regarding persecution today.[6] For example, my friend, New Testament professor Chee-Chiew Lee in Singapore, wrote a recent book about persecution in the New Testament.[7] Earlier, Romanian Christian Joseph Ton wrote a five-hundred-page book on suffering, martyrdom, and heavenly rewards.[8] After being exiled from Romania in 1981, he was invited to teach a course on theological issues in Eastern Europe. He spent half the lectures on being ready to suffer and die for Christ.[9]

Of course, conditions in Eastern Europe are very different now from what they were four or five decades ago, but the lessons Ton preached remain relevant in much of the world today. Illustrations of persecution in some countries today are current as of this book's writing, but as international affairs shift (some undoubtedly already by the time of this book's publication) they will remain no less relevant for our lives than illustrations culled from more distant history.

Many have written books about theodicy, answering questions about God's righteousness in the face of suffering. Though worthy of attention, it is not the primary subject of this book, which is more the *reality* of suffering, a reality from which many of us want to shield our gaze. Still, for the record, I don't believe any alternative worldview offers a more satisfying explanation than the Christian one. Is suffering a punishment for sins in a past life, or working out bad karma? Is it simply personally meaningless, as in atheism? We have a God who suffers with us on the cross, who thereby consecrates our involuntary suffering as worthy of his favor. Jesus's resurrection has guaranteed our future hope of deliverance, comfort, and vindication.

Who Wants More Suffering?

The reality of suffering is so pervasive that I originally wondered why anyone would need to write a book about it. Various charismatic friends, however, have pressed on me the problem that in some charismatic circles, where we expect healing and deliverance, many Christians are confused when it comes to how we should feel about suffering. Does embracing pain express lack of faith? Does suffering reflect God's disapproval, like a spanking or being sent to our room would?[10] These questions might point to imbalance in some of our teachings. In our finitude, even the most zealous Christians sometimes latch onto one truth in a way that obscures other truths.

This problem is not exclusive to my fellow charismatic Christians, nor is this book addressed exclusively to them. But I do keep them in mind and sometimes appeal to them directly. Just as we charismatics rightly believe that the New Testament's spiritual gifts continue, we also ought to believe that New Testament kinds of suffering continue.

Though some of my fellow charismatics believe that faith will *always* heal the sick[11] or can even prevent some persecution,[12] most of us recognize that suffering does challenge us whether we invite it or not. Prayer sometimes averts expected hardships (e.g., 2 Kings 19:20),[13] but sometimes it just gives us strength to face the hardship that is coming (as in Mark 14:38).

Nor does the book address specific end-times views, even though I have one.[14] I have met ordinary Christians who counted on a particular end-time scenario to exempt them from more severe suffering. Yet no view of the end-times suggests that Christians will escape persecution. That would be impossible, especially given the many persecutions Christians have already experienced through history. Whatever we teach, however, some people simply interpret what we or Scripture says to make it say what they would like to be true.

More commonly, some of us think of persecution in terms of friends who tease us about our faith or subtle acts of discrimination (or "microaggressions"). Many of us are familiar with difficulties in paying all our bills or health challenges for us or family members. In the wake of the pandemic, some 36 percent of Americans were suffering from frequent or continual loneliness.[15] An estimated one-fifth of people even in the US suffer from chronic pain and the limitations it imposes on them.[16] But many of us do not want to even entertain the possibility of having to endure still more severe sufferings. Nevertheless, smaller tests can get us ready for larger ones. We should be aware of the kinds of tests that believers face around the world.

Most of us do need to be reminded that God loves to bless his children and that he invites us to look to him with our needs. Some people have experienced so much trauma that they need to hear especially about God's comfort in the midst of sorrow (e.g., 2 Cor. 1:3–5).[17] The balanced kind of book we need most is a book about God's character and his plan to restore humanity at the ultimate cost to himself. That book is the Bible, and there is no need to try to duplicate it here. But many of us also grew up in a culture that relegates all suffering to the same category. For those who have suffered abuse, suffering can feel like God's anger.

Yet most of us who have raised children also recognize that, no matter how much we protect them, children learn some things the hard way. Sometimes we have to balance protecting them with respect for their choices, especially as they become older and must learn responsibility. They will inevitably experience the fruit not only of their choices but also those of others—whether siblings, classmates, teachers, employers, or strangers—from which we cannot always protect them. Sometimes they also suffer for the family's greater good, as when a family must relocate for ministry or even for a safer environment for the children, but the children must leave some friends behind. We suffer with our children when they suffer, but suffering is part of a real world.

The God of the cross is a God who suffers with us. He invites us to work to reduce this world's suffering, but suffering will remain with us until Jesus returns. Death was not God's creation ideal for sinless humanity, but humanity (inevitably?) sinned. In this fallen world, however, the cross demonstrates that obedient suffering can serve God's redemptive purpose.

Romans 8 describes this suffering as pangs that prepare the birth of a new creation (Rom. 8:22). That is, our suffering in this life is not meaningless; Christians suffer in hope, in expectation for the world made new. In the meantime, creation (8:22), we ourselves (8:23), and God's own Spirit (8:26) groan in eagerness for that day. More on that subject in my final chapter.

Suffering Is Coming

Sooner or later, all of us will face suffering—unless we suddenly die first. Whether grief, illness, financial hardship, or another crisis, challenges come unbidden. Given our world's electronic and other vulnerabilities, there is nothing implausible about even the more apocalyptic scenarios some critics offer, such as economic collapse, terrorists contaminating water supplies, outright persecution, or war on our soil. Forewarned is forearmed; recognizing that testing will come (Matt. 18:7; Luke 17:1) helps get us ready. Being faithful to Jesus in our present tests helps make us ready for future ones. Understanding that eternal blessing follows helps us endure even our worst testing. Knowing what others have gone through also provides encouragement that we can make it too.

Suffering is not the most popular topic. Yet we must teach what Scripture teaches, even when it makes us feel uncomfortable. When we stand before the Lord at the judgment, what will matter will not be how big our churches are or how many followers we have on Facebook. What will matter will be that we have prepared disciples who can persevere no matter what.

> If you remain established and firm in the faith, not moved from the hope of the good news. . . . We announce Christ, warning everyone and teaching everyone in all wisdom, so we may present everyone complete in Christ. (Col. 1:23, 28)

When I couldn't stand it any longer, I also sent to learn how your faith was, lest the tempter have tempted you successfully and our labor over you have proved worthless. (1 Thess. 3:5)

Although most of us understand that our suffering is not always the result of something wrong we have done, it can be easy to forget that. My own life overflows with the blessings of family, health, and friends, yet like a spoiled child my heart often still protests the fairness of comparatively minor inconveniences.

Perhaps in an ideal world where the righteous lived perfectly and everyone was righteous, there might be little if any need for the righteous to suffer. But that is not yet the world in which we live.

In contrast with my scholarly books, this one merely skims a vast subject just enough to make the point: Scripture is clear that suffering is a fundamental part of the Spirit-filled Christian life. This is even true—indeed, perhaps especially true—for apostles and prophets (treated in chaps. 2 and 3), two groups that interest many charismatics in particular (and, for apostles and prophets in the Bible, all other Christians as well). But first, let's look at why Jesus is worth whatever cost in this world we need to pay to follow him.

CHAPTER ONE

Jesus Is Worth Everything

Jesus is up front with us that there is a cost to following him. From God's side, the gift of life in him is free—or rather, already paid for by what Jesus suffered for us. But we live in a world that challenges our faith, so from the world's side our faith is bound to cost us hardships. Yet God empowers us by his Spirit to maintain our witness for Christ in this world no matter what.

Jesus Comes Before Everything Else

We could explore various ways that Jesus calls us to make disciples of all peoples (Matt. 28:19), and we will explore one of those ways later in this book. One obvious feature of making disciples for Jesus, however, is teaching everyone to obey Jesus's commands (28:20), not least those that specifically concern being his disciples. Jesus is king in God's kingdom (28:18), so obeying him is paramount.

In Matthew's Gospel, being a disciple of Jesus ranks above job security. Commercial fishermen and tax collectors normally made a better-than-average living, but some members of both professions leave behind their livelihoods to follow Jesus (Matt. 4:18–22; 9:9; compare Mark 1:16–20; 2:14).

Jesus is also above residential security. As Jesus prepares to cross the Lake of Galilee, a prospective disciple offers to follow him wherever he is headed. Jesus makes clear that following Jesus is costly. Foxes and birds have homes, but Jesus's mission leaves him no permanent place to lay his head (Matt. 8:19–20; compare Luke 9:57–58).

Jesus is above financial security. When a person of means asks how to receive eternal life, Jesus summons him to give away his wealth and follow

Jesus. Forced to choose, the man chooses to keep his wealth (Matt. 19:16–22; compare Mark 10:17–22).

Jesus is above family ties. "Whoever loves father or mother more than me is not worthy of me, and whoever loves son or daughter more than me is not worthy of me" (Matt. 10:37; compare Luke 14:26).

Jesus is above all social obligations. Burying one's parents after their deaths was the ultimate act of filial piety; failing to bury one's father could leave one a permanent outcast from one's village. When someone asks to attend to his father's burial before following Jesus,[1] however, Jesus makes clear the necessary priority: "Follow me, and let the dead people bury their own dead" (Matt. 8:22; compare Luke 9:60).

Finally, Jesus is above life itself. "And whoever doesn't take up their cross and follow me isn't worthy of me" (Matt. 10:38; compare Luke 14:27). "Then Jesus said to his disciples, 'If anybody wants to come after me, let them deny themselves and take up their cross and follow me'" (Matt. 16:24; compare Mark 8:34).

The Cost of Discipleship

In his book *The Cost of Discipleship*, theologian Dietrich Bonhoeffer comments more extensively about the rich man who chose to keep his wealth rather than to follow Jesus (Matt. 19:16–22; Mark 10:17–22; Luke 18:18–23). Bonhoeffer remarks that the difference between the rich man and us is that Jesus stood before him so he could not conveniently reinterpret Jesus's words. Bonhoeffer compares a boy told by his father.to go to bed; the boy has studied theology, however, so the boy now can reinterpret his father as ultimately just wanting him not to be tired. Surely going out to play will cure the exhaustion just as well as going to bed, right? All too often, Bonhoeffer complained, professed Christians reason away the Lord's demands in like manner.[2] Bonhoeffer's theology changed over time, but he maintained the path of resisting evil. In connection with this resistance, he was executed under Hitler.

Each of the Gospels qualifies Jesus's radical teachings with narrative, revealing an absolute standard implemented with grace. Jesus's disciples, most of whom were probably teenagers, discovered that while their spirits were willing, their flesh was weak (Matt. 26:41; Mark 14:38). They had abandoned everything else to follow him (Matt. 19:27; Mark 10:28), but when it came time to follow him to the death they all abandoned him (Matt. 26:56; Mark 14:50). When the time came to carry the cross and follow Jesus, Rome's soldiers had to draft a bystander, Simon of Cyrene, because Jesus's "followers," who were supposed to take up the cross, were nowhere in sight (Matt. 27:32; Mark 15:21).

Yet Jesus did not repudiate his disciples. He doesn't lower the standard to what we are, but his patient grace transforms us into what he has called us to be. "Follow me," Jesus promises, "and *I* will make you fishers of people" (Matt. 4:19; compare Mark 1:17). Jesus empowers us by his Spirit (Matt. 3:11; Mark 1:8).

How Much Is Jesus Worth?

Many Christians are familiar with the story of Richard Wurmbrand, who endured fourteen years of torture and imprisonment in Communist Romania. Wurmbrand emphasizes that our identity is determined not by the creed we recite but by what we are "ready to die for." Those who remain faithful when tested by persecution or other hardship reveal what they *really* believe in their hearts.[3] He mentions one young prisoner, a high official's daughter who had become a believer. She loudly recited the Apostles' Creed as she was marched to her execution. She was proclaiming the eternal hope to which the Creed bears witness.[4]

Matthew 26:6–16 offers three contrasting estimates of Jesus's worth.[5] For the woman who anoints Jesus in 26:7, Jesus is worth everything; she lavishes her affection on him, pouring out all her expensive ointment. Whereas others are thinking about their roles and gains in the future kingdom (e.g., 18:1; 19:27; 20:21), and Jesus welcomes the many who seek him for blessings (e.g., 4:24; 8:2–3, 5–17; 9:2–7, 27–30), she comes not for what she can get from Jesus, but what she can offer him. She is a model of the deepest devotion to the Lord.

By contrast, the male disciples, soon to fail the Lord in his time of testing (Matt. 26:40–56), oppose her action as wasteful. They think of other, supposedly better, uses for the resources (26:8–9). Their interest is not selfish per se; they want to expend the resources on the poor, which is in keeping with Jesus's own teaching. After all, Jesus told a young man who wanted to follow him to sell all his goods and give to the poor (19:21). But their focus is distorted; they criticize a particularly devoted follower for lavishing her love on Jesus. God must be the supreme object of our love (22:36–37). Jesus had told that young prospective follower not only to give his resources to the poor but, "Come, follow me" (19:21). Without Jesus being central and renewing us, all our other service, no matter how good, can just burn us out.

The devotion of the woman who anoints Jesus contrasts with the collective attitude of the male disciples, but it contrasts even more starkly with Judas's mindset. Like some professed worshipers of God today, Judas seeks only what he can get from Jesus (Matt. 26:14–16). Once Judas learns that Jesus's kingdom will not profit him materially (and may even cost him his life), he chooses to get what he still can from his lengthy investment in Jesus. He sells his Lord for the Old Testament price of a slave (Matt. 26:15; Exod. 21:32). Like another disciple of old (2 Kings 5:26–27), Judas abandons his spiritual birthright for material prosperity. In saving his own life, he loses it for eternity (Matt. 16:24–27; 27:1–10). Like Judas, some people even today decide that the cost of serving Jesus is higher than it is worth.

Jesus and his kingdom are like a pearl of great price or treasure hidden in a field. Jesus is worth sacrificing everything else for this one treasure that is more valuable than everything else put together (Matt. 13:44–46). The rich young ruler chose to keep his earthly wealth over following the king who grants eternal life. True disciples must follow Jesus no matter what the cost.

Baptism in the Spirit and Suffering

Those of us who value the gift of the Spirit often emphasize how the Lord uses this gift to empower us for mission. Sometimes, however, we forget what that mission may involve.

> Instead, you'll receive power when the Holy Spirit comes on you, and you'll be my witnesses in Jerusalem and all Judea and Samaria and as far as the end of the earth. (Acts 1:8)

> See, I'm sending you out like lambs among wolves. (Luke 10:3)

Luke's two-volume work uses the Greek term *dunamis* ("power") to refer to healing or exorcism more than to anything else (Luke 4:36; 5:17; 6:19; 8:46; 9:1; Acts 3:12; 4:7; 6:8; 10:38). The plural form of this word is usually translated "miracles" (Luke 10:13; 19:37; Acts 2:22; 8:13; 19:11). Vineyard leader John Wimber was right, then, to speak of such witness in terms of "power evangelism." Throughout the book of Acts, the most common means narrated of getting people's attention for the gospel is signs (e.g., 2:12, 16; 3:11–12; 4:29–30; 14:3; 15:12). Luke does not directly associate them with every believer, but neither does he limit them to the apostles (Acts 6:8; 8:6, 13; 9:17–18). The Spirit's role may also include leading us to know how and when God wants us to bring healing in Jesus's name.

Yet such power evangelism is hardly associated with a life of ease. As suggested by Jesus's earlier instructions (Luke 9:3–5; 10:3–4, 10–15), Jesus's agents in Acts must travel fairly simply and face considerable opposition (e.g.,

Acts 12:2–3; 14:5–6, 19; 16:22–23). Already in Acts 4–5, the temple authorities arrest, beat, and consider killing the apostles. Signs don't guarantee that people will be converted. Jesus criticizes many towns whose residents witness his miracles without repenting (Matt. 11:21–23; Luke 10:13–15). Miracles by themselves don't convert people; they just make the gospel impossible to ignore. Some will respond in faith; others will respond by trying to shut down the message (e.g., Acts 14:3–5). That's why we need the Spirit to continue granting us boldness (Acts 4:8, 13, 29–31).

Jesus's warning about what Spirit-empowered witnesses will face appears in all the Gospels, in one form or another:

> When they hand you over, don't worry how you'll speak or what you'll say, because what you should say will be given you in that hour. That's because it's not you speaking then, but the Spirit of your Father speaking by you. (Matt. 10:19–20)

> And the good news must first be preached among all peoples. And when they bring you to court and hand you over for arrest, don't worry beforehand about what you should say. Instead, speak whatever is given you in that hour, because you're not the one speaking it, but the Holy Spirit. (Mark 13:10–11)

> When they bring you before the synagogues and the rulers and authorities, don't worry how you should defend yourselves or what you should say, because the Holy Spirit will teach you in that very hour the things you need to say. (Luke 12:11–12)

> [Initially], they will just throw you out of synagogues; but the time is coming for everyone who kills you to suppose that they are offering worship to God! (John 16:2)

Both in the Bible and today, reaching the lost usually entails a measure of hardship.

Our Model for the Spirit-Empowered Life

Toward the beginning of his Gospel, Mark shows us what Spirit-baptized Christians should expect. Jesus, who baptizes in the Holy Spirit (Mark 1:8), is endowed with the Spirit himself at his baptism (1:10). Jesus thus becomes not just the Spirit-baptizer but also the model for the Spirit-baptized life.

Yet the Spirit does not lead Jesus into a life of ease; sometimes God's call sends us into greater hardships for a greater purpose (see, e.g., Exod.

3:10; Josh. 1:2; 1 Sam. 22:5; Jer. 1:17–19; Acts 9:16; 16:9).[6] The Spirit im-mediately hurls Jesus into the wilderness for testing, for conflict with Satan (Mark 1:12–13). This is how Jesus begins modeling the Spirit-baptized life for those he will baptize in the Spirit! The rest of Mark's Gospel recounts Jesus performing Spirit-filled miracles—and facing increasing opposition from Satan's religious and political agents. Do we *really* want to be baptized with the baptism that Jesus was baptized with (10:38)? Such a price should not surprise us since the servant is not greater than the master (Matt. 10:24–25; John 13:16).

Signs get attention. They do not always get acceptance.

He casts out demons by the ruler of the demons! (Mark 3:22)

It's enough for the disciple to be like their teacher and the slave like their mas-ter. If others have called the head of the house Beelzebul, how much more the members of his house! (Matt. 10:25)

What are we doing about this man doing many signs? If we let him keep doing this, everyone will believe in him! (John 11:47–48)

They came, not just because of Jesus, but also so they could see Lazarus whom Jesus had raised from the dead. So the chief priests decided together to kill Lazarus as well, since many Judeans were going and trusting in Jesus because of him. (John 12:9–11)

Stephen, full of grace and power, performed great wonders and signs among the people. . . . Then they secretly instigated some men to say, "We heard him speak blasphemous words against Moses and God." (Acts 6:8, 11)

So they stayed there for a long time, speaking boldly for the Lord, who testi-fied to the message about his grace by granting signs and wonders to be done through them. But the town's people were divided, some favoring the Jews, but others the apostles. And when both gentiles and Jews, with their leaders, rushed to abuse and stone them . . . (Acts 14:3–5)

Revivals Among the Broken

The Spirit's work is often deepest where people are most desperate for him, and people are often most desperate in hardship. Spirit-filled scholar Jack Deere notes that in general miracles are reported most "where persecution was the most intense and godly people were desperate for God's help."[7]

Iris Global is a Spirit-filled (and in the common sense noted in chap. 2, apostolic) church-planting movement. Its participants have witnessed abundant signs—including healings of blindness and raisings from the dead—with tens of thousands won to Christ. Here is the third among its five core values:

> We look for revival among the broken, humble and lowly, and start at the bottom with ministry to the poor. God chooses the weak and despised things of the world to shame the proud, demonstrating His own strength and wisdom. Our direction is [humbling ourselves] lower still.[8]

Iris's members depend on God alone, rather than worldly power, recognizing that God's power is revealed in human vulnerability.

In biblical times and today, reaching the lost usually involves suffering. Even where the most dramatic miracles are occurring today, suffering is also present—including among those through whom the miracles are accomplished.

In the early twentieth century, Shang-chieh Sung (John Sung), from Fujian Province in southeast China, engaged in the apostolic sort of evangelism with signs and wonders that we see in Acts. He was China's best-known evangelist of that era[9] and is usually regarded as one of the leading early figures of indigenous Chinese Christianity.[10] He has been called "probably the single most powerful figure in Chinese revivalism in the mid-1930s,"[11] perhaps "the greatest Chinese revivalist of the twentieth century,"[12] and "China's George Whitefield."[13] He impacted Asia beyond China,[14] and his strategic form of discipleship through small groups remained important even in Indonesia.[15] Yet Sung spent three years suffering from an agonizing illness that finally took his life.[16]

Conferences about miracles are well attended. Far less common in the charismatic spotlight is the global persecution of Christians. What about conferences on global missions that remind us that spreading good news about Jesus is worth any price?[17] Or those that cultivate empowerment and gifting *for the purpose* of mission?

What about conferences focusing on how revival usually comes to the lowly and the *broken*?[18] Brokenness is often the matrix for revival. Revival is rarer in centers of status.

- Whitefield and the Wesley brothers preached to masses in the fields, much to the dismay of more "proper" churchmen.
- Much of the Second Great Awakening happened on the then-frontier rather than in (and sometimes receiving criticism from) the venerated halls of academia.

- The Welsh Revival (1904–1905) began among miners, who worked in a long-dangerous profession.
- India's Mukti Mission Revival (1905) began among orphan girls.
- The son of former slaves led the interracial Azusa Street Revival (1906–1908).
- The 1907 revival in Korea began after years of suffering and helped fortify the church for sufferings to come.
- The bloody Biafra War (1967–1970) killed between half a million and three million in Nigeria, especially in its southeast. Some estimate that the resultant famine alone killed a million Igbos. In the war's wake the interdenominational work of Scripture Union birthed the massive Nigerian revival.[19]
- More recent revivals include those among repressed or neglected people in, for example, China and Mozambique.

Revival movements often emerge among young people who feel alienated from society's structures. These include the Jesus Movement or, again, Nigeria's student movement through Scripture Union. Briefer college outpourings, such as the life-changing one many of us experienced at Asbury University in 2023, have often come to young people desperate for a fresh touch from God. That is, God is near the lowly (Ps. 138:6; Prov. 3:34; Matt. 23:12; Luke 14:11; James 4:6; 1 Pet. 5:5) and those who hunger and thirst for him (Pss. 42:2; 63:1; Matt. 5:6).

Revival May Prepare Us for Hardship

Sometimes revival comes after hardship, but sometimes it comes to get us ready. An 1857–1859 prayer revival started among businessmen in New York City and led to an estimated million conversions (about 4 percent of the US population at the time)—on the eve of the bloody Civil War (1860–1865). Many of those stirred by the Welsh Revival of 1904–1905 perished on the battlefields of World War I. Recent years of miracles and massive conversions in Mozambique prepared the growing church there for the current wave of martyrdoms and intense persecution the Christians have been facing.

In 1965, God sent a revival in West Timor, Indonesia, during a period of instability. Even greater instability soon struck the nation as a whole. Several days after the revival began, Indonesia claimed a Communist coup attempt, which over the next year led to the slaughter of hundreds of thousands of suspected Communist sympathizers in various parts of the country. In some other parts of the country, dismay at the massive slaughter turned many to Christ.[20] More recently, Mel Tari, a leader in that revival, shared with me the important insight that revival is never the end of a work of God; it is the beginning.[21]

Here I comment especially on the Korean Revival, which strengthened the church in the face of continued foreign domination. Korean Christians understand *han*, a sort of suffering that one cannot translate into English with a single term.[22] Koreans faced unimaginable sufferings from the Japanese occupation during World War II. A particularly hideous example is that soldiers forced an estimated two hundred thousand Korean women into sex slavery, each of them raped an average of twenty to thirty times per day, and most killed afterward to conceal the atrocities.[23]

The overlords forced all students to worship at shrines of Japanese deities. Christians who resisted were mercilessly beaten, had bamboo needles thrust under their nails, and were tortured in other ways.[24] Prisoners were fed such meager rations[25] that one group of them, for example, divided and devoured a cowhide belt.[26] They endured numbing cold; in warmer weather, nocturnal chinch bugs crawled all over them, leaving many bites.[27] One minister recounted, "I have never heard God's voice so clearly as in these days. . . . Only at such times as these of persecution and disorder by the hands of Satan do believers awaken in faith."[28]

Although the Korean Revival started in the north, eventually the church in the north had to go underground. While the proportion of Christians in South Korea is now the second highest in Asia, the repression of Christians is harsher in North Korea than in any other country in the world. In 1950, some three hundred thousand Protestants and fifty-seven thousand Catholics lived in North Korea, but repression came quickly, with Christians being crucified, roasted over fires, and "crushed under steamrollers." North Korea's leader insisted that progress required the state to execute all believers who would not recant their faith.[29] Authorities sent Christians' children to prison camps where they could be "reeducated."[30] Vast numbers, variously estimated from one million to five million, fled south, abandoning their homes.[31]

One Christian torture victim explains that her captors nearly suffocated her, knocked out her teeth, and tore out her nails.[32] She estimates that thirty to forty captives in the camp died each day; prisoners "were so hungry that we would take food from the mouths of dead people, or fight for the undigested corn husks found in animal faeces." "Cells" in her camp lacked roofs.[33] Paul Marshall, Lela Gilbert, and Nina Shea open their book on global persecution with the report of a North Korean woman summarily shot to death when a Bible was discovered in her home.[34] Still, we need not conclude that North

Korea is without hope. Albania once hosted the atheist regime that was the most repressive against faith; today fewer than 4 percent of Albanians are atheists, with 80 percent professing some religious faith.

Conclusion

Jesus is worth everything, and he more than rewards us eternally for any sacrifice we make to follow him. God's Spirit empowers us for his mission in the world. But mission is not always easy—as is true for life itself. Indeed, Scripture illustrates this pattern in the missions and lives of apostles and prophets.

CHAPTER TWO

Apostles and Suffering

For I think that God has displayed us apostles last, exhibited like those condemned to death, because we've been made a public spectacle to the world, both to angels and people. . . . Even to this present hour we go hungry and thirsty and are poorly clothed and beaten and homeless and we endure manual labor. When others ridicule us, we bless them; when we are persecuted, we endure it; when people slander us, we speak encouragement. We're treated like this world's trash, like the scrapings of everything, even until now.

—the apostle Paul, 1 Corinthians 4:9–13

So do not be ashamed of the testimony about our Lord or of me his prisoner. Rather, join with me in suffering for the gospel, by the power of God.

—2 Timothy 1:8 (NIV)

Last of All

It's very popular today to talk about apostolic ministry, though not everyone agrees on the definition. The Gospels usually reserve the term *apostle* for the original Twelve, but Paul uses the term more broadly for those establishing new ground for the kingdom, laying foundations in new spheres (e.g., Rom. 1:1; 1 Cor. 15:7; Gal. 1:19; 1 Thess. 2:6–7).[1] In this chapter, I am using Paul's broader definition.

I met Baba Tambaya Jibirin on July 2, 1998, with my close Nigerian friend Emmanuel Itapson. Emmanuel's father had worked with Baba Tambaya planting churches in northern Nigeria a generation earlier. By the broader Pauline definition, Baba Tambaya was surely an apostle. In one story about him, he boarded a bus and started preaching, and the bus driver ordered him to get off. "All right," Baba Tambaya warned, "I'll walk, but I'll get there before this bus does." It would take days to walk to the destination city! But as soon as he got out and the driver tried to start the bus, the engine was dead. So some people ran after Baba Tambaya and begged him to board the bus again. Once he got aboard, the bus started—and he preached about Jesus all the way to their destination.

Yet Baba Tambaya also suffered for his witness. On one occasion, like Paul, he was stoned and left for dead (Acts 14:19; 2 Cor. 11:25). Some of his fellow Christians thought that the stoning had made Baba Tambaya unstable mentally. Every morning he would sound a call to Christian prayer before the Muslim prayer call. As a night person, I personally can see why some would find this disturbing! But one fully enculturated missionary confided to me, "I sometimes think that Baba Tambaya is really saner than the rest of us."

Whereas Paul lists apostles first among gifts in 1 Corinthians 12:28, in 1 Corinthians 4:9 he describes them as "last," like the climactic spectacle that bloodthirsty Romans would watch die in the arena. Although it is popular today to hail "apostolic" ministries, a key biblical hallmark of such ministry is *suffering*. As Jack Deere points out, "The main proof of [Paul's] apostleship was the sufferings he endured for Christ and the gospel ([2 Cor.] 11:16–33)."[2]

Daniel Kolenda, appointed successor to Reinhard Bonnke and one of the world's leading evangelists today, points out that when people challenged Paul's apostleship, you might have expected him to have "flashed his 'big-A' credentials": "Hey, you'd better listen to me because I'm a big-A apostle!" Instead Paul cites as proof of his apostolic status his suffering for Christ. "In five passages between both Corinthian letters, Paul catalogs his hardships specifically to demonstrate that he is an apostle of Christ."[3]

Hungry, Shabby, Imprisoned Witnesses

In Matthew's Gospel, Jesus sends out his first apostles with a promise of signs (Matt. 10:8) along with far more extensive warnings about suffering (10:16–39). Matthew later revisits ongoing apostolic ministry as the good news goes out to the nations. Although we often apply the phrase "the least of these my brothers" to the poor (and God does reward concern for the poor as service to himself, for example in Prov. 19:17), that is probably not its sense in Matthew 25. In Matthew 25:31–46, "the least of these my brothers" (and sisters) probably refers to those sent to spread the good news. This seems clear when we compare language there with that of the rest of Matthew's Gospel elsewhere.

Matthew 10 and Elsewhere Before Matthew 25	Matthew 25
Good news about the kingdom must be preached among all nations before the end comes (24:14).	The nations are judged at the end (25:32).
God will reward whoever gives disciples even a cup of cold water (10:42).	The righteous fed and gave drink to Jesus's representatives (25:35).
God will bless whatever house takes in Jesus's emissaries (10:11–13).	The righteous took in Jesus's representatives, though they were strangers (25:35).
Jesus's emissaries will face courts, beatings, and persecution (10:16–22).	The righteous visited Jesus's representatives when they were sick or in prison (25:36).
Whoever receives his disciples receives Jesus (10:40).	Whatever was done for Jesus's representatives was done for Jesus himself (25:40).
Jesus's followers are his brothers and sisters (12:48–50).	Jesus's representatives are his brothers and sisters (25:40).
The wicked who do not receive Jesus's representatives will be judged (10:14–15).	The wicked who did not receive Jesus's representatives will be judged (25:41–46).

When others feed them and take them in, they are welcoming Jesus—just as with the apostles earlier sent out in Matthew 10:11–13, 40–42 (compare 2 Cor. 5:20; 6:13). Elsewhere in Matthew, Jesus's true brothers (and sisters) always refer to his followers (Matt. 12:48–50; 23:8–9; 28:10). Likewise, those who reject Jesus's agents and face judgment in 25:41–46 sound like those who rejected Jesus's agents in 10:13–15. Notice again the conditions that may characterize Jesus's agents as they labor for him in Matthew 25: "hungry . . . thirsty . . . needing a place to stay . . . poorly clothed . . . sick . . . imprisoned" (25:35–39, 42–44).[4]

Suffering often occurs in the context of mission. Brother Andrew, founder of Open Doors, emphasized that there is no place in the world that the gospel cannot penetrate, but he also warned about the cost: "Show me a closed door and I will tell you how you can get in. I won't, however, promise you a way to get out."[5]

An Apostle Named Paul

Certainly such suffering was evident in Paul's ministry. When Paul writes from Roman custody, he calls himself "the prisoner of Christ Jesus for the sake of you gentiles" (Eph. 3:1) and speaks further of his sufferings for them (3:13). Following Jesus's teaching (Mark 13:9), Paul views his arrest as an opportunity to spread the gospel further (Phil. 1:7, 12).

Of course, Paul was not *trying* to suffer or go hungry.[6] He simply learned to be content, trusting Christ's power whether he was full or hungry, whether he had more than enough or was in need (Phil. 4:11–13). In a fallen world, suffering was often a necessary part of Paul's mission. It was in fact explicitly part of Paul's calling from the start. Part of the prophetic message that God gives Ananias for Paul is, "I will show him the things he *must suffer* on behalf of my name" (Acts 9:16). Luke, who records that message, sometimes uses the term *must* for God's plan, including for suffering as part of Jesus's own mission (Luke 9:22; 17:25; 24:7, 26; Acts 17:3). Paul and Barnabas later use this same term to tell new believers what *all* Christians must be ready to face. When they exhorted "them to remain true to the faith," they explained, "'We *must* go through many hardships to enter the kingdom of God'" (Acts 14:22 NIV, emphasis mine).

In context, these passages focus on the opposition we may face for following Jesus in a world that does not understand his values.

Apostle to the Corinthians

Paul's emphasis on apostolic suffering becomes especially clear in 2 Corinthians, where Paul will eventually contrast his ministry with that of false apostles.

> For just as we share abundantly in the sufferings of Christ, so also our comfort abounds through Christ. (2 Cor. 1:5 NIV)

> Just as you are sharers in our sufferings, so you are also in the comfort. (1:7)

> We do not want you to be unaware, brothers and sisters, of the affliction we experienced in Asia; for we were so utterly, unbearably crushed that we despaired of life itself. Indeed, we felt that we had received the sentence of death so that we would rely not on ourselves but on God who raises the dead. (1:8–9 NRSV)

> But thanks be to God, who always leads us as captives in Christ's triumphal procession and uses us to spread the aroma of the knowledge of him . . . among those who are being saved and those who are perishing. To the one we are an aroma that brings death; to the other, an aroma that brings life. (2:14–16 NIV)

Rome executed most captives at the end of a triumphal procession. Just as people without faith viewed Christ's cross as failure, so those without faith viewed apostolic suffering as the stench of death. Those who trust God's message, however, experience the aroma of life both in the cross and in what apostles sacrificed to bring others God's message.

That is why, for Christ's sake, I delight in weaknesses, in insults, in hardships, in persecutions, in difficulties. For when I am weak, then I am strong. (2 Cor. 12:10 NIV)

Paul chose to embrace his sufferings for Christ, recognizing that God's grace would be more than commensurate with his suffering.[7]

Listing His Sufferings in 2 Corinthians 4 and 6

Ancient sages sometimes listed their sufferings to prove that they genuinely believed and lived for their message.[8] Paul does the same.

> We are afflicted in every way, but not crushed;
>> perplexed, but not driven to despair;
>> persecuted, but not forsaken;
>> struck down, but not destroyed;
>> always carrying in the body the death of Jesus, so that the life of Jesus may also be made visible in our bodies.
> For while we live, we are always being given up to death for Jesus' sake,
>> so that the life of Jesus may be made visible in our mortal flesh.
>> (2 Cor. 4:8–11 NRSV modified)

> Rather, as servants of God we commend ourselves in every way:
>> in great endurance;
>> in troubles, hardships and distresses;
>> in beatings, imprisonments and riots;
>> in hard work, sleepless nights and hunger;
>> in purity, understanding, patience and kindness;
>> . . . through glory and dishonor, bad report and good report;
>> genuine, yet regarded as impostors; . . .
>> dying, and yet we live on;
>> beaten, and yet not killed;
>> . . . poor, yet making many rich;
>> having nothing, and yet possessing everything. (2 Cor. 6:4–6, 8–10 NIV modified)

False Apostles

Paul's longest list of sufferings comes near the end of the letter. Here Paul contrasts himself with "false apostles" who are pretending to be true ones (2 Cor. 11:13). As noted earlier, there were genuine apostles beyond the twelve original ones (1 Cor. 15:5–7). These included

- Paul himself (Rom. 1:1),
- Barnabas (1 Cor. 9:5–6),
- James the brother of Jesus (Gal. 1:19),
- Silas and Timothy (1 Thess. 1:1; 2:6),
- and others (Rom. 16:7).

Nevertheless, false apostles also existed, requiring churches' discernment (Rev. 2:2). Paul distinguishes these false apostles from himself partly on the basis of fruits of ministry. Paul had founded Jesus's movement in Corinth (1 Cor. 9:2); he sought to lay foundations where churches did not exist before (Rom. 15:20). The false apostles, by contrast, simply tried to come in and take over what real apostles had started, while claiming the title for themselves (2 Cor. 10:12–16).

Paul therefore elaborates the differences between himself and the false apostles. The Corinthians themselves witnessed divine miracles through Paul (2 Cor. 12:12), and he had plenty of visions, though he had learned not to boast about them (12:1–7). But central to Paul's apostolic ministry, proving his genuine commitment to Christ, was not only his ministry or miracles but also his sufferings. Although he mentions visions and miracles, he elaborates on sufferings most extensively by far.

Paul's Qualifications in 2 Corinthians 11

After explaining why he has to "boast" at all, Paul offers a résumé that boasts in the sorts of things that most of his contemporaries instead considered embarrassing:

> Are they servants of Christ?—I am speaking as if insane—I more so;
>   in far more labors,
>   in far more imprisonments,
>   beaten times without number,
>   often in danger of death.
> Five times I received from the Jews thirty-nine lashes.
> Three times I was beaten with rods,
> once I was stoned,
> three times I was shipwrecked, a night and a day I have spent adrift at sea.
> I have been
>   on frequent journeys,
>   in dangers from rivers,
>   dangers from robbers,
>   dangers from my countrymen,

> dangers from the Gentiles,
> dangers in the city,
> dangers in the wilderness,
> dangers at sea,
> dangers among false brothers;
> I have been
> in labor and hardship,
> through many sleepless nights,
> in hunger and thirst,
> often without food,
> in cold and exposure.
> Apart from such external things, there is the daily pressure on me of
> concern for all the churches.
> Who is weak without my being weak?
> Who is led into sin without my intense concern? (2 Cor. 11:23–29
> NASB modified)

Imagine evaluating a résumé for a pastoral search committee that highlighted how many times your beloved government had arrested the candidate! To top it all off, Paul adds a story that some might have considered cowardice—the opposite of the honor given to any (surviving) Roman soldier to be first to scale an enemy wall. When Paul's enemies were guarding Damascus's gates to capture him if he tried to flee, "I was let down in a basket through a window in the wall, and so escaped" (2 Cor. 11:33 NASB).

Crucified with Christ

Paul learned to boast in his weakness so that any credit would go to the one to whom it was due: the Lord working in him. Paul's hard situations made him rely all the more on Christ, on whom he depended literally for dear life. Jesus told Paul that Jesus's power was completed in weakness. Paul thus insisted,

> Most gladly, therefore, I will rather boast about my weaknesses, so that the power of Christ may dwell in me. Therefore I delight in weaknesses, in insults, in distresses, in persecutions, in difficulties, in behalf of Christ; for when I am weak, then I am strong. (2 Cor. 12:9–10 NASB)

In so doing, he was embodying the message of the cross that he preached. Christ

> was crucified in weakness, but he's alive by God's power. In the same way, we are weak in him, but we shall live with him by God's power in us. (2 Cor. 13:4)

Paul was preaching to a church that reflected the values of its culture. Ancient sources show us how much Corinth valued the quest for honor, social power, and wise speech. Paul's preaching challenged these cultural values:

> We preach Christ crucified, a stumbling block to Jews and folly to Gentiles, but to those who are called, both Jews and Greeks, Christ the power of God and the wisdom of God. For the foolishness of God is wiser than men, and the weakness of God is stronger than men. (1 Cor. 1:23–25 ESV)

Similarly, after emphasizing that he has been crucified with Christ (Gal. 2:20), Paul notes that the Galatians had witnessed Christ depicted as crucified in him before their eyes (3:1). While "before your eyes" was a common expression for dramatically narrating an event so that audiences felt that they themselves witnessed it, Paul may have had a more literal visual aid.[9] Just as Jesus showed his wounds after the resurrection (John 20:20), Paul declared that he carried in his body the marks of Jesus (Gal. 6:17). In contrast with his circumcision (see 6:13, 15), these marks—probably scars from past beatings—demonstrated his sharing in Christ's cross (see 6:12, 14). These were his trophies, his medals of honor. Because the apostolic mission requires suffering, Paul elsewhere even says that he rejoices in his sufferings for the church,

> completing in my flesh what remains of Christ's sufferings for his body.
> (Col. 1:24)

In the wider, Pauline sense of apostles as those who lay new foundations for the kingdom, we may, as already noted, apply the label generally to planters of church movements laying foundational new ground in unevangelized areas or spheres. Satan, however, does not surrender ground gladly, and those who break new ground are also often themselves broken in some ways. Although Axum in East Africa, for example, received the gospel peacefully, many other mission fields in history, including many in Europe, were opened through the blood of martyrs.

Apostolic Determination: Other Cross-Cultural Laborers

Through much of history and also today, many laborers have been ready to break new ground for the kingdom, often starting church-planting movements or ushering in major shifts for the gospel. Hardship has long characterized ministries regarded as "apostolic," such as those of medieval missionaries to new regions or early Methodist circuit riders.[10] Estimates are that nearly half of the pioneering circuit riders died before they reached the age of thirty. Church planter Rich Stevenson shared with me some of his conversation with Vineyard leader John Wimber shortly before the latter's death. Wimber mentioned John Wesley's ministry as an example of the apostolic kind and noted that a key evidence of apostolic ministry is suffering for one's calling.[11]

This seems likewise true of the ministries of Francis of Assisi, Francis Xavier, George Whitefield, Francis Asbury, and others. Because of their influence for the gospel we might also include some of the Reformers. I'll focus here on more recent examples.

The Careys, the Judsons, and the Taylors

In 1792, William Carey declared, "Expect great things from God; attempt great things for God!" Soon after he reached India, he and his family suffered destitution until he found some secular work. When his five-year-old son died of dysentery, his wife, Dorothy—who had never wanted to come to India to begin with—snapped mentally. Eventually she even tried to kill William. After twelve years in mental agony, she died in 1807. Carey's original missionary colleague, John Thomas, also suffered from mental illness.

This was not the end of hardship. It had taken seven years from Carey's arrival before he had even one convert, yet he persevered. When a fire in the printing room claimed years of work, including the only copy of the Sanskrit dictionary he had completed as well as ten Bible translations, Carey was devastated. The spiritual battle was surely intense.

Trusting in God's sovereign plan, however, Carey determined to start over.[12] Meanwhile, news of the costly fire brought attention to and more support for the work. With local help, Carey translated Scripture into many of India's languages, laying foundations for the harvest that faith anticipated. Eventually hundreds more came to faith. When Carey died after forty-one continuous years in India, he had laid foundations and a model for missions that were respectful and supportive of local peoples and that deeply influenced following generations.

Two of those influenced by Carey's example were Adoniram (1788–1850) and Ann (1789–1826) Judson, among the first missionaries from the newly formed United States. When England and Burma went to war in 1824, however, Burmese authorities supposed that English-speaking Adoniram was a British spy and imprisoned him for seventeen months. Ann set up a shack outside the prison so she could provide food for her husband. The cramped prison cell lacked toilet facilities, and guards suspended the prisoners in the air by their feet at night. Some prisoners eventually died on a forced march. Ann meanwhile was translating Scripture into Burmese and Thai. Soon after Adoniram's release, however, Ann and their third and only surviving child died. Adoniram continued to serve the gospel and Burma until his death a quarter century later. By then he had translated the entire Bible into Burmese, created the Burmese dictionary, and helped plant many churches.[13]

As a medical missionary to China, Hudson Taylor (1832–1905) chose to adopt local Chinese dress and culture and depended radically on God to supply his needs. Moved with concern for China's spiritual needs, he recruited more missionaries for the interior, founding China Inland Mission (CIM; today, Overseas Missionary Fellowship). Sometimes he was deathly sick; his first wife, Maria, died at thirty-three, and half of their children died in childhood. Serving "China's millions" continued to drive him regardless of the cost. In 1900, Taylor experienced a breakdown; he could do no more than cry out to God as seventy-nine of CIM's missionaries (twenty-one of them children) were martyred during China's Boxer Rebellion. Yet by the time Taylor died in 1905 at the age of seventy-three, his movement had changed the world. From 1865 to 1949, CIM fielded 2,680 adult missionaries to China.[14]

Church Planters in 1960s Congo

That pattern has also held true in more recent times. Many examples are possible, but I begin with 1960s church planters in what is now the Democratic Republic of Congo.[15] Like James and Peter in Acts 12, they faced varying fates.

EXPLOITATION AND VIOLENCE

Foreign church planters in Congo faced a time of severe danger in the 1960s. Before I talk about that, though, I should give some background about foreign abuses in Congo. This was a region primed for suffering. Local believers had suffered terribly, and local nonbelievers had reasons to resent foreigners. Some evils build on earlier evils, and sometimes we get caught in the conflicts.

From 1885 to 1908 the playboy king of Belgium, Leopold II, cruelly exploited Congo as his private slave colony. His abuses led to the deaths of up to ten million people in a genocide often forgotten in the West.[16] Finally, African American missionaries William and Lucy Sheppard and their missionary colleagues got word out to the wider world and Leopold was forced to hand over Congo to the Belgian government.[17] That reduced the exploitation but didn't end it. Indeed, international exploitation of the region continues today, not least in labor for the world's cobalt supply.[18]

When Zaire (now the Democratic Republic of Congo) finally won its independence, it came with convulsions of violence, some directed at foreigners. In 1964, many missionaries were killed or severely abused.

SURVIVORS

Dr. Helen Roseveare had built a hospital and was serving the local population. On October 28, 1964, however, six soldiers surrounded her, struck her, then hurled her to the ground. They then kicked her until she was bloodied and her back teeth were shattered. She was too numb even to pray. Roseveare survived five months in captivity, being raped and beaten. Despite all that, she afterward continued to serve her host country.[19] (I return to her story in chap. 5.)

My current next-door neighbors, Wes and June Eisenman, were missionaries in the Congo at that time.[20] Wes was a pilot with Mission Aviation Fellowship and helped rescue many missionaries who had fled into the jungle to escape being killed.[21] The former owners of our home were also working for Christ in Congo at that time; their participation in celebrating independence and providential timing helped keep them safe.[22]

One Swiss Assemblies of God missionary whom the Eisenmans knew, Jacques Vernaud, remained in Congo during the bloodshed. His wife, Johanna, pretended to drive him to the airport, but he secretly returned in the trunk of the car. I attended Bible college with his daughter Liliane—herself healed of leukemia as a child—and she introduced me to her parents when they visited. Jacques Vernaud was also close friends with my Congolese father-in-law Jacques Moussounga, who received a spiritual gift of healing after Pastor Vernaud laid hands on him. Later, when my wife and I were visiting Congo, Pastor Vernaud also laid hands on my wife and me. We hosted Johanna and sometimes their granddaughter in our home.

Vernaud remained in Congo to continue his ministry even in hard times, and God protected and blessed that work. He planted a vast number of churches, and his great ministry included visible miracles attested by eyewitnesses I know. Even today, I periodically meet people he discipled or pastored. He passed away peacefully in 2011 at the age of seventy-eight.

AND MARTYRS

By contrast, some missionaries were martyred in 1964. One of them was a different Assemblies of God missionary, Jay W. Tucker, from the South Central United States. Simba rebels held Tucker and some Catholic priests prisoner at a Catholic mission, and on November 24, the rebels clubbed Tucker to death and discarded his corpse in the Bomokandi River. The Mother Superior of the captive mission had to report the grim news to Tucker's wife, Angeline. "He is in heaven," she shared, choosing her words carefully. "May God comfort your heart to know he was ready to die."[23]

Grieving, Angeline and her children escaped with their lives. For the children who had grown up there, Congo was home, and she herself wished she could return. "It's hard for us to understand why God took Jay from us when we needed him so much, but we know He had His reasons, and that they will be revealed in due time. . . . I pray daily that the children and I may be faithful to his ideals, and that, with God's help, we may continue to carry on the work he was forced to lay down."[24] Jay had served for a quarter century in his beloved Africa, where he wanted to spend his whole life and be buried.

When I was in seminary, a guest speaker in a missions class told us that Tucker had shared with him his determination to serve Jesus in Congo regardless of the cost. We do not always get to see the reward of the cost in this life, but Tucker's widow grasped it in faith. Citing Tertullian's dictum that the blood of martyrs is the seed of the church, Angeline insisted, "If Jesus tarries, there should be a wonderful harvest of souls in all of northeast Congo."

In this case, Tucker's family lived to see the fruit of his ministry. Although the local Mangbetu tribe had been hostile to the message of Christ, one of Tucker's converts became police chief there. He explained to his people that Tucker's body had been cast into their river. "Since Tucker's blood had flowed through their waters, they believed they must listen to the message that he carried." Thousands came to Christ, with miracles following. Some locals were reportedly even raised from the dead.[25] The seed that fell into the ground and died bore much fruit (compare John 12:24).

The Bakers in Mozambique

I stay in fairly regular contact with Rolland Baker, who, like me, counts Pentecostal scholar Gordon Fee among his mentors. Fresh from master's work at Vanguard University in Southern California, where Fee had been teaching, Rolland and his wife, Heidi, moved to Indonesia in 1985. There they worked with Mel Tari, one of the leaders who had earlier emerged from Indonesia's 1965 West Timor revival.[26] Later they worked with Jackie Pullinger in Hong Kong, serving among the neediest people in the world's densest urban area.[27]

THE BACKGROUND

Eventually, after doing doctoral work in London, the Bakers headed for Mozambique.[28] They chose Mozambique because at the time it was the poorest nation on earth, and they knew from Scripture that God works among the broken (e.g., Ps. 138:6; Isa. 66:2; Matt. 5:3; Luke 1:52). Soon they began taking in many of the children living on the streets, who themselves began sharing the love of Jesus with other children. (For God's special care for children, see, e.g., Mark 9:37; 10:14–15.)

At one point, they grew deathly sick and were burned out, but God renewed them during an outpouring of the Spirit through the ministry of Randy Clark. Trusting God to confirm his message of grace with signs, as in Acts (e.g., Acts 14:3), Heidi prayed for people to be healed. She kept praying for months without any visible results until finally, all in one week, three blind women were healed. I asked Rolland whether perhaps God arranged it this way so they would recognize that the power for healing came from him and not them. Rolland thought so. (Admittedly, I asked with ulterior motives, to stir hope that I might yet see more blind people healed too!)

HOMELESS AGAIN

After their orphanage grew to 320 children, however, a government department ordered them to stop all "religious activity." Heidi recounts, "Our children were not allowed to pray, even under a tree. . . . We could no longer bring in street children, give out clothes or dispense medicine." The children, who had suffered extensively in their previous lives on the street before being taken in, responded with holy defiance. They claimed that they would rather stay "in tents in the fields, with no water and electricity, than remain behind where they were beaten, starved and prevented from worshiping Jesus."

The officials responsible at the time thus gave the Bakers and their colleagues forty-eight hours to abandon the property the Bakers had restored. Incidentally, Heidi was also told that a contract had been issued on her life.[29] Staff labored night and day to salvage from their property whatever they could—for example, dragging bedframes across grass and packing medicine through rain and mud. The only place they could head for at the time was the office space they owned in Maputo, fifteen miles away. The orphans, lacking relatives or places to find shelter, walked the distance barefoot to Maputo. They said some persecutors had beaten them "with large sticks for singing" on the way, but they insisted that they would keep singing because they were committed to God.

Roughly one hundred children showed up at the office. Heidi tried to explain that there was not enough room, but they protested that she had promised that God always provides. Rolland, Heidi, and their own two children were hungry, not having eaten in days, and a kind friend from the US embassy stopped by with food for their family. Opening the door, Heidi showed her the mass of children. "I have a big family!" Horrified, the friend protested that the food wasn't nearly enough, but they prayed and then began giving each person a full bowl. Miraculously, "all our children ate, the staff ate, my friend ate and even our family of four ate."[30]

PHYSICAL AND SPIRITUAL FLOODS

More suffering awaited, however. When three cyclones struck in 2000, floods destroyed more ground than had Mozambique's fifteen years of civil war. Inadvertently, "mothers struggling in neck-deep currents drowned their own babies in their back slings," and communities stranded on high ground "were reduced to eating the decayed flesh of dead cows." Survivors amassed atop buildings perished when roofs collapsed beneath their weight.[31] Prayerful Christians were not spared. At one of the Bakers' orphanage centers, for example, fifty children had malaria, including the Bakers' birth daughter Crystalyn.[32] Out of that suffering arose cries to God. In response to those cries, the church movement began to multiply, planting thousands of churches and caring for some ten thousand orphans in the following years.[33]

The children grew to be laborers for the harvest, many of them planting churches themselves. Rolland and Heidi moved to northern Mozambique to evangelize among a previously unreached people group. As God healed deafness and blindness in one unchurched village after another, churches were planted.

Some Other Recent Church Planters from the US

Church planting and cross-cultural ministry can remain risky today as well. The past century has seen hundreds or thousands of leaders of church-planting movements; here I offer only samples. Most of my wife's mentors in Congo-Brazzaville were Congolese, but they also included Americans Eugene and Sandy Thomas. I later learned that Pastor Thomas grew up just a few blocks from where I (later) grew up in my hometown in Ohio. The Thomases planted churches in unevangelized areas and trained local leaders to continue spreading the gospel farther.[34] Yet these cross-cultural laborers sacrificed much, including living through shelling and shooting.

On the border of Colombia and Venezuela, nineteen-year-old Bruce Olson braved severe sickness, deprivation, and being shot in the thigh with an arrow to reach the Motilone (or Barí) people, among whom he lived for decades. He spread the gospel, established medical and educational institutions, translated the Bible into their language, and worked for justice for Indigenous people—a story described in detail in his moving book *Bruchko*.[35] In 1988, however, guerrillas captured and planned to execute him. This story ends differently than some others. Bruce was released after nine months in captivity, his name defended by the grateful local people among whom he had labored.

When Presbyterian Don McClure began work among the Anuak people of eastern Africa, they were completely unchurched. By the time he relocated to reach other peoples, a fifth of the Anuak had received baptism and another fifth were getting ready for it. God blessed his half century of ministry in Ethiopia and Sudan, and he was known as a joyful man whose prayers God heard. Still, on a final mission requested by the Ethiopian emperor Haile Selassie himself, McClure was murdered by Somali guerrillas in March 1977.[36]

Church planters are not limited to ministry outside their own country. In 1990, for example, I learned much from Dan Taylor, a Chicago church planter who pioneered churches in Cabrini-Green and the Robert Taylor Home, both crime-infested areas at that time. When I asked him whether many Christians in the suburbs came out to work with him, he indicated that this was very rare. The only explanation he could give was that "they aren't ready to die for their faith."[37]

Other US Cross-Cultural Laborers

Davy Lloyd grew up at the Pentecostal mission orphanage started by his American parents in Haiti, and Davy, 23, and his wife, Natalie, 21, devoted themselves to the orphans. Gangs were running Haiti, but the young couple were hopeful that God was bringing change. God had intervened for them in previous crises. One night in 2024 while I was safe at home working on this book, however, gangs burned the orphanage. They killed this couple and a local church leader, Jude Montis, who was with them.[38]

My dear friend and coauthor on another book, charismatic Bible scholar Michael Brown, is Chancellor of the Christ for All Nations School of Ministry. (You might know of Michael from his *The Line of Fire* broadcast, or his role in the Brownsville Revival, or his Messianic Jewish ministry.) One of Michael's American graduates, in his mid-twenties, traveled with his wife and children to serve in a Middle Eastern nation. He was serving materially poor Muslims, teaching English and work skills, and even literally washing their feet. After al-Qaeda terrorists killed the student, "many of the Muslims who knew him (including women in burqas) risked their own lives by marching in the streets, speaking out against his death and commending him as a saintly Christian man who came to serve the poor and the needy."[39]

Michael shared with me his journal entry from the time. "The loss of precious life and the reality of a new widow and her little children is deep and stunning. . . . But this day, we see the true price of Jesus revolution: the blood of . . . a spiritual son."[40] He elsewhere recounts, "I will never forget attending his funeral and watching his four-year-old son, the older of two boys, after his father's casket was lowered into the ground saying, 'Bye-bye, Daddy! I love you!'"[41]

Some Asian Church Planters

Michael travels regularly to India. During one visit there, he talked with a preacher who baptized three hundred people in 2007, after which local radicals stripped and beat him. When they realized that he would survive in the hospital, they sought to poison him there. Getting word, his family took him to a different hospital about 170 miles away. After six days in a coma he recovered—and went back to preaching.

Michael asked, "Are you afraid they're going to kill you?" The evangelist replied, "Never!" and talked about taking up the cross to follow Jesus. There are still threats on his life, but the first man to strike him when he was first beaten has since received Christian baptism.

In 2010 Michael met a mom and her seventeen-year-old daughter in India. The mother had to watch aggressors beat and then behead her husband, a pastor. The daughter said that now that her father had been killed she had a sense of purpose in serving God. The mother and daughter are continuing the ministry for which the father was martyred.[42] They are not angry with those who killed him; they forgive them and want to reach them with the gospel.[43] Michael had participated in her husband's commissioning, and now he wept as he washed the widow's feet. After the foot washing, those who had lost loved ones or been beaten worshiped God joyfully.

During the 1965 revival in West Timor, Indonesian ministry teams traversed jungles and crossed wide rivers to evangelize. They experienced miracles, including healings of blindness, raisings from the dead, and (initially unknowingly) walking on water. But sacrifice, suffering, and a martyrdom also characterized their mission.[44] More recently, Indonesian believer Tandi Randa, a doctor of ministry graduate of Asbury Seminary, has had confrontations with practitioners of curse magic. Though they had previously found their curses effective against others, they were shocked to discover how God protected Tandi. He has led scores of former curse-magic practitioners to Christ.[45]

A Sri Lankan man, angry that his wife had become a Christian, hired a gunman to kill Pastor Neil and his wife, whom I shall call Priya. One May night soon after, while the pastor and his wife slept, the assassin riddled them with bullets. Pastor Neil died immediately; friends rushed Priya to the Colombo hospital. Doctors did their best but did not expect her to survive the night. Prayers were answered, however, and shortly before Christmas 2008, she returned to the house church. Despite a paralyzed leg and hand, she was determined to fulfill the mission she originally shared with her husband.[46]

After Phan became a believer, he preached one message in his village in Laos, leading more than a hundred people to Christ. The village expelled all the Christians, but the new believers witnessed God providing for them.[47] Such forced moves can be part of life for persecuted believers. In India, one effective evangelist and his family have had to relocate 185 times in nineteen years because of death threats.[48]

For the sake of planting churches, Nagmeh Panahi endured persecution in Iran, and she had friends there who were killed for their faith. She survived these crises only to also endure betrayal in her marriage—tragically, by a fellow Christian who had once shared many of the same sufferings.[49]

In Iraq, Karwan planned to convert infidels to Islam. But as he began studying the New Testament to refute Christians, he instead experienced peace and became a Christian himself. He soon began spreading the message about Jesus and planted a church. Now, he says, "Every moment we are waiting for someone to come and kill me. There is no moment in my life without this waiting." He keeps reminding the church members of the example that Jesus set. "We are not higher than our teacher. If he died, if he was executed, of course it will happen for us. It is normal."[50] Is his assessment accurate, at least potentially?

> If anyone wants to follow me, let them deny themselves and take up their cross and follow me. For whoever wants to save their life will lose it, but whoever loses their life on account of me and the good news will save it. (Mark 8:34–35)

"Time Will Fail Me . . ."

Hebrews 11:32 warns that time would fail if the author tried to tell of Gideon, David, and so many other "heroes of the faith." Indeed, we will not in this life know the names of most of those breaking ground for God's kingdom around the world, though we will someday surely celebrate their Spirit-inspired devotion around God's throne. I offer just a few samples here.

Further stories could be multiplied. I will return to Hebrews 11 in chapter 4, but first, just as we have examined apostolic-type sufferings in this chapter, we should look at prophets, prophecy, and suffering in the next.

CHAPTER THREE

Biblical Prophets and Suffering

For an example of hardship and fortitude, brothers and sisters, take the prophets who spoke in the Lord's name.

—James 5:10

[When people persecute or insult you,] rejoice and jump for joy, for your reward is great in heaven, since this is how they persecuted the prophets who were before you.

—Luke 6:23 (compare also Matt. 5:12)

If there is any ministry that many Spirit-filled Christians today regard as next to apostolic ministry, it would be prophetic ministry. So it is relevant to our discussion to note that biblical prophets often both announced and experienced hardships. Jesus notes that prophets are typically unwelcome among those nearest them (Matt. 13:57; Mark 6:4; Luke 4:24; John 4:44).

Killing the Prophets

For some preliminary examples of the prophets' hardships, note the following:

- Jezebel killed the prophets of the Lord, probably most of them friends or mentees of Elijah (1 Kings 18:4; 19:10).
- Joash ordered the murder of his mentor Jehoida's son Zechariah because the latter prophesied against him (2 Chron. 24:20–22).

- "They were disobedient and rebelled against you and cast your law behind their back and killed your prophets, who had warned them in order to turn them back to you" (Neh. 9:26 ESV).
- Jesus's prophetic forerunner, John, is beheaded (Mark 6:27–28).
- "You testify against yourselves that you come from those who murdered the prophets. . . . That's why I'm sending you prophets, wise people and scribes. You'll kill and crucify some of them; you'll flog some of them in your synagogues and pursue them with hostility from one town to the next. This is so you may merit the punishment due all the righteous blood shed on the earth from righteous Abel to the blood of Zechariah, Berachiah's son, whom you murdered between the sanctuary and the altar. Surely, I declare to you: all the vengeance for their blood will climax on this generation! O Jerusalem! Jerusalem! You kill the prophets and stone those sent to you" (Matt. 23:31, 34–37; compare 23:29–37; Luke 11:47–51; 13:34).
- "Which of the prophets didn't your ancestors persecute? They killed those who foretold the Righteous One's coming—and now you have become his betrayers and murderers!" (Acts 7:52).
- "Because they shed the blood of your consecrated ones and prophets, and you have [accordingly] given them blood to drink, just as they have earned!" (Rev. 16:6).
- "Celebrate over her, Heaven, and consecrated ones and apostles and prophets! For God has rendered judgment for you against her. . . . And in her was found the blood of prophets and consecrated ones and of all who have been slaughtered on the earth" (Rev. 18:20, 24).

Revelation has in view continuing prophets rather than just Old Testament ones (compare Rev. 11:18; 19:10; 22:9); this is also the case in Matthew 23:34 and Luke 11:49. Jeremiah escaped death, but lest we suppose his survival normative for the prophetic occupation generally, he narrates the story of the prophet Uriah, who was killed for his message despite his best precautions (Jer. 26:20–23).

Prophets of Peace Get Popular

Most of us recognize that in the Old Testament, true prophecies were not always positive, and consequently people were often unhappy with those who prophesied to them. Shooting the messenger is hardly an exclusively modern practice. In most generations, most people were not living for the Lord, and they did not want to hear what the Lord was really saying. For example,

- King Ahab complained about the prophet Micaiah: "I hate him, because he does not prophesy good concerning me, but only what is bad" (1 Kings 22:8; for the record, Ahab was not fond of Elijah, either—see 18:17; 21:20).
- The idolatrous high priest of Bethel warned Amos not to prophesy there any longer (Amos 7:13).
- Rebellious Judahites urged "the seers, 'Stop seeing [visions]!'" and urged "the visionaries, 'Stop having right visions! Tell us smooth things. Have deceptive visions!'" (Isa. 30:10).
- People said to Jeremiah, "Don't prophesy in the Lord's name, lest you die at our hand" (Jer. 11:21).
- "He'll come and destroy those tenant farmers," Jesus said, "and will entrust the vineyard to other people!" But when the people heard him they cried, "May it never be!" (Luke 20:16).

People Perish with Prophets of Peace

Conversely, people (including myself) usually appreciate those who prophesy happy news. In the long term, however, this is true only when they prophesy correctly! What some charismatics call "prophetic declarations" are really blessings—prayers—not predictions per se. Even "blessings" and "curses," however, are *ideally* prophetic (see, e.g., Josh. 6:26 as fulfilled in 1 Kings 16:34).

- "[Most so-called prophets] have healed the brokenness of my people only on the surface, by declaring, 'Peace! Peace!' when there is no peace!" (Jer. 6:14; 8:11)
- "Then I said: 'Ah, Lord GOD! Here are the prophets saying to them, "You shall not see the sword, nor shall you have famine, but I will give you true peace in this place."' And the LORD said to me: The prophets are prophesying lies in my name; I did not send them, nor did I command them or speak to them. They are prophesying to you a lying vision, worthless divination, and the deceit of their own minds. Therefore thus says the LORD concerning the prophets who prophesy in my name though I did not send them, and who say, 'Sword and famine shall not come on this land': By sword and famine those prophets shall be consumed. And the people to whom they prophesy shall be thrown out into the streets of

Jerusalem, victims of famine and sword. There shall be no one to bury them—themselves, their wives, their sons, and their daughters. For I will pour out their wickedness upon them." (Jer. 14:13–16 NRSV)

- "Where now are the prophets who prophesied that the Babylonians wouldn't come against you?" (Jer. 37:19)

God told Jeremiah to wear a yoke around his neck to symbolize that God was putting the nations, including Judah, under Babylon's empire (Jer. 27:2, 8, 11–12). By contrast, the prophet Hananiah soon prophesied that God would break Babylon's yoke (28:2, 4). Indeed, far from punishing his people through Babylon, Hananiah assured Judahites, God would restore all that Babylon had already taken. Jeremiah confronted Hananiah. "I want all your words to be true," Jeremiah conceded. But that's not what Jeremiah was hearing from God. He explained that an intergenerational succession of prophets had warned about judgment, leaving the burden of proof on any prophet of peace (28:1–9).

How did Hananiah respond? In true prophetic form, he matched Jeremiah's symbolic action (the yoke) with another symbolic action, seizing Jeremiah's yoke and breaking it. Then with even greater assertiveness than Jeremiah he reaffirmed his earlier prophecy, declaring that God said he would break the yoke within two years. He shamed Jeremiah, who apparently was unprepared with an answer from the Lord (Jer. 28:10–11). Jeremiah wasn't playing a game of prophecy; he spoke only what God gave him. Later, however, a prophecy came to him: Hananiah was not going to live long enough (two years) to see his prophecy fail. Hananiah was going to die within the year (28:12–16). Hananiah went on to die a few months later (28:17), but by then no one was paying attention. It was no longer part of Jerusalem's news cycle.

Jeremiah laments false prophets and leaders through much of chapter 23, though he recognizes the true gift of prophecy. "What does straw have in common with wheat?" Jeremiah asks, distinguishing false prophecies from true (Jer. 23:28). Unhappily, the false prophets of Jeremiah's day vastly outnumbered the true ones. Sometimes Jeremiah just wanted to keep quiet. "You made me look like a fool!" he protests to God (20:7–8). But whenever he resolves to quit speaking, the word of the Lord burns within him so he can't stop speaking it (20:9; compare 6:11). As far as others can tell, he remains simply a stubborn naysayer.

Prophets and Priests Persecute the Prophet Jeremiah

One example of why Jeremiah stayed unpopular may suffice. "Do you have a message for me?" King Zedekiah asks him. "Sure do," Jeremiah responds.

"You're toast!" (Jer. 37:17; compare 23:33). His words contradicted the more optimistic prophets, as God had already made clear:

> The prophets prophesy falsely,
> And the priests rule on their own authority;
> And My people love it this way!
> But what will you do when the end comes? (Jer. 5:31 NASB)

Jeremiah certainly wasn't winning the prophetic popularity contest. People expected that God's presence and favor with them rendered their nation immune from judgment (Jer. 7:4), and they naturally gravitated toward prophets who agreed with them. After all, God couldn't judge his *own* people. Everybody in the ancient Near East understood that that wasn't what a god was for. Jeremiah smashing a pot to symbolize the imminent fate of Jerusalem (Jer. 19) did get some attention but really did not go over very well. The priest Pashhur, the temple's chief administrator, had Jeremiah beaten and then put in stocks overnight, again publicly shaming him (20:1–2). (At least the authorities didn't immediately plot to kill him, like they did for Jesus after Jesus made a big scene in the temple in Mark 11:15–18.)

Yet instead of humbling himself and acting more submissively, Jeremiah greeted Pashhur with a fresh prophecy in the morning: "You're a false prophet yourself, Pashhur, and you and the people deceived by you will all die in exile" (Jer. 20:3–6). Imagine! What a great way to win the favor of the temple establishment!

Eventually, priests and prophets rallied the people to seek Jeremiah's death for prophesying against Jerusalem (Jer. 26:8, 11). After Jeremiah warned that God would hold them to account for his blood, however, the people and their officials remembered the long-standing tradition of prophetic immunity (essentially diplomatic immunity for God's ambassadors) and restrained the religious leaders from killing him (26:16). This confrontation, however, would not be Jeremiah's last.

Accusing Jeremiah of being a traitor, another official named Iriyah arrested him (Jer. 37:13).[1] As the political-military situation became more desperate, leaders even resolved to execute Jeremiah because his prophecies were "discouraging" the people (38:4). (One might imagine upbeat preachers today who warn that negative prophecies weaken people's faith in positive outcomes.) The king, who has enough authority to stand for what is right, instead abdicates his responsibility to do so (38:4–5)—and will face judgment (38:18; 39:5–7). We cannot avoid taking sides, especially if we are church leaders; we must stand with the truth and reject false prophecies of "peace, peace."

Even after Jeremiah's prophecies proved true, he experienced the hardships of a prophet living in a time of disobedience. The Babylonians naturally appreciated his recognition that God had given them an empire, and they treated him kindly. They did not force him to exile in Babylon with most others (Jer. 40:1–6). But a group of his own people disbelieved his prophecies (43:1–4) and so forced him into exile with them in Egypt (43:5–7)!

Should All Christian Prophecies Be Positive?

What about prophecies after Jeremiah's time? In some circles, prophecies about a massive influx of new believers and a coming transfer of wealth have reached the status of being standard expectations.[2] That we would appreciate positive prophecies is no surprise, but are we ready to heed warnings as well? Even in the early eighteenth century, God used true prophecies to protect many individual believers,[3] but some increasingly popular prophetic expectations faced disappointment.[4] True warnings can be helpful in preparing for testing (e.g., Acts 11:28–29; 21:11; Rev. 2:10; 3:10) or in inviting correction (e.g., Rev. 2:4–5, 16; 3:2–5, 19).

In Iran, Maryam Rostampour and her sister Shirin both experienced prophetic dreams warning that Maryam would soon be arrested and imprisoned.[5] As with Agabus's prophecy to Paul in Acts 11 or Pharaoh's dreams of impending famine in Genesis 41, these dreams were getting her ready for hardship in advance. A dream warned the imprisoned Korean believer Esther Ahn Kim about the life-threatening test of faith that awaited her that day.[6] Similarly, one of her recent converts in the cell dreamed about meeting Jesus, and that same day the convert was taken out and executed.[7]

Before it was obvious that war would come to my future wife Médine's hometown of Dolisie, Congo, a friend visited Médine's family on January 9, 1997. "I wanted to move here to Dolisie, but the prophet was adamant. 'Don't stay more than two weeks. If you stay till past midnight, Sunday, January 24, you won't be able to get out.'"

Médine's family could not easily relocate, however, since their father was disabled. Médine herself had recently barely escaped fighting in the capital, and she and her sister Thérèse were both recovering from medical procedures. Monday, January 25, began as usual. Thérèse was preparing to leave for the elementary school where she taught. Around six o'clock in the morning, however, they heard a deafening sound. Dolisie was being bombarded; war had come. They had missed the January 24 deadline.[8]

Like Jerusalemites in Jeremiah's day, most of us tend to gravitate to verses and promises we find pleasant. Charismatic conference planners also know the topics that draw crowds: miracles, blessings, success, or even how to get what you want from God (compare 2 Tim. 4:3).[9] And yes, I speak about miracles at conferences where I am invited to do so. Miracles are biblical, but they are not God's whole message. Some foods are healthy in moderation but are not meant to be the whole diet; in the same way, in learning Scripture we need "the whole purpose of God" (Acts 20:27).

What About New Testament Prophecies?

Some people say that prophecies today should always be favorable. The idea that prophecies should never be corrective rests especially on 1 Corinthians 14:3: "The one who prophesies speaks to people for their upbuilding and encouragement and consolation" (ESV). But while Paul usually uses the middle term for encouragement or comfort, which makes sense in a local church setting, this Greek term can also mean exhortation (1 Thess. 2:3; Heb. 12:5), which can have various levels of intensity.

If someone is going to make a mistake in prophesying, a positive mistake is usually less harmful than a negative one. But the idea that all prophecy should be favorable is not biblical—even if one narrows the pool of evidence to the New Testament. The clearest New Testament *examples* of prophecies appear in Acts, where they involve impending suffering: coming famine (Acts 11:28) or arrest (21:11). The next clearest examples would be the letters to the seven churches in Revelation, which include both encouragements and warnings; five of the seven churches receive corrections and reproofs.

One of those warnings in Revelation includes the removal of a church's lampstand, signifying its end as a church. I once had to prophesy these same words to an apparently vibrant church, to my own dismay. (In case we ever meet in person, don't worry; I don't normally do that!) Why would the Lord warn of judgment to this church and not to the many others that I was sure were worse off? This one seemed to be failing only on the matter that the Lord pointed out—in this case, lack of outreach. But within a year the church ceased to exist. We don't have the authority to decide what to prophesy based on our understanding; whether with teaching, prophecy, or evangelism, our job is just to deliver faithfully the message entrusted to us.

The only two churches of Asia Minor in Revelation 2–3 that Jesus does not reprove at all are those in Smyrna and Philadelphia—the persecuted churches. Yet the exhortation to one of even those is sobering:

> You will have suffering. . . . Be faithful to the point of death, and I will give you a crown of life. (Rev. 2:10)

God is warning of impending hardship in Smyrna, not of judgment. Yet judgment may begin at the house of God (1 Pet. 4:17), and God's healing power may be curtailed by our failure to treat one another rightly (1 Cor. 11:29–30). New Testament examples of prophecy and exhortation are certainly not all favorable.

Why Nobody Liked Jeremiah[10]

Most of Jeremiah's people did not like what God gave him to say; they viewed him as an unpatriotic contrarian.[11] Such hostility may be harder on those of us who are sensitive to what others think than on somebody thick-skinned and pugnacious. It was certainly going to be hard on Jeremiah. God's opening assurance, "Don't let them scare you! I'll rescue you!" (Jer. 1:8) gave a hint where this assignment was headed. "But if you give in to them, you're through," God essentially says (1:17; compare 12:5; 15:19). Jeremiah would struggle inwardly, but he would never be free to renounce his saving message to Judah.

Following God's will meant that he would be ostracized and attacked.

> Nobody owes me money, nor do I owe money to anybody else, but everybody curses me anyway! (Jer. 15:10)

God's calling—and the nation's destiny—demanded significant sacrifice. Jeremiah would have to stay single—to spare him from the grief of having to lose a family when judgment came (Jer. 16:2–4). He couldn't attend parties or funerals. Separated by his devotion to God, he fed on God's words and was isolated from what mattered to the rest of society (15:16–17; 16:5–9). His closest friends would turn on him (20:10). He would endure public beating, humiliation, and confinement in stocks for not being appropriately "patriotic" (20:1–3). His own relatives, priests in Anathoth (1:1), would want to kill him (11:21). Most of us hate it when that happens.

For decades, Jeremiah went against the mood of his culture. He was summoning Judah back to the values of God's covenant with them, but they didn't think that they had strayed.

Contradicting Guardians of the Tradition

Most of the common people couldn't read Scripture, so they depended on what their preachers taught them. (Similarly, most people today are able to read Scripture but *don't*, so they depend on what preachers or, more often, social media teach them.)

And most of Judah's preachers assured them that God was with them. After all, they were his chosen people, and they alone of all peoples worshiped the one true God. Granted, they had compromised that allegiance, but they were doing better than any other people. These preachers remembered *part* of the covenant message. Yet they forgot that God expects higher standards for his own people and thus may judge them more strictly (compare Amos 3:2). Although they remembered the blessing part of the covenant message, over generations they had adapted the curse part of the message (see Jer. 2:8; 18:18; Ezek. 22:26). Keeping up with the times meant being more positive. Certainly that helped their view count.

Unfortunately, these leaders' "progressive" adjustments rested not on what God was really saying but on what seemed good to them, which was shaped by generations of tradition and by the climate of public opinion (compare Judg. 17:6; 21:25; Prov. 14:12; 16:25). They didn't want to upset their donation base (Jer. 6:13; 8:10; compare Mic. 3:5, 11). They refused to challenge immorality; after all, the preachers themselves were among those committing it (Jer. 23:14). Even in the New Testament, some attempts to "update" key biblical issues of sexual and theological morality rested on deceptive appeals to the prophetic Spirit (Rev. 2:14, 20).

It could have been different, had the prophets cared more about God's voice than that of their fellow prophets or followers. God told Jeremiah, "I did not send these prophets, but they ran. I did not speak to them, but they prophesied. But if they had stood in My council, then they would have announced My words to My people, and would have turned them back from their evil way and from the evil of their deeds" (Jer. 23:21–22 NASB).

The situation was like that of a century earlier, when the more openly idolatrous northern kingdom of Israel could cry out, "My God, we of Israel know you!" (Hosea 8:2)—even while continuing to honor golden calves at Dan and Bethel. Now, in Jeremiah's day, priests and prophets were still telling God's people how much God delighted in them without warning them of the dangerous judgment to come.

It was indeed true that God loved them. But the God who loves us comes to transform us and invite us into relationship with him, not to leave us wallowing in de facto rebellion against him. Judgments on societies are sometimes wake-up calls (Ps. 78:34–35; Amos 4:6, 8–11; Hag. 2:17; Rev. 9:20–21; 16:9, 11) because God loves us too much to let us continue to be deceived. They come when more direct means of admonition have failed—when people do not listen to God's message through the prophets, or when the prophets fail to speak the full truth of God's message (Isa. 28:9–13; 29:9–12; 30:10–14; Amos 7:12–13). Shorter-term judgments warn people to avoid pursuing the longer-term judgment of alienation from him—our source of meaning and life (Jer. 2:13; Hosea 13:9). People complain about a God of judgment, but people complain even more about its delay—about God's patience with the wicked.[12]

Most prophets of Jeremiah's day focused on the covenant blessings and took encouragement from one another's prophecies (see Jer. 23:30) that they must be saying the right thing. Who was Jeremiah to think that he alone was hearing from God? (Still, he may have had some sympathizers at some point. Some letters that archaeologists recovered from the ruins of Lachish might suggest that more than one Judahite prophet of doom was undercutting "the war effort" with "unpatriotic" warnings.) How could Jeremiah dare to prophesy one thing when everybody else was prophesying something different? And something that *nobody* wanted to hear! And something they thought contradicted Bible verses about God's blessings! Yet the majority of the prophets proved to be wrong about the big picture. They were stealing God's words from one another, confident in the consensus of their peers (Jer. 23:30).

Discerning the Truth

Jeremiah was often discouraged about his mission. To whom could he speak, when the people were closed to his message (Jer. 6:10)? Yet he was full of God's wrath; he could not hold it inside any longer and had to speak (6:11). The prophets and priests had healed his people's wound only superficially, promising them well-being (6:14); but they needed to return to the ancient covenant, to God's Word that he had given long ago (6:16). Listening to a consensus of preachers, even on YouTube, is no substitute for going back to the Scriptures ourselves. Most Judahites were illiterate and lacked this option (Isa. 29:12; compare Jer. 5:4–5), an opportunity more available to most of us.

God explained that his people did not know him (Jer. 8:7), despite their insistence:

> How can you say, "We are wise, and the law of the LORD is with us," when, in fact, the false pen of the scribes has made it into a lie? The wise shall be put to shame, they shall be dismayed and taken; since they have rejected the word of the LORD, what wisdom is in them? (Jer. 8:8–9 NRSV modified)

From prophet to priest, eager for popularity, the leaders had been assuring God's people that all would be well, but it was not what God was saying (Jer. 8:10–11).

Rather than weighing opinion by Scripture or God's prophetic voice, most people follow what is right in their own sight (Judg. 17:6; 21:25; Prov. 12:15;

18:2). We naturally think our own ways are right, but the Lord is the one who evaluates our hearts (Prov. 21:2).

Granted, we know in part and prophesy in part (1 Cor. 13:9), so some of us may hear one part of God's message and others different parts. For example, God might be warning of judgment and encouraging his remnant at the same time. But if the word of the Lord that we hear consistently and urgently calls God's people to awaken, to turn more wholeheartedly to him, how can we hold that inside?

Jeremiah's generation didn't listen to him, but his message turned out to be true. And while Jeremiah himself did not see full vindication in his lifetime, the next generation affirmed his message (2 Chron. 36:22; Ezra 1:1; Dan. 9:2). Together with the exile, Jeremiah's message from God ultimately brought a paradigm shift among his people, who never again turned to physical idols.

Bad News and Bad Prophets[13]

When God gives a promise, we are right to believe it with all our hearts. Some biblical promises, though, are about collective judgment or impending hardship. These promises, too, we must take to heart so we may prepare for them (Gen. 41:30, 36; 2 Kings 8:1). This perspective may not appeal to a generation accustomed to having speakers cater to our wants as consumers. We need, however, to break that consumer habit when it comes to God, who does not work for a service industry.

Unfortunately, we leaders ourselves are vulnerable to being misled. If we do not immerse ourselves in God's voice in Scripture, we can sometimes miss the voice that is genuinely God's when his Spirit speaks to us. As we have seen, that happened in Jeremiah's day.

All the King's Prophets

We encounter the same sort of setting in 1 Kings, back in the time of the prophet Elijah. There all King Ahab's court prophets unanimously promise that their boss will win back the city he is trying to capture (1 Kings 22:6). Yet the God-fearing king of Judah, King Jehoshaphat, is uncomfortable with their unanimous message. That he wants to inquire from a prophet of the Lord (22:7) suggests that he recognizes that the prophets on Ahab's payroll are not speaking for God alone. King Ahab seems to view prophets the same way that some earnest Christians today treat "positive confession": Speak what is positive in the Lord's name and thus help bring it to pass. Without a genuine message from God's Spirit, however, that is a sure formula for false prophecy (see Lam. 3:37: "Who can speak and have it happen if the Lord has not decreed it?" [NIV]).

Ahab's false prophets use symbolic gestures just as true ones do (1 Kings 22:11). They claim to speak in the Lord's name, just as true ones do (22:11–12). Formal features do not distinguish the false prophecies from true ones; only truth can do that. But Jehoshaphat insists on hearing an independent witness, so Ahab reluctantly summons the prophet Micaiah, who consistently confronts Ahab with unpleasant messages (22:7–9). Why should Ahab believe this isolated, grumpy prophet who prophesies coming judgment on Ahab, when despite Micaiah's past prophecies Ahab remains alive? Micaiah will just put a damper on the troops' confidence before the battle!

Ahab's messenger thus warns Micaiah what the consensus of prophets is, and invites him to speak accordingly (1 Kings 22:13). Talk about pressure! Micaiah at first seems to echo the other prophets (22:15), yet in such a way that it seems clear to Ahab that he does not believe their message (22:16). Micaiah is committed to speak what he hears from God (22:14). Thus Micaiah prophesies that the king will die (22:17) and that God himself, as a means of judgment, ordained a false message for Ahab's prophets in order to lure him to destruction (22:19–23). Not every inspiring feeling that anyone has is from God's Spirit.

Better Heed the Right Ones!

As far as Ahab is concerned, this is just contrarian Micaiah, characteristically trying to give his king a hard time (1 Kings 22:18). Moreover, Zedekiah, one of the other leading prophets, strikes Micaiah, thereby publicly insulting and challenging him. Why should anyone suppose that Zedekiah, a renowned royal prophet, heard wrongly whereas isolated Micaiah heard correctly (22:24)? Micaiah informs him that he will know when the Lord's true word comes to pass, and Zedekiah has to hide in a time of judgment (22:25). The king takes precautions to forestall any bad luck from Micaiah's prophecy (22:26–27), as if Micaiah rather than the Lord were the source (22:28). (Despite what others sometimes suppose, those who prophesy judgment may not personally want it to happen; see Jer. 28:6; Luke 19:41–44.) Yet Micaiah's word does come to pass (1 Kings 22:34–37), as does an earlier prophecy of Elijah that had been deferred for a time on account of Ahab's temporary remorse (22:38; compare 21:19, 27–29). Needless to say, this proves to be the end of Ahab and his dynasty.

My African wife taught me to pay more attention to dreams, and now the Lord sometimes speaks to me through them. But not all dreams are from the Lord (Jer. 23:27, 32); some messages come only from people's own minds (23:26, 36). It is often easy to become popular by telling people what they want to hear (2 Tim. 4:3) and then attributing the corporate emotional thrill to God's anointing. Yet cheap thrills from rhetoric alone are not the same as the stirring power of the true word of the Lord in one's heart (Jer. 5:14), and imitations of prophetic form are not the same as the true word of the Lord—God's own voice within us (Jer. 23:28).

The biblical solution is not to throw out the baby with the bathwater, to discard Micaiah or Jeremiah along with the prophets who curry favor. The biblical solution is to use discernment (Jer. 23:28; 1 Cor. 14:29; 1 Thess. 5:20–22), unfortunately a discipline sometimes in short supply. Jeremiah seems to suggest that even the false prophets could have become true prophets had they truly feared and heeded God first (Jer. 23:21–22).

Consensus of people genuinely seeking God is important (Acts 15:28; 1 Cor. 14:29), but when a generation becomes too corrupted by its own desires, the consensus we must heed instead is the transgenerational succession of the true prophetic word (Jer. 28:8). If prophets have been announcing judgment for a land and no major transformation has occurred, then the burden of proof is on prophets who prophesy peace (28:9).

Accurate and Inaccurate Prophecies

Before I say more about false prophecies, I want to emphasize that prophecy can be very accurate, even today. Mesfin Nigusse, an Ethiopian Pentecostal with a track record of very accurate prophecies, did not know that I wrote books. Yet he prophesied to me accurately about two books that were then in process, including information that I myself did not yet know about their publication. Likewise, three different people of prayer in Congo-Brazzaville, who did not know one another, prophesied to Médine Moussounga that she was going to marry a white man with a big ministry. There aren't many white guys in her country, Médine and I weren't dating, and I didn't yet have a big ministry, but the prophecies proved correct.

Keep in mind, too, that in one of the instances Médine thought of a godly white friend in France during the prophecy, whereupon the woman prophesying interjected, "Not that white man, but another one." The woman prophesying in that case was also annoyed by what she needed to prophesy, because she was personally against Black Africans marrying white people, whom she had earlier experienced as oppressive colonialists. This prophecy and the others nevertheless proved surprisingly accurate. I have other dear friends who prophesy so accurately that I could never doubt the reality of the gift. But I am under no illusion that most people prophesy at that level; tragically, some people even abuse the gift or its counterfeit.

Hardships Ahead?

While some offer prophecies of peace and security each January, others have prophesied very differently. Certainly, earlier voices such as Leonard Ravenhill and David Wilkerson called for repentance in the face of coming judgment. For what it is worth, if anything (but I'll go ahead since I'm the one writing this book), I have sometimes felt judgment was coming also. (Judgments on societies are not judgments on every individual who suffers them, but wake-up calls to the societies more generally.) As one example, I wrote down something I felt the Lord was saying in 1982:

> Those who have not drawn near to me will be taken unprepared. Humble your hearts to hear my word, and seek not the prosperity of men—for man's prosperity will fade and wither in the time of famine, but the Lord will not suffer him to be hungry who has faith in him. Put your trust in the Lord; for the earth and its mountains shall be removed, but he who trusts in the Lord shall be firmly planted, as an oak battered by the winds but unshaken. Let my words be to you as the strength and life of your heart: so in the day of adversity you will stand and will not fail.[14]

Later I felt the Lord saying that Christians in North America sometimes acted as though severe catastrophes were only for other places, an attitude of arrogance against our brothers and sisters elsewhere. I had never thought of it that way. Then he went on to say that he would strip us of the things that we valued so we could learn to value what really matters. Sometimes I also felt that there would be a dangerous collapse of our infrastructure.

Someone may say, "Keener, it's been over four decades since then, and I don't see any catastrophes!" Personally, it takes me time to adjust, so I welcome plenty of advance warning. But maybe the US has already experienced more catastrophes than my imaginary critic might suppose—certainly we have experienced some disasters on the scale I was hearing in other countries, not least the tragedy of 9/11. Maybe what I felt was conditional—though I'm not sure I've yet witnessed the sort of repentance that would bring full relief. And naturally I'd prefer to be wrong. Yet I'm sure of one thing: God taught me that day not to exempt my own culture from the hardships that batter others.

Prophesying Amiss

Because prophecies get filtered through human agents (including a few heavy-handed prophetic editors), they can be distorted by deeply held personal convictions or the influence of popular theological fashions. It may be a matter of semantics whether we want to call the heavily redacted versions "prophecies," but their proclaimers and hearers often consider them such. Fashions can influence even the spiritually sincere, as they often have even in otherwise important movements of God's Spirit. At the height of the Moravian revival that birthed the first Protestant missions movement, some Moravians in the 1740s emphasized the blood of Jesus to such an extent that they sang that they were worms sucking Jesus's blood. Jonathan Edwards had to defend the First Great Awakening in the face of some excesses in the same era.[15] At the height of the Second Great Awakening, when leading evangelist Charles Finney was president of Oberlin College, the positive emphasis on healthy eating led to the cafeteria for a time serving especially the health fashion of the day: graham crackers.[16] (Admittedly, they also served vegetables, and 1830s whole-grain graham crackers were healthier than today's modified-for-consumers version.)

Some attempted "prophecies" even reflect mere calculations about the future. There is nothing wrong with futurists studying trends and helping us try to plan ahead. (For example, if the sea level is rising quickly, beachfront property might not be the wisest investment.) But futurism is not prophecy. For well over a century, "prophecy teachers" have tried to predict the future based on biblical prophecies—often taking verses out of context. It is legitimate to look for general principles of God's ways of working, but some of these speakers are just being Christian "futurists" (and also sometimes very speculative Bible interpreters). Some who claim to have the biblical gift of prophecy have blended it with futurism and arrived at very fallible predictions (projections? guesses?).[17]

Worse yet, some prophets speak from spirits other than God's. Once when I was a doctoral student I was invited to a neighbor's "discussion group," where I expected purely intellectual engagement. Instead it was a reading of an occult manual. Supposedly dictated from Jesus himself, it denied that sin and guilt were real.

Then the leader, who seemed very sincere, invited us all to discuss the reading. I pointed out that toward the end of the first century, there were various voices claiming to speak for Jesus (compare Rev. 2:14, 20). But John, who had been with Jesus in the flesh (John 1:14), insisted that the true prophetic voice of God's Spirit was the one in accord with the Jesus who came in the flesh (1 John 4:1–6), the Jesus whose message John had earlier recorded in his Gospel. The denial of sin, righteousness, and judgment reflected not the Spirit of Christ (John 16:7–11) but false prophets with the spirit of antichrist (1 John 4:3). The Spirit of true prophecy will always be consistent with the testimony about the real Jesus (Rev. 19:10).

Grounded in Rightly Understood Scripture

It is too easy to go along with what others tell us rather than stand for what God alone is saying. One true prophet who believed another prophet's "white lie" ended up paying for this error with his life (1 Kings 13:11–25). If we immerse ourselves in what we all can agree is God's Word—Scripture—we will be much more likely to rightly discern God's voice when he speaks to us in other ways.

Today we have Bibles, but we often interpret them according to how the rest of the church is living instead of interpreting how people are living in light of the Bible. We may assume that some commands are not meant to be taken very seriously if no one we know takes them seriously. But what if the problem is simply with the peer group we are using for comparison? Will you stand firm to make a difference for God in your generation? Even if you have to stand virtually alone? You can stand firm if you know, as God told Jeremiah, "I'm with you to help you" (Jer. 1:19).

After I had been a Christian for a couple of years, I began learning to hear God's voice in prayer.[18] I shared about this experience with a new believer whom I'll call Brenda (not her real name). After my first semester of Bible college I returned to my hometown for a visit, and by this time Brenda had gone way beyond me in listening to God. In fact, she was having visions. I had never had a vision, and—displaying my own spiritual immaturity—I got jealous. One day I shared with her something the Lord had shown me that day. "God showed me that *months* ago," she shot back. Spiritual gifts are not the same thing as the *fruit* of the Spirit!

Yet all was well and good until she began explaining her newest revelation (under the influence of an older friend who should have known better). Sometimes God gives people insights while reading Scripture;[19] these friends, however, had gotten this idea while reading the *Chronicles of Narnia* (though C. S. Lewis would not have approved). She shared that we, the church, would become the fourth member of the Trinity. Aside from this "revelation" violating basic arithmetic, it rather glaringly contradicted Scripture and the most basic orthodox theology. She insisted that it just complemented Scripture. "Of course it's not in the Bible," she explained. "It was revealed only last week."

"As far in the future as we see," I protested, based on the Bible's last chapter, "we are still his servants, serving him before his face."

"It's farther in the future than that," she replied. She and her friend began pressuring me for being unspiritual. I felt very stubborn, but I could not see how their point made sense biblically, or even from what I knew of the Spirit's voice. Eventually, Brenda admitted that the idea was wrong. But where had she gotten off the right path to begin with?

Brenda really did have an intimate relationship with God (despite the isolated and temporarily unorthodox anecdote I just offered), but it drifted off course because it was not grounded in Scripture. Brenda explained it this way: "God spoke to people in the Bible, but God speaks to me also. Why do I need to hear what God spoke to them when I can hear God for myself?"

Unlike Brenda, most of us know better than that, but many of us fail to immerse ourselves in Scripture anyway. One reason we need Scripture is that each of us plays just a part in God's larger plan in history (compare Acts 13:36). Paul warns, "We know in part and we prophesy in part" (1 Cor. 13:9) and that all prophecy must be evaluated (1 Cor. 14:29). Lots of people think they hear God, but how do we evaluate what God is really saying and who is really hearing him?

The Measuring Stick

The word *canon* means "a measuring stick." Whatever else Christians have disagreed with one another about, one thing nearly all of us agree about is that the Bible is "canonical"—that is, it is God's Word, and we can evaluate other claims in light of it.[20] In Jeremiah's day, there were lots of prophets, and lonely Jeremiah was the outlier. After Jeremiah's message was fulfilled, however, everybody knew which prophet was right and which prophets were wrong. So guess which one's book made it into the Bible?

Like the book of Jeremiah, the rest of Scripture comes to us tested by time (compare Ps. 18:30). It provides a "canon," a measuring stick we can use to evaluate any other claims to hear God's voice. Certainly, God sometimes has pleasant messages for his people (as in the book of Haggai, for example). But the burden of proof is always on those who speak what people want to hear, especially to those blatantly disobeying God's values. When a false prophet insisted to Jeremiah that all would be well, Jeremiah responded, "The prophets who preceded you and me from ancient times prophesied war, famine, and pestilence against many countries and great kingdoms. As for the prophet who prophesies peace, when the word of that prophet comes true, then it will be known that the LORD has truly sent the prophet" (Jer. 28:8–9 NRSV).

Conclusion

Jesus warned his disciples about coming suffering (John 16:2–3) so they would remember that he told them in advance (16:4) and thus would not fall away in time of testing (16:1). The world would hate them (15:25–16:4), but Jesus reminds us that he overcame the world (16:33). We should beware of supposed "revelations" that leave God's people unprepared for suffering hardship. Scripture urges us to be wise with sober expectations about what is coming: "A wise person sees trouble and hides oneself, but the simple-minded keep going, and pay the penalty" (Prov. 22:3; 27:12).

Clearly, true prophets often delivered messages about suffering and, especially in times of national disobedience, were forced to experience it themselves. Yet suffering is by no means limited to apostles (chap. 2) and prophets (chap. 3).

CHAPTER FOUR

"Ordinary" Christians and Suffering

There is no such thing as "ordinary" Christians, since all of us are born from God's own Spirit (1 Pet. 1:3, 23; 1 John 3:9). But lest anyone protest that biblical accounts about apostles (chap. 2) and prophets (chap. 3) are irrelevant for them, I need to show why suffering is expected for all believers in Jesus.

God demanded a lot from prophets in times when the culture rejected his values. To protect Jeremiah's heart for God in the coming time of judgment, God would not let Jeremiah marry (Jer. 16:2). God would not let Ezekiel mourn when his wife died (Ezek. 24:16–18). Hosea probably wished God hadn't let *him* marry (see Hosea 1:2). God made Isaiah run around fairly naked and barefoot for a few years (Isa. 20:2–3) and, had his wife not been a prophetess (8:3), she probably would've wished she hadn't married *him*.

But when a prospective disciple of Jesus wants to just go and say farewell to his family, Jesus says, "No one who looks back after setting his hand to the plow is a good fit for God's kingdom" (Luke 9:61–62).[1] When Elisha is plowing, Elijah calls him to be a disciple. Elisha requests that he first be allowed to say farewell to his family (1 Kings 19:20). By this he means a little farewell party for himself, where he would turn his back on his many fields and post-famine prosperity (see 19:19, 21). Elijah lets him do it (19:20), but Jesus tells a prospective disciple no. Being a disciple of the kingdom is more radical than being the disciple of an Old Testament prophet. Are we ready to follow Jesus wherever he calls?

Generic Suffering

Lest we think that suffering is only for apostles, prophets, or evangelists, Scripture is clear that persecution and various other hardships can strike anyone. As Paul writes,

Who shall separate us from the love of Christ? Shall

- trouble or
- hardship or
- persecution or
- famine or
- nakedness or
- danger or
- sword?

As it is written: "For your sake we face death all day long; we are considered as sheep to be slaughtered." (Rom. 8:35–36 NIV modified)

Paul quotes here from Psalm 44:22. Whereas some psalms lament God's people suffering his judgment, this psalm laments God's people suffering despite or even because of their faithfulness to him (44:17–18). And whereas the psalmist never saw descendants of the righteous begging for food (Ps. 37:25), Paul in Romans shows that believers, like others, may be caught even in famine. But his list also highlights persecution—my primary focus in the first part of this chapter.

Opposition Is the Norm

One evangelist in India was beaten, driven permanently from his home, and jailed for having shared the gospel. He explains, "Persecution is not an accident. It is the expectation."[2] In some places and periods, the experience is minimal, but we can never take such lulls in history's storm for granted.

Paul on Persecution

Everyone who wants to live in a godly way in Christ Jesus will be persecuted. (2 Tim. 3:12)

After noting his own experiences of persecution known directly to Timothy (2 Tim. 3:11), Paul says he expects this experience to be normal for all followers of Jesus.

For it has been granted to you not only to trust in Christ, but also to suffer on his behalf. (Phil. 1:29)

The Greek term here for "granted" is not the more generic term for "given"; it is a term specifying a gift of *grace*, of unmerited favor. God gives some of his people the *privilege* of suffering for Christ. We might translate it as "God has blessed you not just to trust in Christ but also to get to suffer for him." Paul goes on to say that the Philippians were now experiencing the same sort of suffering they had witnessed him suffer for Christ (Phil. 1:30). Paul had suffered public humiliation, beating, and imprisonment. Perhaps the intensity of their suffering was less, but it was no less real.

To another church Paul wrote that he sent them encouragement to keep them from being distressed by their sufferings:

> You know that we are destined for affliction. For even when we were with you, we warned you in advance that we would suffer affliction, even as also it has happened and you can recognize. (1 Thess. 3:3–4)

In his next letter to the same church, Paul praises those who endure through suffering:

> Among God's churches we boast about your perseverance and faith in all the persecutions and trials you are enduring. All this is evidence that God's judgment is right, and as a result you will be counted worthy of the kingdom of God, for which you are suffering. (2 Thess. 1:4–5 NIV)

As noted earlier, Paul regularly warned new believers to expect coming affliction, urging them

> to remain true to the faith. "We must go through many hardships to enter the kingdom of God." (Acts 14:22 NIV)

Luke is here summarizing not simply any random speech of Paul's but the heart of Paul's message to new believers!

Jesus on Persecution

Jesus had prepared his disciples for the same dangers:

> If the world hates you, you know that it hated me before it hated you. (John 15:18)

> Then Peter spoke up, "We have left everything to follow you!" "Truly I tell you," Jesus replied, "no one who has left home or brothers or sisters or mother or father or children or fields for me and the gospel will fail to receive a hundred times as much in this present age: homes, brothers, sisters, mothers, children

and fields—along with persecutions—and in the age to come eternal life."
(Mark 10:28–30 NIV)

Some more prosperity-oriented charismatics quote part of this passage to
promise a hundredfold return on whatever Christians sacrifice for the kingdom (and sometimes for the charismatic preachers themselves). Yet in light
of the rest of Mark's Gospel (especially 3:31–35), the hundred times as much
probably refers to Christians sharing their resources with their displaced
fellow Christians (see chaps. 8–9). It should therefore imply that we who are
not facing persecution should be partnering with those who are suffering it.
Helpful organizations doing this include Open Doors, Voice of the Martyrs,
Global Christian Relief, and Christian Solidarity International. Additional
organizations, such as Compassion International, Salvation Army, World Relief, World Vision, OneChild, Convoy of Hope, and others, help both believers
and nonbelievers who face other extreme circumstances.

Preachers who quote only part of the passage have sometimes also been
known to leave out the line that promises persecutions (Mark 10:30). Perhaps
Peter did not initially pay it much attention either. He noted that he had
abandoned everything to follow Jesus, but his "everything" was not quite
true—he would soon deny Jesus to save his own life (14:66–72). Yet Peter
later, empowered by the Spirit, continued to preach Christ and eventually
did give his life for Jesus. The Spirit makes the difference, empowering us
with boldness for Christ even in the face of persecution (as in Acts 4:8, 13:
"Peter, filled with the Spirit, spoke. . . . When they saw the boldness of Peter
and John . . ."). Nor is Spirit-empowered boldness for Peter alone. Acts 4:31
refers in context to the entire assembly:

They were all filled with the Holy Spirit and spoke God's message with boldness.

Thus, for example, Mariam Ibraheem, tortured in Sudan and on trial for
her life because of her faith, felt weak in herself. But she experienced the Spirit
giving her supernatural boldness whenever she needed to speak for Christ.[3]

Others, like seed sown on rocky places, hear the word and at once receive it with
joy. But since they have no root, they last only a short time. When trouble or persecution comes because of the word, they quickly fall away. (Mark 4:16–17 NIV)

Jesus speaks in Mark 4 of the seed of God's message sown on four kinds of
ground. Not all those who receive the message persevere. Some get distracted
by the affairs of this life (4:18–19), and others abandon Christ when they face

persecution—like Jesus's disciples the first time around (14:50). Still others, however, become fruitful (4:20). May we be like the fruitful soil.

Real Faith in Hebrews 11

Charismatics often put an emphasis on trusting all of God's Word, and that can strengthen the rest of the church—especially our cessationist brothers and sisters who want to relegate much of the New Testament narrative's theological message to the past. But some of our fellow charismatics are, like cessationists, inappropriately selective. They may highlight only the happier promises, sometimes taking them out of context. Naturally, we pray for the happier outcomes; the Bible provides plenty of models. But faith also entails recognizing the less happy promises.

Some people say that if we have *enough* faith or righteousness we can avoid such suffering. What does the Bible say? God always does what he says, but he does not always do what we might want him to say. Faith means trusting God—both when he does what we want and when he doesn't.[4]

Persevering Faith

Now faith is confidence in what we hope for and assurance about what we do not see. (Heb. 11:1 NIV)

Some popular teachers, whose teachings have influenced millions of people, have read this affirmation of faith as requiring belief that God will answer immediately: "If it's not now, it's not faith!"[5] Happily, this approach is less common today, but originally they based this teaching on the word *now* in Hebrews 11:1. In English grammar, however, *now* is an adverb, so if the Greek term here meant "now," it would modify *is* rather than *faith*. More important is the fact that the Greek term translated "now" is *de*, which does not mean "now" in the sense of time (that might have been the Greek word *nun*). *De* simply means "but" or "and." That is, if these popular teachers had even bothered to look up the term in an interlinear Bible, they would have seen that the verse has nothing to do with time.

This is not to deny the value of taking God at his word now. In the Gospels, people usually express their faith in desperate acts rather than simply hoping they will get better someday. The paralyzed man's friends are ready to tear up a neighbor's roof to get him to Jesus; Jesus recognizes their action as faith (Mark 2:4–5). The woman with the flow of blood actively touches the hem of Jesus's garment, despite the scandal of her touching anyone when she is ritually impure (5:25–29). Jesus calls her desperate action faith (5:34). Instead of taking Jesus's first no for an answer, the Syrophoenician woman humbles herself and explains why just a fragment of Jesus's power will be enough (7:27–28). In Matthew 15:28, Jesus calls her persistence and confidence in his power faith. Blind Bartimaeus cries out all the more for Jesus when the crowd tries to silence him (Mark 10:48), and Jesus commends his faith also (10:52).

But the kind of faith addressed in Hebrews 11 is not "faith that takes the answer now." It's faith that endures, awaiting God's promise. The entire context shows that it is faith for the long haul.

Faith to Endure for God's Future Promise

The preceding context is the endurance of faith. After their conversion, the letter's first audience had suffered insults, confiscation of property, and in some cases imprisonment (Heb. 10:32–34). They had done so because they trusted that in Christ they had a more permanent possession than what they had lost (10:34). "Don't throw away this confidence!" the author exhorts, since it "has a great reward" (10:35). Instead, his audience needs to hang in there, so that after they have done God's will, they may receive what God promised (10:36).

When would they receive this reward? Quoting the Old Testament, the author emphasizes that it will be at the Lord's coming (Heb. 10:37). The righteous are those who persevere for that day in saving faith, rather than shrinking back for destruction (10:38–39). *This* is the faith that Hebrews 11:1 says provides us certainty even before we see it with our eyes (11:1). The God who formed the world from invisible things (11:3) is true even before the outcome is visible.

This future orientation of faith continues through the rest of the chapter, giving examples of our predecessors in the faith (Heb. 11:2). Thus Abraham relocated in faith, living in tents, without yet experiencing the inheritance of the ultimate promised land—a city built by God (11:8–10). The patriarchs

> were still living by faith when they died. They did not receive the things promised; they only saw them and welcomed them from a distance. (11:13 NIV)

Here was their positive confession of faith:

> [They confessed] that they were foreigners and strangers on earth. . . . They were longing for a better country—a heavenly one, [and God] has prepared a city for them. (Heb. 11:13, 16 NIV)

By faith Isaac blessed Jacob and Esau in *regard to their future*. By faith Jacob, when he was *dying*, blessed each of Joseph's sons. . . . By faith Joseph, when his *end* was near, spoke about the exodus of the Israelites from Egypt and gave instructions concerning the burial of his bones. (Heb. 11:20–22 NIV, emphasis mine)

By faith Moses . . . chose to suffer with God's people rather than to enjoy the short-term benefit of sin. He deemed bearing reproach with Christ better than Egypt's treasures, because he looked *ahead* for the reward. (Heb. 11:24–26)

Faith When God Doesn't Deliver Before Death

Hebrews goes on to summarize other people of faith and their victories in 11:32–34. But the author is not concerned only with victories in this life. He mentions mothers who received back from death children who were raised, presumably in miracles worked through Elijah and Elisha (1 Kings 17:23; 2 Kings 4:36–37). But then, probably thinking especially of the Maccabean martyrs, he mentions others who were tortured to death, refusing to compromise their faith to secure release. They endured because they looked ahead to a better, more permanent resurrection than what Elijah or Elisha could bring (Heb. 11:35).

Others experienced the testing of mocking and whipping, and further chains and imprisonment. (Heb. 11:36)

Thinking of stories about the prophets, the writer continues,

They were stoned, sawed in two, murdered by sword, traveling around in sheepskins and goatskins, deprived, afflicted, badly treated . . . wandering in deserts and mountains and caves and pits. (Heb. 11:37–38)

That is, these heroes of the faith experienced severe deprivations for their faith. Elijah, for example, spent much time in the wilderness (1 Kings 17:3–7; 19:4). When Jezebel killed prophets, others had to hide in caves (18:4). Joash had Zechariah stoned (2 Chron. 24:21). Later Jewish tradition says Isaiah's persecutors sawed him in half.[6] In the midst of the list of sufferings, the author adds,

The world was not worthy of them. (Heb. 11:38)

They belonged to a better world than this present one.

But while God commended the faith of all of them, none of them—
including the earlier heroes in the chapter—received the perfected promise
(Heb. 11:39) of the coming city (11:10, 16; 12:22; 13:14) and resurrection
bodies (11:35). These remain in the future.

The original Bible had no chapter breaks; in Hebrews 12:1 the writer mentions the great cloud of those who testified for their faith and calls again for
endurance. But then the writer turns to the ultimate hero of the faith:

> Jesus, the forerunner and completer of the faith. (Heb. 12:2)

Jesus also modeled faith for us by enduring in the present because of confidence in future reward:

> For the joy set before him he endured the cross, scorning its shame, and sat
> down at the right hand of the throne of God. (Heb. 12:2 NIV)

Jesus himself was made perfect through sufferings (Heb. 2:10). By considering what Jesus endured, we can strengthen our own resolve to endure (12:3).

Unlike many of those the author has mentioned, including Jesus, Hebrews'
first audience had

> not yet resisted to the point that your blood has been shed. (Heb. 12:4)

So what, the author asks, do they really have to complain about? God sees our
suffering, the author assures us, but God uses this suffering like benevolent
parental discipline, to make us better (12:5–11). God's discipline for us is not
abusive, but an act of love for our good, so we may share his holiness (12:10;
compare Rev. 3:19).

Testing and Trials

> No temptation has overtaken you except what is common to mankind. And
> God is faithful; he will not let you be tempted beyond what you can bear. But
> when you are tempted, he will also provide a way out so that you can endure
> it. (1 Cor. 10:13 NIV)

> It will be well for anyone who endures testing, because after proving faithful
> in the test they will receive the award of life that God promised to those who
> love him. (James 1:12)

> Loved ones, don't think strange the fiery burning that comes to test you, as if
> something strange were happening to you. (1 Pet. 4:12)

We can stand firmly, even stubbornly, on God's Word; Abraham and Moses appealed to God's character and promises until God answered them (Gen. 18:23–32; Exod. 32:10–14; 33:12–17). The Gospels present as models those so sure that Jesus could help them that they refused to let any obstacle deter them from getting his help (e.g., Mark 2:4; 5:27; 7:28; 10:48; John 2:4–5). Yet Scripture taken as a whole promises not only blessings but also hardship, and even the blessings get tested.

Testing to Prove Versus Testing to Trip Up

In the Bible, both the wicked and the righteous may suffer, but the wicked may experience suffering as judgment whereas the righteous experience it as testing.

"The Lord tests both the righteous and the wicked," the psalmist observes (Ps. 11:5). English Bibles sometimes speak of "trials" or "testing" or "tempting"; these reflect the same terminology in Greek. The Greek words for the verb (*peirazō*) and noun (*peirasmos*) refer to putting us to the test, but the *motives* for such testing may vary, depending on who is testing us. A hard professor may test students at a high level to raise the standard and help them to excel; or (in principle) a mean professor could test them with the objective of flunking them. The Bible speaks of both kinds of testing, the former characterizing God and the latter characterizing the devil ("the tempter," Matt. 4:3; 1 Thess. 3:5) and people like him.

James says that God does not test us (James 1:13–14), in this case meaning that he, unlike the devil, does not seek to make us fall ("tempt" us). Scripture does claim that God tests us, but it is in a different sense; his interest is in solidifying our faith through us enduring the test, strengthening our faith muscles by forcing us to exercise them. God is sovereignly at work even when evil is testing us (e.g., Deut. 13:3), but God's purpose is different from the devil's. God sometimes visibly sorts out those who are his, and proves to the world and the devil that some really do model the faith that others should have had (compare Job 1:8, 12; 2:3, 6). Those who endure may rise up at the judgment and render the rebellious without excuse (compare Matt. 12:41–42; Luke 11:31–32).

Jesus warns us to pray that God won't lead us into testing (Matt. 6:13; Luke 11:4), but he is not implying that we won't be tested. Jesus himself faced testing. Rather, the point is that we won't fall when tested. Jesus uses the same wording later, when he warns his disciples in Gethsemane, "Stand watch and pray, so you won't come into testing. Your hearts are willing, but your flesh is weak" (Matt. 26:41). When Jesus said these words, testing—in the form of the arrest party—was already on its way up the hill. The point was not that they could escape being tested but that they would be ready so as not to fall. Jesus watched and prayed that night, and he was ready when his test arrived. His disciples fell asleep instead of watching and praying, and they were caught unprepared.

Passing Our Tests

God may test our faith as we await the fulfillment of what he has shown us. God refined Joseph like this (Ps. 105:19). God sometimes tests us to show what we are truly made of (Deut. 13:3; Judg. 2:22; 3:1, 4; 2 Chron. 32:31; Jer. 17:10; 20:12). As Mariam Ibraheem learned during her imprisonment for Christ, "Our faith cannot truly be revealed to us until it is tested, and it is not tested during good times."[7]

Abraham passed his ultimate test (Gen. 22:1–19); Israel in the wilderness failed their tests multiple times (Exod. 15:25; 16:4; Ps. 81:7). When God tests us to humble us, though, it is for our good (Deut. 8:2, 16). The psalmist sometimes even invited God to demonstrate the psalmist's righteousness by God's testing the psalmist (Pss. 17:3; 26:2; 139:23),[8] though he probably meant something more like a spiritual CT scan than the kind of testing Job experienced!

> These testings are meant to prove the genuineness of your trust in God. Even though fire proves the genuineness of gold, gold is perishable. But your trust in God is worth far more than gold. The result of such unalloyed trust in God will be praise, glory and honor when Jesus Christ is revealed! (1 Pet. 1:7)

Sometimes we might read 1 Peter 1:7 as if it were saying that our faith is more precious than perishable gold. In Greek, however, it is clear that Peter says that the *testing* of our faith is what is more precious than gold. Anything mortal may perish in fire, but faith *tested* by fire is proven and will not fall away; it is like those in 1 Peter 4:1 who have suffered for Christ and proven sturdy enough to persevere:

> Whoever has suffered in the flesh has given up sin.

As something more precious than gold, faith-testing is in good company, alongside God's Word and wisdom (Ps. 119:127; Prov. 3:14; 8:19).

Commenting on 1 Peter 1, church father Athanasius, a leading defender of the Trinity, explains: "Rather than being hurt by what they went through, they grew and were made better, shining like gold that has been refined in a fire."[9]

Testing ideally produces pure metal (Ps. 66:10; Prov. 17:3; Isa. 48:10; Zech. 13:9), and God desires to make a precious masterpiece of us. Another church father, Hilary of Arles, remarked, "The glory of the redeemed will never fade after they have been raised from the dead, for it will have withstood the fire of temptation, whereas the gold of this world is said to rust."[10]

Jesus's Testing

Because he himself suffered when he was tempted, he is able to help those who are being tempted. (Heb. 2:18)

For we don't have a high priest who's unable to sympathize with our weaknesses, but one who was tested in every way like we are—except without sinning. (Heb. 4:15)

Jesus faced testing at various times (Luke 22:28). One of the most obvious times occurred after the heavenly voice announced Jesus's calling and before Jesus entered his public ministry. I would think forty days without eating (Matt. 4:2; Luke 4:2) would be testing enough, but Satan then tried to get the famished Jesus to use his power to feed himself by turning stones into bread (Matt. 4:3; Luke 4:3). At one point Satan even quotes Scripture out of context to try to manipulate Jesus (Matt. 4:6; Luke 4:10–11). It's no surprise that Satan also uses Scripture selectively today. (Incidentally, Satan may have often heard the verses he quotes here, Ps. 91:11–12; that psalm was a favorite among ancient exorcists!) Jesus, by contrast, responds to testing consistently by quoting Scripture in appropriate ways, making an analogy between his forty days of testing in the wilderness and the forty years that Israel experienced testing in the wilderness.

After God declares Jesus his Son (Matt. 3:17; Luke 3:22; compare Luke 3:38), Satan challenges Jesus's sonship: "So, you're God's Son? Then do this . . ." (Matt. 4:3, 6; Luke 4:3, 9). Satan challenges what God has said (compare Gen. 3:3–5). But Jesus responds by appealing to a passage where God treated Israel as his son (Deut. 8:5). There God teaches Israel that they should live by his promise rather than by mere bread (Deut. 8:3); as God's Son, Jesus therefore depends on his Father to provide for him. When the devil suggests that Jesus throw himself from the temple and wait for angels to catch him, Jesus responds with a nearby passage, Deuteronomy 6:16. Israel had tested God at Massah by refusing to trust his provision (Exod. 17:7); Jesus quotes the verse that warns them against testing God again. Jesus again depends on his Father to provide for him; and after the testing, God does indeed send angels to take care of Jesus (Matt. 4:11).

But the devil's third offer in Matthew might be the most insidious: If Jesus worships Satan, Satan will let him rule the world (Matt. 4:9; Luke 4:7). Jesus, of course, will rule the world anyway. But God's way to the kingdom is costlier, passing through the cross, and Satan offers Jesus the world without the cross. Jesus knows better and refuses, mining again the same context (this time just three verses away, in Deut. 6:13; Jesus knows context). Jesus commands Satan to depart (Matt. 4:10).

Satan is not acting subtly here. But what happens when your best friend, your handpicked student, suggests the same thing as Satan, just more subtly? Right after Jesus commends Peter as a rock for recognizing Jesus as Christ the king (Matt. 16:18), Peter protests that Jesus's kingdom can't include suffering (16:22). We then get a rerun of Jesus's rebuke to Satan in Matthew 4:10. "Go behind me, Satan!" Jesus tells Peter that he has now gone from being a good rock (16:18) to being a bad rock, a stumbling block (16:23). Testing can strike even from unexpected angles.

Some Places Harder Than Others

Jesus warned that we will be hated by all nations (Matt. 10:22; 24:9)—that is, all the world (Mark 13:13; John 15:18). That does not mean, however, that every place will hate us equally at all times. Christians in Corinth experienced relatively little hostility at a time when Macedonian Christians in Philippi and Thessalonica were enduring much (Phil. 1:29–30; 1 Thess. 1:6; 3:4).

The outcome of suffering also differs from place to place: James was beheaded (Acts 12:2), yet Peter was miraculously released (12:7–10). Although it's possible that prayer made a difference in Peter's case (12:5, 12), sometimes the difference is just a matter of God's plan. Jesus promised Philadelphian Christians deliverance from their suffering: "Because you have obeyed my command to endure, I'll also protect you from the hour of testing" (Rev. 3:10). By contrast, he warns Christians in Smyrna that their suffering is about to get worse: "Don't fear the things you're about to suffer. Look, the devil's going to cast some of you into prison so you will be tested, and you'll face affliction for ten days. Stay faithful until death, and I'll give you the award of life" (Rev. 2:10). God would preserve Philadelphia's Christians in hardship but would not prevent Smyrna's Christians from facing death.

The modern Western world and past Western colonial regimes (despite their severe failings) have sometimes protected Christians or offered a measure of religious freedom, leaving a legacy in which such protection is seen as a right. (This despite growing anti-religious sentiment in some of Western culture today, and despite the fact that past Western colonialists often repressed missionaries and especially some indigenous Christian movements.)[11] Many of the cultures that emphasize hospitality also value tolerance. But not everyone everywhere today shares these perspectives; evil prevails more in some places than in others (e.g., Ps. 12:8; Prov. 29:12).

The modern Western legacy of religious freedom should not blind us to global realities. I discuss persecution more extensively in chapter 6. Like Peter during Jesus's arrest, some of us Christians in the United States might want to defend Jesus or ourselves with a worldly sword (John 18:10)—without which we would rather flee or follow only from afar. But Jesus calls true disciples to pick up not a sword but our cross to follow him (Mark 8:34; compare Matt. 26:52). This is not to deny the importance of speaking for justice (e.g., Mark 12:38–40; James 5:1–6), including for ourselves (compare Luke 22:48; John 18:23; Acts 23:3). In the final analysis, though, the one thing we can always control is not how others treat us but how faithfully we follow Jesus.

Many cultures even disdain Christianity as a Western import—even though Jesus birthed his movement in western Asia (in the Middle East) and an estimated 80 percent "of the most active Christians" in today's world live outside the West.[12] Some plausibly suggest that church attendance may be higher in China today than in all of western Europe put together.[13] Jihadists attacked the home of my acquaintance, Bishop Benjamin Kwashi, who soon after became Anglican archbishop of Jos, Nigeria. He complains that Islamists treat the African church as a convenient scapegoat and proxy for the West.[14] Yet Christians flourished in much of what is now the Muslim world before the birth of Islam—for example, in Persia (Iran) from the second century onward.[15] Egypt, Syria, and Turkey were strongly Christian, and Christian faith remained strong in many of these lands into the late Middle Ages[16] and early twentieth century[17] (and in Egypt even today). The western Asian kingdom of Armenia (AD 301) and the eastern African kingdom of Axum (330s–350s) became Christian before Christianity became the official religion of the Roman Empire (380).[18]

Because most Western Christians right now do not face imprisonment or death for their faith, in contrast to many early Christians, I will defer models of major persecution for chapter 6. Those who are severely persecuted, too, are ordinary Christians. But in less conspicuous ways, at least in most of the West, we are aware of some non-Christians' prejudice against us for our faith. (Indeed, most religious and cultural minorities experience prejudice, although this book's focus is on Christians.) Our suffering isn't always due to our faith, though; we as believers often suffer the same things other people do so they can see our distinctive, eternal confidence. If Christians never suffered, the world would convert for the wrong reasons, and their conversions might dissolve when they are tempted (compare perhaps the situation envisioned in Rev. 20:7–8). Paul's "trouble or hardship or . . . famine or being poorly clothed" (Rom. 8:35) includes facing difficulties beyond those provoked by our faith. It's a supreme blessing to be human, but part of being human is hardship. We undoubtedly have much to learn from our brothers and sisters who suffer more than we do (again, more of their lessons appear in chap. 6).

Ridicule

Sometimes hatred is expressed simply in ridicule (e.g., Ps. 44:16), something most of us have experienced for various reasons, not least for our faith. (In the US, this may vary by region and social groupings.) Scripture treats this experience as normal, and warns us not to respond in kind but rather to be gentle.

> Blessed are you when people insult you, persecute you and falsely say all kinds of evil against you because of me. (Matt. 5:11 NIV)

> Blessed are you when people hate you, when they exclude you and insult you and reject your name as evil, because of the Son of Man. (Luke 6:22 NIV)

> When we are verbally abused, we bless. (1 Cor. 4:12 NASB)

> Behave well among the gentiles. That way, those who slander you as wrongdoers for something may see your good works and honor God on the day when he comes. (1 Pet. 2:12)

> Don't pay back wrong for wrong. Don't answer an insult with another insult— instead, bless your mockers! Because God called you for this lifestyle, so that you would inherit blessing. (1 Pet. 3:9)

> They're amazed that you don't join them in their wasteful excesses. That's why they say terrible things about you. (1 Pet. 4:4)

In this we follow the model of our Lord:

> When others abused him verbally, he didn't abuse them back. When he was suffering, he didn't threaten his abusers. Instead he handed himself over to the one who judges justly. (1 Pet. 2:23)

People make fun of others for many reasons, especially now that they can do so anonymously online. Before I was a Christian, some people thought I was strange because I was an atheist (and others thought I was strange just because I actually am, well . . . idiosyncratic). So after I became a Christian, it didn't surprise me too much that many people thought I was strange because I was a Christian. I made fun of Christians when I was an atheist, and when I became a Christian some people made fun of me; in that sense I knew what I was getting myself into. With some notable and appreciated exceptions, non-Christian acquaintances avoided hanging out with me because they couldn't put up with my incessant talk about Jesus! But by standards of suffering in the world, this is extremely mild.

A larger problem is when we and therefore our message get misrepresented because of people's prejudices. It is heartbreaking when others twist our diligent labors for the gospel to misrepresent it. People sometimes misrepresent the gospel as racist, sexist, imperialist, greedy, or abusive. Some people who claim to be Christians do misrepresent the Christian faith in these ways, and then others—through stereotyping and slander—paint all Jesus's followers with the same brush.

Yet even this is not unexpected, though we labor however possible to challenge the misconceptions. Paul had to endure misrepresentation and slander, putting up

> with honor and dishonor, with negative press and good press. (2 Cor. 6:8)

Sadly, some misrepresentations come from fellow believers. Many Jerusalemite believers zealous for the law had heard that Paul taught Jews to abandon their ancestral, biblical customs (Acts 21:20–21). Some people even twisted his preaching of God's forgiveness and charged that he supported sinning (Rom. 3:8)! Similarly, some of Jesus's critics twisted his transformational welcome for sinners to claim that he supported their sin (Mark 2:15–17; see also Matt. 11:19; Luke 7:34). Some even represented him as forbidding paying taxes to Caesar (Luke 23:2)—despite his earlier public statement to the contrary when they bothered to ask (Luke 20:24–25)!

Jesus promised:

> You are blessed when people insult you and throw out your name as evil. (Luke 6:22)

Sometimes those hostile to God's message enlist compromised members of God's own people to make common cause with them (e.g., 2 Kings 18:22), as when atheist skeptics recruit Christian skeptics to help undermine the message. When others slander us, we can turn only to God, who puts everything else in the right perspective (Pss. 31:13–14; 119:69, 78, 86; 120:2–4). God has our back, and his honor will be vindicated in the end (compare Matt. 11:19;

Luke 7:35). In the 1800s, local malicious slander endangered Hudson Taylor's group of missionaries in China, followed by misrepresentation in the British press. But God protected their mission.[19] In the former Soviet Bloc, government propaganda exploited both false accusations[20] and real cases of fallen or weak Christians[21] in trying to discredit the gospel. In one case in Tajikistan, misrepresentation in local media led first to more inquirers about the gospel, but then to the church planter's martyrdom. That in turn, however, precipitated the conversion of the martyr's son.[22] In Egypt, local gossip distorted a church's teaching as insulting Muhammad, leading some five thousand people to surround the church; several people were killed and ninety injured.[23] Slander obviously continues today—even if we could otherwise forget, every election season in the US would remind us!

Conclusion

We have already looked at apostles, prophets, and "ordinary" Christians. Now let's look more at the hero who climaxes the list of faith heroes in Hebrews 11:4–12:3: Jesus, the author and finisher of the faith, whom Hebrews offers as the supreme model for enduring suffering (12:1–3).

CHAPTER FIVE

Sharing with *Jesus* in Suffering

You don't know what you're requesting. Are you able to drink the cup from which I drink or be baptized with the baptism with which I am baptized?

—Mark 10:38

Just as Christ's sufferings abound in us, even so our comfort abounds through Christ.

—2 Corinthians 1:5

My goal is to know Jesus and the power of his resurrection and a sharing in his sufferings, so that being conformed to his death I may in some way reach the resurrection from the dead also.

—Philippians 3:10–11

I complete in my flesh what remains of Christ's sufferings for the sake of his body, which is the church.

—Colossians 1:24[1]

Instead, to the extent that you're sharing Christ's sufferings, be glad, so you may celebrate with joy when his glory is revealed.

—1 Peter 4:13

Sharing Christ's Sufferings

A key biblical feature of intimacy with Christ is sharing in his sufferings. If the world hated me, Jesus warned, it will hate you (John 15:18). A Sudanese imam flogged Mariam Ibraheem for two hours for her refusal to deny Christ, leaving her back bloody. Yet she renewed her strength by identifying with Christ. Noting John 15:18, she reasoned, "My Savior had also been whipped, so why would I expect anything better?"[2] In Nepal, as Surita's Buddhist father-in-law beat her head with her Bible, she contemplated Christ's much greater pain on the cross.[3]

> Whoever heeds you heeds me, and whoever rejects you rejects me; and whoever rejects me rejects the one who sent me. (Luke 10:16)

Of Saul, who was persecuting the church, the Lord demanded, "Why are you persecuting *me*?" (Acts 9:4). Jesus's words here evoke again what he told his disciples in Luke 10:16. Whatever they do to us as we are serving Christ, they do to him. (This may be especially the case for what they do to the lowliest and humblest of believers; see Mark 9:37, 42; Matt. 18:5–6.) In chapter 2, I mentioned the terrible abuse Dr. Helen Roseveare experienced in Congo. She recounts that while she was being abused and felt too numb to pray, she experienced God's dramatic presence. Not everyone experiences grace this same way during suffering, but we can all learn from her experience.

"Twenty years ago," she heard the Lord say, "you asked me for the privilege of being a missionary. This is it." She understood: the privilege is identification with Christ. As she was being beaten, she felt the Lord saying: "These are not your sufferings. . . . These are *my* sufferings. All I ask of you is the loan of your body." This assurance didn't reduce the pain or humiliation, she notes, but it gave it new meaning: "the inestimable privilege of sharing in some little way in the fellowship of his sufferings."[4]

Son of Man and Sacrificial Lamb

Jesus's self-designated title "Son of Man" implies his suffering with us as well as our suffering with him. This image goes back to Daniel 7. Daniel has a vision of four evil empires and their kings as beasts. But then he speaks of God's own, final kingdom and king not as a beast but as one that looks human, "like a son of man" (Dan. 7:11–14). Identified with the people of God's kingdom, this Son of Man suffers under the final beast (7:21–22, 25), which Jesus's contemporaries understood as Rome. Afterward both God's people and their king would be exalted to reign in glory forever (7:21–27). Yet the king in *God's* kingdom is not only human but divine, receiving *worship* (7:14). Jesus is the divine human, the ultimate Son of Man, who reigns in God's kingdom.

Identifying with his Jewish people, he suffered with them before beginning to reign. His people were expecting a conquering messiah who would overthrow Rome, but Jesus instead suffered with his people under Rome. Instead of crushing Rome, Jesus let Rome crush him—indeed, on the ultimate symbol of its imperial brutality: a cross. At his first coming, Jesus's mission was not about conquering Rome—Rome was small fries. Destroying one empire without destroying the spirit of empire merely makes way for other empires. Jesus's mission was far more urgent and fundamental. Jesus came to conquer sin and death, and thus to begin to transform the world from the inside out. The glory of the new covenant is not external, like that of the Mosaic covenant, which brought plagues and judgment and embodied a revelation even fatally holy. Instead, new covenant glory works internally, conforming us to God's heart revealed in Christ (2 Cor. 3:6–18).

When the book of Revelation speaks of a "beast" (Rev. 13:1–2), it actually blends the imagery of all four of Daniel's beasts (Dan. 7:3–7) as the spirit of evil empire more generally. The beast seeks to supplant the lamb (Rev. 13:11), as Babylon strives with the new Jerusalem (contrast Rev. 17:4–5 with 21:2, 18–21). In terms of worldly power, in any conflict between a "beast" and a lamb, most people would place their bets on the beast. But they don't know that the lamb is the *lion* from the tribe of Judah. The future belongs not to the conquering beast and his followers, but to the martyred lamb and his followers (compare Rev. 13:16–14:1).

In Revelation 5, John hears about a conquering lion, symbol of power and of the victorious Messiah. But when he turns, he sees a slain lamb, the epitome of weakness and vulnerability (Rev. 5:5–6). At his first coming, Jesus conquered not by force but by submitting to God's plan on the cross. Now, as the sacrificial Lamb, he begins to open the seals that guide the rest of history (5:5; 6:1).

One of the seals opened by Jesus reveals those who died for him. These martyrs would not be completely avenged until the rest of those destined to be martyred would die (Rev. 6:9–11).[5] John describes these martyrs as souls "under the altar," slain because of God's message and their testimony (6:9). Why were they under the altar? When priests sacrificed animals, they poured out the animals' blood at the base of the altar (Exod. 29:12; Lev. 4:7). Just as Jesus was slain like a sacrificial lamb (Rev. 5:6; 13:8), those who share in his death appear as sacrifices. Most of the time we are living sacrifices (Rom. 12:1), but whether in life or in death, sharing in Christ's sufferings is the privilege of his true followers.

How Far Will We Follow?[6]

> If anyone wants to follow after me, let them deny themselves and take up their cross and follow me. (Mark 8:34)

Early Christian memory is probably right to recognize Mark as a protégé of Jesus's famous disciple Peter. Mark tells his Gospel especially from Peter's perspective. Mark starts with Jesus calling Peter (Mark 1:16–18) and then follows Peter's perspective through Peter recognizing Jesus as the Messiah (8:29), his resistance to Jesus's impending suffering (8:32), his fumbling at the transfiguration (9:5–6), and to his denial (14:66–72). Peter's absence at Jesus's crucifixion becomes conspicuous, but Mark soon resumes with Jesus's promise to restore Peter (16:7). God may have used prayer to help spare Peter from early martyrdom (Acts 12:5), but Peter was eventually martyred for his faithful witness.

As best as we can reconstruct Mark's setting, he writes to a suffering audience. They have survived persecution in Rome, when the emperor Nero was burning Christians alive as torches to light his gardens at night. Some of their friends died for their faith; some others may have escaped martyrdom by denying their faith and now are ashamed. Mark reminds them that the great apostle Peter, whom many considered a hero, failed the first time too. Ultimately, the only real and perfect hero of our faith is Jesus, who embraced his own death to give us all life. And as Peter matured and became the fisher of people Jesus originally called him to be (Mark 1:17), so too can we.

The question now is whether we stay on the road following Jesus cross-ward or whether we abandon him even in our current tests. Jesus is worth everything (Matt. 13:44–46), but admittedly we need help. That is why Jesus taught us to pray, "Lead us not into testing"(Matt. 6:13; Luke 11:4). That is also why he invites us to ask the Father for the power of his Spirit (Luke 11:13; compare Ps. 143:10), who accomplishes in us more than we could ask or think (Eph. 3:16, 20).

Jesus Is the Messiah

When I get to know some of my living spiritual "heroes," I discover that they are flesh and blood like me, gifted by God and recognizing their dependence on him. Some have even failed him at times. No matter whom we might admire in this world, all of them put together can't hold a candle to Jesus. Yet the greatest hero came with a secret identity.

Peter was in awe of Jesus—but not nearly as much as he should have been. It takes the first half of Mark's Gospel for Peter to recognize: "You're the

Messiah!" (Mark 8:29). It takes the second half of Mark's Gospel for Peter and his fellow disciples to understand what Jesus's messiahship entails: Their king will be enthroned on a Roman cross, crowned with thorns.

Peter's confession of Jesus's messiahship and Jesus's explanation of what that means is a turning point in Mark's Gospel. When Peter confesses that Jesus is the Messiah, Jesus warns his disciples not to tell anybody (Mark 8:30). This warning fits Jesus's pattern of controlling unnecessary publicity wherever possible (1:44; 3:12; 5:43; 7:24, 36; 8:26). One reason for this is the danger of overcrowding that the publicity created (1:45; 2:2–4; 3:9–10; 5:24; 6:31). Another reason is that Jesus's popularity made him a target of those who wanted all the attention for themselves and their own teaching (2:7; 3:6; 7:5; 15:10). The biggest problem is politics: If people viewed Jesus as the messianic king, guardians of public order would want him dead. That was because they would view Jesus as a threat to the current order. They did not understand what it *meant* for him to be the messianic king.

The heart of Jesus's public message was that God's kingdom was coming (Mark 1:15). The good news about the kingdom is really the good news about Jesus Christ as Lord, the kingdom's King. But it was not yet time to proclaim his kingship publicly, since that would precipitate his execution prematurely. The secret of the kingdom (4:11), therefore, was the secret identity and mission of that kingdom's King. This secret of the kingdom was revealed at first only to a handful who even themselves barely comprehended it. God's future reign was already present in a veiled way because the King was present, but at the moment it was just a tiny seed of what the kingdom will look like when Jesus returns to consummate it (4:30–32).

Mark summarizes Jesus's message in terms of the kingdom (Mark 1:15; 4:11, 26, 30; compare 10:14–15, 23–24; 14:25). Yet instead of Mark's narrative climaxing with a lavish, public display of power, Mark's "king" language climaxes with the "King of the Jews" enthroned on a cross, crowned with thorns (15:2, 9, 12, 17–18, 26, 32).

What It Means for Jesus to Be the Messiah

We think of the world today as being moved by prominent figures—Trump or Putin, Netanyahu, or fill in the blank for your own time and place. When Jesus's contemporaries thought of kings, they thought of rulers who exploited power over others (Mark 10:42). They thought of people like Herod Antipas. Mark calls Antipas a "king" (6:14), since many Galileans viewed him that way because he was a powerful heir of King Herod the Great. But politically, Antipas was just a governor who was a wannabe king.[7] And while Herod

Antipas pretended to have power, his wife and stepdaughter exploited his own reckless passions that he, lacking power even over his own heart, failed to bridle (compare Prov. 16:32). They manipulated him into beheading a prophet at his own birthday banquet (Mark 6:19–28). Meanwhile, Jesus serves a different banquet, feeding the hungry masses by God's power (6:41–42).

Herod, of course, isn't the Gospel's real king. Toward the end of Mark's Gospel, the language of "king" applies exclusively and repeatedly to Jesus—as a mocking accusation and charge from his enemies.

People expected the real king to conquer Rome by force. But instead Rome conquers Jesus by force. The real King does not exploit others to serve him; he serves others to the death (Mark 10:45). What kind of king is this?

Once Peter confesses Jesus as Messiah (Mark 8:29), then Jesus is ready to clarify what it *means* for him to be the Messiah: Jesus is the promised suffering Son of Man (8:31). As in Daniel 7, the Son of Man would reign (see also Mark 8:38). Even at Jesus's first coming, throughout Mark's Gospel, spirits, sickness, and storms are subject to him; human beings alone are given a choice. And sinful humans choose power to hurt others.

Satan's Theology

Have you ever had to comfort someone who felt like God did not come through for them the way they expected? Have you ever faced such a disappointment yourself? Sometimes false expectations about God or his purposes set us up for disappointments. In Mark 8, Peter had some seriously false expectations. In this case, they risked more than disappointment.

So long as Jesus spoke in parables, his disciples requested explanations (Mark 4:10, 34). In 8:32, however, Mark says that Jesus speaks "plainly"—that is, not in parables—this time. Now Peter *does* understand Jesus's message—and therefore *opposes* it! Peter has been happy to follow a conquering Messiah; he did not sign up for following a martyr to the death. So Peter decides to "rebuke" his own master (8:32)!

Mark says that Peter took Jesus aside rather than reprove him publicly; this was because Peter recognized that disciples were not supposed to correct their teachers. But Jesus turns and rebukes Peter openly in front of his colleagues (Mark 8:33). Jesus himself taught, as did other Jewish teachers, that we should start any correction process privately. This occasion is, however, a special emergency (not the last time an exception will be made to Peter's dismay; see Gal. 2:14). In a culture that valued honor and feared shame, Jesus shames Peter in front of his fellow disciples! They probably shared Peter's opinion, so Jesus makes Peter's failure an object lesson for all of them.

"Get behind me!" Jesus demands (Mark 8:33). Disciples were supposed to *follow* their teachers, not lead them. Jesus's first recorded words to Peter in Mark's Gospel were, "Follow me" (1:17). Now he has to remind Peter of his proper place.

But Jesus goes beyond simply reminding Peter of his place. As noted earlier, he calls him Satan! What does Jesus mean by calling Peter Satan? Satan's kingdom opposes that of Jesus (Mark 3:23–26). Satan therefore seeks to blind people to Jesus's message (4:15). Now Peter takes on Satan's role by denying Jesus's message and seeking to turn him from his mission to the cross.

Rejection of Jesus's cross (Mark 8:32), and of our sharing in Jesus's cross (8:34), is satanic theology (8:33). Those who would reign with Jesus must first suffer with him and for him.

What It Means to Be a Disciple of the Messiah

Earlier in Mark, Jesus calls as disciples whomever *he* wishes (Mark 3:13). Now Jesus invites *whoever* wishes to follow him as disciples.

> Whoever wants to be my disciple must deny themselves and take up their cross and follow me. (Mark 8:34)

Disciples by definition were supposed to be followers of their teachers. Jesus is no ordinary teacher, however, and following him means following him in an extraordinary way—even to his cross.

People in the Roman Empire understood what it meant to take up the cross. A criminal condemned to death would carry the heavy horizontal beam of the cross through an often mocking mob out to the site of execution. There the condemned would be tied or nailed to the cross naked, to die a slow and agonizing death, especially from dehydration, blood loss, and finally shock. This is where King Jesus is headed, and this is where his disciples must follow.

But guess what? This is not quite how it works out later in the Gospel. When the time comes for Jesus's disciples to take up the cross to follow him, they're in hiding. The Roman execution squad thus has to draft a bystander, Simon of Cyrene, to pick up Jesus's cross (Mark 15:21). That's because another Simon—Simon Peter—is missing. Simon Peter, who insisted, "Even if I have to die with you!" (14:31).

After calling all his followers to follow even to the death (Mark 8:34), Jesus shifts in 8:35–37 to accounting language and basic math. No amount of profit matters if one isn't alive to enjoy it. While studying at a university, I explained this basic math to a freshman named John who had just bombed his calculus test. That ten is more than one is simple math; likewise, that a year is more than a day. On an incomparably greater scale, eternity is infinitely greater than the present life. It makes sense to invest our lives in what counts eternally. John soon gave his life to Jesus and became one of Jesus's most radical followers on the campus, leading far more of his fellow students to Christ than I did.

Jesus warns that whoever wants to save their life in this world by refusing the cross will lose life eternally, and that whoever loses their life to follow Jesus will gain that life eternally (Mark 8:35). Scripture already emphasized that no price in the world is enough to ransom one's life eternally (Ps. 49:7–9). Even gaining the whole world at the cost of oneself is thus a losing proposition. There is, however, one exception regarding losing one's life to gain the world. By giving his life, Jesus, the infinitely worthy one, ransomed the whole world (Mark 10:45).

What light does this reasoning shed on Peter's behavior? Instead of denying himself, as Jesus urges (Mark 8:34), Peter will end up denying Jesus three times (14:66–72). Like the rich ruler in 10:21–22, Peter makes a bad calculation: He values this world more than eternal life. In God's mercy, though, Peter got a second chance, and God used him greatly.

Suffering Successfully

In virtually all cultures, human beings respect advantages such as power, status, beauty, health, and wealth. This respect raises theological problems for us when these respectable conditions don't always apply to those we otherwise consider the "best" people. Theologically, we're tempted to ask, "Why do the righteous suffer?" as if God should make everything better for his own people.

Jihadists persecute and kill our brothers and sisters in northern Nigeria, Burkina Faso, and Mozambique. Christians currently face collective repression in Myanmar and in Manipur, India. God's children flee deadly gang violence, drug cartels, and hostility in Venezuela, Colombia, and much of Central America.[8] My wife was a refugee for eighteen months in her nation of Congo.

In the US we sometimes think that our democratic system of government or some actions that we (or our forebears) have done right protect us from such suffering. Somehow, catastrophe can't come our way because, in some sense, we don't "deserve" it. This underlying rationale doesn't always protect us from fear, however. When a loved one dies, we lose a job, or somebody slanders us, we may ask, "What did we do to deserve this?" When public opinions against evangelicals, charismatics, or other Christians rest on caricatures or the worst examples, we reasonably cry, "Unfair!"

Most people in the Bible thought this way too: If you do what's right, good will come your way. Proverbs shows us that good does *usually* follow, but how many psalms also lament unjust suffering? Job's friends recoil to think that a just God could allow Job to suffer if he hadn't done something wrong. But in the Bible, suffering is not always judgment. Sometimes it is testing. Sometimes it is bad people hurting good people. Often in the New Testament it involves sharing Christ's sufferings for God's honor.

The Longest-Range Standard for Success

American culture emphasizes success in this life. It values sacrificing for goals, so long as one achieves success and popularity, wealth and honor. But just as Jesus invites us to value eternal life above life in this world, he invites us to value eternal honor above any honor in this age. When he returns, even the secrets of our hearts will become public knowledge (1 Cor. 4:5; compare Mark 4:22).

In Mark 8:38, Jesus continues his response to Peter's denial of Jesus's cruciform destiny. This narrative shows Peter himself as an example of someone ashamed of Jesus and his words, the words that Jesus had just spoken about his death (8:31). Jesus thus warns,

> If anyone is ashamed of me and my words in this adulterous and sinful generation, the Son of Man will be ashamed of them when he comes in his Father's glory with the holy angels. (Mark 8:38)

The transfiguration that follows this warning (Mark 9:1–8) is a foretaste of the promised future glory at Jesus's return. It is that glory, not glory in this age, that we should live for. We must therefore weigh our decisions in this world in light of eternity: What will count forever?

Jesus's first disciples didn't get it, though they should have. Jesus didn't choose highly educated scribes, aristocratic priests, or other "important" people. Jesus defended the poor and marginalized (e.g., Luke 4:18; 6:20–21, 24–25). He restored hope to the physically sick and those whose sins had alienated them from polite society. But contemplating Jesus's coming kingdom, Jesus's own disciples soon begin to think like this world's "important" people (Mark 9:34). They want to protect their hero from the needs of mere children (10:13–16) or a blind beggar (10:46–52). They fail to understand that caring for others' needs is what Jesus's mission was really about (10:14–15).

Indeed, as noted earlier, two disciples get the idea that they deserve the seats on Jesus's right and left in his kingdom. Recognizing that many others

will covet those seats, James and John want to submit their request in advance
(Mark 10:37). Jesus replies,

> Can you drink the cup I drink or be baptized with the baptism I am baptized
> with? (Mark 10:38)

Jesus's cup is the cup of his death (Mark 14:22–24, 36). Like Peter, confident
that he is ready to die for Jesus (14:31), James and John assure Jesus that they
are ready for his cup and baptism (10:39). Their spirit indeed is willing, but
their unprepared flesh will soon prove weak (14:38). They don't understand
that the places to Jesus's right and left belong to two robbers (15:27), hanging
beside Jesus's cruciform throne, as he is crowned king of the Jews.

Their fellow disciples are upset with James and John for trying to get ahead
of them (Mark 10:41), presumably because they *all* want to be the greatest
(9:34). So Jesus has to explain again that the first will be last and the last first;
whoever *serves* is the greatest (9:35; 10:31, 44). The supreme illustration of this
principle is Jesus himself. The Son of Man, whom Daniel said would reign in
glory forever, came first to serve and give his life as a ransom for others (10:45).

The values of Christ's kingdom invert this world's values. Those who honor
Jesus in this world, even at the expense of their own shame, will receive eter-
nal honor when Jesus returns to judge the world. Those who are ashamed of
Jesus in this world will bear eternal shame when Jesus returns (Mark 8:38).
The real question for us is whether we actually trust Jesus's message enough
to stake our honor and life in this world on him. If we *really* trust him, we
will live for his promise. "Jesus has many who love His Kingdom in Heaven,"
Thomas à Kempis lamented, "but few who bear His Cross."[9]

Another Chance

As we know from Jesus's predictions in Mark and from the book of Acts,
Peter was eventually restored. He went on to serve Jesus for the remaining
decades of his life. Church tradition says that he eventually did take up his
cross to follow Jesus to the utmost, crucified upside down in Rome. Mark's
early hearers in Rome would remember Peter as a hero who lived what he
preached. But Mark wants us to remember that Peter started out just like any
one of us. Jesus is the real hero. *He* is the one who *makes* Peter—and us—into
fishers of people (Mark 1:17).

If we want to follow Jesus, he invites us to take up our cross and follow.
Someday this could entail literal martyrdom; our lives in this age become
forfeit the moment we call Jesus Lord. But from day to day this also entails

rejecting Satan's theology of success and power, rejecting those human interests that defy God's interests.

> If someone wants to come after me, let them deny themselves and take up their cross *daily* and follow me. (Luke 9:23)

> Why are we also in danger every hour? By the boasting I have about you in Christ Jesus our Lord: I die daily! . . . I fought wild beasts at Ephesus. (1 Cor. 15:30–32; compare 2 Cor. 1:8–10)

It means that we share Jesus's definition of success and honor in light of eternity, rather than valuing it the way the world defines it. True success—to truly overcome—means denying ourselves in this life rather than denying Jesus and his words.

Jesus as Our Model

Jesus is the ultimate model. Luke emphasizes this point by underlining the many parallels between Jesus in the Gospel of Luke and Jesus's followers in the book of Acts. For example, the Spirit empowers Jesus while he is praying (Luke 3:21–22), an experience that Jesus explains from Isaiah (Luke 4:18). Likewise, the Spirit empowers the church while they are praying (Acts 1:14; 2:4), an experience that Peter explains from Joel (Acts 2:17–18). Luke likewise underlines the continuity of suffering for the mission. That is why the first Christian martyr's final sayings echo some of Jesus's final words:

Jesus in Luke 22–23	Stephen in Acts 7
"They led Jesus away to their Sanhedrin. . . . He said to them, 'From now on the Son of Man will be seated at the right hand of God's Power'" (Luke 22:66–69).	"They brought Stephen to the Sanhedrin . . . and he said, 'Look! I see the heavens opened and the Son of Man standing at God's right hand!'" (Acts 6:12; 7:56).
"Father, I entrust my spirit into your hands" (Luke 23:46).	"Lord Jesus, receive my spirit!" (Acts 7:59).
"Father, forgive them" (Luke 23:34).	"Lord, do not hold this sin against them" (Acts 7:60).

Lest anyone suppose that Stephen acted presumptuously and wrongly because the ensuing backlash scattered the church, Luke shows us that God was working through his martyrdom. Stephen's final speech publicly lays out a biblical theology for the church's mission beyond Jerusalem: Contrary to the ideas of his accusers (see Acts 6:13–14), God was not localized in the temple (7:2–5, 10, 17; especially 7:33, 43–50). Through that message, a seed was sown in one of his hearers (7:58; 8:1) that was later reaped on the road to Damascus, and Paul later on began carrying out the culturally universal theological vision that Stephen had articulated. Meanwhile, the ensuing persecution that scattered the Jerusalem church (8:1, 4) led to the church spreading elsewhere (8:5; 11:19)—as the Lord had always wanted (1:8).

Jesus the king carried his cross, enduring suffering in light of the promised joy beyond it (Heb. 12:2). He invites us who trust him to do the same.

CHAPTER SIX

Learning from the Persecuted Church

Continue to remember those in prison as if you were together with them in prison, and those who are mistreated as if you yourselves were suffering.

—Hebrews 13:3 (NIV)

Stay disciplined and watchful. Your opponent the devil prowls around like a roaring lion, looking for somebody to devour. Stand firm against him in faith, knowing that your spiritual family throughout the world is experiencing the same sorts of sufferings.

—1 Peter 5:8–9

Be faithful even to the death, and I will give you the victor's wreath of life. Let anyone who has ears heed what the Spirit is saying to the churches.

—Revelation 2:10–11

I know where you live—where Satan has his throne. Yet you remain true to my name. You did not renounce your faith in me, not even in the days of Antipas, my faithful witness, who was put to death in your city—where Satan lives.

—Revelation 2:13 (NIV)

It is probably no coincidence that nearly all of the earliest non-Christian references to John the Baptist, Jesus, Jesus's brother James, and Jesus's other early followers mention them dying for their devotion to God.[1] Persecution varied by place and generation after that, but it has hardly vanished.

Tortured for Christ

Romanian Lutheran pastor Richard Wurmbrand endured years of torture, drugging, isolation, near starvation, and malnutrition-related disease for his faith.[2] He recounts how his Communist torturers in Romania sometimes made him stand motionless for hours in a tight container surrounded by inside nails that would pierce him if he relaxed.[3] His wife, Sabina, and other prisoners often suffered the same torture.[4]

Even more frequently, Sabina was kept in crowded cells that sometimes held eighty persons, rendering movement nearly impossible.[5] Through malnutrition she and many other prisoners suffered from scurvy and other deficiency diseases; dysentery was also pervasive.[6] After one woman mocked Sabina for her faith, a guard entertained himself by tossing Sabina into the Danube River. Rocks there broke two of her ribs and left much of one side of her body discolored, but the labor camp's overseers would not excuse her from work. Only God's healing intervention enabled her to continue.[7]

The Wurmbrands share others' stories as well. Sometimes guards hung believers upside down and beat them so hard "that their bodies swung back and forth under the blows."[8] Tormentors drove starving rats into one prisoner's cell, forcing him to remain awake continually to defend himself.[9] Guards regularly beat Adventists on Saturdays, when they faithfully refused to dishonor the Sabbath by working.[10] One work colony was a virtual death camp for "elderly men, many in their seventies," who were forced to haul loads barefoot.[11]

Soviet authorities exiled medical doctor Vera Yakovlena from Ukraine to a Siberian labor camp for ten years. Among the minority of survivors, she recalled, "Every day people died, collapsing from overwork in the snow."[12] After guards caught her sharing her faith, she was forced "to stand for hours barefoot on ice."[13] One day she strayed into a prohibited area, and for ten minutes a guard tried to shoot her, yet found his arm immobile only during those minutes. Afterward, he correctly acknowledged that she must have a praying mother.[14]

Richard Wurmbrand invited Western Christians to help the persecuted church by sharing their lives of sacrifice and joining them in praying for their persecutors' conversions.[15] Yet he found the complacency of Western Christianity more shocking and painful than the persecutions he endured from open enemies of the cross.[16]

Global Persecution Today

While news programs often limit the level of graphic violence they display, friends in different continents sometimes send me firsthand videos of

Christians experiencing persecution for their faith. These include churches targeted and set on fire, Christians' homes burning as mobs chant in unison against them—usually incited by false accusations—or Christians being terribly beaten. Sometimes they include the bodies of dead fellow Christians. The most horrific, heart-rending video sent by a friend showed the bodies of recently slaughtered young Christian mothers. In this case, the killers had spared their babies, who were clinging to their mothers' fresh corpses and mostly still crying.

At least 70 percent of the world's population lives in countries with significant restrictions on religious freedom.[17] While many faith groups face prejudice, this is particularly true, at least numerically, for Christians; at least 200 million of them globally face significant intolerance.[18] Other recent estimates are higher. Open Doors, known for careful research, estimates that at least 380 million Christians face severe discrimination and sometimes even violence.[19] Some researchers estimate that Christians are the object of three-quarters of all "acts of religious intolerance" globally.[20] By contrast, Christians constitute less than one-third of the world's population. (Meanwhile, some 85 percent of countries with the greatest religious freedom for all have a Christian heritage.)[21] Noting the regress of religious freedom around the world, the US secretary of state in 2012 lamented, "The world is sliding backwards."[22]

Open Doors reports that in 2023, over fourteen thousand churches, Christian schools, or Christian hospitals were attacked or forcibly shut down, especially in China and India. Global Christian Relief documented the destruction of nearly five thousand churches and Christian homes in India in 2024.[23] Facial recognition technology has facilitated greater government control in China, requiring further decentralization of urban churches there.[24] Global Christian Relief documented the arrest of 1,559 Christians in China in 2024. While this is a tiny percentage of Chinese Christians, it puts China ahead of Eritrea, Nicaragua, Russia, and apparently even North Korea in the number of Christians arrested for their Christian activity.[25]

One caveat before I proceed: Although I have more examples of persecutors from some religious groups (especially Muslim extremists) and some nations (such as Nigeria or India), they do not by any means represent the actions of all their religious or national compatriots. Islamic extremists dominate official lists of terrorist organizations, but in some cases (e.g., at times in northern Nigeria and in Mindanao, Philippines) Muslims have protected Christians, and most people in Nigeria and India, for example, do not support religious violence. While millions support violent jihad, most Muslims globally do not.[26] The examples reflect merely my sources and my focus. I offer these examples for prayer and exhortation, not to incite enmity. I offer fewer examples from North Korea simply because I have fewer on hand, yet that is currently the most repressive state for Christians.

Christians face significant hardships in places like Iran and Pakistan, but Western Christians should embrace Iranians and Pakistanis with love and prayer not least for the sake of our many brothers and sisters there. Indeed, governments that oppress Christians should recognize that true Christians elsewhere love these governments' peoples all the more because we have brothers and sisters among them. The world should also know that the God of heaven shows more collective mercy on them because of his people among them.

Nigeria

I spent three summers in Plateau State, Nigeria, in the late 1990s, most often in Plateau's chief city of Jos. Everyone I met welcomed me hospitably, and the university and seminary students seemed eager for whatever I would teach them about the Bible. Where I taught in Plateau State, churches were everywhere, and often entire villages attended morning prayer. For the first time in my life I witnessed what looked like a (majority) practicing Christian civilization that, if it ever existed in the United States, no longer did, at least where I have lived.

Yet Nigeria in general and the northern region near Plateau in particular have become a major epicenter of Christian martyrdom. Terrorist group Boko Haram's violence led to an estimated two thousand deaths and harm to twenty-six churches in Borno State in 2009.[27] In 2012, Boko Haram demanded the removal of millions of Christians in the north.[28] From 2009 to early 2023, an international commission estimated the murder for religious reasons of more than fifty-two thousand Nigerian Christians.[29] In 2023, from May 15 to 17 alone, more than three hundred Christians were killed for their faith just in Plateau State.[30] In that year, more than four thousand Nigerian Christians died for their faith[31]—on average, ten a day, or one dying for her faith nearly every two hours. In December alone that year, attacks displaced ten thousand people. To put that more pointedly, ten thousand more people are now homeless because of these attacks. These may be low estimates. Based on concrete sources, Global Christian Relief reports that in 2024, nearly ten thousand (9,814) Nigerians were murdered because they were Christians.[32] Since many northern states introduced sharia law, tens of thousands of people have died, "most of them Christians or adherents of traditional religions."[33]

Some secular observers try to minimize the religious dimension of the conflict. While other factors are also involved, a purely secular explanation displays little understanding of the prominent role of religion in most of the world's experience. For example, on Christmas Eve 2023, jihadists targeted full churches celebrating Jesus's birth. They slaughtered 170 Christian worshipers in Plateau State, evoking earlier bombings on Christmas there such as those in 2010 and 2011. Elsewhere, armed by jihadists, Fulani militants burned a church to which residents of a village had fled for sanctuary. The residents cried in agony as they burned to death; the forty-four victims included the pastor's "wife, four of his seven children, and two of his grandchildren." At the mass funeral the next day, the killers returned and slaughtered others.[34] Citing Job 2:10, the pastor insisted that they must accept hardship as well as blessing from the Lord.[35] Militants slaughtered at least fifty more Christians, many in their sleep, on Palm Sunday 2025.

Genocide in Nigeria

One woman shared the gospel with some Muslim youths in Niger State on June 28, 2006. When their elders learned what she had done, they falsely accused her of insulting Muhammad, and hundreds pursued her. The local police rescued her, but the crowd so overwhelmed the police that, concerned for their own survival, they abandoned her to her fate. The crowd then clubbed her to death.[36] Before reading this account, I first heard about it—as I have many others—from my Nigerian friends.

Since 2009, the extremist violence has killed at least thirty-five thousand people (with many estimates even higher), and more than two million have been displaced from their homes. In 2010, a single attack in a Christian farming community in Plateau State killed 483 people, now entombed in a mass grave.[37] An early 2025 mailing from Voice of the Martyrs begins, "Islamic attacks have widowed more than 10,000 of our Christian sisters in northern Nigeria in the past 20 years."[38]

A couple of years ago, Nigerian friends who had not seen each other for a while were visiting Médine and me. Discussing jihadist attacks in Nigeria's Middle Belt, they caught each other up on who they knew who had been killed recently.[39] An update from Voice of the Martyrs laments, "Nearly all Christians in northeastern Nigeria have lost family members or friends in attacks by Boko Haram or militant Fulani Muslims."[40] (I will talk more about the difference between these groups below.)

In Benue State, a surge in attacks displaced farmers into eight camps. These camps are so crowded that men normally sleep outside; the displaced receive rations of corn stew. When one couple ventured back to their farm, militants killed the husband and sent the wife back to their camp with the warning: "We have taken over. Don't come back."[41] Traumatized farmers sometimes panic now if they see a cow, assuming that Fulani herders are nearby.[42]

Another friend explained the irony. Much of the world complains that Muslim herders (who want to graze on Christian farmers' land) and Christian farmers just can't get along. But if you find a driver's dead body and then somewhere down the road someone driving the deceased's car, you might suspect the new driver of having had something to do with the former one's murder. When herders have now settled in deceased farmers' homes and taken over their land, however, many refuse to draw the logical corollary.[43]

Suzanne is one of the recent victims of Boko Haram in Nigeria. After killing her father, a terrorist shot Suzanne through the temple. Astonishingly, she survived, though she is now blind and must be led around by others. She loves Jesus even more than before.[44] Amina, attacked with a machete by a Fulani militant in Nigeria, was left for dead. During her four months in the hospital, she eventually found grace to trust God's sovereign plan. When she later met her assailant, she forgave him.[45]

In another village, Boko Haram ordered thirty members of Habila's church to convert to Islam or die. Refusing to deny Christ, all thirty were killed. Habila too was shot through the head with an AK-47 and left in a pool of blood. Nevertheless, he survived and experienced miraculous healing. He prays daily for God to forgive and save his persecutors.[46] Such survivors, though, are a minority. Nigerian jihadists praised a seven-year-old boy for finishing off one Christian by cutting his neck.[47]

Heartbreak for My Friends

While I was in Nigeria, some of my Nigerian pastor friends also shared about some of their own pastor friends, often classmates from seminary, martyred in the north. They also shared reports of jihadist mercenaries from outside Nigeria. One Nigerian friend, now an Anglican priest, told me that before he began teaching he was doing campus ministry at a religiously mixed university in the north. One day anti-Christian riots broke out in the city; they were supposedly spontaneous, but militant Islamists had already mapped out where local pastors lived.[48] Many pastors were hacked or burned to death; my friend, his wife, and their two precious young children lived to recount the story only because their downstairs Muslim neighbor went outside and declared that this was a house of peace.

When I first visited Nigeria, Sani Abacha was the dictator, and he ruled with an iron hand. My first week in the country, I attended a meeting of some church leaders who discussed a march to protest government repression. Media was so tightly controlled that those present did not even know that police had raided the university where I was staying that morning, driving out students because of protests. As the only foreigner present, I had no business speaking, but I nevertheless pleaded against the march, because it would surely cost many lives. The church leaders agreed about the cost, but they responded that everything else had been attempted and failed, so they resolved to march. By God's grace, it turned out that there was no need for the march—that week Abacha died.

The next summer I was in the country when former general and political prisoner Olusegun Obasanjo, a Christian from the southwest, was sworn in as president. Nevertheless, jihadist attacks remained a threat. I was invited to teach at a denomination's headquarters church about one of Revelation's seven churches of Asia Minor. I explained that while churches in some regions have to resist materialism, churches in other regions have to be ready for martyrdom. Obviously this was not news to them; indeed, a few years later a jihadist's plan to blow himself up in a crowded service at that church was stopped only by a providentially timely (but sadly fatal) motorcycle accident outside the sanctuary.[49]

The New Testament teaches often about persecution, which means that New Testament professors also must teach about it. But it felt harder for me to teach about it in central Nigeria than in the US, because in Nigeria it was obvious that my very sober hearers were not merely hearing a random Bible lesson but counting the cost for their own lives. I felt this pain most personally during one of the weeks I spent teaching Nigerian missionaries preparing to reach unreached (mostly polytheistic) people groups. One of my students there had already been expelled from her Muslim family in the southwest for becoming a Christian. Although her outreach would not be focused on Muslims, she was very cognizant of the real possibility of facing death for preaching Christ in unreached areas.

News in September 2001

In September 2001, I received frantic news from close friends in Jos.[50] Riots had begun during the Friday, September 7, Muslim prayer services, and Christians were being slaughtered. One of my previous students, a Nigerian lawyer, was trapped in a church under siege for three days with a corpse and no water.

During the first three days of slaughter, I desperately tried to contact US news organizations, hoping that someone would pay attention and get out urgent pleas for help. Instead, one journalist responded reluctantly that if the news wasn't dealing with terrorism impacting the US, oil prices in the US, or something else that people in the US care about, they couldn't cover it. News organizations in the US compete for viewers, and consumers allegedly don't care what happens in most other places—especially, I was eventually given to understand, if the people in those other places aren't white Americans. If 1 percent of those deaths occurred in events in North American or European suburbs, they would be headline news, barring competition from events elsewhere of greater popular magnitude (for instance, happenings in the lives of celebrities).

Concerned journalists themselves lament the information problem. *New York Times* columnist Nicholas Kristof notes that television networks neglected crises in Darfur and Congo because coverage of them brought lower ratings. Indeed, he complains, "*Christianity Today* ended up covering Darfur more assiduously than either *Newsweek* or *Time*."[51]

Rupert Shortt, religion editor for *The Times Literary Supplement*, notes that over the course of three decades, Sudan's government had precipitated "the deaths of 2 million Christians and other non-Muslim civilians." Likewise, over the final three decades of the twentieth century, the Indonesian government killed one hundred thousand Catholic civilians in East Timor—a sixth of the population.[52] What do the lower ratings say about the interests and thus hearts of their viewers? Shortt points out that whereas Western media can portray Muslims in the West as a minority needing protection, they usually remain silent regarding Muslim genocide against Christians in much of the world. "There is scarcely a single country from Morocco to Pakistan in which Christians are fully free to worship without harassment."[53]

Because US media must give consumers what they believe they want, secular media remain largely silent about thousands of faithful Christians genocidally martyred in northern Nigeria, or jihadists slaughtering hundreds of Christians in Mozambique. This is the case even though the death toll of Christians murdered in Nigeria rivaled the death toll from ISIS even at the latter's peak.[54] Had another religion been targeted, the coverage might well have been higher. (Happily, CBN is now covering it.) Location and the availability of footage are also issues. The news magazine to which I once subscribed finally devoted a half page to genocidal war in Congo-Kinshasa only after some three million people had perished, and never did mention the war that had displaced a quarter of the population of my wife's smaller Congo-Brazzaville.

Almost immediately after September 7 in Nigeria, on September 11, jihadists attacked the US too, and three thousand people died. I grieved, having also a special love for New York City from my summer in urban ministry there. Yet I thought that finally this attack would awaken the world to the genocide in Nigeria due to the common thread of jihadism. Instead, the events here drowned out even further any attention to Africa. Over the course of the year, the death toll in Jos grew much higher than in New York.

Even Nigerian news coverage was not always even. On various occasions the media reported a few casualties in northern Nigeria, faith unspecified, killed in northern riots; my friends on the ground countered that so many Christians had been killed that morgues and refrigeration units could not hold them all. When I did try to publicize my accounts of what was happening in northern Nigeria, a Nigerian from the south declared that I was merely producing Christian-biased propaganda. I think he must know better by now.

Not Just Boko Haram

Today the world talks about Boko Haram, founded in northern Nigeria in 2002. Boko Haram became famous in April 2014 by kidnapping 276 girls from a secondary school in Chibok. Initially even some in Nigeria ignored the kidnapping because it was merely "one more tragedy" among hundreds;[55] within several months, in fact, the estimated total of kidnapped minors came to two thousand girls and ten thousand boys, the latter forced to fight for Boko Haram.[56] Their captivity finally went viral after women's rights supporters in the West joined the online protest.[57]

Most of the Chibok girls were from Christian families; some of them were children of pastors and Bible translators.[58] Their captors forced them to memorize Qur'an passages, teaching them that women brought sin, that democracy was sinful, and even that the world is flat.[59] The girls were told to marry young so as to bear many children (who would be raised in the movement);[60] they were given the choice between being slaves or marrying the male fighters, who were considered theologically justified in forcing sex on them.[61] When one leader insisted that a student named Naomi marry or be gang-raped, she refused marriage, so he struck her, leaving a scar.[62] (Elsewhere, too, Christian girls are kidnapped or forced into Muslim marriages to bear children for Islam.)[63]

After being captive for two years, the girls began to starve.[64] Although negotiations brought the release of many girls (including Naomi, mentioned above), roughly a hundred remain missing to this day. Negotiations also released some other students taken captive on later occasions, but these did not include fourteen-year-old Leah Sharibu, taken February 19, 2018. Her captors kept her prisoner because she refused to deny her Christian faith, despite her friends' pleas that she merely pretend conversion as they had done. As of 2024, she is twenty-one years old. Reports have circulated that her captors married her to a rebel commander. She is likely unaware of the protest marches that have pleaded for her release, or of the courage that her story has stirred among other Christians. In 2024, more than nine thousand Nigerian Christians were kidnapped for money or to be forced brides of jihadists.[65]

But as should be obvious from my pre-2002 examples, jihadist attacks were occurring well before the founding of Boko Haram.[66] Certainly they occur much more widely now. Fulani militants once had only sticks, but Islamic extremists, expanding their reach, eventually armed them with automatic weapons. Radicalized Fulani herders now kill and displace more people than Boko Haram does.[67]

In an earlier period Islamic rulers had tried to subdue the Middle Belt, but conquest mattered more than conversion. Islamic law permitted the enslavement of Africans so long as they didn't convert to Islam.[68] Under British rule, however, the Islamized Hausa-Fulani were given administrative control over northern Nigeria.[69] Plateau State is overwhelmingly Christian, but as the Sahara expanded southward, more northern Fulani began grazing on Plateau's farmlands. What an opportunity for Christians to show love to Muslim neighbors! Yet letting herders graze one's farmland is hard on farmers, and genuinely as well as nominally Christian farmers resisted. Meanwhile, some Islamist teachers have proved eager to indoctrinate and recruit other Muslims with certain Qur'anic teachings about conquest.

Retaliation or Escape?

It was not only Christian noncombatants who died in the wake of September 7, 2001. Many Christian youths, fed up with their elders always "turning the other cheek," eventually armed themselves and burned local mosques, some of them even killing Muslim noncombatants. A Muslim woman in Jos told one of my Christian acquaintances there, "Our people started this, but your people went too far in responding!" The overall loss of life was horrific.

The vast majority of Christians do respond nonviolently, but when local Christians have dared to fight back and kill their assailants, Islamic militants mock them for violating Jesus's teachings about peace and nonretaliation. Years ago a Nigerian friend and I wrestled over this question. I insisted that discipleship meant nonresistance and martyrdom; he talked about genocide and caring for one's family. If their government can't or won't defend residents, should residents simply surrender their homes to invaders and settle in refugee camps? Farmers who had worked their land for generations lose their livelihoods (and sometimes their food access) when they flee, and no other territory will simply give them new land. US Christians critical of others who retaliate should remember US actions in Afghanistan and Iraq in reprisal for attacks here. In any case, the farmers are so outgunned now that without government intervention self-defense might be suicidal.

I support Christian nonretaliation based on Scripture, but I also recognize that I have not earned the personal right to stand in judgment. Nobody has been killing my family members or forcing us into a refugee camp. My friend and I each found the other's arguments persuasive. He significantly qualified my virtual pacifism (beyond the personal level) while also recognizing Jesus's teachings on nonretaliation. Where we could certainly agree was that even by historic just-war principles, it is wrong to kill noncombatant Muslims in retaliation for the murder of noncombatant Christians. With one hand tied behind our back while our aggressors use both hands, we must depend radically on the Lord.

Retaliation in Yelwa, Forgiveness from Kaduna

When I was in Nigeria's Middle Belt, I taught a large group of local pastors in the area of Yelwa Shendam, which is part of Plateau State. I accumulated quite a few mosquito bites overnight, but I knew that the pastors had provided me the best accommodations available, better than their own. The local pastors who hosted me were financially poor, but they banded together and gave me a chicken to thank me for my teaching. While eating with them (not the chicken), I noticed a foreigner who appeared to be perhaps from the Middle East, gesturing menacingly toward me while talking with some local Muslims.[70] The pastors took it in stride; menacing looks are common but normally harmless.

A few years later, Muslim extremists there slaughtered many local Christians, including some inside a church, although other Christians escaped. Afterward they reportedly declared an Islamic state and turned the many local churches into latrines. At the time I saw no media coverage and just heard from close friends in the area. When Tarok tribespeople in the surrounding region later responded by massacring an even larger number of Muslims in Yelwa, suddenly it made global news. Muslims controlled most of the regional media.

In nearby Kaduna State, Muslim youths marched in the state capital to demand the implementation of sharia; Muslims outnumber Christians in the northern part of the state, where the capital is. Christians, the majority in the southern part of the state, then organized a march in the state capital to protest sharia. Peaceful protesters, the majority women and youths, were quickly met with automatic weapons. My student Sunday Agang, who later became a seminary president in Nigeria, was panicked; some of his unarmed relatives were killed, and he hadn't heard from his wife, whom he believed had been part of the march (happily, he was wrong about that). As we prayed together, I prayed for the God of vengeance to arise like a mighty warrior. I thought I prayed the language of the Psalms pretty well. After I finished, Sunday prayed. "God, please forgive our oppressors. If we die, we go to heaven, but they die without hope."[71]

Both were biblical prayers, but Sunday prayed more faithfully than I did. Jesus teaches forgiveness (Matt. 6:12; Luke 11:4; Matt. 18:21–22, 35; Mark 11:25; Luke 17:3–4); Scripture also enjoins us to avoid vengeance (Lev. 19:18), leaving judgment to God (Deut. 32:35; 1 Sam. 24:12; 25:26; 2 Sam. 22:48; Ps. 18:47; Rom. 12:19). Forgiving those who hurt us is not an act of weakness; it requires great strength and trust in the God who has our back. Sunday embodied that spirit better that day than I.

Two Recent Students' Testimonies

Yakubu Philemon, my PhD student, grew up near Gwoza in Borno State. After Boko Haram attacked the state capital, Maiduguri, Christians fled to the state's villages, whereupon Boko Haram began systematically attacking the villages. Boko Haram had AK-47s; local Christians had sticks. Boko Haram intercepted Christians traveling on roads and killed them if, as usual, they refused to convert to Islam. (They killed some who did convert anyway, not trusting their loyalty.)

The military ordered all men in Yakubu's area, which was predominantly Christian, to gather on June 3, 2014. Instead of Nigeria's military, however, they found Boko Haram militants dressed in captured military uniforms. The militants gunned down the men from the area—Yakubu estimates tens of thousands. Muslims had been warned in advance not to come, so the men gunned down were Christians. Boko Haram then took the young women as sex slaves, as war plunder, and the children to be groomed as terrorists. Happily, Yakubu had left the area shortly before this happened. While most Christian men died for their faith, many discouraged survivors in the area compromised it, reverting to African traditional religions that promised charms to protect them from bullets.

Another student, Ayooluwa Olawole, a counseling major at Asbury Seminary, shared how her parents had been counseling children who had escaped from Gwoza and the rest of Borno. Traumatized, the children suffered from nightmares and flashbacks and experienced regression. Because Boko Haram likes to document its atrocities, Yakubu also showed me some of their video footage. Boko Haram leaders sent a warning to Christians not to return to Gwoza, and then axed to death the Christian prisoners on the video—men, women, and youths—as if they were simply cleaving meat. I could not finish the video.

The world usually ignores genocide, ethnic cleansing, and in this case religious cleansing. Our media accounts instead fill up with the lives of celebrities and comparatively trivial matters.

Persecution Elsewhere in Africa

I recount events from Nigeria because I have closer connections there, but similar events could be recounted from around the world. Elsewhere in Africa, for example, jihadists from Mali have slaughtered civilians, especially Christians, in Burkina Faso. Their raids have displaced more than two million people from their homes and work, and at one point jihadists controlled 40 percent of the country. They raped women in Pastor Soré's village, then burned it, warning Christians that the time of Christianity was over and that they should convert to Islam or die.[72] Keep in mind that Christians represent roughly a quarter of the population; the Assemblies of God, as the largest Protestant denomination there, has more than a million adherents.[73]

Those who know the history of the US abolitionist and civil rights movements, which were mostly motivated by Christian conviction, also understand that standing for justice can be costly. The International Fellowship of Evangelical Students had sixty Bible study leaders in the universities at the time of the Rwandan genocide of 1994. They were known for promoting ethnic reconciliation. Nearly all were murdered.[74]

In Mozambique, jihadists kill Christians and force non-Christians into their violent form of Islam. Already several years ago it was possible to document scores of attacks on churches and hundreds of Christians slaughtered.[75] Global Christian Relief documented 262 more Christians killed for their faith there in 2024,[76] and twelve thousand Christians displaced.[77] Jihadists reportedly nailed pastors to church doors, boiled babies alive and force-fed them to their mothers, and hacked teenagers to death. Pastor Armando escaped with his life, but his four-year-old and seven-year-old children remain unaccounted for.[78] Another pastor hid in the forest with his older sons; after the raid he returned to the ruins of his hut to find his four-year-old youngest son beheaded. His wife and other son remain missing.[79]

Some Christians have been crucified. More often, jihadists have hacked to death and beheaded Christians, including many children, while often sparing one relative to go spread word of what others should expect if they persist in their faith. In one largely Christian region, thousands have fled into the bush to evade being murdered. A report in *Christianity Today* notes that "boys as young as 10 are made to enlist as child soldiers and girls as young as 12 are forced into marriage as child brides—and anyone who does not comply is killed. There are also reports of sexual assault incidents involving women as old as 60."[80] Most Muslims in the region oppose these atrocities; but it is the extremists who are receiving foreign funding and automatic weapons. Nominal Muslims who cannot prove their orthodoxy are also the militants' targets.

Eritrea's totalitarian government has arrested thousands of Christians from banned churches, starting in the early 2000s; more than 350 remain in prison, with eighty more already arrested in the first five months of 2024.[81] For example, Pastor Gebremedhin Gebregergis was imprisoned in November 2004. He has remained in prison, unable to care for his six children, even though his wife died in 2022.[82] Youth minister Mussie Ezaz was detained without trial in 2007 and remains in a maximum security prison.[83]

Eritrea locked many prisoners in metal shipping containers, which are unbearably hot during the day and freezing at night, without access to sanitation or toilets. One of those so detained, gospel singer Helen Berhane, remained imprisoned from 2004 to 2006. The refrain of one of her songs runs, "Christianity costs you your life, but at the end, its outcome is victory."[84] Berhane was released in 2006 because she was severely sick and authorities did not want her to die in custody. An Eritrean government spokesman condemned Amnesty International for protesting her conditions. Denmark granted her asylum and medical treatment, however, and she continues to speak for justice today.[85]

Persecution and Genocide Globally

When ISIS invaded Mosul in northern Iraq in June 2014, they gave four choices to Christians: By July 19 they needed to convert to Islam, hand over money to demonstrate submission, leave, or die. Tens of thousands of Christians left, with ISIS soldiers stripping them of any resources they tried to take with them. They chose to lose all property, employment, and proof of education rather than renounce their faith.[86]

After three days inside their home during ISIS attacks in Syria, Samia's husband ventured out to forage for food. After another day and a half Samia went outside to look for him, finally finding the remains of his corpse. She escaped to her family, but they soon discovered that in that place "Islamists had a list of Christians' names to target for execution." They fled to a neighboring country, where they have had to settle with other refugees in tents.[87] Life can be difficult for refugees seeking safety, since not every location welcomes them. In the Nazi era, the United States turned away a ship carrying nine hundred Jewish refugees from Germany. Over 250 of them ended up dying in the Nazi Holocaust.[88]

Egypt (on the continent of Africa but usually associated culturally more with the Middle East today) was predominantly Christian before the rise of Islam, and a large percentage of Christians remain there.[89] Many, however, are among impoverished outcasts, surviving by garbage collection.[90] Under Hosni Mubarak (i.e., before the government current as of 2024), police arrested three Christian converts and tortured them for ten months "by methods that included electric shocks to the genitals, beatings, cigarette burns, sexual humiliation, and isolation in cells too small to enable detainees to lie down," until they recanted their conversions.[91] Another convert was tortured in custody, which included his captors extracting his toenails.[92] When assailants began attacking a church, a Christian who ran to seek police help ended up detained himself.[93] In another case, when captured monks refused "to spit on a cross, deny their faith and accept Islam, the monks were beaten, whipped, and had thorns stuck into the soles of their feet."[94]

A court sentenced a Coptic priest to five years of prison for performing the marriage of a Coptic Christian man and a woman he did not know was a Muslim convert to Christianity. (The couple had used forged papers so they could marry.) While Muslim men may marry Christian women and raise children as Muslims, Muslim women may marry only Muslim men; because the woman's background was Muslim, the court did not recognize her legally as Christian because conversion was legal only to and not from Islam.[95]

Precedents for Modern Genocides

Some earlier events assured the world's aggressors that they could murder religious and ethnic minorities with relative impunity. One of these was the Armenian genocide of 1915–1916. Ottoman leaders forced 800,000 to 1.2 million Armenians on death marches to the Syrian desert, raping, robbing, killing, and using concentration camps. As Rupert Shortt laments, "Women were gang-raped and horseshoes were nailed into men's feet"; in a single province, "about half a million Christians were killed."[96] To this day, Turkish authorities deny that the mass murder was genocide. Indeed, despite thousands of death threats, one reporter there who affirmed the genocide was denied police protection. He was convicted of "insulting Turkishness" and was soon gunned down in the street.[97]

Unsurprisingly, a generation after 1915, Hitler assumed that Germany could get away with mass murder also. Germany had earlier gotten away with genocide against the Herero and Nama peoples in southwest Africa (in what is now Namibia) in 1904–1905. Turks got away with the Armenian genocide; the US government's earlier detainment and forced march of Cherokees—many of them Christians—also served as a model for concentration camps. The scale of Hitler's genocide was larger, but only Nazi Germany's loss of World War II kept him from "getting away with" more murder of Jews, Roma people, and others. In the 1930s Stalin also killed, imprisoned, and starved millions—including many for their faith.

Despite Nazi death camps and persecution, though, many remained faithful to their callings. Most Christians know the stories of the ten Booms and of Dietrich Bonhoeffer. In Auschwitz, Father Maximilian Kolbe volunteered to die in place of another inmate. The commandant granted his request, sending him to starve in an underground cell. During his slow and painful death, the other inmates heard his prayers and songs to God.[98]

Blasphemy Charges in Pakistan

When atheists in Sweden burn Qur'ans, Islamists burn Christian homes in Pakistan in supposed reprisal.[99] In Pakistan and elsewhere, Christians are often charged with blasphemy against Muhammad, and sometimes convicted solely on the testimony of accusers; under Islamic law, a Muslim's testimony is worth more than a Christian's.[100] For example, after a false rumor that Christians desecrated a Qur'an, mobs burned forty Christian homes, in which "eight Christians, including a child," were burned alive.[101] When a Catholic official and a Muslim official protested the abuse of blasphemy laws, both were quickly assassinated.[102] When business rivals charged a Christian and his Muslim colleague with blasphemy, the court exonerated the accused Muslim but sentenced the accused Christian to life imprisonment "on the basis of the same evidence." The imprisoned Christian was often beaten, and he died under very suspicious circumstances.[103] A few days after an examination showed that a blasphemy charge against one Christian minister was fabricated, he was "shot dead while in police custody."[104] (Obviously we need police, but police forces are not equally helpful everywhere for everything.) After some Christians filed a complaint that their pastor was assaulted, police retorted that "unrecognized" religions "were unwelcome."[105]

A video shows, and local witnesses recount, the recent attack on a Christian businessman in Pakistan. Jealous of his business success, some neighbors falsely accused him of blasphemy, and for four hours a mob "kicked him, threw bricks and stones at him, and insulted him and his [Christian] religion." They left him in a coma and burned down his business and his home.

"Meanwhile, 200 Christian families fled for their lives during the onslaught and don't know when they can safely return to their homes."[106]

False blasphemy accusations are not a recent invention. Jesus's detractors accused him of blasphemy (Mark 2:7; 14:64). The irony is that it was his accusers who were blaspheming him (15:29, using the same Greek term). Rejecting even the Spirit's testimony to Jesus through his ministry, they risked eternal judgment (3:2–29). On the day of judgment, people will give account for every word they have spoken (Matt. 12:36–37).

Elsewhere in Pakistan, a brother named Kazim was beaten, tortured, and threatened with death in his village. He was falsely imprisoned and his property was confiscated.[107] When a sister named Gulnaz rejected a Muslim man's sexual harassment, the man burned much of the skin on the top of her body with acid.[108] Young women, especially from minority Hindu and Christian backgrounds, are sometimes kidnapped and forced into Islamic marriages, bearing children to be raised in Islam.[109]

Other Examples

In the 1980s, Shining Path revolutionaries and a Peruvian army determined to crush them killed countless church members seeking to avoid the conflict. The Marxist guerrillas sometimes executed pastors for taking church offerings, which they viewed as exploiting the poor.[110] Even in the midst of the tragedy, God protected some. When guerrillas blew up one church, only three women were unable to escape the collapse. Those three women, however, were safe inside an air pocket in the rubble and were quickly rescued.[111]

But God does not stop every incident of human depravity. When in 2018 jihadists targeted Surabaya Central Pentecostal Church in Indonesia, 85 percent of Fenny Suryawati's skin was burned in the explosion. She lost her hearing, but unlike many, she survived.[112] On October 29, 2005, Islamic militants in Indonesia beheaded "three teenage schoolgirls . . . as they walked to their Christian-run school"; the militants deposited one of the heads "on the steps of a local church."[113] Happily, the current government in Indonesia supports freedom of religion. However, whether due to laws or local sentiments, religious freedom is not equally available everywhere.

On October 31, 2010, ten al-Qaeda agents murdered more than fifty unarmed worshipers in a church in Baghdad. When one mother could not make her infant stop crying, a terrorist gunned down the infant and then the mother and the rest of that family. During the massacre, in an event I find too heartbreaking to shake off, "Three-year-old Adam Udai also begged one of the terrorists to 'please stop.'" He was immediately killed.[114] One survivor, Samer, recounts his own experience. After he and others barricaded themselves in the sacristy, he heard his friend Raghda begging to enter and he let her in. Her husband had just been shot dead. Unable to force their way into the sacristy, the militants hurled weapons into the ventilation shaft. Raghda bled to death in Samer's arms. Security forces took five hours to arrive.[115]

Shukri, a new believer in Iraq, shared Christ boldly with Muslims, as the Lord would lead him. One day he told his wife, "I felt like the Lord said to me that I am going to see Him today."[116] Later that day soldiers from ISIS captured, tortured, and executed him.[117] Yet when his body was recovered, "he was smiling."[118] Also in Iraq, an imam and his family became secret Jesus followers; but some relatives caught some of them and exulted in torturing and burning them.[119] Jesus began appearing to Rafia Abbar, a professor of sharia at an Islamic university in Saudi Arabia, helping bring her to himself.[120] An uncle beat to death one of her students who became a Jesus follower. Two of Rafia's uncles likewise tried to kill Rafia, but Jesus stood in front of her and stopped them.[121]

When a moderate Muslim cleric in Europe denied that Jews and Christians were infidels, a Saudi grand mufti declared the cleric an infidel, who could therefore be subject to assassination with impunity.[122] In some countries, underage Christian girls are kidnapped and forced to "convert" to Islam, then made brides to sometimes polygamous Muslims to raise more children for Islam.[123] Christian girls are sometimes raped and forced to marry the rapist or are punished themselves for having "unlawful intercourse."[124] In one school, a Muslim teacher egged on students as they beat to death a Christian boy who was part of the class.[125]

India

As the world's largest democracy, India seems an unlikely location for persecution. Christian tradition in India traces its origins to the first century. Beyond dispute, a non-European, Middle Eastern form of Christianity was well established there in the first few centuries.

Many of the more extreme Hindu critics, however, denounce it as a Western religion. The original architects of the modern Hindutva nationalist ideology traded in the same sort of racial ideas as Hitler's Aryan supremacy. In its purest form, Hindutva demands the subjugation of non-Hindus to Hinduism if they wish to remain in the nation; it offers particular advantage to the highest castes. Hinduism itself is a diverse faith with many forms, and most Hindus are tolerant, as exemplified by the late Mahatma Gandhi and his allies. Those pressing for Hindutva, however, seek to marginalize non-Hindus.[126]

While Hindus abroad send funds back to support Hinduism, the government increasingly restricts funds from other religious groups outside the country. Compassion International supported more children in India than in any other nation, but the government expelled the organization from the country.[127] Global Christian Relief reports that Prime Minister Narendra Modi's government has revoked the licenses of "more than 19,000 NGOs . . . mostly Christian and Muslim groups."[128]

As just suggested, Christians are not the only minority to face prejudices. Some Hindu extremists have lynched Muslims as "cow-murderers."[129] After the massacre of an estimated eight hundred Muslims in the state of Gujarat in 2002, a Hindu extremist celebrated a "successful experiment."[130] Observers accused the state government of complicity; its top official, Narendra Modi, ordered police not to intervene in the killings. Although branded a criminal by the US government, Modi's role in the riots fueled his political success. Modi is now India's prime minister, and he is now welcome in Washington because of essential US interests in India.

Discrimination is widespread, and incidents of violence are increasing as Hindus marginalize the history of non-Hindus even in school curricula. Christians who help leprosy victims or Dalits (those at the bottom of the social pyramid) are often falsely accused of bribery, hence "forcing conversions" (more on this below) and offending local (i.e., Hindu) religion, and thus are subject to legal penalties.[131] For thirty-four years, Australian Graham Staines served leprosy victims in India, but in 1999, a militant Hindu mob burned Staines and his two young sons alive, despite the attempts of more appreciative local Hindus to intervene. Staines's widow, Gladys, and daughter, Esther, forgave the aggressors and continue to serve leprosy victims.

Unlike Staines, the vast majority of victims of Hindu extremism make less news—because they are Indian. Open Doors offers an example from 2024. Partly in connection with many healing miracles, Laxman's church grew from a handful to hundreds. But Hindu extremists falsely accused Laxman of bribing converts; "anti-conversion" laws are often used in this way to depict any benefits offered—even divine healing in response to prayer—as tools for "forced conversion." The police summoned a member of Laxman's church and threatened to destroy his house unless he signed a blank piece of paper. After he signed it, they added above the signature a "confession" that Laxman had bribed him to convert. "Laxman was put in jail, where he was again beaten with wooden canes, kicked, abused and tortured mercilessly by the policemen." When he was finally released, he saw that the extremists had also destroyed his church. The believers now had to meet in smaller groups, all under surveillance. Far from offering protection, his state's Hindu nationalist government has closed hundreds of churches.[132]

In Orissa state, India, in 2008, Hindu militants killed at least ninety persons—both Christians and some tolerant Hindus who tried to protect them—and displaced some fifty thousand people.[133] The state transferred a police superintendent who warned in advance that persecutors of Christians would be prosecuted.[134] Although most camps for displaced victims closed by 2010, one reporter afterward found two to three thousand still living in tents.[135]

In 2023, members of the mostly Hindu Meitei people assaulted members of the mostly Christian Kuki-Zo people in the Indian state of Manipur. The death toll exceeded two hundred, the majority of deaths being Kuki. Although the Kuki tried to defend themselves and some retaliated, they were clearly unprepared and outgunned. While multiple factors played into the conflict, the national government's rhetoric supporting Hindu militants amplifies the conflict's religious dimension. Mobs destroyed some four hundred churches in Manipur. Global Christian Relief has reported some seventy thousand people "displaced—mostly believers." Militants destroyed some seven thousand homes and more than a hundred villages.[136]

A subsequently viral video showed two Kuki women being forced into a mob of abusers, who stripped and gang-raped them. The younger woman, Glory, was traumatized both by rape and by witnessing the murder of her father and brother, both of whom had been beaten to death. Her mother recounts, "My husband was a church elder. He was soft spoken and kind. . . . My son was in the 12th grade, a gentle boy who never fought with anyone. . . . He was killed because he ran after them [the mob] to try to save his sister."[137] Some have alleged that police, far from protecting the women, abandoned them to the mob.[138]

Still more recently, after Pastor Praveen Pagadala received many death threats, his body was found covered with wounds on March 27, 2025. Blood-stained sticks lay nearby, and the autopsy confirms that he was tortured. Nevertheless, the government initially called it an accident and refused to investigate further. I leave my source anonymous, but he included a photograph of the bloodied body.

A Few Cases Closer to Home

While patterns of persecution are more prominent in some parts of the world than in others, individuals have also targeted churches in the US for various reasons—racial, marital, or religious.[139] In examples from the news that are recent as I write this paragraph, God stopped attempted church shootings by the gun jamming (and a deacon's fast action) near Pittsburgh on May 5, 2024,[140] by the quick action of parishioners in Louisiana on May 11, 2024,[141] and by on-site security in Houston on February 11, 2024. Parishioners or security also limited deaths at churches in White Settlement, Texas (December 29, 2019), and Laguna Woods, California (May 15, 2022).

Still, sometimes Christians die in church shootings, such as nine at a Bible study at Emanuel AME Church in Charleston, South Carolina, on June 17, 2015, or twenty-six (roughly a third of them children) in the shooting at First Baptist Church in Southerland Springs, Texas, on November 5, 2017. The former shooter was a white supremacist and the latter an anti-religious atheist.

Church shootings, however, are currently among the least common sufferings most Christians face in the US. There are of course venues in the US where one can be beaten or killed for sharing one's faith; at the beginning of the book I gave one example of a beating I endured. On Flatbush Avenue in New York, a man threatened to shoot me for my witness for Christ. (He did apologize the next day, however, saying that he had been a bit drunk but that now he and his wife wanted to visit my church.)

And even in a small town in North Carolina, one Muslim told my friend and coauthor on a book, Pastor Glenn Usry, that it might be necessary for us to be killed. Nevertheless, what passes as persecution here is normally quite limited, and most of us have more to learn from brothers and sisters elsewhere. May we learn well, lest, like the disciples in Gethsemane, we be caught unprepared. Remembering the cost of our faith and committing to pass the daily tests of life is an important part of being prepared.

People in the US, however, are not immune to suffering, whether in this way or others. In all parts of the country they can face joblessness, floods, fires, prejudice, insensitive coworkers, abusive superiors, pharmaceutical addictions, family disputes, and the list could go on. I met a sweet, normal, inquisitive fourteen-year-old girl named Shonda whose mother (we later learned) sold drugs. Shonda ran away a number of times because her mom got hooked on the drugs she was selling. The mother owed her own dealers money, and Shonda knew what was coming. When Tammy, my friend who was her counselor, found out what was going on, she called social services. She would have taken Shonda into her own home, but she had been previously reprimanded for doing that. Social services was busy that day and then closed for the weekend. On Monday, Shonda and her mother were found in their apartment, both strangled to death.[142] That was three decades ago. Shonda should have been in her forties now. Meanwhile, Tammy told me that many of the drug dealers' clients were wealthy undergraduates at the university where I was doing my PhD.

But even if such stories do not resonate with some of my readers, eventually *everyone* faces death, and, if we live long enough, grief over other people's deaths. In the US, my dad and my doctoral mentor both passed on the same day in May 2016; in Africa, my brother-in-law Emmanuel Moussounga, still young and at the height of his career as a scientist, passed suddenly and unexpectedly on August 31, 2020. We might try to avoid the subject of death, but only the eternal perspective offered by the eternal God offers true eternal hope.

Our hope cannot be in this temporary life; it must be in the apostolic promise:

> When the perishable has been clothed with the imperishable, and the mortal with immortality, then the saying that is written will come true: "Death has been swallowed up in victory." "Where, O death, is your victory? Where, O death, is your sting?" . . . Therefore, my dear brothers and sisters, stand firm. Let nothing move you. Always give yourselves fully to the work of the Lord, because you know that your labor in the Lord is not in vain. (1 Cor. 15:54–55, 58 NIV modified)

Where we have resources, freedoms, and other blessings because of Christian forebears, we should use them for the kingdom. As a chemistry professor, my brother-in-law Emmanuel labored to provide better medicines and greater productivity for Congo-Brazzaville. Yet he labored under such greater pressure and with such fewer resources than I have available for my work in the US. Knowing his sacrifice and how hard others work with limited resources motivates me to work sacrificially with my resources to make up for what they did not have available.

After surviving torture and long imprisonment in Sudan, Mariam Ibraheem was able to relocate to the United States. Knowing that others still languish under such conditions, however, she uses her current advantages to serve others. "The message of Jesus Christ is not for me to live a comfortable life in a Christian country. It is for me to walk in the footsteps of the disciples and sacrifice for those who have never heard."[143] Alluding to Revelation's Laodicean church, she aptly diagnoses many Western Christians' spiritual condition. They are "fed spiritual sugar and artificially processed Scriptures that transform them into obese believers. Sick, untrained, comfort-seeking Christian soldiers are ineffective in the kingdom of God."[144] Instead of our spiritual immune system responding to real outside threats to the faith, we too often look inside Christ's body and turn on one another.

The only two churches of Revelation's seven that Jesus did not reprove at all were the persecuted ones. Today, as then, we have much to learn from suffering churches.

CHAPTER SEVEN

In Sickness and in Health

> Erastus stayed on at Corinth, but I left Trophimus sick at Miletus.
> —2 Timothy 4:20

In his *The Disease of the Health and Wealth Gospels*, Pentecostal scholar Gordon Fee critiques unbiblical approaches to healing and wealth. He nevertheless points out (correctly) that the case with healing is a bit different from the case of wealth. The New Testament does, after all, say a *lot* about people getting healed. We can still trust God as healer today.

Not least in the Western church, we usually need to be reminded of God's grace and power to heal us more than we do of the reality of sickness. That was one reason I wrote *Miracles Today*, and I suspect that is one reason the Gospels expend a whole lot more space recounting healings than recounting sicknesses. But because people sometimes get the wrong idea or even feel guilty if they are physically afflicted, we also need reminders that we are still on the "not yet" side of the "already/not yet" of the kingdom. "Sick" or "disabled" Christian is not an oxymoron.

Who's to Blame?

If we are going to cite Scripture to encourage our faith when praying for healing, we will naturally cite texts about healing. (We don't ordinarily pray for God to make us sick, unless perhaps we're unprepared for a midterm.) But unless we are also biblically aware that God does not heal everyone in this life, we can also run the risk of blaming the victim, as Job's friends did. The victim could be ourselves or someone else.

When God doesn't heal, or when a loved one passes, God is not guilty of negligence. Our lives were his gift to begin with, and every day we have is a gift from him. Protesting is a natural part of grief (e.g., Pss. 10:1; 44:23–24; 74:1); David is angry at God when God strikes a friend (2 Sam. 6:8; but compare Job 2:9–10). But we can also remember that God is not the one who introduced death to humanity (John 8:44; Rom. 5:12; 1 John 3:12). Jesus treated sickness as an enemy to be overcome (Acts 10:38; compare Heb. 2:14; 1 John 3:8), just as do health care workers. Jesus's resurrection defeated death, but that "last enemy" remains until his return to resurrect us (1 Cor. 15:26). We might wish that the kingdom's fullness had already arrived. But had God's day of justice and restoration come sooner, those now living might neither have been born nor had opportunity to repent (compare 2 Pet. 3:9).

Bill Johnson is known for teaching people to strive in faith for God's promises. At the same time, he recognizes that God remains God no matter what. He stood in faith for his wife's healing, but when she passed, he resolved to mourn in hope. God is faithful and worthy of trust even when life is hard. God "doesn't work for me," he explained. "I work for him. He never owes me an explanation." In the midst of the greatest pain, Johnson offered God the sacrifice of costly trust.[1] Such an attitude expresses not mere faith *that* (God will do something); it expresses a relational trust *in* the God who merits our trust no matter what. (I turn to some biblical examples of nonhealing later in the chapter.)

God can also use our infirmities for his purposes. That's not to suggest that we volunteer for such infirmities, but rather that when we face them, we welcome what God might do with them. Sometimes God glorifies himself through our healing (compare John 9:3). At other times God glorifies himself by showing what Christian faith and hope can mean in the midst of suffering. God has used Joni Eareckson Tada's injury to change the world, not least in her role as a Christian disability advocate. Similarly, because of the remarkable accomplishments of Nick Vujicic, who was born without arms and legs, he is able to evangelize from his platform as a motivational speaker.

Doing Research with Attention Deficit

I haven't earned the right to speak to such major health issues myself, but at least I can use my own lesser stories as illustrations without owing anybody else royalties. Of the first six times I lectured about miracles after my first miracles book came out, I was sick with one malady or another for five of them. For example, when I spoke for a Society of Vineyard Scholars conference, my left ear was so clogged that I could not hear through it. When I gave examples about miracles at the Special Divine Action conference at Oxford University, I had such a bad cold that I reluctantly even missed Alister McGrath's important plenary session. Without denying the possibility that the enemy wanted me to shut up, I also believe that the Lord had something to teach me. Through these experiences the Lord kept reminding me that his power is perfected in weakness and that he can bring his message through very unimpressive vessels, including me.[2]

Longer-term, from childhood I had ADHD before that was a label (these days we have much more respectable labels such as "neurodiverse"). Several years ago I asked my friend Randy Clark, leader of Global Awakening, to lay hands on my head and pray for my brain to be fixed. He sort of did, but he also said something like, "Lord, please don't let this prayer mess anything up in this useful brain." As a kid, my ADHD made me want to drop out of elementary school (though my mom wouldn't let me). Later, sitting still as an author felt like torture in the early years, requiring painful discipline to write books. (I enjoyed research, however, perhaps benefited by ADHD's side effect of hyperfocus.)

It became dangerous, however, when my wife, Médine, and I were going to speak about ethnic reconciliation to seventeen hundred pastors in Côte d'Ivoire. A travel doctor put us on Lariam, an antimalaria prophylaxis, which, unknown to us, was contraindicated for nervous conditions. Médine got nightmares, but I ended up having a series of hellish panic attacks and continuous nervous anxiety. Because I didn't yet know what a panic attack was, I panicked about the panic, creating a cascading cycle of terror. Prayer quieted my spirit periodically, but the panic attacks would eventually start up again. Continuous anxiety is hard on the heart.

Eventually this led to me being put on an expensive treatment regimen. In the process, I ended up on a treatment for my ADHD that ended a background anxiety I had experienced all my life. I had always tried to control it simply with diet and exercise. I hadn't known that life could be any different, but the past decade on this medicine has been much more tranquil. (Having grandkids probably helped too.) I had long enjoyed learning and began experiencing spiritual joy after my conversion, but now I enjoyed ordinary life itself. In the long run, then, that crisis was for my benefit. But it wouldn't have done much good had I not survived those first two years of crisis on the edge!

Miracles and Death

Faith teacher Kenneth Hagin notes that he has seen wonderful Christians die and they are now in heaven. "I would not speak despairingly of them at all, because they just didn't know what faith is."³ Healing, he argues, is "not a promise" but "a statement of fact."⁴ While most of us could learn genuine principles about standing in faith, however, faith does not resolve all ailments. Our present bodies are not immortal, and Scripture itself provides examples when God did not heal his servants in this life.⁵

Whereas the reality of persecution for following Jesus pervades the New Testament, it does not need to say as much about (unhealed) sickness or death. There is no need to encourage our faith that these things happen; we're all familiar with them from our ordinary experience. Although it is true Jesus healed all who came to him, it's also obvious that none of them is alive today. Everyone in this age still dies—though because of Jesus we who trust him will ultimately share in his resurrection.

Raisings from the Dead—Sometimes

Elisha fell sick with the sickness from which he would die. . . . And while they were burying a man, they saw a band of raiders and they threw the man into Elisha's grave. When the man touched Elisha's bones, he came to life and stood up on his feet. (2 Kings 13:14, 21)

Although Elisha's bones were so full of power that they resuscitated a corpse, Elisha himself died from sickness.

My earlier books on miracles recount the experience of Dr. Chauncey Crandall, a cardiologist in West Palm Beach. Emergency room physicians had labored for forty minutes to revive flatlined auto mechanic Jeff Markin, to no avail. Finally Crandall was summoned to certify that no more could be done. Markin was not just dead, Crandall told me, but very obviously dead; though Markin was a white person, his oxygen-starved face and hands had turned black.

After signing the death certificate, Crandall returned to his rounds, only to feel prompted by the Holy Spirit to go back and pray for Markin to have a second chance to know the Lord. Feeling little faith but determined to obey the Holy Spirit, Crandall returned and prayed for Markin while the nurse glared at him as if he were insane. Crandall then ordered Markin shocked with the paddle one more time, even though irreparable brain damage begins after six minutes without oxygen. After Crandall's colleague shocked Markin once, his heartbeat immediately sprang to normal. Markin did come to know the Lord, without brain damage, and today Crandall and Markin sometimes share their testimony together.

But there is a crucial backstory to all this. Crandall had once prayed for someone else who died—his own son. Despite many prayers concerning his son's leukemia, the son died, and no raising followed. At that point Crandall realized he could either lose faith or continue to trust God, and he resolved to do the latter. Thus on the day that God sent him to pray for Jeff Markin, he felt little faith—but he was obedient. God is worthy of our trust when he answers the way we want—and when he doesn't.

During my summers in Nigeria I spent time with Dr. Leo Bawa. I had noticed that most of my African friends had witnessed at least a few miracles, so when I was writing my first book about miracles I asked Leo whether he had seen any. "Not many," he admitted, so he sent me just seven pages of his recollections. Among these was an occasion when he was doing research in a village and neighbors brought to him their child, who had just died, asking him to pray. After a few hours of prayer, he handed their child back to them alive. Wondering whether perhaps Leo just prayed for everybody who was dead and once in a while the death was misdiagnosed, I asked how often he had prayed for God to raise the dead. "Only twice," he replied. The other had been for his best friend, who stayed dead. God has not promised to raise on every occasion, though he honored his name by raising the child in the non-Christian village.

Staying Dead for Now

Even those with the greatest faith recognize that everyone in this age dies, unless the Lord's coming interrupts that process. While I know healthy octogenarians and nonagenarians (disproportionately represented among those with healthy lifestyles), I have yet to meet a 150-year-old.

When we consider what God created us for before humanity's fall into sin, and the eternal destiny that God has prepared for us, it seems clear that God's ideal purpose for humanity is not sickness or death. We should work for his ideal, caring for our and others' health.

But it's also clear that God's ideal is not always fulfilled in this world. The greatest heroes of the faith from the past are no longer with us; of Jesus's first apostles, only one remained alive by the end of the first century. When the Bible speaks of sickness or death without healing, it seems to take for granted that this is the ordinary course of nature (e.g., 2 Kings 4:1; 13:14). The Bible takes for granted that death remains in this age; consider the repetition of "and he died" in the various generations of Genesis 5:5, 8, 11, 14, 17, 20, 27, 31, with only Enoch excluded.

Although God may allow some variables in response to prayer (Isa. 38), God is ultimately in charge of when his servants die. Thus God said to Moses, "The days when you will die are near" (Deut. 31:14; compare Gen. 47:29; 1 Sam. 26:10; 1 Kings 2:1). Indeed, those whom Jesus himself raised from the dead, some of whom were reported to live into the late first century,[6] eventually died again.

Everett Cook, who used his retirement income to run the Pentecostal street mission where I once helped, confided in me there one day that the Lord told him that he was going to take him home within a year. Brother Cook and I used to prophesy to each other, and his prophecies were normally spot-on. Nevertheless, I tried to object. This time he cut me off. "The Lord told me to get things in order" (I now realize he was evoking 2 Kings 20:1 and Isa. 38:1). "I just wonder about some of the things he called me to do for him that I haven't done yet."

Sure enough, some months later doctors diagnosed him with cancer. Before he died he became so weak that he couldn't speak, yet through signals in response to questions he indicated that he experienced no pain. It was, his wife explained, just God's way of taking him home. "The things God told you to do that you haven't done yet," I told him at his bedside, "I and your many other mentees will carry on." (For the principle, see 1 Kings 19:15–16; 2 Kings 8:13; 9:1–3.) He lifted his hands to praise God.

Most of those involved in the ministry of healing have accounts of times when God dramatically healed and accounts of times when he didn't. Sometimes the latter also included uplifted hands at the end. Jack Deere, author of *Why I Am Still Surprised by the Power of the Spirit*[7] and a close mentee of John Wimber, shares one account of his anguish when, despite fasting and daily prayer, a close family friend passed away. The lack of healing devastated him, yet the friend's faith to the end, expressed as she exerted her final strength to lift her hands to God, challenged him to deeper faith.[8]

Learning Healing and Its Limits the Hard Way

We rightly celebrate healing, but we can also celebrate God giving us special grace to persevere in cases where physical healing has not yet happened; that too is God's blessing in this life. Early in my Christian life, I began learning to hear God's voice. I celebrated the intimacy with the Lord that I experienced, which was deeper than any relationship I had had with anyone else. I sometimes saw people get healed or otherwise spiritually zapped when I prayed for them. But in time, for about a year, I became increasingly absorbed with a version of faith teaching that almost reduced healing to a formula. One day during my freshman year I was coughing so badly that I passed out in class and had to be carried back to my dorm room. To the dismay of the wise campus nurse, I insisted that I was healed, apart from "symptoms." As she left the room after reproving me, I felt God say, "Would you go to a doctor if I wanted you to?"

Well, when he put it that way, what was I supposed to say? "Yes, Lord," I responded. "But I don't have any money. So please heal me or provide me the money." He healed me on the spot, but I hadn't learned my lesson. During my sophomore year, I had a case of bleeding hemorrhoids and passed out in the hallway en route to class. When I regained consciousness, I couldn't see anything, but I could hear people say, "He's started breathing again! He's not purple anymore." After maybe forty seconds my sight returned, but this time the school insisted on sending me to a doctor, and the bill was sent to my parents. My parents were not believers at the time, but I had boasted to them about God's healing power. Now I was embarrassed.

Soon after that I was praying upstairs at the mission where I helped out. Addicted to my formulas, I protested, "God, how could you let this happen to me?" And then I uttered one of the worst blasphemies possible. "I thought you loved me!"—implying that maybe he didn't. There was a moment of silence, and then a still small voice. "My child, I let this happen to you *because* I love you." That was all he had to say, and instantly I understood. I had traded my intimacy with God for formulas. God works for our good, but he is not controlled by formulas.

A Brief History of Modern Healing and Foibles

In the 1700s and 1800s, most US Protestants believed that the afflicted should passively accept their condition rather than work against it.[9] Many associated physical suffering with God's blessing[10]—for example, seeking out an amputee who could provide prayer and spiritual counsel.[11] By the 1870s, however, a reaction set in, as people realized that restoration of health was beneficial when it was available, whether through now-improved medical means or through spiritual means.[12]

For example, Jennie Smith wrote in 1876 about how she had learned to submit to God's will and accept her sickness.[13] By the next year, however, she was considering whether God might want her to exercise faith for healing.[14] On Tuesday evening, April 23, 1878, her physician, her sister, some Methodist and Presbyterian ministers, and some others began praying with her, for two hours. She asked for God's will again, felt strength, and then sat up. Finally, she stood up, for the first time in sixteen years. She walked around the room and remained whole thereafter. She became an evangelist preaching to men on the railroad until she died in 1924 at the age of eighty-two.[15] The period includes many other testimonies of bedridden people being permanently healed once they began to pray for healing.[16]

Sometimes, however, the reaction against earlier passivity went too far, now rejecting medicine in favor of faith alone. Many medical treatments from an earlier period, such as siphoning blood from patients, were harmful; songwriter Fanny Crosby lost sight in infancy due to a quack physician. Nevertheless, medical knowledge advanced significantly in the late 1800s, after which resisting medical help more often had negative consequences. Faith missionary Rowland Bingham, founder of SIM, realized the weakness of his theology when he barely survived the sickness that killed his missionary colleagues. While he continued to pray for the sick, witnessing many healings, he recognized that prayer did not heal everyone.[17] Methodist bishop William Taylor lamented the antimedicine view that cost the life of his assistant; while affirming that Christ's death provided "for bodily as well as spiritual restoration," he noted "that the work of physical redemption would not be completed until the resurrection."[18]

Many early Christian Alliance (now Christian and Missionary Alliance) and Pentecostal missionaries died from malaria in Africa until the missionaries started accepting medicine.[19] John Alexander Dowie had a significant ministry of healing, but some of his followers died after refusing medical treatment.[20] When his own daughter accidentally burned to death, Dowie blamed this tragedy on her sin.[21] While some attributed all lack of healing to inadequate faith,[22] others who affirmed divine healing, such as A. J. Gordon and D. L. Moody, sought a more balanced approach, which eventually became the movement's prevailing view.[23] For example, R. Kelso Carter, who authored the famous hymn "Standing on the Promises" in 1886, initially rejected medicine and expected healing to come exclusively through prayer. After finally needing medical treatment, however, he publicly modified his position, allowing a greater element of mystery.[24] While appreciating the spiritual commitment of those who died refusing medicine, Pentecostal leader Donald Gee questioned "their sound judgement."[25]

As historian Paul King notes, history provides us many examples of balanced "faith teaching," such as (to name only a few examples) George Mueller and Hudson Taylor in the nineteenth century, and Christian and Missionary Alliance missionary John MacMillan in the twentieth.[26] Of course, as in Hebrews 11, heroes of faith include both those we honor by name and a multitude of others whose honor awaits the Lord's return.

Today most Pentecostals and other renewalist Christians recognize that God often heals in this life but also that full healing awaits Jesus's return.

God Answers—in Various Ways

God shows his faithful love, but he also likes to surprise us so we can't confine him to our formulas or boxes. For years I had prayed for God to pour out the Spirit again at Asbury University and Asbury Theological Seminary. I held tight to God's promise in Luke 11:13, which seems to be exemplified in outpourings of the Spirit after prayer in Acts (1:14; 4:31; 8:15). Still, I must confess to some mixed motives. I often would suggest, "God, I am preaching in chapel next week. That would be a really good time to pour out your Spirit."

But when God did it in February 2023, he did it in an unexpected way that nobody could take credit for except him. The people near the center of it—such as the gospel choir and the humble Pastor Zach Meerkreebs—absolutely refused to take any credit. (Zach in fact initially thought that his sermon had bombed that day.) God's holy presence inspired so much awe that none of us who sensed it dared boast of anything in his presence. It also turned out so much bigger than the merely local experience I had been praying for. God answers prayer, but he often likes to do it in ways that surprise us. That way he can remind us that yes, he hears us, but it is God acting and not the product of some special formula we used.

Peter Chin's wife underwent needed chemotherapy for cancer, while God protected her unborn child from its negative effects. God "did not answer a single prayer in the way that I had asked," he notes, "but instead gave me things so much deeper and richer."[27]

When doctors diagnosed my son, David, with acute liver failure, I prayed for his healing with some confidence. A few months earlier, I had been among those praying for a blinded eye when it was instantly healed in front of us. But this time God answered prayer and encouraged my son's faith in a different way. He was listed for a liver transplant one day, the next day they found a match, and two days later he had a new liver. The usual wait for a liver can run from a month to five or more years. His old liver was so decayed that doctors were amazed that his kidneys had not shut down and that other bodily systems had not been affected. They were even more astonished that he had run a 5K several days before the surgery. Unknown to him, the genetic defect that led to liver failure had been gradually destroying his liver all his life, but God preserved him until the condition could be diagnosed and a new liver would be ready for him.[28]

We continue to pray for him because of side effects from the post-transplant medicine, but we thank God and the researchers for the medical technology God used, technology that was not available just a few decades earlier.

How Come *Africa* Gets More Miracles?

When I ask my African friends why they see more miracles in Africa, they point out the greater need for miracles there. "You should thank God for the medical resources he has given you," they point out, resources much less often available to them.

My godly African parents-in-law died from illnesses that probably could have been treated had they lived in the US. It was not that they lacked faith for healing. When my father-in-law, Papa Jacques, prayed simple prayers, many people were healed. When Médine and I were visiting Congo, periodically we would run into people even on the street who remembered being healed when Papa Jacques prayed for them.

But despite miracles sustaining many individuals in Africa, average longevity is considerably lower there than here. The availability of health care and health education makes a big difference. Christians in the West tend to live much longer than our African counterparts, with less frequent need for dramatic miracles. God does not do miracles merely to entertain us; he does them when they are needed. Jesus fed the five thousand, but afterward he told his disciples to collect the leftovers (John 6:12). They wouldn't *need* a miracle for their next meal.

We can thank God for the eventual medical fruits of the sixteenth- and seventeenth-century scientific revolution. Most of the founders of modern science worked from Christian premises; the scientific revolution began because Christians who believed in an orderly God began inductively exploring nature, including the nature of the human body.[29] Often medical technology today produces results that otherwise could be produced only by a miracle.

But economic limitations are so severe and supplies so limited that many doctors leave Africa; only those most committed to serving patients there stay. In 2018, the US had 25.7 doctors for every ten thousand people; the Democratic Republic of Congo had *one* for every ten thousand people (about 4 percent of the US figure). One should not assume that this situation is God's ideal for his people. Estimates of self-identified Christians in the US are some 63 percent, with an estimated church attendance of about 30 percent. By contrast, some 95 percent of people in the Democratic Republic of Congo identify as Christians. Roughly a quarter of the nation is charismatic.[30]

In 2020, in some countries such as South Sudan or Nigeria, more than one mother died for every hundred live births, more than triple the rate in the US. In 2023, on average four infants died for every hundred live births in those countries, close to eight times the average in the US. The rate of infant mortality was even higher in some areas: In Somalia, it was more than eight per hundred. Beyond Africa, in Afghanistan, it was more than ten. Mothers in Africa and Asia do not love their babies less than North American mothers do. Many, however, have less access to resources.

Nonhealing in the Bible

> And Ahijah wasn't able to see, because his eyes were set because he was old. And the LORD said to Ahijah, "Look, Jeroboam's wife is coming to seek a message from you about her son . . ." And when Ahijah heard the sound of her steps coming to the door, he said, "Come in, Jeroboam's wife!" (1 Kings 14:4–6)

Whereas the Bible encourages our faith for healing by recounting many examples, it doesn't need to tell us that some people stay sick or that most dead people aren't raised; we know that from ordinary experience.[31] We don't need much encouragement to believe in sickness!

The only person whom the Bible explicitly mentions as healed from a skin disease in Elijah's day was the Syrian Naaman (2 Kings 5:14), though there were Israelites with the same condition (7:3–10). Jesus specifies that Naaman was indeed the only one healed of that condition in that generation (Luke 4:27).

Sickness sometimes comes as judgment (Deut. 28:21–22, 27–28; 2 Chron. 26:20; Rev. 2:22; compare Pss. 38:3; 39:9–11), but sometimes comes, even lethally, to spare people from harsher judgment scheduled around them (1 Kings 14:12–13; compare Isa. 57:1–2; Rev. 9:6). Sometimes God uses sickness or physical weakness even to facilitate the preaching of the gospel, as in Paul's own case:

> You know that it was on account of a physical weakness that I first preached the good news to you. (Gal. 4:13)

There is no one-size-fits-all reason for sickness. (Though we know that quite often, spiritual factors aside, it relates to microorganisms!)

In the Bible, David became physically weak, declining with old age. Indeed, this once ambitiously polygamous king did not have any intimate relations with the young lady his attendants brought to keep him warm (1 Kings 1:1–4). Whereas Moses retained his strength and eyesight at the age of 120 (Deut. 34:7), the prophet Ahijah was physically blind in his old age—yet so spiritually sighted that he could reveal who had just come to his door (1 Kings 14:6). We learn in passing that the prophet Elisha died of a sickness (2 Kings 13:14), even though his bones remained so full of God's power that a corpse thrown on top of his bones came back to life (2 Kings 13:21). Obviously, Elisha's sickness is not a negative comment about God's power in his life.

New Testament Examples

Although Jesus enacted God's kingdom ideal by healing all who came to him, he also left instructions regarding those who would not be healed: "When you throw a party, invite those who are destitute, disabled, lame or blind" (Luke 14:13).

Jesus's first missionaries not only faced hunger, thirst, travel, and imprisonment for his sake, but they sometimes incurred sickness as well (as noted earlier, Matt. 25:35–36 probably refers to missionaries). This has also been true for many groundbreaking apostolic ministries since then (using the broad definition of "apostolic" from chap. 2). Pioneering faith missionary Hudson Taylor, for example, witnessed miracles,[32] but his bright and devoted eight-year-old daughter Gracie died of sickness, as did his youngest son.[33] He eventually lost his devout, thirty-three-year-old wife, Maria, and her newborn to the same,[34] and he endured breakdowns and sickness himself as well.[35]

Like Paul, Epaphroditus is an example of experiencing health challenges in the course of carrying out one's mission. When Epaphroditus was sick close to the point of death after a difficult voyage, Paul did not say, "We claimed his health and he was instantly well." Instead he celebrates, "God had mercy on him" (Phil. 2:27); by God's grace, Epaphroditus recovered. (Gradual recovery is also God's gift; compare Ps. 41:3.)

Paul left Trophimus sick at Miletus (2 Tim. 4:20) and does not feel the need to offer any theological justification or explanation to Timothy. Nor does he offer a rationale for not urging (further?) prayer for healing when he instructs Timothy to use healthier means than before to take care of his digestive issues (1 Tim. 5:23).

Do I think everybody Jesus ministered to got healed? Yes. (I think this includes those who came to him, but otherwise just a few persons, like the one man out of the many at the Pool of Bethesda in John 5:3, 5. Jesus was not emptying hospital wards.) Do I think everybody Paul prayed for got healed? It doesn't look like it.

Job as a Good Example, Not a Bad One

Some advocates of greater faith (itself a good thing) have suggested that Job's low expectations invited his troubles:

What I fear comes on me! (Job 3:25)[36]

They neglect to mention that he also lamented,

> When I expected good, evil came. (Job 30:26 NASB)

Part of the point of the book of Job is that God permitted Satan to afflict Job *even though* Job

> was blameless and upright, one who feared God and turned away from evil. (Job 1:1 NRSV)

His offerings on behalf of his children (1:5) were not acts of unbelief; the author recounts these to make clear that Job did everything right to avoid trouble and did not in any way deserve what happened to him. The book of Job is emphatic that despite what he suffered, Job did not sin (1:22; 2:10). Later in the book Job does say some theologically questionable things, but these are the words of one in despair (6:26). After setting Job straight, God reproves his accusers:

> You have not spoken what is right about me, as my servant Job has. (Job 42:7)

Perhaps some seek fault in Job in hopes of discovering how to avoid sufferings like his for themselves: "You see [my] calamity, and are afraid" (6:21). Yet James declares,

> We consider those blessed who remained steadfast. You have heard of the steadfastness of Job, and you have seen the purpose of the Lord, how the Lord is compassionate and merciful. (James 5:11 ESV)

Kingdom Now and Not Yet

We do not receive every aspect of the kingdom now; what we have now is a foretaste, not the consummation. Canon Andrew White recounts some people being raised from the dead during his ministry in Iraq. Yet more than a thousand of his church members in Iraq were killed, many in random or sectarian violence but most simply for being Christian converts. As he points out in *Faith Under Fire*, "From the time of the resurrection of Christ to His second coming, God's kingdom exists alongside the kingdom of darkness"[37] (compare Matt. 13:29–30, 47–49; Rom. 9:22–23).

When John the Baptist faced impending death in Herod's prison, he heard that Jesus was healing people. This was nice and obviously prophetic, but it wasn't what God had shown John about the coming one. John's expected kingdom bringer would baptize in the Holy Spirit and fire (Matt. 3:11; Luke 3:16), and John has not heard of any fire. So John sends messengers to Jesus to ask whether he really is the coming one, as John originally thought, or whether John has it wrong (Matt. 11:2–3; Luke 7:18–20).

John's messengers see the healings, and Jesus makes their eyewitness experience part of his message: Blind people see, lame people walk, people with skin diseases are cleansed, deaf people hear, dead people are raised, and good news is preached to poor people (Matt. 11:5; Luke 7:21). Using these words, Jesus appeals to John's knowledge of Scripture. The coming restoration, the time of the kingdom, would include such blessings: Blind people would see, deaf people would hear, lame people would walk (Isa. 35:5–6), and the Lord's anointed would preach good news to poor people (Isa. 61:1).

The fullness of the kingdom will bring the expected total healing and restoration of God's people and indeed of all creation (Isa. 35:1–2, 10; 61:4, 11; 65:17–19). In the meantime, though, Jesus was already doing *kingdom* works. Healing and bringing good news to the disenfranchised constitute a genuine foretaste of the kingdom. Jesus was saying, "Yes, John, I *am* the kingdom bringer." But everything would be in its own time. The kingdom comes first like a tiny mustard seed before it becomes something massive (Matt. 13:31–32; Mark 4:31–32; Luke 13:19). It comes first like yeast concealed before it becomes the kingdom banquet (Matt. 13:33; Luke 13:21).

Likewise, Jesus warned his opponents that his widespread deliverance of the needy from evil spirits meant that the kingdom had come upon them (Matt. 12:28; Luke 11:20). The kingdom has invaded the world, and Satan is not able to supplant it, though he continues to rage until his final removal (Rev. 12:12).

After World War II, scholars began comparing this already/not yet character of the kingdom to the difference between D-Day and V-Day. Once the Normandy invasion succeeded (D-Day), the outcome of the war was clear; the Nazi regime's defeat was just a matter of time. But battles continued until the final collapse of the Nazi regime (V-Day). We too live between the times of the spiritual D-Day and the final V-Day, continuing the war but now with full knowledge of the outcome. As South African Vineyard scholar Derek Morphew points out, "Whenever someone is healed, it bears witness to the fact that the kingdom is here. Whenever someone is not healed, it bears witness to the fact that the kingdom is not yet here."[38]

We are not yet in the fullness of the kingdom, although that is what we strive for as we seek kingdom purposes in the present and work against this world's evils. Nevertheless, the works of the kingdom in the present remind us that God has not forgotten his promise.

We may not individually receive every miracle that we would like, but anyone else's miracle is also a gift to the rest of us. Any miracle is a kingdom foretaste and thus an encouragement to all of us to trust the future God has promised, when God will bring streams in the desert (Isa. 35:6) and renew the heavens and the earth (Isa. 65:17; Rev. 21:1). In that day, war will be no more (Isa. 2:4; Mic. 4:3). There will be no more sickness and no more suffering. Indeed, God

> will wipe every tear from their eyes. Death will not happen anymore. Nor will mourning or crying or pain be anymore, for the first things have passed away. (Rev. 21:4; compare 7:16–17; Isa. 25:8; 49:10)

The Lord God will dwell among us in fullness.

Healing Often but Not Always

Rolland and Heidi Baker and many of their Mozambican colleagues have been stoned and escaped various attempts on their lives as they have planted churches in Mozambique. Serving in areas with little medical help and much disease, they have also faced health challenges. Heidi had an infection so serious that doctors wanted to amputate her legs, but God healed her. Rolland was on his deathbed from long-term cerebral malaria, his memory gone and his kidneys failing, when God healed him completely in one day. But while they have experienced dramatic healing, they emphasize that there is no formula that will always yield healing. God heals sovereignly, and they seek to follow his leading.

Heidi reports that right after seeing a blind woman healed, her eyes visibly changing "from white to gray to brown," she prayed for a blind man, expecting the same sort of miracle. He was not healed, though he came to faith and a Christian doctor who was visiting from abroad was able to remove the man's related tumor. God miraculously and instantly healed other blind people at this time, but not everyone.[39]

In a 2012 interview with John Lathrop for *Pneuma Review*, Heidi Baker spoke of a blind girl named Albertina in the village of Mieze. Albertina was about twenty months old, and her eyes were completely white. In front of local villagers and foreign visitors, "Albertina's eyes turned from white to gray and finally to beautiful dark brown. We sobbed as we watched her actually see her mother for the first time."

But at the conclusion of that same interview, Heidi adds, "I hug lots of people every Sunday, people in wheelchairs who don't get out of them. As many blind people as we see healed, we also have homes for blind people who aren't healed. We have cottage industries for blind people. It's all about God and giving His love to others. Love accomplishes God's will even if a supernatural miracle doesn't happen. The biggest miracle is love."

Emphasizing the importance of missions, Dr. Helen Roseveare insists that if God calls you somewhere swept by disease, God will take care of you there. If you get the disease, God may use that to open doors for you to share with others who have it. "How's that for success?" she asks. By the world's standards, we are crazy—and by our standards, they are the crazy ones. If we truly believe that Jesus is the only savior, "we've only got this short life to get others to know the same truth."[40]

God often heals, but sometimes we stay sick for a while; whether it's short or long, that need not mean that something is wrong with us spiritually. William Wilberforce, for example, suffered much of his life, enduring ulcerative colitis and spinal curvature, yet he lobbied for decades for the abolition of slavery in the British Empire. On July 26, 1833, Wilberforce learned that the bill for abolishing slavery would pass; his greatest mission in this life accomplished, he died three days later at the age of seventy-three.[41]

Imprisoned for their faith in Iran, Maryam Rostampour and Marziyeh Amirizadeh shared Christ with their cellmates. They had experienced the Lord's miraculous leading and protection. Nevertheless, they still endured severe sickness at times in prison, and this was part of what they endured for Christ.[42]

In Russia, Aida observed her brother becoming more alive even as cancer increasingly ravaged his body. He faced death with confidence in his destiny with Christ. It was this experience that brought Aida to trust in Christ for herself, after which she became an unwavering witness for Christ despite opposition.[43]

Conclusion

When we pray for healing, we can pray expectantly; Scripture appears to even suggest that, barring other factors, healing is the normal expectation (Ps. 103:3; James 5:15). God delights to bless his children (e.g., Ps. 37:4), so it is good to pray with expectant faith.[44] The God who shows himself faithful in so many details of my life is surely to be trusted even when the world around us might seem, from our finite vantage point, to be out of control. As Jesus assures us, not a hair from our head falls to the ground without our Father's care (Matt. 10:29–30; Luke 12:6–7).

Nevertheless, the "not yet" part of the already/not yet character of the kingdom maintains a tension. Biblical wisdom not only shows us that God normally blesses the righteous, the diligent, the hardworking, and so forth (e.g., Prov. 6:6–8; 10:4; 12:11, 24; 13:4, 11; 14:23; 21:5; 22:29; 28:19). It also shows us that, as in the case of Job, there are exceptions (compare Eccles. 7:15; 8:14; 9:13–16). The complementary perspective of Ecclesiastes is valid: Enjoy God's gifts in this life (Eccles. 2:24; 3:13; 5:18; 8:15; 9:7–9). But that book's perspective is limited to events of this life (compare Luke 12:19; 1 Cor. 15:32, drawing on Isa. 22:13). If there were no afterlife to finish distributing just rewards, then it would be true: The righteous and wicked share the same fate (Eccles. 9:1–3). Happily, we can look beyond our death to eternal hope because Jesus is risen.

CHAPTER EIGHT

For Richer, for Poorer

Don't give me poverty or wealth. Feed me with the appropriate allotment of food, so I won't get satisfied and deny truth by saying, "Who is the LORD?" or become poor and steal and so abuse the name of my God.

—Proverbs 30:8–9

Give us today our bread for the day.
—Matthew 6:11

I recognize that trusting God's provision for us, like trusting him for healing and other needs, is biblical. When I started my bachelor's degree, I was working maintenance and doing yard work twenty hours a week, alongside eighteen hours of classes, including Greek and Hebrew. Then a couple offered to pay much of my tuition with one string attached: that I wouldn't say that *God* provided for me. As a matter of conviction I had to refuse the condition, noting that it was God who would supply my need one way or the other. Soon after this they dropped the condition and God provided through them. We can be grateful to human agents (in this case, the nearer cause) while being also grateful to God (the ultimate cause).

Likewise, the day before I was going to call Duke University and tell them that I couldn't come to do my PhD because I had no funds, money unexpectedly came. After graduation, I could not immediately find a teaching position and I was not sure how I was going to support myself. Less than a day after

I figured how much I would need to live on that year and cried to God with very weak faith, InterVarsity Press unexpectedly offered me an advance on my *IVP Bible Background Commentary: New Testament*. Amazingly, it was for the exact dollar amount I had calculated the night before. So let no one suppose I am belittling God's provision.

But God's provision is based on need and calling, not on keeping up with neighbors. Note what we are to seek and not to seek, and the basics God provides in Matthew 6:31–33 (here NASB): "Do not worry then, saying, 'What are we to eat?' or 'What are we to drink?' or 'What are we to wear for clothing?' For the Gentiles eagerly seek all these things; for your heavenly Father knows that you need all these things. But seek first His kingdom and His righteousness, and all these things will be provided to you."

Prosperity Teaching

> Listen, my beloved brothers and sisters! Didn't God choose the poor of the world to be rich in faith and heirs of the kingdom that he promised to those who love him? (James 2:5)

James here almost certainly refers back to a saying of Jesus:

> How well it will be for you who are poor, for God's kingdom belongs to you! (Luke 6:20)

I confess that academic work doesn't leave me much time to keep up with popular-level teaching. My summary of some prosperity teaching here therefore uses my old notes on prosperity teaching as it was circulating in the 1980s, when I was a pastor needing to address it in my congregation. I apologize if some of the following quotations do not reflect the writers' latest thinking; I use them merely to illustrate that my concern about prosperity teaching does not come from thin air.[1]

Kenneth Hagin himself, often hailed as the father of the modern faith movement, later in life did express concern that some were abusing prosperity teaching for personal wealth rather than to serve God's kingdom.[2] Indeed, an author with inside knowledge notes that "Hagin met privately with some of the major 'prosperity teachers,' including Kenneth Copeland, Creflo Dollar, Jerry Savelle, Jesse Duplantis, and others, and gave them an opportunity to adjust their messages and correct their errors before the release of his book. Some did, while others did not."[3] So my quotes from Hagin's earlier works (below) should be read in light of his later warnings.

This chapter will be short, but it could be a book. A couple of decades ago I was collecting biblical material for a critique of unbiblical prosperity teaching. When Craig Blomberg published his excellent *Neither Poverty nor Riches*,[4] however, I decided that his treatment of biblical wealth and possessions was more than sufficient—no need for the same book from two Craigs. The biblical material on the subject is vast, and there is no need to rehearse more than a sample of it here. (The original prospective publisher that invited my treatment of prosperity teaching also disliked my approach: I noted that prosperity preachers at least respect Scripture enough to seek a theological justification for their practice, whereas most of the Western church practices rampant, selfish materialism without caring what Scripture actually says about it.)

Kenneth Hagin's Teaching

Hagin says that he sacrificed many years before the prosperity he confessed materialized.[5] Yet godliness, he says, is profitable both in this life and in the life to come (1 Tim. 4:8),[6] with Hagin taking "profitable" as *financially* profitable in this life. (The Greek term simply means "beneficial," and in context applies also in a lesser way to physical exercise.) On his view, God "said that if His children would listen to Him, He would make them wealthy. He isn't opposed to their being rich, only to their being covetous."[7] That God isn't opposed to wealth is true as far as it goes (may God bless donors to good causes!), but in the same letter (1 Timothy) *seeking* to get rich for one's own sake counts as covetousness (1 Tim. 6:9–10).

The point of the "cattle on a thousand hills" being God's in Psalm 50:10 is that (unlike pagan gods) God doesn't need our sacrifices (50:8–14). Hagin, however, reasons that God put them there for us.[8] Don't let the devil make you poor, he advises.[9] Hagin says that we have been redeemed from poverty's curse.[10] "The first thing that God promised to Abraham was that He was going to make him rich. Do you mean that God is going to make all of us rich? Yes, that is what I mean." He clarifies that he does not mean millionaires, but he speaks of abundance.[11]

Hagin is right to contrast the blessing of Abraham with the law's curse, from which Jesus redeemed us (Gal. 3:13–14). The blessing of Abraham is inheriting the earth (Rom. 4:13). But we inherit the earth in the future; the foretaste Paul promises us in the present is not wealth but the promise of the Spirit (Gal. 3:14; compare 5:5; Rom. 8:23; 2 Cor. 1:22; 5:5; Eph. 1:13–14).[12] Although the covenant blessings in Deuteronomy 28 are for obedient Israel in the Holy Land, there is likely a relevant principle of collective material blessing on God-fearing societies. Nevertheless, as individual believers in the present, it is explicitly the Spirit who is the down payment of our future blessing in Abraham (Gal. 3:14).

If you need money, Hagin urges, loose it; it's in the earth realm, so God won't send it from heaven, or he'd be a counterfeiter.[13] "The Lord told me never to pray for money," he explains. "He said for me not to ask Him to give me money, for it was down here. He instructed me that in the name of Jesus I should command the money to come. Whatever I wanted or needed, I should claim it. He said that He wanted His children to have the best."[14] "If you pray to God to give you $100, you are putting all the responsibility upon Him. But the responsibility is on our part [contrast Deut. 8:3]. . . . From that day to this I never pray anymore about money. I just tell Satan to take his hand off my money. I always say that I claim so much money. I always say that angels are ministering spirits who are sent to minister."[15]

So instead of praying to God for resources, one addresses Satan? Where is that in the Bible? As for commanding angels to fetch it (based on *ministering* angels in Heb. 1:14),[16] the verse says not "sent to render service *at the command of*" but rather, "sent to render service *for the benefit of.*" While on earth, Jesus himself would have asked his Father for angelic help rather than commanding angels directly (Matt. 26:53; compare 4:6, 11). Likewise, guardian angels remain subject to God's command rather than ours in Psalm 91:11 ("*He* will command his angels concerning you"); placing them at our discretion seems closer to how Satan uses the passage in Matthew 4:6 and Luke 4:10–11.

Kenneth Copeland and Charles Capps Go Further

Kenneth Copeland proclaims, "You must realize that prosperity is the will of God for you."[17] "Decide on the amount you need. Be careful not to cheat yourself. God is not a skinflint. He is a giver. He is a lover. God is love."[18]

Charles Capps claims authority to choose prosperity and refuses "to accept . . . poverty, or any other thing of the devil."[19] Copeland notes that the responsibility for choosing lies solely with us.[20] When Jesus says to lay up treasures in heaven (Matt. 6:20; Luke 12:33), Copeland says this is a literal financial investment—money laid up in heaven till we need it, and then we can take it. "The rust and corruption," he claims Jesus told him, "is inflation and depression." In the Gospels, the promise of treasure in heaven follows using one's resources to help the needy (Mark 10:21; Luke 12:33), and it has to do with entering eternal life and the kingdom (Mark 10:17, 23–24). It is reserved for the future ("the treasure . . . for the future," 1 Tim. 6:19 NASB).

Copeland claims that Jesus went on,

If I gave you one thousand dollars today, in nine months' time it probably wouldn't be worth more than seven hundred fifty dollars. You need to learn to exercise your faith in the fact that you have this money on deposit, and when you need it, all you have to do is call for it. Make your deposits with Me according to the rate of exchange which My Word guarantees and operate under My system of finance instead of the world's system. We can make it work at the current rate of exchange at that time. It won't matter if it takes a billion dollars to buy a loaf of bread—I [God] can afford it![21]

Copeland claims that Jesus attributed the rich young ruler's wealth to his keeping the commandments. "The Lord said, 'Do you think I would ask something from him that I hadn't given him in the first place?'" Jesus only wanted him to give up his money so he could bless him all the more. In fact, "He had intended to give the rich young ruler a hundred times what he had!" This man would have been the replacement for Judas, Copeland's Jesus said.[22] The hundredfold return, he insists, is guaranteed to us today as well.[23] Yet in Mark 10:30, the hundredfold for those who lose everything for the kingdom comes because they share in a new spiritual family (compare Mark 3:35); our spiritual brothers and sisters are to be our safety net.

Citing Proverbs 13:22, Capps declares that "the wealth of the sinner is laid up for the just" and that "it is beginning to change hands. When you and I begin to act on the Word of God; when we get our speech in line with the Word we will see God move in our behalf."[24] Some of it may "change hands" because God's people are normally hard and honest workers, but this is not a matter of simply "claiming" wealth.

Nor are prosperity teachers all simply advocating a good day's work. As Copeland notes, "Well, I could look at my dad and see that this wasn't working in his life. He made more than a good living, but he worked for every dime he got."[25]

Many use 3 John 2 to declare that one can pray for and receive financial prosperity.[26] But 3 John 2 is a prayer, using the precise literary form often used in ancient letters to wish someone well.[27] Although as a pastor I explored a fuller range of arguments used by prosperity teachers, examining them all would extend this chapter beyond its appropriate length and objective. I simply encourage interested readers to examine proof texts in context.

Prosperity as Provision

In challenging what many people mean by "prosperity teaching," I am not disagreeing with faith for provision (which is what some people mean by that label). When we pray for our daily bread (Matt. 6:11; Luke 11:3), we are not praying for mansions. Especially when conjoined with a prayer for God to protect us from testing (Matt. 6:13; Luke 11:4), some of us might pray more like Agur, Jakeh's son, a prayer with which this chapter opened:

> Give me neither poverty nor riches . . .
> So that I will not be full and deny You and say, "Who is the LORD?"
> And that I will not become impoverished and steal,
> And profane the name of my God. (Prov. 30:8–9 NASB)

Of course God does invite us to trust him for provision for what we need for our life and ministry (Pss. 23:1; 33:19; 34:9–10; 37:19). At the height of the Great Depression, Pentecostal Bible college student Louise Jeter had no money, but someone gave her a dollar. On March 7, 1933, she and the women's dean prayed that God would multiply it so she could go to Peru. God provided the funds, and on June 7 she sailed for Peru, the beginning of sixty years of service in Latin America.[28] Everett and Esther Cook, the couple who ran the mission where I helped, also told me about the times God provided for them when they were planting churches during the Great Depression and World War II.

At the age of twenty-three, Lillian Trasher heard God telling her to break her engagement to a minister and move to Africa; in 1910 she arrived in Egypt. When a dying mother entrusted her baby to Trasher's care, it shaped the course of Trasher's future ministry. An increasing number of orphans were entrusted to her care, and initially she had to beg from locals to feed them. She established the nation's first orphanage. At different times she was associated with the Church of God and Assemblies of God denominations. But World War II brought new trials. She refused to abandon her children by leaving Egypt, but German tanks approached Cairo while bandits from the south plundered the orphanage's city of Asyût. One bandit had already climbed the orphanage compound walls when a stray bullet struck him—after which the other bandits fled. The war, however, cut off food supplies, and one day there was insufficient food for the next day's meals. In chapel, Trasher led the children to pray in Arabic for their daily bread.

They could not know that two days earlier a British captain, informed that Italian submarines were coming to sink all British ships in Alexandria's harbor, received orders to evacuate. Given the urgency, he planned to scuttle the cargo, which consisted of food crates intended for British troops. One Scottish sailor pleaded for the crates to be sent to an orphanage he knew about. The captain allowed the donation if it could be accomplished expeditiously. The sailors laboriously unloaded all the crates and sent them by railway cars to Asyût. Three hours after the children prayed for their daily bread, the crates arrived. This was merely one of the many times God acted on their behalf.

By her death in 1961, she was known around the world as "Mother of the Nile." Her ministry had cared for some twenty-five thousand children. The orphanage today continues to house four hundred orphans.[29] Similar stories of tested faith are told of George Mueller, who ran an orphanage in the nineteenth century.[30]

For most of us, promised provision means the basics:

> We'll be content to have something to eat and wear. (1 Tim. 6:8)

Such an idea goes back to Jesus himself, who invited us to trust God for our food and clothing.

> Don't worry about your life, what you can eat or what you can drink; or about your body, what you can wear. . . . So don't worry, saying, "What can we eat?" or, "What can we drink?" or, "What can we wear?" For pagans seek all these things—but your heavenly Father knows that you need all these things. Seek first God's kingdom and his righteousness, and all these things will be added to you. (Matt. 6:25, 31–33)

Prosperity Is Relative

Diligence "makes rich" (Prov. 10:4; 12:24; 13:4; 21:5), but prosperity is relative. God provided a meal a day for Médine's family during the war in her country, and an end to the war before they would have died from malnutrition (compare Ps. 33:19). When Jerusalem fell, God rewarded faithful Baruch, Jeremiah's scribe, not with great things but simply with his life (Jer. 45:5). In Roman custody, Paul's chains presumably limited his material advancements (compare 1 Cor. 4:9–13; 9:5–6; 2 Cor. 6:4–10; 11:23–33; Phil. 4:10–13).

For Paul, contentment and sufficiency were themselves prosperity.

> Reverence for God along with being content with what one has is great gain. (1 Tim. 6:6)

Compare that to the psalmist's words:

> You have put gladness in my heart more than when their grain and wine abound. (Ps. 4:7 NRSV)

Above the level of basic needs (unmet for many people living on benches or tenement roofs or in abandoned buildings or shacks), poverty is a relative term. A family too poor to buy its children video games might not be poor by the standards of poverty in Calcutta.

Remember again also Paul's words, which apply not only to direct persecution but also to limited access to basic necessities such as food and clothing:

> Who shall separate us from the love of Christ? Shall trouble or hardship or persecution or *famine or nakedness* or danger or sword? (Rom. 8:35)

Jesus also spoke of earthquakes, wars, famines, plagues, and other hardships as characteristic of this age until the time of the end (Mark 13:7–8; Luke 21:10–11); he calls them merely "the beginning of birth pangs" and notes that "the end is not yet" (Mark 13:7–8; compare Rev. 6:1–8).

How Jesus Wants Us to Use Our Resources

Let us grant, however, that we may trust God's provision for what he has called us to do for him (e.g., Luke 10:7–8). As I mentioned at the beginning of the chapter, I myself have experienced this blessing. But I want to spend most of this chapter looking at what Christian love urges us to *do* with our resources. Scripture promises its blessings of provision especially to the generous (e.g., Deut. 15:10; Ps. 37:21–22; Prov. 11:25; 22:9; Luke 6:38).

One goal for which we trust God's provision is that we can help others:

> Anyone who was a thief must stop stealing; instead he should exert himself at some honest job with his own hands so that he may have something to share with those in need. (Eph. 4:28 NJB)

> Instruct those who are rich in this present world . . . to do good, to be rich in good works, to be generous and ready to share, storing up for themselves the treasure of a good foundation for the future, so that they may take hold of that which is truly life. (1 Tim. 6:17–19 NASB; compare Ps. 62:10)

> If a brother or sister is poorly clothed and lacking in daily food, and one of you says to them, "Go in peace, be warmed and filled," without giving them the things needed for the body, what good is that? (James 2:15–16 ESV)

> We know love by this, that he laid down his life for us—and we ought to lay down our lives for one another. How does God's love abide in anyone who has the world's goods and sees a brother or sister in need and yet refuses help? (1 John 3:16–17 NRSV)

This ministry brings honor to God:

> This service that you perform is not only supplying the needs of the Lord's people but is also overflowing in many expressions of thanks to God. Because of the service by which you have proved yourselves, others will praise God. (2 Cor. 9:12–13 NIV)

When Rwandan genocide widow Denise Uwimana first saw the relative wealth of Manhattan, she thought of completely homeless widows and orphans in her country. "Couldn't America spare a scrap of its wealth to put roofs over my people?"[31] None of us merited to be born or raised where we were. Many of the needy in today's world—including many refugees displaced by fighting in Africa or drug cartels in Central America—are our brothers and sisters in Christ. Christians may represent nearly half the world's migrants today.[32] In some places in the Western world, such Christian migrants are even a counterforce to a culture's abandonment of religion. In the Bible, sharing of course includes our neighbors (Luke 16:20–23), but it can also extend beyond geographic boundaries when we know the needs of believers elsewhere (Acts 11:27–30; 1 Cor. 16:1–2; 2 Cor. 8–9).

Nations that are generous will be blessed, but since I write to fellow believers, what is specifically our role? Some say Christians should influence governments for righteousness; others, that caring for needs is the financial responsibility only of the church. On the latter approach, the church has plenty of opportunity to put its money where its mouth is. Some estimate that more than two billion people (a quarter of the global population) lack access to safe drinking water, and nearly half lack access to safely managed sanitation.[33] Some estimate that resolving this problem would cost about $114 billion annually.[34] Some other solutions are less expensive. An estimated one thousand children under the age of five die from malaria daily, mostly in Africa (with its strong concentration of our fellow believers, but also of malarial mosquitoes); $7.8 billion annually can address much of this need.[35] As believers, we cannot insist that we are responsible only for people in our own nation. If Jesus is truly our Lord, then fellow believers are our fellow citizens even more than national compatriots are. (In free countries, we don't even get persecuted for saying that.) If someone values earthly country over brothers and sisters in Christ, are they really a true Christian?

Sharing Possessions

One aspect of Spirit-filled experience following the day of Pentecost was sharing possessions with those in need (Acts 2:44–45), repeated again during the book's next reported outpouring of the Spirit (Acts 4:31–35).[36] This fits a pattern of expectations for kingdom living in Luke's narrative:

- "What should we do?" (to show the repentance John is preaching; Luke 3:10)
  - Those with two tunics should share one with the person who has none; same for food (3:11)
- "What shall I do to inherit eternal life?" (Luke 10:25)
  - Love and help your neighbor as yourself (10:27–37)
- "What shall I do to inherit eternal life?" (Luke 18:18)
  - Sell everything, give to the poor, and follow me (18:22)
- "What should we do?" (Acts 2:37)
  - "Repent and be baptized" (2:38; ongoing life includes sharing life [2:42, 46] and possessions [2:44–45])
- "What must I do to be saved?" (Acts 16:30)
  - "Trust in the Lord Jesus" (16:31)

The last command, trusting in Jesus, may seem incongruous with the other commands, but it is instead simply another side of the same truth. We who truly trust in Jesus stake our lives on his truth and learn to live accordingly. In Acts 16:30, the jailer addresses Paul and Silas as "sirs" or "lords" (*kurioi*), but in 16:31 they respond that he must trust in *the* Lord (*ton kurion*), Jesus. The jailer responds so radically that he removes them from their cell to wash their wounds and lets them wash him and his family in baptism. He eats with them, which was against the rules for a prison keeper. He lays his job and perhaps his own freedom on the line, showing radical trust in God as in the other cases noted above.

Often God's provision comes through others—our new, spiritual family (remember again Mark 10:29–30). This can go beyond individual or local support (again, Acts 2:44–45; 4:32, 34–35) to collective support for believers in different regions. Concerned for the needs of the poor in Jerusalem, believers in Antioch supplied them with resources. They did so even though the coming famine would impact the whole Roman world—including Antioch (Acts 11:28). Paul continued to care for the destitute in Jerusalem with a collection from among his circle of churches farther north (Rom. 15:25–27; 1 Cor. 16:1–4; 2 Cor. 8–9).

More on Sharing Possessions

Jesus further tells the story of a rich man who let a poor beggar, Lazarus, starve to death at his doorstep. This is the only sin recorded of this rich man, yet he faced eternity in hell (Luke 16:25). Of course, most of us Western Christians can piously protest, "There are no poor beggars at our doorstep." That is true; our modern society is too sophisticated to let the destitute poor get that close to our doorsteps. Much as many of us rightly insist on honoring and obeying Scripture today, we sometimes strain out gnats while missing a major theme there: More than a hundred passages talk about the poor, most of them inviting us to make sure their basic needs are met, warning against mistreating them, or speaking of God's care for them.[37] To take just a handful of examples from Proverbs:

- Prov. 19:17: "Whoever is generous to the poor lends to the Lord, and he will repay him for his deed" (ESV).
- Prov. 21:13: "Whoever closes his ear to the cry of the poor will himself call out and not be answered" (ESV).
- Prov. 22:9: "Those who are generous are blessed, for they share their bread with the poor" (NRSV).
- Prov. 28:27: "Those who give to the poor will lack nothing, but those who close their eyes to them receive many curses" (NIV).
- Prov. 29:7: "The righteous is concerned for the rights of the poor; / The wicked does not understand such concern" (NASB).

Resources are of course limited, and wise stewardship includes determining which needs are most severe and which methods are most sustainable. *How* best to meet those needs is a legitimate matter of discussion, welcoming expertise, for example, in economics, drilling water wells, microfinance, and the like. *That* we must seek to meet those needs, however, is such a plain teaching in Scripture that no one who denies it should pretend to love the Bible.

Although the teaching about financial sacrifice is for all Jesus's followers, it applies especially to those regarded most as Jesus's ministers and representatives (Luke 12:41–48). It was a standard church rule that church leaders must not be greedy (1 Tim. 3:8; Titus 1:7; 1 Pet. 5:2)—that is, they must not love money (1 Tim. 3:3; compare Acts 3:6; 20:33). (One should note at this point that despite common complaints about a few pastors being paid millions of dollars, the vocation of most ordinary pastors is itself sacrifice, a less lucrative profession than others they could have chosen.)

> If somebody has this world's resources and sees a brother or sister in need, yet shuts their heart against them, how does God's love live in that person? Children, let's not love just with our words or our mouths but by deeds and for real. (1 John 3:17–18)

If we feel like something is missing in our lives, this could be it.

> This is how we'll know that we belong to the truth and we'll reassure our hearts before God. (1 John 3:19)

> What good is it, my brothers, if someone says he has faith but does not have works? Can that faith save him? If a brother or sister is poorly clothed and lacking in daily food, and one of you says to them, "Go in peace, be warmed and filled," without giving them the things needed for the body, what good is that? So also faith by itself, if it does not have works, is dead. (James 2:14–17 ESV)

If someone's church tradition says that James 2 sounds too legalistic to belong in the Bible, they could follow Martin Luther's lead in questioning whether James is fully inspired. But if we accept such passages as fully inspired, we need to engage what they say rather than denouncing the stewardship beliefs of those bold enough to quote them.

Wesley and Other Voices from History

Illustrations of sacrifice for the kingdom are not difficult to find in church history. When the era of mass martyrdom ended in the Roman Empire, monastic movements took over as an expression of devotion to Christ. Leading church father Athanasius wrote an account of the demon-fighting Saint Anthony. Anthony actually took literally Jesus's call to abandon everything and follow him, and signs followed his ministry. In times of massively bloated church bureaucracy, Francis of Assisi, John Wycliffe, and others called Christians back to what they believed was apostolic poverty.[38] Early Anabaptists and Moravians embraced Jesus's teachings about sacrificing possessions; Hutterites even pooled their possessions literally.[39] Such sacrifices also characterized the early Pentecostal movement in China known as the Jesus Family[40] and some elements in the North American Jesus Movement of the 1960s–70s.[41] Until the mid-twentieth century, signs and wonders were more associated with living simply than with wealth (compare Matt. 10:8–10; Acts 3:6; Rev. 11:3–6).

John Wesley (1703–1791) was an evangelical Anglican leader in a revival that birthed the zealous early Methodist church, a forerunner of the Holiness and Pentecostal traditions. Wesley preached total commitment to Christ, including in the area of finances.[42] For Wesley, defying lust for material prosperity was part of holiness, separation to God away from the things the world valued.[43] He warned that riches would increase believers' conformity to the world, and he attacked those who preached the accumulation of wealth.[44] He felt that Acts 2 remained the standard—including the part about sharing possessions (2:44–45).[45] In contrast to most contemporary Christians, Wesley felt that "stewardship means giving to the poor. . . . *We give to God not by giving to the church, but by giving to the poor.*"[46] (One might add some qualification to the dictum today,[47] but only after letting its raw demand shake us regarding what God cares most about—people in his image.) If one did not give all one could, Wesley taught, one was in disobedience to Jesus's teaching and would end up in hell.[48]

My former colleague, ethicist Ron Sider, summarizes Wesley's teaching on possessions:[49] earn all you can, but keep for oneself only the bare minimum, "plain, wholesome food, clean clothes, and enough to carry on one's business," giving the rest to the poor.[50]

> Unfortunately, Wesley discovered, not one person in five hundred in any "Christian city" obeys Jesus' command. But that simply demonstrates that most professed believers are "living men but dead Christians." Any "Christian" who takes for himself anything more than the "plain necessities of life," Wesley insisted, "lives in an open, habitual denial of the Lord." He has "gained riches and hell-fire!" Wesley lived what he preached. Sales of his books often earned him fourteen hundred pounds annually, but he spent only thirty pounds on himself. The rest he gave away. He always wore inexpensive clothes and dined on simple food. "If I leave behind me ten pounds," he once wrote, "you and all mankind bear witness against me that I lived and died a thief and a robber."[51]

Whereas many Western observers today complain about the extravagant lifestyle of some preachers, we can imagine them complaining that Wesley must be legalistic. Yet Wesley's preaching is no more emphatic than that of John the Baptist or Jesus. Luke's Gospel particularly underlines this point. When ordinary hearers asked John what their saving repentance should look like (Luke 3:7–10), he demanded,

> Whoever has two tunics should give [one] to the person who doesn't have one, and whoever has food should do the same. (Luke 3:11)

Even just wanting one's just share of an inheritance (a matter that Judeans sometimes invited rabbis to arbitrate), Jesus calls greed (Luke 12:13–15). This is a form of greed because one's life cannot depend on one's possessions

(12:15). Jesus then illustrates the point with the parable of the rich fool, which emphasizes that treasures are worthless in death (12:16–21). Jesus's opposition to greed "therefore" entails not worrying about even food or clothing (12:22–23)! (I won't pretend that I have always succeeded at that virtue.)

What would this say about some people's "needs" for more video games, flashy cars, and other possessions to entertain them or raise their status in others' eyes? What does it say about those who, to justify their own lifestyles, would dismiss John Wesley or Charles Finney (I discuss Finney below) as legalists or proto-Marxists? Granted, Jesus (and John the Baptist, Wesley, and Finney) may be speaking hyperbolically, but the purpose of hyperbole is to grip our attention and force us to consider our ways, not so we can ignore the demands by saying, "That's *just* hyperbole!"

Charles Finney and Others

Charles Finney (1792–1875), a leading figure in the Second Great Awakening in the US, was uncompromising regarding biblical demands for following Christ. We may not lose our possessions, jobs, or property at conversion, he granted; but we *do* lose our *ownership* of them. If Jesus is our Lord, then everything we "own" must be at his disposal, "so that we shall never again for a moment consider it *as our own*. A man must not think he has a right to judge for himself how much of his property he shall lay out for God."[52]

But, sadly, he complained, many do not acknowledge this fact:

> Men have been led to suppose that they could be Christians, while holding on to their money. It is an undoubted fact, that the church has funds enough to supply the world with Bibles, and tracts, and missionaries immediately. But the truth is, that professors of [those who profess] religion do not believe that the "earth is the Lord's, and the fulness thereof." Every man supposes he has a right to decide what appropriation he shall make of his own money. And they have no idea that Jesus Christ shall dictate to them on the subject.[53]

Later, he notes: "Young converts should be taught that they have renounced the ownership of all their possessions, and of themselves, or if they have not done this they are not Christians."[54] Here Finney is simply taking Jesus at his word:

> Any of you who does not renounce ownership of all their possessions cannot be my disciple. (Luke 14:33)

The context is one of demand.

If anyone comes to me and doesn't "hate" their own father, mother, wife, children, brothers and sisters—and indeed their own life—they can't be my disciple. Whoever doesn't carry their own cross and come after me can't be my disciple. (Luke 14:26–27)

After giving examples of counting the cost beforehand so that one will follow to the end (Luke 14:28–32), Jesus continues:

So in the same way, any of you who doesn't renounce interest in all their possessions can't be my disciple. So salt is good; but if salt loses its saltiness,[55] what will you season it with? It's of no use for the soil or the dung heap, so it gets thrown out. Whoever has ears, let them take heed! (Luke 14:33–35)

Some have endured hunger for the sake of serving others. Desperate to feed her Chinese friends, Southern Baptist missionary Lottie Moon died from her own malnutrition.[56] I am not presenting this as a model of ideal self-care. Nevertheless, she acted in desperation to save others when her pleas for outside support fell on deaf ears.

Greater love has no one than this: to lay down one's life for one's friends. (John 15:13 NIV)

Generosity

Some teaching about prosperity is meant to counter defeatist identification of poverty with piety. Scripture provides much guidance for wise and honest business practices, including diligence, perseverance, and thrift. It does not encourage earning less; rather, it emphasizes generosity with what we have.

Let one labor, working with one's hands to produce what is good, so one may have something to share with someone else who has need. (Eph. 4:28)

The issue is not how much one makes (ideally, the more the better) but what one *does* with what one makes. A Christian leader should encourage those who are wealthy

to do good, being rich in good works, to be generous and to share, so treasuring up for themselves a good foundation for the time to come, so they make take hold of *genuine* life. (1 Tim. 6:18–19)

This exhortation may echo Jesus's warning to someone who owned much property and asked how to have eternal life: He should give to the poor and so lay up heavenly treasure (Mark 10:17, 21). The inquirer realized that he lacked something necessary (Matt. 19:20; Mark 10:21; Luke 18:22) to have eternal life (Matt. 19:16; Mark 10:17; Luke 18:18). Jesus invited him first to surrender his rival affection, and second to follow Jesus himself (Matt. 19:21; Mark 10:21; Luke 18:22). Jesus suggested that it is harder for the well-endowed to follow him and be saved because they have more to lose (Matt. 19:22–24; Mark 10:23–25; Luke 18:23–25).

First Timothy does not call the wealthy to divest themselves of all their capital, but to enjoy what God had given them and to pour their resources into serving the needy (1 Tim. 6:17–19). By serving those in need, they invest in what will count forever. Yet only those who *genuinely* trust Jesus's promise about forever stake their lives on his claim in this manner. Wealth thus holds a special temptation.

> But those who want to be rich fall into temptation, a trap and many foolish and harmful desires that submerge people in ruin and destruction. For love for money is a root of all kinds of evil. Some by pursuing it have strayed from the faith and have impaled themselves with many griefs. (1 Tim. 6:9–10)

Pursuing wealth risks straying. One may pursue it to have more to give (Eph. 4:28), but most who pursue it are motivated by "love for" it. Believers should not be impressed with wealth (James 2:1–9) or pursue it for its sake (Prov. 23:4–5; 28:20; Matt. 6:31–33; Luke 12:29–31; 1 Tim. 6:9–10). When Jeshurun grew fat, she kicked (Deut. 32:15); when Israel became prosperous, she forgot God, the source of her blessings (see Deut. 6:10–12). Some trust their resources rather than God (Ps. 52:7), though riches prove worthless in death (52:5). But if we desire only God (Ps. 73:25), versus the wicked's temporal prosperity (73:3–12), God will surely grant our desire (37:4).

The rich in Jesus's day were often oppressive landlords whose land the poor worked; New Testament statements about the wealthy are not directly applicable to all the wealthy today. But *reliance* on wealth risks spiritual poverty, as in the case of the Laodicean church (Rev. 3:17–18; compare 1 Tim. 6:17), whereas the poor could be spiritually rich (Matt. 5:3; Luke 6:20; James 2:5), as in the case of the persecuted church in Smyrna (Rev. 2:9).

Israel's prophets repeatedly address this temptation. God granted safety and prosperity to his people in the time of Jeroboam II (2 Kings 14:25–27), after Israel's rival, Aram, had been destroyed. Assyria had troubles at home, giving Israel opportunity to expand. In that time of blessing (Hosea 1:1), however, Israel attributed her prosperity to sources other than God (Hosea 2:5–13), and both Isaiah in the south and Amos in the north thundered the Lord's judgment against his people. They began a refrain that would sound again and again by the prophets until both Israel and Judah were carried away into captivity. The true fast and the true sacrifice is to care for those in need (Isa. 1:17, 58:6–7; Zech. 7:3–10). To fail to institute justice for the oppressed, when it is in our power to establish it, is to invalidate our prayers (Amos 5:21–24).

Where More Resources Are Needed

God does supply our needs. But when God gives us more than we need, it is often so we can be God's gift to others by meeting their needs:

> Our desire is not that others might be relieved while you are hard pressed, but that there might be equality. At the present time your plenty will supply what they need, so that in turn their plenty will supply what you need. The goal is equality. (2 Cor. 8:13–14 NIV)

God had provided the Corinthians enough resources to go around, giving some the privilege of sharing what was beyond their needs with others who still had needs.

Many Believers Are Poor

As I walked through parts of Kinshasa in a largely Christian part of Africa, I witnessed many barefoot children playing near open sewers, piles of rubbish, and streets strewn with broken glass. It is estimated that Christians, though some 30 percent of the global population, represent nearly half the world's migrants today.[57] Many of them migrate, seeking better jobs to provide for their families. Many others are refugees from wars or persecution. By the end of 2023, more than 117 million people were living forcibly displaced from their homes; roughly 40 percent are children.[58]

By Western middle-class standards, many believers around the world are materially poor. The same was true of many of our forebears in the faith. In a narrative that contrasts young Mary with the aged and honored priest Zechariah, Mary cries out that God casts down rulers and exalts the humble (Luke 1:52); he fills the hungry with good things and sends the rich away empty (Luke 1:53). Likewise, James declares that God will exalt the poor and cast down the rich (James 1:9–11).

Believers can be hungry or otherwise needy (1 Cor. 11:21; Phil. 4:12). When I helped in street missions, I met Christians who lived on the street and ate at the mission because they had no choice. One who had gotten off the street let me spend the night with him in his room in a condemned building swarming with insects, lines of them marching up and down the walls. Becoming a Christian did not immediately resolve his housing problem. (I couldn't invite him to my place because I still lived in a dormitory and that wasn't allowed.)

The Stats

While it is possible that many casualty estimates run high in the interest of increasing donor support (and some readers might mistrust some of the reporting organizations for other reasons), common estimates provide at least an order of magnitude.

- In 2008, long before the recent food shortages caused by Russia's invasion of Ukraine, the United Nations estimated that 25,000 people—more than 40 percent of them children—died each day from hunger-related causes.[59] This averages out to more than seventeen people (about seven children) per minute, more than one life every three seconds. This is equivalent to the direct loss of life in the 9/11 attacks eight times each day, or every three hours. World hunger, however, does not make the news, because it is not new—it keeps killing daily.
- The World Health Organization estimates that in 2021 up to 828 million people—more than 10 percent of the global population—were suffering hunger. This was an increase of more than a fifth since the COVID outbreak.[60] Yet in 2022 other households wasted an estimated one trillion dollars' worth of food per day.[61]
- In 2022, Food Research & Action Center estimated that 12.8 percent, or one in every eight households, even in the United States, "experienced food insecurity, or lack of access to an affordable, nutritious diet."[62] The same report indicates that the rate was higher in rural areas (14.7 percent) and among African American (22.4 percent) and Latino/a (20.8 percent) families.
- The World Health Organization estimates that in 2023, some 733 million people were malnourished (some 9 percent of the world population), including roughly one-fifth of people in Africa. More than two billion people (a quarter of the world's population) faced food insecurity, including more than half the population of Africa.[63] By 2050, Africa could have as many Christians as the next two continents combined.[64] Those of us celebrating the high proportion of Christians in Africa should take heed to the numbers suffering hunger there; sub-Saharan Africa accounts for 60 percent of the world's poor.[65]

- As of 2023, the Christian organization World Vision cites sources estimating that two billion people—more than a quarter of the global population—lack access to "safe drinking water, while 3.6 billion (46%) lack access to safely managed sanitation."[66]
- UNESCO estimates that more than 240 million school-age children in the world lack access to education.[67]
- The World Bank estimates that half the world's population lives on less than seven dollars per person per day.[68] About one-sixth of the world lives on less than two dollars per day. Middle income is between ten and twenty dollars per day.[69]
- Due to inadequate health care, nearly five million children below age five die each year from diseases that are mostly preventable or treatable.[70] The mortality rate for these young children in sub-Saharan Africa runs some fourteen times higher than that in North America or Europe.[71]
- An estimated 1.6 billion people globally lack adequate shelter,[72] and about 150 million people lack not only adequate shelter but any shelter at all—they are homeless.[73] One hundred fifty million people would be 43 percent of the United States if they all lived here. Half a million of them *do* live here.[74] Meanwhile, someone without children to support whose income is $60,000 per year after taxes is in the wealthiest 1 percent of the world's population.[75]

Yet Larry Ward, founder of Food for the Hungry,[76] lamented that statistics were not enough to convey the pain of starvation. Each statistic had a face and a name: "I see those statistics in terms of that little girl in Laos, her pretty face now like a skeleton . . . as she dies of ordinary dysentery. At last a hot bowl of rice has been placed beside her, but her little body is too weakened from long-term malnutrition. All she can do, as she lies there and dies, is take one little grain of rice at a time and transfer it to the tip of her tongue."[77]

He describes meeting a boy in Cambodia whose ankle and leg, even above the knee, he could circle with his thumb and forefinger. He discovered that the boy was nine years old, but severe malnutrition had stunted his growth.[78] Eighty percent of brain development occurs by age two; inadequate access to protein during formative years leaves children mentally retarded, sometimes with underdeveloped craniums and brains.

Some accuse those who speak of such needs of being guilt manipulators. Guilt isn't the best response to these needs. But *compassion* is. And surely every real Christian, who has Jesus in his or her heart, experiences compassion (compare Matt. 9:36; 15:32; Luke 10:33, 37).[79] Admittedly, resources are limited, and sometimes the needs are so many that it's tempting to shut our hearts. Unlike God's infinitely large heart, we can't endure all the pain. What then can we do?

Western Wastefulness

Many Western Christians seek to finance "necessities" that, in light of the lifestyles of most of the world's people, are mere status symbols. Although churches in the New Testament period normally met in homes, church buildings have their usefulness in many cultures, both for outreach and for shelter. But what might Jesus say about our *priorities*, considering US religious institutions spent nearly three billion dollars in 2023 on building construction alone?[80] Unimpressed with the splendor of a physical temple, Jesus chose to build one of people instead (Mark 13:1–2; 1 Pet. 2:5). But physical buildings are not the costliest of our expenditures.

We should consider whether we can live more simply to be more faithful in using the resources he entrusts to us. Indeed, sometimes God's calling requires that of us. When someone volunteered to follow Jesus, as already mentioned, Jesus responded,

> The foxes have their dens and the birds of the sky have their nests, but the Son of Man doesn't have anywhere to lay his head. (Matt. 8:20; Luke 9:58)

When Jesus sent the Twelve, he commanded them

> not to take anything for the journey, except a staff. That means no bread, no bag, no money in their belt, though they would wear sandals. "And don't wear two tunics." (Mark 6:8–9)

After visiting ministers serving in Western New Guinea (Indonesian Papua), charismatic leader Jamie Buckingham praised their sacrifices and criticized our Western waste of resources on things we don't need.[81] Comparing them to Eli's corrupt sons Hophni and Phinehas (1 Sam. 2:12–17), Buckingham denounced corrupt modern prosperity preachers. He quotes Catholic charismatic leader Francis MacNutt's words from the 1976 Holy Spirit conference in Jerusalem: "If Jesus were on earth He wouldn't be here today. He couldn't afford the registration." Criticizing morally compromised television preachers, Buckingham concluded, "The only way we will ever restore our lost credibility is to pick up our wounded, renounce what we have become and re-commit to be like Jesus."[82]

Some people object, "I give to meet some needs; I just have a nice lifestyle, too," as if we're being generous. If Jesus is truly Lord of all our life and all our possessions (Luke 14:33), however, it is not very generous to rescue a few people from starvation while letting others die so we can buy mere status symbols. Do our resources belong to us, or are we called to be stewards (1 Chron. 29:14)? If we squander our resources mainly on ourselves, do we really believe that it is more blessed to give than to receive (Acts 20:35)? Of US Christian finances devoted to God's work, some estimate that only 4 percent reaches the 94 percent of the world's population outside the United States. Jesus warned us not to be tricked by the allure of money ("the deceitfulness of wealth," Mark 4:19 NASB, NIV). If we truly believe that we can lay up treasure in heaven worth eternally more than treasure on earth, what we do with our resources will show where our heart is (Matt. 6:19–21).

What to Do with What We Have

[Your father Josiah] upheld the cause of the poor and needy. So things went well for Judah. The LORD says, "That is a good example of what it means to know me." (Jer 22:16 NET)

No one can serve two masters; for either he will hate the one and love the other, or he will be devoted to one and despise the other. You cannot serve God and wealth. (Matt. 6:24 NASB)

That is why you must kill everything in you that is earthly: sexual vice, impurity, uncontrolled passion, evil desires and especially greed, which is the same thing as worshipping a false god. (Col. 3:5 NJB)[83]

. . . people of depraved mind and deprived of the truth, who suppose that godliness is a means of gain. But godliness actually is a means of great gain, when accompanied by contentment. . . . And if we have food and covering, with these we shall be content. (1 Tim. 6:5–6, 8 NASB)

Many of us could live with less, but a key purpose of most advertising is to delude us into thinking that we need more.

Covetousness is not a matter of one's income. It is possible to have a very high income and be very generous with it; God provides members in the body of Christ with this gift (Rom. 12:8). Contrary to some common misinformation, a needle's eye back then meant what it means today, not something larger. The point of the image is something impossible. Nevertheless, *God*, who accomplishes the impossible, can squeeze even a camel through a needle's eye—that is, he welcomes anybody into his kingdom who is truly willing to abandon all for Jesus (Matt. 19:25–26; Mark 10:26–27;

Luke 18:26–27). Joseph of Arimathea becomes one such example (Matt. 27:57–60; Mark 15:43–46; Luke 23:50–53; John 19:38). He was clearly willing to lay his wealth, reputation, and even life on the line by standing for Jesus; requesting the body of someone executed for treason (Matt. 27:58; Mark 15:43; Luke 23:52; John 19:38) could lead to the requester being charged with the same offense. Governors were especially happy to pin capital charges on the wealthy to confiscate their property.

Other persons of wealth also entered the kingdom after making sacrifices commensurate with their resources (e.g., Acts 4:36–37). When one rich man (Luke 19:2), Zacchaeus, was converted, he expressed his faith in two ways: (1) he gave half his goods to the poor; and (2) he paid back fourfold anyone he had ripped off (19:8), treating his white-collar crime as theft (Exod. 22:1, 4; 2 Sam. 12:6). Once Zacchaeus announced his intention to make restitution, Jesus announced that Zacchaeus was saved (Luke 19:9–10). His second action provides a model for those who gain wealth dishonestly; his first action provides a model for all persons who have more than they need (compare Luke 3:11).

Views vary on how best to generate wealth, and I am no economist. Most agree at least that helpful approaches include accountable NGOs establishing microfinance, job training and job creation, and education. Partnership on projects is also valuable. Principles that foster self-support and indigenous initiative are far more effective in the long term than are practices that foster dependence.[84] At the same time, urgent crises such as famines and displacement require more direct interventions, and these are massive issues today.

We're All Vulnerable

Some Americans suggest that the poor should just "pull themselves up by their bootstraps"; but as Tom Skinner pointed out, most of the poor are children. How can children pull themselves up by their bootstraps? An estimated 20 percent of children even in the US suffer hunger, with cases in nearly every community.[85] An estimated half of low-income homes with children in the US are headed by single mothers with limited means; nearly one-third of households led by single mothers face food insecurity.[86] Many of us who have not lived our entire lives in privilege can remember when we ourselves were just a paycheck, medical crisis, or job loss away from vulnerability or dependence.

In my early ministry, I pastored a small congregation for free while working in a fast-food restaurant to support myself. Although God provided my basic needs—groceries and rent for the cheap basement apartment that stank for a week whenever it flooded—I often wanted to eat the more nutritious food I saw other people throwing away. When the restaurant where I worked closed down, I quickly found another job, but after a couple weeks that employer began laying off the new employees when it became clear that the program was under-enrolled. I could have been on the street had it not been for one generous couple in the congregation who secretly helped those in desperate need.

There were several other times in my life when I was one of those people just a paycheck away from being homeless. It took twelve years of college to get the academic qualifications required for me to teach in my discipline; I often lived hand-to-mouth until I finished, though the Lord provided my tuition and essential needs every year, sparing me from debt. During my first winter doing PhD work I could see my breath while bundled up in my apartment because I couldn't afford the heat bills. I looked to God, and he did supply my needs—but needs differ from preferences, and life was not always easy.

May our own vulnerability motivate us to greater compassion for those in need.

CHAPTER NINE

Examples of Other Kinds of Hardships

At times during the Cold War, the world teetered on the edge of a nuclear holocaust. Several accidents led to very close calls,[1] from which God spared us. But if we experienced a nuclear war, which would presumably impact the Global North most directly, it would surely touch the lives of Christians. Many of Japan's fairly small number of Christians lived in Nagasaki when a US plane dropped the atom bomb code-named Fat Man on August 9, 1945. This act immediately reduced the proportion of Christians in Japan. Radiologist Takashi Nagai had recently become a Christian when the bomb fell. His children were safe in the countryside, but he returned home to find his Christian wife just a pile of bones in what had been the kitchen. Clutched in the bones of her hand he found her cross—the only thing that made sense now in the vast devastation around him. When he made his way to the local cathedral, ground zero for the bomb, among the incinerated ruins he found the church's bell astonishingly intact. Ringing the bell, he summoned Christian survivors together to celebrate hope and the faith to begin rebuilding their lives.[2] Despite deterrents in place and reduction of the world's nuclear arsenal, the potential for vast devastation remains.[3]

One could trace examples of the various sufferings Paul lists in Romans 8:35–39 (such as famine, poverty, accidents, war, death) or John lists in Revelation 6:1–8 (conquest, war, famine, plagues, and animal attacks). Mental anguish or losing a child can be among the most horrible sufferings, but space here is limited, so any categories are merely illustrations. The general principles apply to a range of hardships, so I illustrate in this chapter with just a few categories, some more dramatic than others: displacement, family conflicts or losses, other disappointments, and challenges to success.

Don't Blame the Victims

While the sufferings in Revelation 6:1–8 are judgments, they are judgments on humanity or societies, not normally on the individuals who suffer them. God may raise up people to protect others from the deadly effects of natural disasters (Gen. 41:25; 45:5; 50:20; Acts 11:28–29). Moreover, Jesus warns us not to presume that disasters can strike only particular people (Luke 13:1–5).

One response to compassion fatigue, however, is to implicitly blame the victims, individually or collectively. When I lamented dictators abusing their people (see Prov. 28:15), a close relative responded that it will always be that way until the people rise up, like "we" did in the American Revolution. Granting his ultimate point that we cannot expect our own governments to intervene in situations everywhere else—resources are limited—revolutions do not all succeed. When a democratically elected president in Congo-Brazzaville, my wife's country, tried to renegotiate oil prices with Elf, the French oil company, Elf helped arm the former ruler to return to power. In the ensuing war, a quarter of the nation became refugees, and the former president (1979–1992) returned to power (1997–current). Whether one sees the outcome as positive or negative might depend on one's region of origin, but the point remains that wars have losers as well as winners. Except in cases of direct or indirect genocide, difficult governments are often easier on civilians than is war.

One form of implicitly blaming the victim is to shrug and say, "They chose to live in that place." Yet people have no choice where to be born, even if sometimes they can migrate. Moreover, what happens when migration transgresses national boundaries? Fulani herders clash with Christian farmers in Nigeria because the Sahara is spreading southward, and the herders seek better pasture for their cattle. Where can farmers go to start over? Gang violence in Central America drives many northward to escape death threats and forced recruitment, but the US immigration services lack resources to process and properly investigate all claims.

Those of us in the Midwest lament West Coast earthquakes and forest fires while reasoning that people could relocate to more stable ground. (Kentucky, where I currently live, also includes an earthquake fault that just hasn't moved for a long time.) Those in the Northwest can wonder why anyone would choose to live in the Midwest tornado alley. Why would anyone choose to live on the Gulf Coast or Florida with their hurricanes? Why live in the North with its ice storms or the South with its summer heat? Low ground is more susceptible to floods and high ground to tornadoes. Meanwhile, weather patterns are changing, and previously less vulnerable locations are becoming increasingly vulnerable. Some places have more drugs, some places have more shooting, some places have less access to emergency medical help. Many of us have to move for work or to be able to afford housing, despite these other factors.

Geography keeps some nations chronically poor. Although this situation impacts many nations, I will take just one nation as an example. Bangladesh is subject to repeated disasters. From 1960 to 1970, roughly 5,000 people died from natural disasters there every year, "excluding the estimated 500,000 deaths from the 1970 cyclones."[4] Annual monsoon floods can cover one-third of the country, and in May 1985 a storm and tidal wave "killed between 5,000 and 15,000" people.[5] In 1988, when three-quarters of the country was submerged by flooding,[6] an estimated 30 to 40 million became homeless,[7] or roughly one-third of the population at that time.[8] Many died of bites from displaced snakes or drinking contaminated water.[9] Disease proliferated, with diarrhea a factor in most deaths.[10] The flooding contributed to thousands of deaths.[11]

In 1991, a cyclone and massive tidal waves killed between 135,000 and 145,000 people along with a million cattle, with up to 10 million left homeless.[12] A few years later, an Assemblies of God support letter notes again that 40 million lost their homes.[13] Monsoon floods submerged over half of Bangladesh in 2004, affecting a quarter of the population and again leaving as many as 25 million homeless.[14] This tragedy was soon followed by the December 26 Indian Ocean tsunami, which impacted multiple countries and left more than 200,000 dead.

One expert warns that "by 2050, Bangladesh will lose 17% of its territory due to rising sea levels, resulting in the loss of 30% of the country's agricultural lands." Right now 85 percent of households in rural areas there depend on agriculture. People fleeing the coast settle in cities, competing for scarce work and limited health and food resources.[15]

Obviously, the current situation looks unsustainable. So, one may ask, why don't people relocate? Yet as of 2022, Bangladesh had 171.2 million people, with more than 1,300 people per square kilometer of land. That is, it has about half the population of the United States living in a nation the size of the US state of Wisconsin. Many of the people have deep ties to ancestral lands and family, but more critically, surrounding countries are not prepared to simply absorb massive numbers of Bangladeshis as immigrants. So yes, people continue living in vulnerable places. But many have little choice. A better response than blaming them is compassion, thus working toward potential solutions insofar as we can, while recognizing our own vulnerabilities.[16]

Displacement and Homelessness

In many nations where governments persecute Christians most severely, Christians do not buy or build homes, since "they will be confiscated at their first arrest."[17] Again:

> The foxes have their dens and the birds of the sky have their nests, but the Son of Man doesn't have anywhere to lay his head. (Matt. 8:20; Luke 9:58)

Although Jesus had lived in Bethlehem, Egypt, Nazareth, and Capernaum, his itinerant ministry now left him no single place to stay. Jesus's family had to flee targeted violence in Judea (Matt. 2:13–14, 22). Sometimes the only place to lay his head was in the stern of a Galilean fishing boat (Mark 4:38). The demands of his ministry were the price of his faithfulness.

More generally, in winter 2023, the US Department of Housing and Urban Development estimated that more than 650,000 people in the United States were homeless, including nearly 112,000 children. More than a third of the total number lacked any shelter at all.[18] At a church-sponsored homeless shelter in Washington, DC, I talked with people who live on the street simply because they lost their jobs and had nowhere else to go. One was a fellow professor who gave up on life when he lost his wife. Some are Christians, who depend on God's provision like the rest of us do but normally experience it through homeless shelters and missions.

Some years ago, when I was witnessing to male prostitutes in Chicago with a friend from Chicago Teen Challenge, a man confessed to us that he just let gay johns pick him up so he'd have a warm place to stay at night. "If my girlfriend found out I was doing this, she'd kill me," he said. He is probably right about the last point now; we talked with him before AIDS became widely known. He could have become infected and infected her. He sounded interested in going through the program to get off the street, but most people never learn about that opportunity.

Homelessness sometimes results from alcohol or drug abuse, but there are other reasons for homelessness—certainly for the more than one hundred thousand children mentioned above. And whatever the circumstances of homeless persons in the US, displacement is an even larger problem worldwide. We could talk about many parts of the world, from the Middle East to Myanmar, Ukraine, and various other nations.[19] Open Doors estimates that 16.2 million Christians are displaced in sub-Saharan Africa, many because of severe persecution.[20] In this section, however, I offer three examples just from French-speaking Africa: (1) believers currently displaced at a camp in the Democratic Republic of Congo; (2) the earlier displacement of my wife and her family in Congo-Brazzaville; and (3) some experiences from the 1994 Rwandan genocide, particularly the stories of Denise Uwimana and Immaculée Ilibagiza.

The Kigonze Camp

Rory Randall is a kindhearted charismatic friend who filmed interviews with many faithful Christians from the Democratic Republic of Congo in the Kigonze camp for internally displaced persons.[21] International aid organizations—at the time of his interviews stretched thin amid recent conflicts in Ukraine, Gaza, and elsewhere—have stopped supplying food (maize flour and peas) and medicine, leading to many deaths.

Many people in the camp are mutilated from war or disabled. Many have been in the camp for five years and can find little work. Some find work washing clothes or helping on farms near the camp for something like forty cents a day, sometimes to feed a family of ten. They hope that someday their children can attend school again; the schools near the camp are too full for the refugees. They want their children to read the Bible and serve God, just as do godly Christian parents in the West. Most of the interviewees said that they are surviving only by depending on God. As one mother declared, "I have a shepherd who never fails; he is the one fighting for us. God does everything according to his perfect will." Two young people said that they want to be teachers, but the war displaced them from school, each at fifth grade. "What keeps me going," one teenage girl declared, "is only faith in Christ Jesus." The camp pastor says attackers murdered some of his friends and family members before he was displaced.

Christians in the camp keep praying for the fighting to end so they can return home, work their own land, and send their children to school. Some of the warfare, though, is fueled by other countries wanting control over the land's rich mineral resources—a prosperity that brings trouble to the civilians. The coltan used in Western cell phones is a key focus.[22] Similarly, as mentioned earlier, in my wife's smaller Congo (Brazzaville), the French oil company Elf helped arm one side in the war to maintain more favorable prices for Congolese oil, at the expense of civilian suffering. A portion of the West's prosperity comes at the expense of other nations' suffering.

As I write, the terror in the eastern Democratic Republic of Congo does not appear likely to end any time soon. The very wealth of its minerals invites exploitation from other countries and their militias. Thousands of rapes and killings are documented annually. One recent report claims the horrendous mass rape and subsequent burning alive of more than a hundred women;[23] the same week saw reports of hundreds of corpses left in the streets of Goma.[24] In general, more than 1.5 million women in the nation report experiencing rape.[25] One Christian hospital has treated more than 70,000 rape victims, a third of them minors, some of them infants.[26] Despite scanty US media coverage, from 1998 to 2008, war and consequent malnutrition and diseases killed an estimated 5.4 million in the DRC. This is more than the population of Alabama or Denmark or Ireland or Lebanon or New Zealand or Singapore— some seventeen times the number of US deaths in battle in World War II. It would thus be front-page news if it were in a part of the world the West tends to care more about. Nearly half the victims are children under the age of five, who are particularly vulnerable to malnutrition and disease.[27] We are rightly outraged that Hitler killed 6 million Jews while the world looked the other way. From what does the world look away today?

My Wife's Family During War

Desperation can drive us to exertion, including the exertion of radical dependence on God. Médine and her family were among the last to flee their neighborhood as shooting and bombing drew near. They had only a few hours to decide which items they could pack and carry on their backs or heads; other things, including family photographs and other precious mementos, they would have to leave behind. Médine had to abandon her camera, her guitar, and the cooking utensils she had acquired when studying in France. Nevertheless, they hoped that fighting would end soon and they could return home.

Little did they know that they would be displaced in the jungle and at the edges of villages for the next eighteen months. During those months one family member or another was often close to death from malaria, typhoid, or other sicknesses. Drinking water was contaminated with human waste and the remains of dead bodies. Médine often walked five miles a day through snake-infested swamps and fields of army ants to get basic food for her family to eat for one meal a day.

When they were finally able to return home, Médine and her siblings worried how their parents would respond to the war-ravaged remains of their town. Her father had invested his life savings in their home; their culture had no home insurance (and had it existed, the war would have bankrupted the insurance companies anyway). Many other elderly people, finding their homes destroyed, died from stroke or heart failure.

When they arrived, Papa Jacques quietly surveyed the ruins of his home as his children held their breath, fearing for his life. Finally, he spoke, lifting his one hand that was not disabled. "Let's thank God. These are just things. But all of us remain alive." The neighborhood, once bustling with the sound of children playing, was now silent; most neighbor children died during the war. But despite typhoid, malaria, dysentery, and shooting, not a single one of the Moussounga family died during the war. They had also learned a deeper dependence on God's answers to their prayers.

One agnostic friend told me that he couldn't believe in a God who would allow so much suffering in the world, including hardships like people being refugees. When I asked my wife how she would respond to such an insistence, she considered it strange that some Westerners use experiences of suffering such as hers to deny God. During her time as a refugee, she notes, refugees turned to God; without him they could not have endured their hardship. It's trust in God that gives us hope. And the heart of our faith, the cross, shows us a God who chose to embrace our pain in person.

Rwandan Genocide

Racism and ethnic prejudice are not a uniquely North American or South African problem. Along with Uganda, Rwanda was at the center of the East African Revival of the 1930s. But after six decades, evil had grown enough to strike back in one of the most massive and horrific genocides of modern history.[28] The 1994 Rwandan genocide followed years of discrimination against Tutsis and the government allowing only Hutus in the army.[29] Starting on April 7, 1994, Hutu militants began slaughtering every Tutsi and moderate Hutu they could find. The death toll from April 7 to July 19 is estimated to be some eight hundred thousand to even a million. That is like the horrific death toll from the September 11, 2001, attacks in the US—multiplied by three every day for all one hundred days of the Rwandan killing spree.[30] In one region, Tutsis organized and held off aggressors for two days; their heavily armed assailants, however, managed to annihilate them after a few days.[31]

Like Hitler's Nazis, the Hutu extremists were organized and brutally efficient. Extremist Hutus disseminated fear among majority Hutus with fake news about Tutsi aggression.[32] Meanwhile, on April 12, for example, one locality called all men to a "peace meeting"; once the Hutus were ordered out, exits were sealed and the hundreds of Tutsi men inside were burned alive.[33] Tutsis fled by the thousands to churches, which in the past had always provided sanctuary. So many crowded inside these churches that the doors could not shut. This time, though, the aggressors burned them alive inside the churches, gunning down anyone who ran out.[34] At one large church, extremists slaughtered an estimated ten thousand fugitives.[35] The killers even slaughtered babies en masse.[36] One survivor recalled her four-year-old boy's last living words: He promised not to wet his bed again, thinking the killers had come to punish wrongdoing.[37]

Many killers were teenagers motivated by propaganda; they afterward spent years wracked with guilt.[38] As human rights investigator Gary Haugen discovered in Rwanda, mass murder does not require "pathological" killers: "When all restraints are released, farmers, clerks, school principals, mothers, doctors, mayors and carpenters can pick up machetes and hack to death defenseless women and children."[39]

HAUNTED BY MEMORIES OF LOVED ONES

Denise Uwimana deeply loved her faithful husband, Charles, and God had even sent someone to prophesy to them about their relationship before Charles left their home for his work the final time. Soon after this, the genocide began; she and her children never saw him again.[40] Killers armed with machetes then burst into her home, murdering the young relatives staying with her.[41] After taking the watch and shirt of a relative who saved Denise's life, they sliced off his head.[42] Denise and others who escaped to sanctuary had to endure hearing the screams of loved ones being tortured to death;[43] aggressors often taunted them by boasting of other loved ones they murdered.[44] Plagued with survivor's guilt, Denise wondered whether she could have acted differently and perhaps saved young Aline, Thérèse, or other guests.[45] Meanwhile, it took years before she could come to terms with the fact that her beloved Charles would never come home.

Denise and many other Tutsi survivors owed their lives to Hutu followers of Jesus who risked their own lives to shelter them.[46] While nearly one hundred Rwandan pastors gave their lives to try to protect others, however, most pastors kept silent, and a few even joined the killing.[47] After the war, many survivors lost their faith.[48] Others protested to God, "Where were you when the soldier raped me? Where were you when my parents were murdered?"[49] A majority of survivors were women, the vast majority of whom had been raped. An estimated 70 percent of the quarter million rape survivors were now HIV positive.[50] Girls as young as nine, and occasionally as young as four, were traumatized by rape, and on occasion even raped by French soldiers who were supposed to be their benefactors.[51]

Denise found herself angry at Hutu pastors with the nerve to preach that Tutsi survivors should forgive their murderers. Most of these pastors had not risked their lives to protect Tutsis, yet now they wanted those who had lost everything to forgive.[52] Jesus himself, however, taught Denise to forgive, as she confronted ashamed Hutu plunderers and offered forgiveness to those who wanted it.[53] It was hard, since she knew which neighbors still used her looted furniture or the gifts her beloved husband had once given her.[54] After years of work to bring healing to other survivors, she married Dr. Wolfgang Reinhardt, a respected researcher on revival and a German advocate for genocide survivors.

Widows sharing their pain openly with one another learned to find solace in God and seek healing for others.[55] Finding hope and meaning only in the cross,[56] they ultimately released their hatred and forgave the killers.[57] Because of Jesus, Denise's friend Beata ultimately forgave the man who killed and discarded the bodies of five of her children.[58] A teenage neighbor named Emmanuel killed the husband and five of the children of another friend, Cancilde; the genocide leaders rewarded him with Cancilde's house. Tormented by guilt, however, he ultimately begged for forgiveness; eventually, she forgave him, and he became like a son to her and she a mother to him.[59] Grace is intensely costly, not cheap. But it ultimately contributed to collective healing for a new generation that has abandoned the artificial and divisive Hutu and Tutsi labels.

HORRORS IN A SMALL RWANDAN BATHROOM

One Hutu pastor hid Immaculée Ilibagiza and seven other Tutsi women in a bathroom four feet long and three feet wide for three months. Keeping them safely hidden meant that some of the women were literally on top of others, cramped in the heat.[60] They couldn't flush the toilet unless someone in the nearby bathroom flushed, lest anyone hear them. Sometimes it took a few days before the pastor could slip them food; Immaculée shrank from 115 pounds to 65.[61] Unable to wash themselves during this period, they developed body lice, and Immaculée developed a 105-degree fever and a urinary tract infection.[62] During their hiding, killers often crowded into the adjoining bedroom, forty to fifty at a time, searching the premises for any trace of Tutsis who might be hidden there.[63]

Outside they could hear the screams of young mothers, elderly women, and others being slaughtered—sometimes people they knew being murdered by other people they knew.[64] Immaculée spent much of those three months in prayer; those prayers initially felt hollow until God gave her grace to forgive even the killers.[65]

When French and Tutsi forces were finally near, the pastor snuck the fugitives out and handed them over to the French. But given orders not to fight, the French troops soon abandoned them in the midst of armed Hutus to meet their fate by bullets or machetes.[66] Now emboldened by God, Immaculée defied those ready to kill them, announcing that Tutsi troops were nearby. She then began walking toward the Tutsi camp, and God brought about the rescue of her party.[67] Initially, though, even reaching the Tutsi camp did not guarantee safety. Tutsi soldiers suspected Immaculée and her colleagues of being spies, since the soldiers believed that all local Tutsis were dead.[68] Finally, however, the soldiers admitted the ragged band into the camp. Once Immaculée got news, she learned how government propaganda had driven longtime Hutu friends to reject her parents and siblings, all of whom they betrayed and murdered.[69] Others protested to their rescuers, "Why didn't you come sooner? Why did you wait till my children were dead?"[70]

Just before the genocide began, General Roméo Dallaire wanted to confiscate the Hutu extremists' weapons, but his superiors at the UN would not allow it. With fifty-five hundred soldiers, he insisted, he could avert the genocide, but once it began officials actually removed 90 percent of their troops, repeatedly delaying any intervention.[71] Thus the vastly outnumbered UN peacekeepers withdrew, abandoning the Tutsis to their fate.[72] Meanwhile, despite Hutu government broadcasts ordering the eradication of all Tutsis, the US initially reportedly denied a genocide was happening, fatally delaying any response.[73]

The world that looked the other way during the Armenian genocide and declared, "Never again!" after the Nazi murder of six million Jews did too little, too late in Rwanda. Afterward, the world again declared, "Never again!" while ignoring that the instability from Rwanda simply spilled over into neighboring countries. As the world washed its hands, genocide continued elsewhere, such as in the eastern part of the Democratic Republic of Congo. God knows this world's hypocrisy: "Rescue those being led away to death; hold back those staggering toward slaughter. If you say, 'But we knew nothing about this,' does not he who weighs the heart perceive it? Does not he who guards your life know it? Will he not repay everyone according to what they have done?" (Prov. 24:11–12 NIV).[74]

Slavery Today

We are rightly horrified by the injustice of slavery in history, including the brutal ways it was practiced in the Americas. But slavery continues in many parts of the world. Over several decades, Soviets and their dependents deported millions to their labor camps. Romanian Sabina Wurmbrand recounts her brutal experience of several years of slave labor in a Communist labor camp.[75]

It is right to escape abuse whenever possible (Matt. 10:23; 1 Cor. 7:21–23), but there are settings where that is not physically possible. Although a few early Christians belonged to the elite, most were poor and many were slaves. The slaves had little choice but to obey their slaveholders and, in many cases, endure harsh treatment. First Peter addresses their situation. Peter does not want them to suffer, but that situation is not under his control. What he can offer is encouragement that God will eternally compensate them for what they suffer:[76]

> Do this because it brings God's favor when, for the sake of one's conscience before God, one puts up with grief while suffering unjustly. For what kind of credit do you merit for enduring being beaten as a result of sinning? But if instead you endure suffering as a result of doing right, this brings God's favor on you. (1 Pet 2:19–20)

This passage illustrates that, even when we suffer for our social status or other reasons besides our faith, God cares about the injustice.[77]

This sort of suffering was not limited to the ancient world, but today we are more able to fight it. Sex trafficking and other forms of slavery remain common today.[78] The Global Slavery Index estimates some fifty million people today remain in bondage through debt slavery, involuntary child labor, involuntary prostitution, and the like.[79] Immigrant workers lured with promises of jobs are often paid only enough to survive and not enough to repay the "cost" of their transportation to the destination country.[80] Most of the following information regarding global slavery is from research I did for a different book a couple of decades ago, but sadly much of it remains relevant today.[81] A 1993 newspaper report in India's state of Orissa complained that some people there were selling children "for the price of a bowl of chicken curry"—roughly sixty-five US cents at the time.[82]

In the Islamic Republic of Mauritania, Arab-Berber Muslims from the north have long held Black African slaves from the south;[83] as *Newsweek* reported in the 1990s, "More than 100,000 descendants of Africans conquered by Arabs during the twelfth century are still thought to be living as old-fashioned chattel slaves. Aside from the shantytowns and a strip of land along the Senegal River, virtually all blacks are slaves, and they are more than half the population."[84] Many slaves are indoctrinated to minimize their condition: "Only the children," some explain, "get beaten." One slave interviewed declared, "Naturally, we blacks should be the slaves of the whites."[85] But while Mauritania officially rejected slavery in 1980, slaveholding became a prosecutable offense only in 2007. Despite further advances in 2015, slavery continues there.[86]

In Bangladesh, slave traders kidnap three- to six-year-old boys or buy them from parents for the equivalent of twenty years' worth of wages and empty promises of hope for the boys. The boys are then used as camel jockeys as gamblers in Persian Gulf nations bet on them. Some wealthy residents of those nations buy twelve- to twenty-five-year-old Bangladeshi females at auctions as well: Those considered more beautiful may fetch as much as two thousand dollars from sheikhs; brothels employ those considered less attractive, who typically bring a price of two hundred dollars.[87] As of 2023, some estimate there to be 1.2 million slaves in Bangladesh.[88]

The Arabian peninsula officially abolished slavery in 1962,[89] but even then official proclamations seem to have had little effect.[90] In the mid-sixties it was still being estimated that Saudi Arabia alone held a quarter of a million slaves.[91] In 1953 a high-level witness reported that some Saudis were recruiting pilgrims in the Sudan and West Africa to visit Islamic holy sites. Once in Saudi Arabia, these pilgrims were being enslaved.[92] (The "curse of Ham" myth, already circulating among some Muslims by the ninth century, was long used to justify enslaving Africans, sometimes even fellow Muslims.)[93] Besides such traditional, hereditary slavery there, many migrant workers in that region likewise continue to be *virtually* enslaved—bound to their masters, unable to leave or complain, and paid only about thirty dollars each month.[94] Some estimate Saudi Arabia still has as many as 740,000 slaves as of 2021.[95]

Sudan has been a particular offender, especially under Omar al-Bashir and the Janjaweed militias. Besides its thousands of extrajudicial executions in raids on villages,[96] the government enslaved many women and children for domestic use.[97] Arab militias burned villages, killing the men and seizing women and now-orphaned children for chores and as concubines. They also exported slaves to the Persian Gulf, Libya, Chad, and Mauritania.[98] A Sudanese lawyer noted that northern armies recruited the children to convert them to Islam so they could join in fighting their homeland in the south. "They are also used as a living blood bank for northern soldiers. . . . Every time there is a major battle, they are rounded up to donate their blood."[99]

Sudanese troops' ethnic cleansing among the Nuba mountain people sometimes targeted Christians in particular.[100] They took many Christian slaves;[101] one US scholar visiting that region told me that he personally was shown sales receipts for "Christian slaves." Mariam Ibraheem notes that Sudanese slave traders recruit Ethiopian Christian girls with promises of good jobs, then force them to work for free and subject them to rape. Eventually they may falsely accuse them of stealing, handing them over to prisons where, unable to pay their fines, the enslaved young women may remain indefinitely.[102] As of 2021, some estimate more than 174,000 people remain in forced labor or forced marriage in Sudan.

Estimates of those forced into labor or marriages in Pakistan vary from nearly two hundred thousand to four million people, many of them Hindus or Christians. Using a system of intergenerational debt, some wealthy Pakistanis use many Christians as bonded slaves at kilns in brick factories. The quota for each family can be 1,500 to 2,500 bricks per day.[103]

May the God who liberated Israelite brick-making slaves in ancient Egypt do the same for his people elsewhere. The list of items in which a doomed evil empire trades in Revelation 18:12–13 climaxes with "human bodies and lives"—the slave trade.[104]

Family Conflicts

A form of suffering far more common in the West than physical persecution is family hardship. Many experience anguish in their families when their children stray from the faith. We are grateful that our children love Jesus, but we also share their pain over some other afflictions, including our (adopted) daughter's hardship in her family of origin. Keren, a strong young woman of God, was originally my wife's niece. We invited her to stay with us partly because her birth father warned us that her situation in Congo was very dangerous. While she was in school here, her birth father and birth mother, both of whom she loved deeply, died. Keren excels in her studies, but she also struggles with grief over childhood memories that can never be revisited in person.

One form of family hardship is intrafamily conflict, which also appears in Scripture and around the world (Mic. 7:6; Matt. 10:34–36; Luke 12:51–53). Saul's attempts to kill David forced conflict on Saul's son Jonathan and daughter Michal (1 Sam. 19:1–17; 20:1–42). Jesus summons us to love our families, but not at the expense of neglecting our love for our rightful master (Matt. 10:37; Luke 14:26).

Conflict for Christ

Sometimes family strife follows directly from our love for Christ. "Don't suppose that I came to bestow peace on the earth: I didn't come to bestow peace, but instead a sword! For I came to turn a man against his father and a daughter against her mother. . . . Whoever loves father or mother more than me doesn't deserve to have me" (Matt. 10:34–35, 37).

In 1936 in Kaduna State, Nigeria, Byang Kato's father "dedicated him to carrying on the family tradition as a fetish priest." But at age twelve Kato became a Christian. "When his father learned of Kato's public commitment, he beat him, refused to give him food, and took his shirt away."[105] Yet Kato grew to have an enormous impact for Christ in Africa, refusing to compromise the gospel. He became the first African general secretary of the Association of Evangelicals in Africa. One of my friends in seminary, Peter Yamusah, an Assemblies of God Bible school leader from Ghana, likewise had to flee from his parents when he became a Christian. In Chad, Zarah's Muslim husband divorced her and took their son when she became a Christian.[106]

Conversely, some have won their families to Christ. My friend and former student, Dr. Charlemagne Nditemeh, head of the Cameroon Baptist Convention, brought his Muslim family to Christ. So did Rwandan Anglican priest Cedric Kanana—though of course Cedric's being publicly raised from the dead at his funeral (after Jesus rescued him from hell) commanded a lot of attention from his family.[107]

But things do not always work out the same way. Tara had to flee from place to place because her Pakistani father and brothers, shamed by her conversion to Christianity, were hunting her. They were seeking to execute an honor killing.[108] Likewise in Pakistan, when the parents of teenage Sameera discovered that she had become a Christian, they doused her with gasoline and set her on fire, "causing 40 per cent burns from her neck to her knees."[109] She survived and went into hiding, but a different convert burned by his family was then reportedly murdered by his brother-in-law.[110] In Nepal, Kamal, though not yet a believer himself, was cast out by his parents and had to abandon his inheritance because he defended his wife's right to follow Jesus.[111]

In Iraq, one religiously tolerant but ethnically intolerant region expelled Ibrahim al-Medina because he was ethnically Arab; but when he returned to his family in a predominantly Arab region and pleaded with them to accept Christ, his father blew off his head with an AK-47.[112] Brought to Christ partly by the online testimonies of many Muslims who had dreams about Jesus, Fatima al-Mutairi of Saudi Arabia began sharing her faith online with others.[113] When her brother discovered his twenty-six-year-old sister's faith, he determined to remove the family shame. He beat her, amputated her tongue, and then burned her alive.[114] Such believers will welcome us in heaven someday.

I was sometimes physically abused growing up when a particular family member had been drinking too much. I usually avoid talking much about that. It did at least help get me ready for some later experiences of abuse for my witness. After I was converted from atheism, I shared Christ with my ten-year-old brother Chris. Despite my very immature witness, he readily embraced Christ because he witnessed the radical change in my life (not least in that I stopped mistreating him). Unfortunately, my parents would not let him attend church with me. "We already lost one son," they reasoned, fearing that I belonged to an extremist cult. (I had some Catholic and mainline spiritual mentors, but the people who led me to Christ were Baptist and my church was Pentecostal, both of which seemed strange to my parents at the time. And my life was now consumed with Jesus.)

My father also forbade me to talk with my younger siblings about Christ. "Do you understand?" he demanded. "I understand, but . . ." I began. "Good, then!" he responded, and walked off, before I could finish protesting. I knew the Bible commanded obedience to parents—quite in contrast with my preconversion attitude of rebellion (it was 1975, but the sixties were still quite fresh for my generation)—yet I also knew that I had spiritual responsibility for my siblings, so I felt conflicted inside. I resolved that the lesser of two evils in this case was what one might call civil disobedience, so I met with my brother downstairs to disciple him before my parents got up in the morning. I also went for "walks" with him to introduce him to some other Christian friends I had waiting around the block. I took him "swimming" at a park so friends and I could baptize him. (Indeed, even for my own baptism I slipped out the side door with a change of clothes in my bag, hoping to avoid conflict.) Eventually Chris was allowed to attend (an approved) church, and once he went to college he joined InterVarsity Christian Fellowship. By that time my mother understood me much better, so she checked with me to make sure InterVarsity was safe. Thrilled, I of course assured her that it was.

Following Christ can be painful in families. Jesus brings division (Matt. 10:34; Luke 12:51), sometimes within families (Matt. 10:35; Luke 12:52–53). Sometimes this division even involves rejection or abuse, as in examples above and the following ones. In Turkey, after Baris was converted from Islam through experiencing visions and reading the Bible, his wife abandoned him, and his brother committed him briefly to a psychiatric hospital. Baris nevertheless continues to share his faith with others.[115]

The father of a Muslim convert in Iran turned him in and offered to help hang him; guards broke the convert's legs and fingers.[116] The mother of a Muslim convert in Egypt locked her in a room for two years.[117] In one Middle Eastern nation, Bassam's family rejected him. His wife denounced him, his in-laws beat him, and his father disowned him. "His relatives could kill him as an apostate," Voice of the Martyrs reports, without risking more than two years of prison.[118]

When Our Families Suffer Because of Our Faith

Sometimes family suffering involves the agony of losing family members. If we live long enough, all of us face grief over the loss of loved ones, although

Christians have comfort in knowing that fellow believers are with the Lord (1 Thess. 4:13–14, 18).[119]

Yet sometimes we experience the pain of family members suffering for our faith. Although they knew it would provoke Richard's arrest, Sabina Wurmbrand urged her husband to speak the truth about an evil regime: "I don't need a coward for a husband."[120] Later, the secret police additionally arrested Sabina; the government confiscated everything they had. This left their young son Mihai dependent on charity—in a country where it was illegal to help prisoners' families. The friend who took him in and helped other political prisoners' children was beaten until the police broke her bones and knocked out her teeth. The state assigned her an eight-year prison sentence.[121] Mihai finished elementary school, but government rules at the time prohibited further education for political prisoners' children.[122]

The Wurmbrands, however, also recount others' family suffering on account of the gospel. Communist authorities permanently confiscated some children to "protect" them from their parents' faith.[123] Government policy punished prisoners' families. When one pastor refused to recant his faith despite much torture, guards began to beat his fourteen-year-old son in front of him. Finally the pastor cried out that he would recant, but his son intervened. "Father, don't do me the injustice of having a traitor as a parent!" The bloodied son died praising Jesus; the pastor never fully recovered from witnessing his son's martyrdom.[124] Persecuted believers could only cling to Jesus's warning: "Whoever loves father or mother . . . [or] son or daughter more than me doesn't deserve to have me" (Matt. 10:37).[125]

When the state imprisoned one pastor, his two eldest daughters lost their jobs at the factory, risking the starvation of the sick mother and six children. A young man courted the eldest daughter until he gradually recruited her and her sister into prostitution. Their fifteen-year-old brother was so disillusioned when he discovered their moral failure that he ended up in a mental institution. The pastor, when released, was so distressed that he prayed to return to prison. The prostituted daughters' pimp quickly facilitated the prayer's answer by betraying to the authorities information about the pastor's continued preaching. When Sabina and the eldest daughter were imprisoned together, Sabina helped her return to Christ.[126]

Muslim-background believer Ibrahim planted twenty-three churches and faced many sufferings. In Ibrahim's decades of witness, however, his greatest hardship was when his clan took away his wife and children, keeping them "as 'guests' at the Saudi Arabian embassy in Nairobi."[127] Hana was just six in 2004 when Eritrean authorities arrested her gospel-preaching father, Tekleab Mengisteab. An Orthodox pastor, medical doctor, and one of the national leaders in the World Health Organization, he remains in custody without charge two decades later.[128]

The Allied Democratic Forces (ADF) is an ISIS-affiliated group committed to stamping out Christianity in a majority-Christian region of Congo-Kinshasa. The ADF wants to establish an Islamic caliphate. In 2024, they and some other groups killed a recorded 390 Christians.[129] They killed many in Luce Ibara's village. She and her husband escaped with their lives but lost everything else, including their twelve- and eighteen-year-old daughters.[130] The ADF made Margurette watch while they killed her brothers, abducting her for other purposes; although she escaped, she is still too traumatized to speak.[131]

Jerome and his family fled destitute after ADF terrorists killed his son and burned down his home with everything in it.[132] One attack on the village of Tchabi killed 182, including the principal of the Christian school when he refused to deny his faith. They smeared excrement all over the church's inside walls to desecrate it.[133] Because it was so macabre, news outlets reported when the ADF beheaded seventy Christians inside a church building in early 2025, yet the ADF had already murdered far greater numbers.[134] Another attack burned worshipers alive inside a church; a nine-year-old survivor was burned over 48 percent of her body.[135]

In Nigeria, Muslim neighbors killed Solomon's father in front of him and set Solomon on fire; Solomon survived and forgave them.[136] On an island in Indonesia, Adel tried to comfort her scared, hungry, seven-year-old son as they hid from jihadists. When the jihadists discovered them, they killed Adel's son in front of her; Adel was then enslaved and sexually abused until she and her fellow enslaved Christians were freed.[137]

Sometimes family members can be targeted for our witness. In 2019, local officials in China seized a mainstream Christian couple's four adopted children, saying they were protecting the children from a "religious cult."[138] In Yemen, Khaled's thirty-three-year-old wife, Samira, was burned to death; before succumbing to her injuries, she urged her husband to forgive the killers.[139] Decades after Abdulmasi left his life as a Nigerian jihadist and became a Christian, jihadists murdered his college-age son. The chief murderer's son, however, came to learn about the gospel from Abdulmasi.[140] A few days after Iran's Anglican Bishop Hassan Dehqani-Tafti narrowly escaped an attempt on his life, assassins murdered his son Bahram.[141]

In Somalia, six-year-old Amiir loved his father, Diya, and treasured his father's Bible. When a militant caught Amiir reading the Bible, he assaulted the father. When young Amiir cried out, "Papa!" the militant killed him and his mother, Diya's wife, Aniso. Diya and his other two sons survived, grieving but entrusting their hope to God.[142]

Also in Somalia, Azzam Azziz Mubarak is a powerful witness for Christ, prepared for martyrdom.[143] After Azzam's conversion through visions of Jesus, his father wanted to kill him, so his mother helped him escape. When he received a parcel from his father, he thought maybe his father had forgiven his conversion; instead, he found his mother's dismembered body inside. Half the members of a group of new believers he joined were martyred within a week.[144] Azzam later led two of his mother's hired assassins to Christ, and they now join with him in risking their lives for their witness.[145] Pirates have kidnapped Azzam's son three times, but God has always restored him.[146]

Many in the village of Satpura, in Bihar, India, mistreated Pastor Sushil and his wife for years, but in 2024 their only son was strangled to death for his faith. They were so traumatized that they both had to be hospitalized.[147]

Some accounts have more favorable outcomes in this life. In Iran, Ebi was beating his daughter Shahnaz for her refusal to turn from newfound faith in Christ. Then he suddenly stopped and began begging her forgiveness. "As I was beating you, I saw Jesus with his left arm wrapped around you. With his right arm he motioned me to stop the whipping. . . . I realized as I was swinging the belt that I was beating Jesus." Ebi eventually became a believer himself.[148]

Broken Love

The Bible lets us in on some conflicts in even what we might regard as model family relations in many respects—conflicts stemming, for example, from Abraham's inequitably blended family in Genesis 16:5 and 21:9–11 or the pressures of Rachel's childlessness in Genesis 30:1–2. Real life and independent perspectives make some family conflict inevitable. Sometimes, as with Joseph and his brothers, such conflicts become potentially lethal.

More common in our culture is divorce and the dysfunctions it typically introduces. God never designed our hearts to have to be broken the way they are for many spouses and children in broken marriages. Intimacy flourishes in a context of commitment; broken trust kills it.

We like to claim Acts 16:31:

Believe in the Lord Jesus, and you and your household will be saved.

But the household also has to believe to be saved; it is not automatic. And while God forbids breaking up one's marriage, he does not guarantee that one's marriage cannot be broken by another partner.

"How do you know, wife, whether you will save your husband?" wrote Paul in 1 Corinthians 7:16. "Or how do you know, husband, whether you will save your wife?" Many Corinthians married before their conversion, and their spouses did not always convert with them. While Paul forbids the believer to walk out of the marriage, he also warns them not to battle the unbeliever who chooses to leave (7:15).

My relationship with my parents grew better over the years following my conversion; I think they and I grew to appreciate each other much more. My story of family sorrow that follows is a different one with more enduring pain. Although an element of the story involves suffering for Christ, without going into those details it can especially illustrate family suffering more generally.

I had married a friend, fellow student, and fellow worker in ministry (in *Impossible Love*, I gave her the pseudonym Cass). When we married, she and I shared a radical commitment to Christ. But testing sometimes has a way of whittling away at radical commitment, especially when some close associates criticize that commitment. Three years after our marriage, in a time of ministry hardship and uncertainty, Cass entered an affair with another of my colleagues, her best friend's husband. He had reportedly had affairs before, but this time he left his wife and kids to be with Cass.

I was less muscular and less attractive to my wife than was my new rival. He was also more personable and well-adjusted socially; besides having ADHD, I'm a nerd (though not on purpose). When Cass filed for divorce to clear the way for her to marry him, I contested the divorce for as long as legally possible, praying and pleading that she would return. Seven years after our wedding, the divorce went through, and Cass married her former best friend's now ex-husband. I felt like I was a twig being bent in God's hand and ready to snap; I already knew that God works everything for good to those who love him, but I was afraid my faith might not hold out long enough to witness that outcome.

I can't describe the anguish I went through after Cass left. To this day, I still care about her and the man for whom she left me. It was love, in fact, that made the pain so painful. I remained single for the next fifteen years. Neither she nor her paramour acted deliberately to hurt me; though my scars took long to heal, that was my responsibility rather than theirs. Yet I met many insensitive Christians who glibly assumed that because I was divorced, I must have been less faithful than they, my judges. Although I celebrate with Christians who were able to save their marriages, more brothers and sisters than I can count have shared with me experiences similar to mine. Because some parts of the church still think they are opposing divorce by punishing divorced persons, however, I choose to tell my own story rather than someone else's. And for those prone to cast stones, may the Lord who knows all hearts be the judge between us.

And yet it was the brokenness of those years that drew my heart more deeply into the Lord's heart for the broken. That was when I began to cry more vocally for racial and global justice. It was also when I learned how the African American church, through its centuries of hardship, knew how to put broken people together. I found so much healing in African American churches in North Carolina. I ended up serving as an associate minister in gracious African American churches in North Carolina and Philadelphia, mostly while teaching the Bible in urban-oriented seminaries. (I talk more about the African American church and what I have learned from its members in some other books.)[149]

This was also the period in my life when I learned that only the Lord could fulfill what he called me to do. Some of my own Pentecostal and evangelical ministry circles rejected me (temporarily) at that time, but that rejection taught me the transitory nature of human favor so I would know better than to compromise God's message for its sake. When you are stripped of everything you think matters to you, you realize that the one thing that matters is what no one can separate you from: God's love in Jesus Christ. I might have become a scholar without experiencing what I suffered. But I would be less of a man of God.

Médine (the friend I married fifteen years later) also faced family tragedy. She grew up deeply loved by her parents, who also deeply loved each other. But the man she first married was not the Christian he was pretending to be. Unknown to her, he was already married to another wife and sleeping with yet another woman. Because Médine was working he wanted access to her money, but he threatened her life. He abused her periodically, and one day he began strangling her to death, but the Lord saved her through a timely interruption. The man then abandoned her during war—after seizing her possessions. Médine and I both came to our new marriage to each other with histories of trauma to be worked through, but over the past twenty-three years our love for each other has grown even deeper than it was at the start.

Disappointments

> You know that everyone in the province of Asia has deserted me. (2 Tim. 1:15 NIV)

In what is probably the final extant Pauline letter, Paul laments the apparent collapse of his ministry in the center where it had been most successful (Acts 19:10, 17, 20). Paul did not live to see the long-range fruit of his ministry through history: hundreds of millions of gentile Christians.

Many psalms (e.g., Ps. 88) exude anguish. Some of God's servants, whom we now honor highly, were so disappointed by others' rejection of their mission that they wanted to die (Num. 11:15; 1 Kings 19:4) or cursed the day of their birth (Jer. 15:10; 20:14, 18). This also happened to those broken by other sufferings (Job 3:1; 6:9). Jesus experienced emotional anguish in Gethsemane and on the cross. "My heart hurts so much," he lamented, "that it could almost kill me" (Mark 14:34). Consider also Paul:

> We were afflicted in everything: conflicts on the outside, fears on the inside. (2 Cor. 7:5)

> And, besides all the external things, there is, day in day out, the pressure on me of my anxiety for all the churches. If anyone weakens, I am weakened as well; and when anyone is made to fall, I burn in agony myself. (2 Cor. 11:28–29 NJB)

Jeremiah, forcibly relocated to Egypt, did not live to see the three books of the Bible that announced the fulfillment of his promise of restoration. Nor did he live to see that because of his ministry Israel never again turned to physical idols. William Tyndale died while translating the Bible into English, not knowing that his translation would form the basis for the major English translations of the Bible over the next few centuries. (How I wish that more Western Christians today, appreciating the price that their forerunners paid, would *read* the Bible.)

We experience some disappointments because, unlike God, we do not see the future. The parents of George O. Wood labored hard in China, but when the church they founded reopened after Mao's persecution, it had just thirty people. A decade later, when Wood visited, it had thirty-eight hundred baptized adults—having grown more than a hundred times over in the intervening years.[150]

We experience life in the short term, but as God brings us through our testing we learn to trust that he is in control of the long term.

Challenges to Success and Popularity[151]

Disappointment comes in many forms. In some parts of the world, being a Christian disqualifies you from getting a job and perhaps even from freedom. In the US, by contrast, even some ministers become addicted to worldly success. The American dream shapes those who grow up here, instilling the idea that you can be or get anything you want if you try hard enough. Social media naturally amplifies the success stories. Apart from privileged families, however, adulthood often confronts us with harder realities. In various circles, genuine racial, educational, or socioeconomic barriers exist (as well as limitations in the job market). So at times do religious barriers.

A colleague was turned away from a PhD program because of his faith; some others were rejected or released from jobs when their faith surfaced. I myself, when I was looking for work to support myself when starting studies for my master's degree, experienced something like this on a very small scale. The manager at one fast-food restaurant immediately terminated the interview after discovering that I had graduated from a Bible college. Having had experiences with Christians that he did not like, he said, "We've had enough of that kind here."

Even where opposition for our faith is rare, we can face more ordinary challenges to success, challenges like those anyone else faces. Shooting for the moon gets us much further than just aiming for the window, so it has its advantages, but eating lunar green cheese is not the standard for success. When my son David moved to Nashville to start his career in Christian music, he was an anointed worship leader who had just completed his worship arts degree at Asbury University. Hundreds of other gifted worship leaders, however, have naturally had the same excellent idea, and David's big break didn't come. Writing and performing Christian music had been his dream since childhood. In contrast to some Disney theology, however, we sometimes have to let our dreams die so that Jesus can resurrect them in his way and time. David has taken various secular jobs to support his young family, for now relegating his music to church, demos, and social media.

Life can be tough. The Bible shows us that real life, and especially following Jesus, can entail hardship and sacrifice. The cross itself illustrates that God forges his purposes on the anvil of suffering.

Many of us may feel spiritually insecure around megachurch pastors, evangelists converting hundreds of thousands, or Christian media personalities. We know that what God desires most is faithfulness in our own calling; we also know that even those servants of God we most admire are people just like us. The last thing *they* need is for people to put them on pedestals and hold them to superhuman expectations. Yet it's hard to resist the celebrity ideals that media regularly highlight for us.

Given our need for encouragement, it's no surprise that success stories usually score higher YouTube or Instagram view counts than sad endings. At the moment I have requests for interviews about my miracle books coming out my nose (for readers of English as a second language, that is a metaphor); I expect fewer for a book about suffering. I myself post mostly pleasant news on Facebook; usually I reserve accounts of my struggles for my wife or another prayer partner.

When Christians in the US think of success in ministry, they often think less of martyrs or those sacrificially breaking new ground for the kingdom and more of highly visible leaders. US culture in general is oriented toward what is big and flashy, and toward communicators who can teach us to be big and flashy too. Celebrities, influencers, and others in the public eye are the really *important* people.

Exaltation comes from the Lord (compare Ps. 75:6–7, 10), however, and our goal should be to please Jesus rather than people (Gal. 1:10; 1 Thess. 2:4).[152] Humbling ourselves in his sight welcomes him to exalt us in the best way, in this life as needed and certainly eternally (Matt. 23:12; Luke 14:11; James 4:10; 1 Pet. 5:6).

Jesus's first disciples faced the same temptations we do. Jesus didn't choose scribes or priests; he chose relative nobodies (fitting the prior biblical pattern; compare Deut. 7:7; 26:5; 1 Sam. 15:17; 2 Sam. 7:8; 1 Cor. 1:26–28). But as his disciples began considering their roles in Jesus's coming kingdom, they began to compete with each other for greatness (Mark 9:34; 10:37). Throughout Mark's Gospel, Jesus invites them instead to embrace his posture—that of a suffering servant (10:45).

Even Boring Academicians Have Some Challenges

I will end the chapter with a few stories of my own. They are not comparable to martyrdoms, homelessness, and other examples in the book; they illustrate the kind of everyday struggles that I think most of us face on occasion. Ministry is full of challenges, and when I pastored I carried in my heart the confidential burdens of half the members of the congregation individually going through one crisis or another at any given time. And then once in a while one experiences some special excitement, such as when I was trying to reach out to someone and he grabbed a harpoon from the wall and began pacing angrily. Both he and a table lay between me and the door. I hate it when that happens.

I have noted challenges faced by those on the front line of mission, often including persecution. But even those of us working mostly out of sight face at least some challenges. I offer a few examples here not because they match other accounts in the book (they are far lighter than the others) but because they're mine (so I can share them without many endnotes or the need to reword them).

If a good name is better than wealth (Prov. 22:1), an academician can sometimes be poor indeed. One professor told me that I was his most encyclopedic student; however, he admitted that, because of my faith, I would not have been allowed into the doctoral program had it been up to him. (He used to say that any professor who publicly admitted faith in God should be fired.) At a scholar's meeting, another scholar publicly demeaned me and a colleague as less than true scholars because we supported the historical authenticity of the Gospel accounts under discussion. Some of us writers also joke with one another about how often reviewers comment on books without first actually reading them. When we publish, we stick our necks out, inviting our critics' rhetorical machetes.

Years earlier, when I was in seminary, I spent months working for my master's thesis on a theme close to my heart (biblical teaching about hearing God), with my professor's blessing. When the dean heard about it, however, he summoned me into his office and reprimanded me: "Our professors are too busy already!" He forbade me to write a master's thesis—which by that point I had already written. I found a quiet place to pour out my heart before God, and he comforted me so deeply with his Spirit that I cried out, "Oh Lord! A thousand times as much pain if I could have a thousand times this beautiful comfort to go with it!" Happily, the professor got the dean to reverse his decision, and my thesis went forward. Less happily, more significant pain did await me (the abandonment of my first wife, already recounted).

Sooner or later, most people face health problems. When I started my four-volume Acts commentary, I was forty years old. I was working too hard and not sleeping enough, and I ended up dehydrated, dizzy, and in the hospital. I spent ten years working on the Acts commentary, my back aching because my nearsighted eyes required me to bend close to my research. (As occupational hazards go, however, professors naturally have much less to complain about than most other people.) Toward the end of composing what turned out to be my first draft, eight months after I had submitted the commentary to the originally contracted publisher, the top editor decided it was too long and canceled my contract (which did not specify length). The situation did indeed plunge me into deep prayer! During the decade of writing, I had regularly wrestled with whether the project was worth it: Would I reach more people by witnessing on the street? Now did it look like I had wasted a decade of my ministry that spanned my forties? Thankfully, Baker Academic later agreed to publish the manuscript (by that time improved but even longer; compare Jer. 36:32). I was in the hospital again (this time for stomach bleeding caused by prescribed medicine) when editor Jim Kinney delivered the first volume to me.

More unusually, when I was nearing completion of that book, a tree split at the roots right where my wife and I had been standing a few moments earlier; it would have crushed us to death had we still been standing there.[153] I mentioned earlier a prophecy from Mesfin, a brother from Ethiopia. He explained the falling of the tree as the devil wanting to take me out because of two big books that I was writing, the second one bigger than the first, but he said that God protected me and the books. I was skeptical: How could I write a bigger book than the one I was writing? Yet Mesfin had prophesied about the books without even knowing that I was a writer, and it turned out that my 1,100-page, two-volume book on miracles (which at that time was just a two-hundred-page draft) came out before my 4,500-page, four-volume work on Acts. Some spiritual assault or other has accompanied many of my most important books. One might joke that it is safer to write only unimportant books!

Hardship comes in multiple forms. Some are more ordinary; others threaten even life or livelihood. Yet God's grace is commensurate for each of them. The ultimate hope God gives us outweighs them all.

CHAPTER TEN

Suffering in God's Will

Let those who suffer according to God's will entrust their lives to the trustworthy Creator. You entrust yourself to him by continuing to do what's good.

—1 Peter 4:19

This is what God wants: by doing good you may silence the ignorance of foolish people.

—1 Peter 2:15

For it is better to suffer for doing good, if this is God's will, than to suffer for doing wrong.

—1 Peter 3:17

Part of the Mission

As Peter learned from following Jesus (see chap. 5), sometimes it can be God's will that we suffer for a greater purpose. When Peter wrote his letter from Rome, Nero was emperor, and suffering lay on the horizon. Soon Nero would be burning Christians alive to light his imperial gardens at night. Both Peter and Paul would die in Rome—Paul the Roman citizen quickly, by beheading, but Peter slowly, by being crucified upside down. Yet Peter was ready.

In light of this, since Christ suffered in the flesh, get your own hearts ready to suffer! Do so because whoever has suffered in the flesh has given up sin. Thus they no longer live the rest of their lives for human passions; instead, they live it for God's will. (1 Pet. 4:1–2)

As Peter suggested, those who have already proved their faithfulness through testing have no reason to fear failing further testing of the same kind; they have already counted the cost (Luke 14:28–32) and proved their loyalty. Like Peter and Jesus's other disciples, Nagmeh Panahi had failed an earlier test of her faith;[1] she determined not to let it happen again. Later, persecuted by the Iranian government for her witness, she was often afraid of being detained, raped, and possibly killed. But when faced with a decision the next time, she refused to deny Christ.[2] "It was not until I was actually arrested and threatened with rape and death that I knew I could stand firm in my faith, through God's grace, and proclaim that I was a Christian."[3]

How can we prepare for tests harder than what we have already faced? By being faithful in the tests that now come our way, learning to depend on God there. Daniel and his three friends refused to compromise themselves with the king's food (Dan. 1:8–16); they were thus ready for larger tests that led to a burning fiery furnace (3:8–27) and a lion's den (6:5–23).

> "Abba, Papa!" Jesus cried. "You're able to do anything! Take away this cup from me! Nevertheless: don't do what I want, but what you want." (Mark 14:36)

Sometimes, when God says no to us, it is for our good (e.g., Mark 10:37–38), but sometimes it is for others' good. Jesus's Father would grant almost anything his beloved Son Jesus asked him, just as he loves to grant our prayers when our hearts are like Jesus's heart, when we pray in his name. Not for Jesus's sake, but for *ours*, God's will was for Jesus to go to the cross.

> Yet it was the LORD's will to crush him and cause him to suffer. (Isa. 53:10 NIV)

When Jesus sends disciples to share the good news, he comforts them not with the idea that human hostility will vanish, but with the assurance that God will be with them. He urges them not to "be afraid of those who kill the body, and after that have nothing further to do to you." Not a sparrow falls to the ground "without your Father," but "you are more valuable than many sparrows"; God knows every hair on your head (Matt. 10:28–31; Luke 12:4–7). He sees the whole world but views his children in a special way (Pss. 33:13, 18; 138:6). In an ideal world, sharing Christ with others might not result in suffering, but in a world where many people are hostile to Christ, Christ may send us as lambs among wolves (Matt. 10:16; Luke 10:3).

When we forgive those who hurt us rather than taking vengeance into our own hands or hearts, we express our trust in the God who has our back (see Mark 11:25 with 11:22–24; Matt. 6:12; Luke 11:4). Throughout this book, I have noted many examples of Christians who experienced God's grace by forgiving.[4]

God Works Things for Our Good

Scripture often speaks explicitly of suffering according to God's will, but it also reveals hardship's (frequent) short-term and (inevitable) long-term rewards.

God Still Has Everything Under Control

People who recognize that the Spirit helps our weakness (Rom. 8:26) can also recognize that God works all things for our good (Rom. 8:28).[5] Scripture does not claim that all things feel good, look good, or actually *are* good in themselves. It does not suggest that everything people do to us they intend for good. But it does suggest that God arranges it all for our good, collectively and often individually, in accordance with his larger good purposes in history. (Even natural evils serve a purpose. For example, earthquakes are a necessary corollary of plate tectonics, which are necessary for advanced life on the earth's surface.)[6]

This is not the place to get into a debate about whether God micromanages all events. Certainly I do not believe (and most Christians do not believe) that God directly causes people's evil choices, including their rejection of him (compare 1 Tim. 2:4; 2 Pet. 3:9). God does hand them over to blindness that they have (individually or corporately) chosen (Rom. 1:18–28; 2 Thess. 2:10–12).[7] But God gives space for humans to act while also watching over his plans for the world and, with the most caring attention, over even the hairs on the heads of his children. As Ingrid Betancourt, the Colombian presidential candidate captured and held for six years by rebels, insisted, humans' wrong choices rather than God's *direct* activity causes most suffering.[8] Some things make no sense to us as God's direct action, although we can see God working around them, through them, and in response to them—and quite often in limiting them.

Still, I am confident that when we know as we are known, even these events will make sense within God's larger plan, where he sovereignly allows some play for evil (rebellion against God) to reveal its horrible character while God nevertheless ultimately and exquisitely fulfills his ultimate purposes in history. That is, we may see them in terms of limited divine permission for free choices of human and extrahuman forces, without God allowing them to prevent his ultimate word from being fulfilled. What Romans 8:28 and other passages do affirm clearly is that God accomplishes his ultimate purposes, and we can entrust ourselves into his caring hands in the meantime no matter what else comes our way.

Robbers spent a night abusing the Beebes, a US Assemblies of God missionary family of four. "Where was God when they hurt us?" the eleven-year-old daughter asked, but then God gave her a vision of Jesus interceding for them, and she understood that Jesus had been with them. God may not give each of us visions to assure us, but he has already provided all of us that assurance in Scripture. Nevertheless, the doctor warned that the injured father, Darrell Beebe, needed brain surgery and that he probably wouldn't survive. Yet the surgery soon proved unnecessary, and the family was able to continue ministry. Darrell even declared, "If [the robbers] had killed us, what the devil meant as a defeat would have been a victory, because God would have welcomed us into His kingdom. The enemy may win some battles, but he will never win the war."[9]

Whether God delivers us in this life or not, we cannot betray our loyalty to our Creator and Savior:

God . . . is able to rescue us, . . . but even if he does not . . . (Dan. 3:17–18)

Compare also Caleb's humble, qualified confidence:

Perhaps the LORD will be with me, and I will drive them out just as the LORD has spoken. (Josh. 14:12 NASB)

Human Evil

Just as God does not force humans to accept his gospel, neither does he force them to welcome its agents. If the world hated me, Jesus warned, it will hate you (John 15:18). God will avenge the blood of his servants (Rev. 18:20, 24), but he does not always prevent its shedding. God can be glorified not only by blessing us (Ps. 67:1–2, 6–7) but also by our deaths for him (John 12:23–24; 21:19). Of course, we look to him to keep us and use us as long as there is more for us to do for him (Phil. 1:21–26). And we will not suffer harm without God allowing it (Matt. 10:29–30; Luke 12:6–7).

The nations and their rulers may plot against the Lord, but he laughs at them (Ps. 2:1–4). The earliest church applies this warning especially to rulers gathering against Jesus—thereby fulfilling God's own plan.

For in this city, in fact, both Herod and Pontius Pilate, with the Gentiles and the peoples of Israel, gathered together against your holy servant Jesus, whom you anointed, to do whatever your hand and your plan had predestined to take place. (Acts 4:27–28 NRSV)

In Exodus, Pharaoh's abuse of Israelites (Exod. 1:8–22) led to their cries for deliverance (2:23), which God heard (2:24–25; 3:7–9). Yet God had already taken this all into account in his larger plan announced centuries before: God would bring his people back from Egypt with many goods (Gen. 15:13–16). The next Pharaoh's heart was hardened, sometimes by himself (Exod. 8:15, 32; 9:34) and often (complementarily) explicitly by God (Exod. 4:21; 7:3, 22; 8:19; 9:12, 35; 10:1, 20, 27; 11:10; 13:15; 14:4, 8). Yet God had a purpose in raising up such a hard-hearted Pharaoh:

This is why I raised you up:[10] to show my power and to declare my name throughout the world. (Exod. 9:16)

God was acting so that even the Egyptians (and other gentiles) would discover that he was the Lord (Exod. 9:14); the legacy of this event would shape history (compare also 1 Sam. 4:8). (The later initial return from exile in Persia was voluntary and required little force, but it did not require wholesale relocation of the entire people.)

Without entering debates about the origins of particular sufferings, we can affirm that God uses them for our good. When Joseph's brothers sold him into slavery, they meant it for evil—but God meant it for good (Gen. 50:20). God used the hardship to train Joseph in administration in Potiphar's household and to begin learning a new language and culture. God then used the false accusation of Potiphar's wife to bring him into administration in a prison where he would also meet the contact who would later introduce him to Pharaoh. God used the entire chain of circumstances, in his own time, to ultimately bring good for Joseph, for his brothers, for Egypt, and for an entire region afflicted by famine (Gen. 45:5, 7; 50:20). As he did for Joseph, God can also more than make up to us for our earlier days of affliction (Job 42:10–16; Ps. 90:15; Joel 2:25).

God may intervene for us in ways we initially resent. Lot resisted even some clearly angelic counsel, so that angels finally had to *compel* him and his family to leave Sodom (Gen. 19:16). Leaving one's home under duress is unpleasant, but God acted here precisely because he was being "merciful" (NIV, NRSV); the Lord's "compassion" was on him (NASB).

Biblical examples show us that God often vindicates us in our lifetimes, as in the case of Joseph, because we hear the story past Joseph's abuse to his exaltation. Our perspective shapes where we leave off in telling a story. For example, if we leave off with crowds following Jesus, we might finish with a "happy" ending. If we leave off with the cross, we might finish with a tragic ending. Yet as Christians, we look beyond the cross to Jesus's resurrection, his present rule, and our future with him, all of which underline God's gracious plan in the cross. God has told us the future outcome of our story, grounded in Jesus's story.

As participants in the Dutch resistance against the Nazi occupation during World War II, Corrie ten Boom and her sister Betsie were sent to the death camp Ravensbrück for hiding Jewish fugitives. Betsie heard from God that they would be released by the end of the year, and that they could then testify that there was no pit so deep that God was not deeper still. Betsie noted that people would recognize the truth of their testimony because they had been in Ravensbrück. By the end of the year, Betsie was released by death, and Corrie by a clerical error. In the decades that followed, Corrie shared around the world Betsie's message of hope: God is enough.[11]

Long-Range Perspective

My wife and I wrote a book together called *Impossible Love*. If the book had ended at many points in the story (e.g., in the midst of Congo's civil war), it might have been considered tragic. As it is, we ended on a happy note with our wedding, reserving further items for a brief epilogue. Yet whatever else happens beyond that epilogue, including someday our deaths, we—along with all other followers of Jesus—belong to a larger story. Our *ultimate* future is happy, with and because of Jesus.

Romans 8 looks beyond even the good that God accomplishes in the stories of our current lifetimes. It declares that God works all things for the good of "those who love him," who are "called according to his purpose" (Rom. 8:28). The God who knew us before we existed has already planned our future glory with him—"conformed to the image of his Son" (8:29–30). That is what Paul means by the completion of our "adoption" when Jesus returns (8:23): Jesus is the firstborn among many brothers and sisters, because we will all be fully conformed to his image, fully glorified. Even our bodies will be "conformed" to his glorious body (Phil. 3:21). That is the ultimate good toward which our present sufferings as birth pangs are leading us.

Meanwhile, he is already working in us to conform us to his image. Paul uses a related expression for being "transformed" by our minds being made new (Rom. 12:2).[12] This comes partly as we get to know Christ better and better, being "transformed" into his image (2 Cor. 3:18). It also comes by being "conformed" to Christ's death as we share his sufferings, preparing for our resurrection (Phil. 3:10–11).

If we can trust that God works sufferings for our benefit, we can take greater courage in the midst of them.

Working Matters for Good in This Age

"The blood of martyrs," declared the North African theologian Tertullian, "is the seed of the church."[13] Nevertheless, in some regions massive persecution decimated the church,[14] while God grew the church in other regions of the world. But our sacrifices count in God's sight, and normally the harvest more than compensates for all the seed sown. Following is a series of vignettes that can illustrate the principle.

Often God works suffering and even martyrdom for good in ways visible to some already in this life. China Inland Mission, committed to principles of indigenous church autonomy and dependence on God, faced repeated challenges. But they also observed that "times of trial, as by a spiritual law, always led on to enlargement and blessing."[15]

This process looks different at different times. Once the Soviet Jewish doctor Boris Kornfeld became a believer in Jesus, he refused to help authorities facilitate the deaths of prisoners in the Gulag. Thus he survived only long enough to share Christ with one patient before being killed himself. The impact of this one faithful testimony, however, proved incalculable: The patient, who soon became a Christian, was Aleksandr Solzhenitsyn.[16]

Pastor Pavel was planting churches in his central Asian nation, but one day robbers intercepted him to steal his vehicle. "Before you kill me," Pavel announced, "I have a message from God for you." He explained how God sent his Son for their salvation, whereupon all but one of the robbers committed their lives to Christ.[17]

Sometimes God miraculously protected some Palestinian believers from martyrdom; their would-be killers suddenly became distracted or simply left.[18] But it does not always work that way. Pauline's husband, Rami Ayyad, worked for the Palestinian Bible Society in Gaza, and she could not understand his willingness to die for Christ. She was in her second trimester with their third child when he was murdered, and Romans 8:28 made no sense to her. What good could come from his martyrdom? Following the lead of her oldest child, however, she forgave the murderer, and God used her witness to touch many hearts.[19]

In the 1940s, as bleeding scabs spread through Esther Ahn Kim's cell, Korean prisoners under foreign occupation turned to the Lord in prayer; not only did the scabs depart, but more of the prisoners grew in reverence for God.[20] A prisoner converted through Kim's ministry became grateful for being a prisoner, because she thereby received the gospel.[21] When Kim's party later fled south during another invasion, a rainstorm drenched and temporarily blinded them; but they soon realized that it had also prevented hostile soldiers from seeing them as they escaped.[22]

Most of us usually face smaller trials, yet we often can see God's hand in retrospect, even in delays that frustrate us Westerners. For example, one missionary was detained at the border of Communist Bulgaria, frustrated and concerned about whether he would be able to enter. Eventually the matter was resolved, but it was precisely because of the delay that he was able to share Christ with someone who had been seeking to understand the gospel.[23] Similarly, when I was a fairly new Christian attending a summer journalism conference, one fellow Christian student I learned of there was a Lutheran who really wanted to be able to pray in tongues. When we were finally able to catch up, Marilyn had only a few minutes to pray with me for the gift because it was the end of the conference, and her parents were supposed to pick her up at any minute. We ran over by fifteen minutes, but she resolved to stay and pray no matter what happened, and she quickly burst into tongues. She ended up not being late at all; her parents were delayed by road construction, so the timing was perfect.

Some Hardships Have a Good Purpose

God works our hardships for good for the sake of his gospel and, when we cooperate, he often does so also for the sake of our own spiritual maturation, which is of eternal worth. This is not to suggest that we go around looking for trouble—enough comes without us looking for it (Matt. 6:34)! God does not endorse masochism, and he invites us to celebrate the gift of life. When leaders at Iris Ministries, now known as Iris Global, articulated its core values, they worded the fourth one prudently: "Suffer for Him, *if necessary*."[24]

Because God is with the righteous, we need not fear bad news (Ps. 112:7). That might be hard for someone traumatized to grasp. Bad things may happen, but God is with us; although the righteous fall seven times, they will get up again (Prov. 24:16). "Though I walk in the midst of trouble," the psalmist affirms, "you will make me live" (Ps. 138:7). The righteous have trouble, but in it the Lord is our strength (Pss. 37:39; 91:15). Usually, then, in ordinary circumstances we *can* expect God to deliver us in our affliction rather than leave us there permanently (Pss. 34:19; 41:1; 91:14–15), and God does hear the prayers of the righteous (Pss. 33:18; 34:15–18; James 5:16).

But trouble does come, and we should embrace it from the right—especially eternal—perspective.

The Gospel May Spread Through Persecution

A Romanian Christian about to be executed for his faith made his last request to his wife: His persecutors did not know what they were doing, so she should share his love and forgiveness for them. Richard Wurmbrand recounts, "These words impressed the officer of the secret police who attended the discussion between the two. He later told me the story in prison where he had been sent for becoming a Christian."[25] Persecuted Christians also won other persecutors to Christ, including Romania's former prime minister.[26]

One Indonesian witness during the revival in West Timor reportedly worshiped God as some practitioners of indigenous religion cut off his arms before cutting off his head.[27] Mel Tari shared with me that his "blood was not shed in vain"; "today there is a growing and vibrant church in that region."[28]

In the book of Acts, God used persecution to spread his church all the more widely:

> On that day a great persecution broke out against the church in Jerusalem, and all except the apostles were scattered throughout Judea and Samaria. . . . Those who had been scattered preached the word wherever they went. (Acts 8:1, 4 NIV)

Luke then zeroes in on Philip as a key example of the point. After Stephen's death, Philip ministered, ahead of the Jerusalem apostles, in Samaria and to a God-fearing gentile (Acts 8:5–40). The scattering did not stop with Philip's mission, however; it led to an entire church movement among gentiles.

> Now those who had been scattered by the persecution that broke out when Stephen was killed traveled as far as Phoenicia, Cyprus and Antioch, spreading the word only among Jews. Some of them, however, men from Cyprus and Cyrene, went to Antioch and began to speak to Greeks also, telling them the good news about the Lord Jesus. (Acts 11:19–20 NIV)

Paul recognizes this pattern also in his own ministry. In Roman custody, Paul could no longer travel to spread the gospel, but God was using his chains to spread the gospel in another way:

> I want you to know, brothers and sisters, that the things that have happened to me have brought about a greater advance of the gospel. Because of this, the whole imperial guard and everybody else know that my chains are for Christ.

And because of my chains, most of the brothers and sisters have become confident in the Lord to speak the message much more boldly, without fear. (Phil.
1:12–14)

This pattern held true also as the Roman Empire martyred many Christians, prompting Tertullian's earlier mentioned dictum about the martyrs'
potent blood. I don't fully agree with the idea, often attributed to P. T. Barnum,
that all publicity is good publicity; nevertheless, when a minority has little
voice in society, bad publicity is sometimes the only way to get any exposure.
As Christians suffered publicly for their faith, more people learned about this
new faith that inspired readiness to die among its adherents.

At the turn of the twentieth century, word spread in China of the growing
Boxer Rebellion. Stationed there, Australian missionary David Barratt appealed for more laborers for the harvest and wrote, "I am like the ox, ready
for either the plough or the altar." His own mission would lead to the altar.
In another letter, he declared, "Our blood may be as a true center . . . and
God's kingdom will increase over this land. Extermination is but exaltation.
. . . 'Fear not them which kill'" the body. His martyrdom soon after these
letters motivated more laborers as well as a massive turning to Christ where
he had ministered.[29]

Protestants lost many missionaries and their families in the Boxer Rebellion—135 adults and 53 children—and far more local Christians. Yet indigenous Chinese Protestants more than doubled in number over the next six
years.[30] "Thousands upon thousands came to Christ as a direct result of the
slaughter of Christians in 1900."[31] By the time of Communism's triumph in
China, the nation had three million Catholics and a million Protestants.[32]
Far more effectively than the Boxer Rebellion, Chairman Mao's Cultural
Revolution brutally suppressed the church,[33] but afterward Christians again
multiplied, this time into tens of millions. Protestants alone may have multiplied twenty times over.[34] A church purified by suffering is always a stronger
witness than a shallow church whose values are indistinguishable from those
of the surrounding world.

Individual accounts could be multiplied. Pentecostal missionaries Frederick and Lulu Leader moved into a mud house in a largely unevangelized
region of Congo in 1922. As local people began to follow Christ, the Leaders
helped equip them to reach their own people, turning over most leadership to
them directly. In 1930, however, Frederick contracted a fever that eventually
exceeded their ability to measure, and despite Lulu's fervent prayers, he died.
Lulu and her three-year-old son Fred returned to the US. Six decades later,
Fred began learning more about his father's ministry and returned to see his

father's gravesite. There local Christians explained to him, "Because your father came, the gospel has spread throughout this entire region."[35]

Missionaries Stan Dale and Phil Masters died trying to share Christ with an unreached people group. Within the year their successors baptized thirty-five new Christians there—including many of those who had earlier participated in killing the missionaries.[36] More familiar to most is a similar story of transformation among the Waorani people in Ecuador after the killing of the first five missionaries who tried to reach them.[37]

When Dori saw a couple of kind Christian neighbors lynched naked in Damascus, it began her own journey to Christ, confirmed through many dreams from Jesus.[38]

God loves irony. A Christian prisoner named Sergei led another prisoner named Viktor to Christ. Years later, after Sergei was free and doing ministry, Muslim assassins killed him in his home. One of the assassins was imprisoned—and Viktor ended up leading him to Christ.[39] Other cases of divine irony abound. Putting his arm around an Ethiopian evangelist, another minister, named Haji, explains, "I used to beat him." Haji used to lead a radical Islamic group attacking Christians, but as this evangelist repaid Haji's hatred with love, he eventually won over Haji. Now Haji faces persecution himself, but he responds with joyful love.[40]

Suffering Does Not Stop the Gospel

It is on account of this that I have to put up with suffering, even to being chained like a criminal. But God's message cannot be chained up. (2 Tim. 2:9 NJB)

The church in Nepal began with twenty-nine baptized Christians in 1959, when the punishment for baptizing someone could include a six-year prison sentence. Despite such penalties (and atrocious prison conditions), by 1985 there were an estimated fifty thousand believers, with an estimated four hundred thousand by 2000.[41]

After working nine years and gaining just forty-eight converts, SIM missionaries to the Wallamo people in Ethiopia were expelled by new colonial authorities in 1937. Afterward, authorities persecuted the fledgling local church, lashing some members more than a hundred times. When missionaries were finally able to return in 1943, six years later, they discovered that the tiny church they had planted had grown to eighteen thousand in their absence. The indigenous Wallamo church was sending out its own missionaries to evangelize elsewhere.[42]

Ugandan believers sang to Christ while a young king, influenced by Muslim Arabs hostile to Christianity, was burning the believers alive. At roughly the same time, an approaching Anglican bishop, about to be speared to death, announced, "Tell your king that I have purchased the road to Buganda with my death."[43] The gospel long outlived the oppressive king, and Christianity became the majority religion in Uganda. Later, in 1971, Muslim dictator Idi Amin seized power and soon killed an estimated three hundred thousand people, with Christians among his chief targets. One martyr was Anglican archbishop Janani Luwum, who, summoned before Amin, whispered to Bishop Festo Kivengere, "They are going to kill me. I am not afraid."[44] He was reportedly praying for his captors when he was shot. Bishop Kivengere escaped but later returned to Uganda, preaching Christ's forgiveness and reconciliation. Today, roughly 84 percent of Uganda professes faith in Christ, a higher proportion than in the US.

Communists came to power in Ethiopia in 1982. They confiscated church buildings and imprisoned many church leaders, forcing many churches underground. During the ensuing ten years of repression, the gospel spread; Mennonites, for example, multiplied tenfold.[45] Most of the denominations, including the Lutheran (Mekane Yesus) church, also became effectively charismatic. My dear friends Melesse Woldetsadik and his brother Tadesse, charismatic Lutherans, were among the refugees in Kenyan camps. During that time, they led thousands of people to Christ. (They are so full of the Spirit and so prayerful that when I would reach the threshold of their apartment in North Carolina I would experience an unexpected, special sense of God's presence.)

"Underground" church is still church. In the New Testament, the church normally met in homes, understanding that God's church is his people, not a building. I am not opposed to large churches, having served in megachurches as well as in house churches. The one place in the Roman Empire that provided public access for worshiping the one God was the Jerusalem temple, so Jesus's followers in Jerusalem were able to have megachurch meetings alongside small groups (Acts 2:46). But when persecution or fuel shortages make commuting impractical, the church remains a family. It has to do with relationality far more than venue.

Iran hanged Pastor Soodmand for following Christ. Members of his church, who had not always been cooperative with him before, concluded, "If he died for his faith, we are also ready for martyrdom." His assistant succeeded him as pastor and was often interrogated. The assistant's wife provided extra motivation for his perseverance, warning him, "If you ever deny Christ, then you can move out and return to" his parents. They stood firm in their faith.[46]

After years of Abdi's witness and service among Somalis, he was gunned down on February 7, 2013. Seven years later, his wife learned that after Abdi's death his witness had become even more well known among Somalis.[47] Boko Haram murdered over fifty of Ishaku's church members, yet some other Boko

Haram members came to Christ, including one who was converted as he heard Christians praying for their persecutors.[48]

Suffering Can Make Us Better

In terms of God's ideal for us, sometimes other matters take precedence over healing or other blessings. God can use various sorts of afflictions to draw us closer to him. And who in this life would protest that we are so perfectly close to him that we cannot be drawn closer (1 Cor. 13:10, 12)? Hear the psalmist:

> Before I was afflicted I went astray,
>   but now I obey your word. . . .
> It was good for me to be afflicted
>   so that I might learn your decrees. . . .
> I know, LORD, that your laws are righteous,
>   and that in faithfulness you have afflicted me. (Ps. 119:67, 71, 75 NIV)

The psalmist mentions his persecutors and oppressors (e.g., 119:84, 86, 122, 139, 157, 161) but clings to God's word in hope.

King Hezekiah speaks similarly about his life-threatening illness:

> Surely it was for my benefit that I suffered such anguish. In your love you kept me from the pit of destruction. (Isa. 38:17 NIV)

Part of God blessing us is God also allowing some hardships to make us better rather than letting us get spoiled (Heb. 12:4–12).

Maturing Our Character

If we respond rightly, suffering can build our character:

> We celebrate in hope of the glory of God.
> And not only *this*, but we also celebrate in our tribulations,
> knowing that tribulation brings about perseverance;
>   and perseverance, proven character;
>   and proven character, hope. (Rom. 5:2–4 NASB modified)

> Consider it all joy, my brothers and sisters, when you experience various kinds of testing. This is because you know that the testing of your trust in God brings about endurance! But let endurance have its ultimate impact, so you may be mature and complete, not lacking anything. (James 1:2–4)

I mentioned earlier the fourth among Iris Global's core values: suffering, when necessary. "We understand the value of suffering in the Christian life. Learning to love requires willingness to suffer for the sake of righteousness. Discipline and testing make saints out of us, and produce in us the holiness without which we will not see His face and share His glory."[49] This affirmation in part evokes Hebrews 12:7, 14 (NASB): "It is for discipline that you endure. . . . Pursue peace with all people, and the holiness without which no one will see the Lord."

Many quote the saying that suffering makes you bitter or it makes you better, depending on how you respond. Helen Keller, who certainly earned the right to speak about hardship, said, "We could never learn to be brave and patient, if there were only joy in the world."[50] Or as Philip Yancey points out, "the deepest strength only comes through testing."[51]

Imprisoned for nine years and often tortured, Iranian pastor Mehdi Dibaj celebrated his opportunity to devote more time to prayer. Sentenced to execution, he announced, "I . . . accept the court verdict with joy and peace." Assemblies of God superintendent Haik Hovsepian, one of just two pastors in Iran who publicly refused to turn away Muslim converts, defended Dibaj's cause and welcomed him into his home after his release. Two days later, on January 20, 1994, Hovsepian "disappeared" at the age of forty-nine. Ten days later his body was found near a police station, and authorities demanded an immediate funeral, which of course permitted no time to examine the corpse. On July 5 of the same year, Dibaj also "disappeared." Hovsepian earlier insisted that the Islamic Revolution in Iran had proved "a great blessing for the church, because we have learned so many lessons that we otherwise wouldn't have learned."[52] Dibaj had declared, "It is a terrible waste for a Christian to die a natural death."[53]

Sometimes people respond to suffering by turning from God, but sometimes suffering turns people to him. When Air Florida Flight 90 slid into the icy Potomac River on January 13, 1982, seventy-four people died, but some survivors turned to God for the first time. One, flight attendant Kelly Duncan, confessed, "It's the first time I had ever prayed."[54]

Raju (a pseudonym), leader of a Hindu extremist group, sent men to dismember and kill a Pentecostal pastor who had ministered in the area for twenty years. But when, soon after the murder, Raju himself was injured and in the hospital, a Christian woman lovingly shared Christ with him. Raju became a Christian but then had to flee for his own life. A pastor took him in, after which Raju planned to return and take the place of the pastor he had killed.[55]

Egypt also has its share of martyrs.[56] But God also has his plans for those who survive. A member of the Muslim Brotherhood ordered Yousef, with a nine-inch knife to his throat, to convert to Islam or die. "I will never bow to anyone other than my Savior, the Lord Jesus Christ!" he answered.[57] Yousef was ready to meet Jesus, but his antagonist stood frozen for a minute and finally simply walked off. Yousef could only reason that God still had work for him to do.[58] An assailant shot Akhom three times in the head and once in the stomach; another assailant slashed his cousin Hassani's face with a machete. Akhom and his cousin survived, and the attacks drew both closer to God. Jesus suffered, Akhom reasons, so "it is a privilege to us" to follow in his steps.[59] Muslims in India detained and interrogated some Christian schoolgirls for six weeks, but the girls' faith grew all the more because of their experience.[60]

Comforting Others

The Lord comforts us in our hardships (e.g., Pss. 86:17; 94:19), including as we think about his Word (Ps. 119:50, 52). Part of that comfort is knowing that we are not alone; others have shared such troubles (1 Cor. 10:13; 1 Pet. 5:9). The Lord also may call us to comfort others, as God used Isaiah to comfort Israel with the promise of future restoration (Isa. 40:1).[61]

Suffering also uniquely equips us with the ability to comfort those who face similar circumstances:

> God comforts us in all our hardships so we can in turn comfort others facing hardships, using the same comfort God has given us. . . . If we suffer hardships, it's for the sake of your comfort and salvation; if we're comforted, it's for the sake of your comfort, which enables you to endure the same sufferings that we suffer. (2 Cor. 1:4, 6)

Sharing the comfort we have received in our afflictions helps others to bear with the same kinds of afflictions.[62] It gives them hope that God does give grace to endure. As just noted, this is true even if the afflictions are like those Paul and his apostolic colleagues suffered.

When Floyd reached back to grab his cowboy hat, the jeep veered toward a ditch. In his panic, he hit the accelerator instead of the brake. As the jeep exploded, Floyd's friend Kc Kopaska rolled in the grass, trying to extinguish the flames burning his flesh. The emergency room doctor concluded that burns covered 70 to 80 percent of Kc's body; the prognosis for his survival was grim. Unlike Floyd, however, Kc survived. Kc didn't understand why, but several years later he met Jesus and began sharing his faith with others. I met Kc when we were in seminary together. Soon after seminary, Kc began ministering among Native Americans, and his scars and experience of suffering bonded him with this people who also had experienced tremendous suffering.[63]

The experience of abandonment helped me write more compassionately (and passionately) about divorce. Witnessing the hardships of some women friends motivated me to stand for justice for them. Having survived abuse in her first marriage, Médine is able to comfort those who experience such abuse. The pain of our miscarriages helps us minister more compassionately to those who have shared the same experience. We can let suffering harden us, or we can let it break our hearts with compassion for others experiencing brokenness.

Suffering Doesn't Always Make Short-Term Sense

While we sometimes recognize positive by-products of suffering, we cannot necessarily reason from such by-products back to divine purposes in the suffering. Sometimes even the by-products seem obscure. Thousands were praying for God to heal my friend Nabeel Qureshi, and some ministers particularly well known for healing prayed for him. Even so, he died of cancer. He did leave a testimony: Despite some critics exhorting him to return to his previous religion, he proved the genuineness of his faith, remaining confident in the truth about Jesus to the end. As I have prayed, I have felt that we will someday understand the spiritual dynamics involved in such tragedies (perhaps like the insight readers get into Job's suffering in Job 1–2—an insight Job himself does not get). But in natural terms, Nabeel's death was certainly a great disappointment for us. More generally, suffering reveals the fallen world's true colors; as Philip Yancey says, "The Cross exposed the world for what it is: a breeding ground of violence and injustice."[64]

When God announces that he is sending Babylonians to judge Judah, Habakkuk protests. Why would God judge his people by those even more wicked than they are (Hab. 1:12–17)? God responds merely by promising also to judge the Babylonians in the right time (2:8–17). Likewise, when Assyria arrogantly conquered nations, God used them to judge Israel. Assyria did not recognize God's hand in exalting them, however, and God would ultimately judge Assyria (Isa. 10:5–15).

> If the righteous are repaid on earth, how much more the wicked and the sinner! (Prov. 11:31 NRSV)

In the same way, God may choose to purify the church by allowing others to repress us, before he judges our oppressors.

> But if any of you suffers for being a Christian, don't be ashamed of that. Instead, give honor to God by this name. Be ready for such hardship, because it's time

for judgment to begin with God's household. And if it begins with us, what will be the outcome for those who disobey God's good news? And "If it's hard for the just to be saved, what can we expect for the irreverent and sinners?" Keeping this pattern in mind, let those who suffer according to God's will entrust their lives to the trustworthy Creator. You entrust yourself to him by continuing to do what's good. (1 Pet. 4:16–19)

My God, Why Have You Forsaken Me?

Rational explanations of suffering (such as the best of all *possible* worlds) are valuable, but what matters to the broken more when they are hurting is an answer to the cries of their wounded hearts. That Jesus cried, "Why have you forsaken me?" (Mark 15:34) shows, as in the psalm he quotes, that we are allowed to ask why. "Our whys," noted one of my professors, "were answered by Jesus on the cross."[65]

Sometimes we charismatics need to be reminded that our feelings do not determine God's faithfulness. The psalmist, and Jesus who quotes him, felt abandoned by God—in Jesus's case, even right before he died. Yet Scripture is explicit that Jesus died in the Father's will (Mark 14:36). And when Jesus died, his Father vindicated him, rending the temple veil (15:38). This discovery encouraged me when I saw it, because sometimes I wondered, "What if I *feel* forsaken at the point of death?" Feelings are temporary; God's faithfulness is eternal.

When Jesus cries, "My God, my God, why have you forsaken me?" his cry of anguish reflects not unbelief but faith. Jesus is not denying God; he hails him as "*my* God"! Moreover, as the biblically literate people who regularly prayed psalms would know, the psalm that starts with, "Why have you forsaken me?" ends with God delivering the psalmist. Jesus already knew that he would rise from the dead (Mark 8:31; 9:9, 31; 10:34). As commentators sometimes point out, we may forgive a dying man for not bothering to recite all thirty-two verses of the psalm, but for Jews who knew Scripture, quoting part of a text could evoke the whole. In fact, it is surely no accident that the crucifixion scene echoes other verses from this same psalm (including Ps. 22:7 in Mark 15:29 and Ps. 22:18 in Mark 15:24)!

Even more obviously, those who recited psalms were familiar with the psalmist's frequent protests that God had turned away his face and forgotten him (e.g., Pss. 10:1; 44:23–24; 88:13–18; 89:49–51), rejected his people (Pss. 60:1, 10; 108:11), hidden his face (Pss. 13:1; 30:7; 44:24), and the like. Yet nearly all these psalms also included continued prayers for and celebration of deliverance! The reality of a faithful God offers hope even when we feel forsaken.

To feel abandoned and to honestly express that feeling to God is not unbelief. It is trusting God enough to be real with him about what's in our hearts. In the next chapter, we turn to a different kind of worshipful response that expresses trust in a different way. Psalm 22 begins with an expression of despair, but ultimately it gives way to trust and triumph.

CHAPTER ELEVEN

Rejoicing in Suffering

Joy in suffering expresses faith.

> Even if the fig tree doesn't bud, and no grapes appear on the vines . . . and the
> fields produce no food . . . I will be jubilant in the LORD; I will rejoice in the
> God who delivers me. (Hab. 3:17–18)

> Now I rejoice in my sufferings for your sake. (Col. 1:24)

Paul's joy in Colossians 1:24 shows that one can demonstrate one's love for
God and others by (when necessary) suffering for them.

Responding to militant Islamist attacks, Evangelical Church Winning All,
a Nigerian-based evangelical denomination with an estimated ten million
members, made its theme for 2018 "Joy in Suffering," using 1 Peter 4:13.[1]

> That's why you celebrate. Granted, now for a brief period various necessary
> testings have grieved you. These testings are meant to prove the genuineness of
> your trust in God. . . . Thus, though you don't see him now, you trust him and
> celebrate with inexpressible and glory-filled joy. (1 Pet. 1:6–8)

> Loved ones, don't think strange the fiery burning that comes to test you, as if
> something strange were happening to you. Instead, to the extent that you're
> sharing Christ's sufferings, be glad, so you may celebrate with joy when his
> glory is revealed. (1 Pet. 4:12–13)

First Peter focuses especially on ridicule and suffering for our faith. But we
may also apply the principles to other significant hardships. As noted earlier,

God counts them in our favor, so long as we respond to them *for* and *in* the Lord, as also described by Peter and James:

> Slaves, submit to your masters with all respect, not only to those who are good and tolerant, but even to the corrupt ones. Do this because it brings God's favor when, for the sake of one's conscience before God, one puts up with grief while suffering unjustly. For what kind of credit do you merit for enduring being beaten as a result of sinning? But if instead you endure suffering as a result of doing right, this brings God's favor on you. (1 Pet. 2:18–20)

> Consider it all joy, my brothers and sisters, when you experience various kinds of testing. (James 1:2)

As a whole, the letter of James focuses especially on the plight of people who are poor and exploited, who might be tempted to lash out at their oppressors. But as stated up front, the letter's principles apply to "*various* kinds of testing." The principle of celebrating during suffering because we trust our heavenly Father's benevolent sovereignty applies to multiple forms of hardship.

Still Learning

Rejoicing in suffering is not a discipline that I would have chosen to write about on my own, because I am not very good at it. (This is true while the suffering is going on, though some of it makes for great stories afterward.)[2] I suspect that I may not be alone; describing suffering, the author of Hebrews notes that

> no discipline seems pleasant at the time, but painful. Later on, however, it produces a harvest of righteousness and peace for those who have been trained by it. (Heb. 12:11 NIV)

The Psalms abundantly illustrate the appropriateness of lamenting and complaining to God when we suffer, and Paul reminds us to weep with those who weep (Rom. 12:15). Both psalms of lament and imprecatory prayers have their place for those traumatized by injustice.[3]

Nevertheless, the Bible does offer the genuine possibility of celebrating suffering that is meaningful—especially when we are suffering for Christ. Not all suffering is equally meaningful. If I suffer "as a murderer, or thief, or evildoer" (1 Pet. 4:15), consequent suffering might help bring me to repentance, but it is not the same as suffering for doing what is right (4:16).

When we trust that God uses suffering for our good, we can embrace it with greater confidence and hope. One of my close friends who helped motivate this book—who has faced tremendous suffering but also found strength in God's joy—was adamant that I needed to address the question of joyous courage and confidence in the face of suffering. Since I respect my friend's wisdom and especially the Bible's teaching on the subject, I gave in, despite my own need to grow in this practice. (But blame him for this chapter. He courageously asked to remain anonymous!)

More Joy in Suffering

Iris Global is on the front line of ministering to the needy in Mozambique. Their fourth core value, as already noted, is suffering for Christ, if necessary. The fifth core value is the one most relevant to this chapter: rejoicing in the Lord. "The joy of the Lord is not optional, and it far outweighs our suffering!"[4] As Rolland Baker puts it, "Suffering for the Gospel was never intended to be a miserable experience, but rather one in which indescribable joy and seasons of hardship intertwine in a way that only God could imagine."[5] Rejoicing in Jesus when life is hard is an act of resistance against evil, an act of trust that the Lord is indeed watching over us.

New Testament Models

As noted in the last chapter, Jesus experienced joyless anguish in the face of death—though he endured it in light of the joy set before him (Heb. 12:2). In normal kinds of hardship, though, joy (without denying the reality of the hardship) is ideal. Paul, who urged continual joy and celebration in God (Phil. 4:4), also confessed great sadness concerning the resistance of his beloved people (Rom. 9:1–3), and daily concern for the state of all the churches (2 Cor. 11:28). How can sorrow and joy coexist? Paul models it

as sorrowful, yet always rejoicing. (2 Cor. 6:10 NASB)

Trust in God's faithful concern for us and his plan, that he ultimately works all things for our good, is a reason for joy:

Our heart rejoices in him, because we trust in his holy name. (Ps. 33:21)

It is also a major reason we can praise him in the face of hardship. Officials in Philippi had Paul and Silas publicly stripped naked and whipped with rods. Then they had them thrown into the most secure part of the prison, immobilized in stocks (Acts 16:22–24). Stocks were blocks of wood with holes so prisoners' legs could be stuck in various positions. Prisons were crowded and dirty and lacked toilet facilities. The apostles' backs, caked now with dried blood, were likely up against a wall. Moreover, Paul and Silas could be concerned how the local people they had won to Christ would react to this humiliation. What new hardships would this public sentiment against the gospel's agents cause the converts (2 Cor. 11:28)? Yet Luke explains:

> Now about midnight Paul and Silas were praying and singing hymns of praise to God, and the prisoners were listening to them. (Acts 16:25 NASB)

Christians in nearby Thessalonica knew what Paul suffered in Philippi (1 Thess. 2:2). They too had suffered persecution (1 Thess. 1:6; 3:3). Yet Paul's closing exhortations to them include the following:

> Rejoice always, pray continually, give thanks in all circumstances; for this is God's will for you in Christ Jesus. (1 Thess. 5:16–18 NIV)

These exhortations immediately precede his charismatic exhortation not to despise prophecies. Paul also emphasized rejoicing in the Lord always to the Philippians themselves (Phil. 4:4), as well as prayer with thanksgiving (4:6). In fact, joy is a frequent refrain throughout Philippians (1:4, 18, 25; 2:2, 17–18, 28–29; 3:1; 4:1, 10)—a letter Paul sent from Roman custody (1:7, 13). Paul would either get to keep working for the Lord, or he would depart and be with the Lord undistracted (1:20–24). Though ultimately he expected that he would be released (1:19, 25–26), he viewed both potential outcomes of his custody as win-win situations.

Paul also describes the Spirit-filled life in Ephesians 5. In contrast to being controlled with wine, Paul exhorts,

> Be filled with the Spirit, speaking to one another with psalms, hymns, and songs from the Spirit. Sing and make music from your heart to the Lord, always giving thanks to God the Father for everything, in the name of our Lord Jesus Christ. (Eph. 5:18–20 NIV)

Paul wrote Ephesians, as he did Philippians, while in Roman custody (Eph. 3:1; 4:1; 6:20). Paul's emphasis on joy in hardship reflects a wider consensus among Jesus's first followers.

You suffered along with those in prison and joyfully accepted the confiscation of your property, because you knew that you yourselves had better and lasting possessions. (Heb. 10:34 NIV)

Any suffering in this life is temporary, and it is often followed by joy (Pss. 30:5, 11; 126:5), true even for the intense period of suffering during Jesus's passion (John 16:20–22). Jesus endured the cross for the sake of the joy set before him (Heb. 12:2). We often sing, "This is the day that the LORD has made" (Ps. 118:24) as if the psalmist meant *every* day. While there is truth in us rejoicing daily (Phil. 4:4; 1 Thess. 5:16), the joy in the psalm reflects a special occasion, regarding a special day. The context runs like this:

> The stone which the builders rejected has become the cornerstone;
> This is Yahweh's doing, and we marvel at it.
> This is the day which Yahweh has made, a day for us to rejoice and be
>   glad. (Ps. 118:22–24 NJB)

Ancient Jewish application of the psalm seems correct about its original idea: David, rejected and pursued by Saul, eventually was exalted. The New Testament applies the principle to the ultimate Son of David, Jesus, whom God exalted after the leaders rejected him (Matt. 21:42; Mark 12:10–11; Luke 20:17; Acts 4:11; 1 Pet. 2:7). When we sing this song, we can remember Jesus's death and exaltation as the ultimate basis for our celebration.

John Chrysostom remarked, "What is required is not only to suffer for Christ, but to endure what we suffer nobly and with all gladness."[6] As archbishop of Constantinople, he often spoke boldly for justice and fairness for all and denounced the ostentatious materialism of the imperial court. Facing consequent political enmity, Chrysostom was banished to Armenia on June 20, AD 404. His enemies still feared him, however, and they ordered him relocated—on a forced march. He died in transit on September 14, AD 407, at the age of sixty.

Modern Examples

Lest we think the ideal limited to the New Testament or ancient times, many today have also offered models of rejoicing in hardship. God often provides his children special grace in times of hardship. Richard Wurmbrand recounts that prisoners understood the rules: Whoever preached the gospel to other prisoners would be beaten. With dark humor he adds, "We were happy preaching; they were happy beating us, so everyone was happy."[7] He recounts that even as believers endured torture, the joy God's Spirit gave their hearts proved more than worth their suffering.[8] His wife, Sabina, discovered the same principle. "In prison the guard used to tell us before we got a beating, 'You wanted to be martyrs, so now suffer!' And we did. But even at the worst times there was the joy of knowing that it was for Jesus."[9]

Here are some examples (with more later in the chapter):

- Under the former Communist regime, Romanian Christians sentenced for singing about Jesus in public knelt and thanked God for the privilege of suffering for Christ.[10]
- As already noted, Iranian pastor Mehdi Dibaj responded to his death sentence by declaring, "I . . . accept the court verdict with joy and peace."
- Among Iraqis displaced by ISIS and living in an encampment of tents, a family of Muslim converts to Christianity declared, "We have everything we need. We are happy!"[11]
- After six months in prison for hosting a Chinese house church, Sister Tong explained that prison had been "a *wonderful* time," because she felt Jesus's presence with her there like never before.[12]
- Driven from his home for following Christ, Iraqi convert Zarguos spent six months sleeping in a cemetery. "It was a wonderful time for me," he explains. Noting God's special presence, he considered it "the best time of his life with God."[13]
- In Vietnam, Pastor Cuong had unfortunately kept too busy to pray much, but his six years in prison gave him six hours a day to pray, and he was grateful to the Lord.[14]
- Mr. Xi described his persecution as a privilege, and his father joyfully thanked God that Mr. Xi had this privilege.[15]
- When arrested for sharing her faith, Iranian Christian Marziyeh Amirizadeh declared, "I am honored to serve Christ this way,"[16] and, like Paul in custody (compare Acts 28:20; 2 Tim. 1:8, 16; Philem. 1), "We are proud of these handcuffs, because we're wearing them on account of our faith in Jesus Christ!"
- Refusing to bow before Shinto idols, underground Korean Christians considered it "more than an honor to die for the Lord," with persecution providing "a joyous blessing . . . that I was able to truly experience God's presence and trust his promises" in a special way.[17]
- The widow of a Muslim convert to Christ declared that it was "an honor . . . to die for Christ," and "to have been married to a man that God would choose and bless with the gift of martyrdom."[18]

- After a period of Islamist attacks in Egypt, one Christian affirmed, "We live in Egypt today with hearts full of peace and joy, realizing that even as we are on that boat . . . Jesus will . . . show up walking on the waves."[19]
- A Nigerian jihadist grew angry upon finding Christians singing and celebrating Jesus even though he had recently bombed their church. He decided that he could eliminate them only by infiltrating their ranks; once there, however, he was won over by their love and became a follower of Jesus.[20]
- Before being beheaded for refusing to convert to Islam, Nigerian Pastor Georgi Orji asked a colleague to relay his message: "Tell my brothers I died well and am living with Christ."[21]
- After his pastor, Wang Yi, and over 160 other members of their Early Rain Covenant Church were arrested, a believer named Ran recounted, "I think persecution is quite a blessing from God. . . . I think the gospel in China will flourish more."[22]
- In the Middle East, Malik insisted, "Every Christian should go to jail at least once in life because of their faith in Christ. It's good for you!" Jesus fills the loneliness, he explained: "My deepest spiritual lessons were learned" there.[23]
- Kham La, arrested in Laos through a misunderstanding, thanks God for his temporary experience in prison, through which he was able to share the gospel with his sixty-two cellmates.[24]

C. J. Wu, a missionary who spent seven years in a Chinese prison for sharing the gospel, recounts his perspective:

> I knew that sooner or later I would be persecuted for my faith. Jesus said we will go through what he had experienced. For whosoever will pursue his life shall lose it, and whosoever will lose his life for the Lord's sake shall find it. Also, I have been to every province in China, where I visited many Christians who were persecuted, beaten, and imprisoned. I've heard their testimony. So when the day came, I had a great peace in my heart. I knew I would pay a price for my faith, so I felt very joyful.[25]

At age thirteen, Purnima refused to deny her faith in Christ that had begun when the name of Jesus healed her big sister. Ordered to leave Bhutan, she trekked with other Christian exiles to Nepal. There at age fifteen she was abused by police for sharing Christ, then sentenced to imprisonment on false charges. Realizing that they were imprisoned for Christ, she and her fellow believers recognized that they were "privileged to be called to suffer for Christ."[26] Another of the Christians, Ashok, was beaten within inches of his life by cellmates,[27] but some of Purnima's cellmates were converted before the Christians' release after some fourteen months.[28]

Insurgents in northern Mozambique have killed thousands and so far displaced roughly a million people.[29] As already noted, Christians, including children, are beheaded and sometimes crucified. Yet pastors who have escaped with their lives are praising God for allowing these circumstances. Many followers of the region's other main religion have seen how their religious compatriots are the ones killing and displacing them, while Christians instead care for them. This has led many to turn to Christ. When asked, "Do you think more people will go to heaven?" because of these attacks, "the pastors responded unanimously with a resounding 'Yes!'"[30] A pastor whose family is missing explained that because he is serving the Lord, he remains happy.[31] Such happiness does not displace all grief, but it sustains us in it.

Why Joy?

Surely a key element of charismatic worship today is joy. The Psalms mention joy more than one hundred times. The Psalms are of course also honest about sorrows, and our prayer lives should exhibit such honesty too. God welcomes our emotions, though I understand that expressing emotion is harder for some cultures and personalities (including mine) than others. Contrary to what some traditional Western expositors insist, Scripture is explicit that God's Spirit touches our emotions as well as our intellect. Joy is even a fruit of the Spirit (Gal. 5:22).

Invitations to Celebration

But while some exuberant worship today shies away from talk of suffering, the New Testament emphasizes that we should rejoice even in the face of hardship. This practice makes sense if we trust that God works all things for our good (Rom. 8:28). Like Old Testament psalms, worship can include some of each.

> Pray, if any of you is going through a hard time; sing, if you're cheerful. If any of you is sick, call for the elders and let them pray. (James 5:13–14)

Paul, who wrote, "Rejoice in the Lord always!" (Phil. 4:4), also wrote, "I'm always very sad and have continual anguish in my heart" for the sake of his people Israel (Rom. 9:2). God's servants sometimes experience anguish (Mark

14:34; 2 Cor. 2:4; 7:5; 11:28–29; 1 Thess. 3:5). We are not always happy and not always sad, but celebrating God's grace during hardship is an act of faith that welcomes God's infinitely longer-range perspective on our trials.

We rejoice in suffering partly because suffering puts us in good company. The Lord himself taught us:

> How good it is for you when people hate you, and when they ostracize you and insult and dismiss your reputation as evil because of the Son of Man. Rejoice when that happens and jump for joy! Do so because (see!) you have a great reward in heaven, and because your enemies' [spiritual] ancestors treated the prophets in just the same way. (Luke 6:22–23)

Jesus here gives two reasons to celebrate when we are mistreated for Jesus, one about the future and the other about the past. We celebrate, first, because we recognize that our reward from God ("a great reward in heaven") is worth far more than sufferings inflicted by people. Paul says the same thing: Our present afflictions are light compared to the much weightier glory they bring us in God's presence forever (2 Cor. 4:17). If we suffer with him, we'll be glorified with him (Rom. 8:17; 2 Tim. 2:12). We celebrate, second, because of how our sufferings connect us with the past. We are just like the prophets and Jesus himself, who suffered unjustly but whom we now recognize to be right.

Despite Jesus's clear warning in Luke 6:22–23 and other passages, his disciples abandoned him in Gethsemane. It was different, however, after they experienced the power of the Spirit at Pentecost.[32] In Luke's second volume, he describes how Jesus's disciples responded when the authorities whipped and threatened them. Their backs sore from the beating, the apostles

> left the council, celebrating that they had been counted worthy to suffer shame for [Christ's] name. (Acts 5:41)

Suffering for Christ is a *privilege*, they understood, because it is an opportunity for us to prove our loyal love for him.

Celebrating Character Formation

Another reason to rejoice in suffering is because of what it does for our character. When suffering comes our way, we can choose to use it to learn to show our trust in God. Again, Paul encouraged Jesus's followers in Rome (Rom. 5:2–4 NASB, modified):

> We celebrate in hope of the glory of God.
> And not only *this*, but we also celebrate in our tribulations,
>> knowing that tribulation brings about perseverance;
>> and perseverance, proven character;
>> and proven character, hope.

Paul frames these verses with a Greek word that we translate as "hope" (Rom. 5:2, 5). But in the way Paul uses the term, *elpis* means more than what we often mean by the English word *hope*. It is not just something that we *wish* would happen; it entails confidence and expectation. The reason we can endure suffering is that our confidence in the Lord increasingly develops as the Lord walks with us through sufferings.[33] Still, even weaker levels of confidence can have value. After surviving a dark night of the soul, I have been able to better encourage the discouraged that their future need not always be like the present that they are suffering. Psychologist and Holocaust survivor Viktor Frankl (1905–1997) observed that, on average, those who lost hope died much faster in the concentration camps than those who maintained hope.[34] Frankl's existential courage differs from Christian expectation, but it demonstrates the human need for meaning beyond our finite limitations.

The term that the NASB translates "celebrate" in Romans 5:2 can mean "boast" or "take pride in," and Paul uses it three times in this passage. We boast because we share the expectation of God's glory (5:2), because our sufferings shape us for that expectation (5:3–4), and finally, in summary, we boast in God through Christ (5:11). Little did Paul's first audience know how seriously they would need to take his words. Less than ten years after Paul sent this letter, the emperor Nero began burning Christians alive as torches in his gardens.[35] Christians at that time needed perseverance to endure that wave of deadly persecution.

Paul was not the only inspired writer to encourage joy in the face of suffering. Again, James writes, "Consider it all joy, my brothers and sisters, when you experience various kinds of testing. This is because you know that the testing of your trust in God brings about endurance! But let endurance have its ultimate impact, so you may be mature and complete, not lacking anything" (James 1:2–4).

So also Peter, whose counsel we have already mentioned:

> You are celebrating in God's eternal promise, even though now, if necessary, for a short period you have been grieved by various kinds of testing. The purpose of this testing is the proving of your trust in God, a proving worth more than perishable gold refined by fire. In this way your trust in God will bring praise,

glory and honor when Jesus Christ is revealed. . . . You rejoice with joy that is beyond describing and glorious. (1 Pet. 1:6–8)

Peter is contrasting perishable gold (1:7) with our imperishable inheritance in heaven (1:4). He promises that our salvation will be revealed (1:5) when Christ is revealed (1:7). And just as gold is tested in fire, so our trust in God is tested by our hardships (1:7). Sufficient heat refines gold by separating it from impurities; the same is necessary in our lives.

Peter is not speaking flippantly; he deliberately draws on an earlier biblical image. God's people were tested as if refined by fire (Ps. 66:10; Isa. 1:25; 48:10; Zech. 13:9; compare Dan. 11:35; 12:10; Mal. 3:2–3). Sometimes this testing came as judgment, but always it came for their good. The Lord tests hearts like furnaces refine metals (compare Prov. 17:3; praise also can test us, Prov. 27:21); he desires us to emerge like gold (Job 23:10). As Mr. Xi said after being jailed at times for Christ in China, "Persecution is like fire. . . . If we want pure gold, we have to let it go through fire." Those who embrace Christianity because it feels "cool" quickly fall away; persecution weeds out those who aren't serious about following Christ himself.[36]

God Is Near the Broken in a Special Way

God takes into account our afflictions; he counts them in our favor (Pss. 56:8; 132:1). In fact, God is especially near the lowly and the broken, the "poor in spirit" (Matt. 5:3), a theme recurrent in Scripture:

- "For you save a suffering people, but you bring down proud eyes" (Ps. 18:27).
- "For the LORD is exalted, but he watches over the lowly, while he knows the proud only from far away" (Ps. 138:6).
- "A person's proud eyes will be brought low, and people's pride will be brought low, and the LORD alone will be exalted in that day. For the LORD God of armies has a day for the proud and uplifted and for all the exalted, and they will be brought low. . . . And human pride will be humbled and human exaltation will be brought low, and the LORD alone will be exalted in that day" (Isa. 2:11–12, 17).
- "For this is the message of the exalted and high One, who lives forever, whose name is holy: 'I live in an exalted and holy place—and with the broken and lowly in heart, to bring life to their lowly heart and to bring life to the heart of the broken'" (Isa. 57:15).
- "The lowly will be high and the high will be brought low" (Ezek. 21:26).

- "Anybody who lifts themselves up will be humbled, and anybody who humbles themselves will be lifted up" (Matt. 23:12).
- "He has pulled down princes from their thrones and raised high the lowly" (Luke 1:52 NJB).
- "For anybody who lifts themselves up will be humbled, and whoever humbles themselves will be lifted up" (Luke 14:11; 18:14).
- "That is why Scripture says: 'God opposes the proud but shows favor to the humble.' Submit yourselves, then, to God. Resist the devil, and he will flee from you. . . . Humble yourselves before the Lord, and he will lift you up" (James 4:6–7, 10 NIV).
- "Likewise, those of you who are younger should submit to those who are older. Now *all* of you: clothe yourselves with humility, since God 'stands against the arrogant, but bestows grace on the humble.' So humble yourselves under God's powerful hand, so that he may exalt you at the right time" (1 Pet. 5:5–6).

If we want to walk close to God, humbling ourselves before God and others is an important part of the process. (Keep in mind I am not talking about allowing other people to be abused when we can help them; Prov. 24:11–12.) Revival history—from the cries of Welsh miners to the girls in Pandita Ramabai's orphanage to Chinese farmers and Mozambican orphans—has repeatedly reinforced this theme.

Joyful Praise During Hardship

Of course, we don't praise God during testing only because the testing might be good for us. We praise God during testing also for the same reason we praise God at other times: He deserves our praise, both for who he is and for what he does (Ps. 150:2). Even our very existence gives us enormous reason for gratitude. Most human embryos conceived never survive to birth. The odds of an undesigned universe producing any life at all are virtually infinitesimal, and the odds of any of us with our distinctive genetic identities existing are far less. Whether it seems short or long, any amount of life is an undeserved gift. Life is a privilege; eternal life, at the price of Jesus's death for us, an even greater one. How could we deny thanksgiving to our rightful Lord?

Rejoice in hope, keep enduring your hardship, continue praying. (Rom. 12:12)

Hearing good news about his converts in Corinth, Paul declared that he was "overflowing with joy in all our affliction" (2 Cor. 7:4 NASB).

> In a severe test of affliction, their abundance of joy and their extreme poverty have overflowed in a wealth of generosity on their part. (2 Cor. 8:2 ESV)

> You accepted the message in the face of severe hardship, with joy from the Holy Spirit. (1 Thess. 1:6)

Although hostile people ran Paul and Barnabas out of town (Acts 13:50), their new converts "were filled with joy and the Holy Spirit" (13:52).

> To the extent that you share Christ's sufferings, rejoice, so you may also rejoice and celebrate when his glory is revealed! (1 Pet. 4:13)

More Modern Role Models

Dietrich Bonhoeffer resisted Hitler and helped Jews escape Nazi Germany. As he languished in prison before his execution, he often faced discouragement. Nevertheless, he wrote, "I believed that we ought so to love and trust God in our lives, and in all the good things that He sends us, that when the time comes we may go to Him with love, trust, and joy."[37]

After a ten-minute sham trial, Pastor Richard Wurmbrand's Communist captors sentenced him to twenty years of hard labor. To those who tortured him, he explained that he was ready to meet God. When one of his tormentors demanded, "What are you praying for?" Wurmbrand responded, "I am praying for you." As Richard was being taken to his second imprisonment, he urged Sabina, who was now free, to give his love to the informer who had turned him in. Altogether, Richard served fourteen years in prison, able to see Sabina during only one brief interval. Later freed with international Christian help, he founded Voice of the Martyrs, one of the key organizations serving the global persecuted church.[38]

Virginia Prodan took on cases defending Christians in dictator Nicolae Ceausescu's Romania. She was harassed, isolated under house arrest, and subject to assassination attempts—ultimately leading one of her would-be assassins to Christ. Despite her traumatic experiences, she thanks her persecutors in her book's acknowledgments "for helping me trust God to teach me to love you as I never thought I could. I am a better person because of you."[39] As she recounts, "It is an honor to suffer for Christ."[40]

I am no expert on church-state relations in China, but I can only admire the hope of joy in the face of persecution expressed by many Christians there. For example, Wang Yi, an urban church pastor arrested in China, resolved that if God "through persecution . . . continues disciplining and building up his church, then I am joyfully willing to submit to God's plans, for his plans are always benevolent and good."[41] An elder from his church wrote, shortly before his arrest, "May the whole world know that we are joyfully willing to receive this persecution for the sake of our faith."[42]

Admittedly, rejoicing in hardship is often easier said than done, and often coexists with a measure of concern or sorrow. As I have noted, I include advice on it because it's in Scripture, not because I have come close to mastering it myself. One day after college, when a job I was counting on did not come through, I remembered that we are supposed to praise God in all things.[43] So I thanked God that he had a better plan for me, and on the way home I stopped at what seemed a less likely place of employment. There I was hired on the spot. That was one of my better days.

I must confess that I didn't rejoice when I have been beaten. Yet these experiences nevertheless stood me in good stead in the long run. When my PhD was nearly complete, one of my professors told me that I might not be allowed to graduate because I was too openly religious. He was a lone voice, but I was indeed concerned. Nevertheless, I had already been beaten and had my life threatened for my witness for Christ. Why would I let a professor's words intimidate me into silence about my Savior?

There was a time in my life, before my PhD, when I told God that I loved him so much that nothing else mattered compared to him. A few months later, I lost the two things in life that I valued most: my marriage and my ministry. So far as I could tell at the time, I had lost them permanently. When someone goes through a crisis, a glib "All things work for good" can feel insensitive.[44] But I had already accepted that affirmation theologically, so now I held on to it for dear life. A few years later, when I told God again that I loved him more than anything else, I understood better what I was committing to. If we really love our Lord more than anything else, then no one can take from us what matters to us most—because nothing can separate us from his love (Rom. 8:35, 38–39).

I conclude this chapter by referring again to the ultimate model. Jesus set the example for us: "For the joy set before him, he endured the cross, despising its shame, and sat down at God's right hand" (Heb. 12:2).

CHAPTER TWELVE

Conclusion: Overcomers

Suffering in Christ is not meaningless. This world's sufferings are birth pangs of the coming world, and we endure in hope. Christ's victory over death has established our future, making our expectation firm. The promised future is more than worth every affliction we endure in the present.

The Spirit's Birth Pangs: Resurrection Power in the Already/Not Yet

> For we know that the entire creation is groaning and experiencing birth pangs even till now. And not only creation, but also we ourselves who already have the first fruits of the Spirit. We too groan within ourselves as we wait expectantly for adoption as God's children—the liberation of our bodies. . . . Likewise, the Spirit also helps us in our weakness. For we do not know how to pray the way that we need to, but the same Spirit intercedes with groanings too deep for words. (Rom. 8:22–23, 26)

God performs signs of the coming kingdom, but until Christ returns suffering continues to characterize the present age. The overlap of future glory and present suffering creates a tension that will be resolved fully only at Christ's return.

As all of us recognize and mothers attest personally, birth pangs are excruciating. The Bible often uses this image of pain presaging something important. Jesus's death was like that: agony for him and his disciples, yet followed by joy at his resurrection (John 16:20–22). Paul spoke of being in fresh labor over the Galatians, until Christ would be formed in them more enduringly (Gal. 4:19). His experience of birth pangs mirrored a much wider one for all creation.

199

The Groaning of Creation, Believers, and the Spirit

Describing the present world's sufferings, Paul speaks of a threefold groan-ing. He declares that all creation "groans and travails," like a mother preparing to give birth (Rom. 8:22). Not only that, he emphasizes that we who have the Spirit also groan (8:23). Moreover, the Spirit himself groans (8:26), no less eager than we for the transformation of the world at Christ's return.

Here is the fuller context of Paul's claim. As God's children, we suffer with God's Son so we may share his glory (Rom. 8:17). Our present sufferings can't even begin to be compared with the glory that awaits (8:18). Indeed, our glory will transform the world, delivering it from the devastation we humans have inflicted on it in our sin (8:19–21). It awaits freedom from its current slavery (8:21). That's why the world groans in childbirth now (8:22), ready to bring forth a new world when Jesus returns.

We too groan, awaiting our full experience of adoption at the redemption—that is, the liberation—of our bodies (Rom. 8:23). In Egypt, Israel cried out for generations because of their slavery, but God heard their groaning and redeemed them (Exod. 2:23). In the same way, God will set us free from all the death and decay of this age when he resurrects our bodies. We already have the guarantee of that future, because the Spirit who will raise us already lives in us (Rom. 8:10–13). That is why Paul says we have the "first fruits of the Spirit" (8:23).

First fruits (*aparchē*) was the biblical expression for the actual beginning of the harvest (Exod. 23:16, 19; 34:22, 26; Lev. 23:10–20), and its meaning is very similar to the term (*arrhabōn*) Paul elsewhere calls the "pledge" (NASB, Douay-Rheims) or "guarantee" (ESV, NIV, NRSV) of the Spirit (2 Cor. 1:22; 5:5; Eph. 1:14). Ancient business documents used that term for the "down payment," the first installment paid down on what is to come. We know that we have the promised future in the Spirit because we already experience the Spirit now (e.g., 2 Cor. 5:1, 5; Gal. 5:5; 1 John 3:24). As Paul says elsewhere, our eyes and ears cannot reveal what God has prepared for those who love him, but God's Spirit gives us a foretaste of them (1 Cor. 2:9–10).

Finally, Paul declares that the Spirit also groans within us (Rom. 8:26). Paul speaks elsewhere of praying in tongues with his spirit and praying in his own language with the understanding (in context, the interpretation of the tongue; 1 Cor. 14:13–15). Many scholars also believe that he refers to tongues in Romans 8:26, and possibly some of the less articulate tongues today might be more like Romans 8:26 than full-fledged tongues. But I believe that here Paul speaks of an even deeper prayer, one too deep for us to articulate in words—in *any* language. When the struggle of still living in the present age is too painful for us to even know how to pray about it, the Spirit intercedes for us with "inarticulate groanings" (8:26). I had been praying two hours a day before my first wife left me. Afterward I could do no more than utter the name of Jesus over and over. I had no strength to pray or to exercise faith—yet God was graciously still there. God hears his Spirit interceding within us (8:27), just as he hears Christ interceding for us at his own right hand (8:34). *This* is the context where Paul also explains that God works all things for our good (8:28).

More Than Conquerors

Paul ultimately concludes Romans 8 with a rousing call to victory. The God who gave his own Son for us has an entire future world prepared for us; no one can keep that from us (8:31–34). None of this means that we will not face testing in this world. In this very context, Paul is explicit otherwise! But none of these tests can *ultimately* affect what matters most. Nothing can separate us from God's love for us in Christ.

Far more than a dollar pales in comparison to a trillion dollars, no short-term suffering compares with a destiny that lasts forever.

In the end, and forever, followers of Jesus overwhelmingly win no matter what we face in the short run (Rom. 8:35–39 NIV):

A   Who shall separate us from the love of Christ?
  B   Shall trouble or hardship or persecution or famine or nakedness or danger or sword? As it is written: "For your sake we face death all day long; we are considered as sheep to be slaughtered."
    C   No, in all these things we are more than conquerors through him who loved us.
  B′ For I am convinced that neither death nor life, neither angels nor demons, neither the present nor the future, nor any powers, neither height nor depth, nor anything else in all creation,
A′ will be able to separate us from the love of God that is in Christ Jesus our Lord.

Yet our suffering qualifies us for greater glory, which testifies to the God who works in us. We suffer now that we may reign with him:

• "We suffer with him so we may also be glorified with him. For I consider that the sufferings of the present time are not worthy to even be compared with the coming glory to be revealed in [or to] us" (Rom. 8:17–18).

- ". . . always carrying in our body Jesus's dying, so that Jesus's life may also be revealed in our body. For we ourselves who live are always being handed over to death on account of Jesus, in order that Jesus's life may be revealed in our death-destined flesh" (2 Cor. 4:10–11).
- "For our momentary minor affliction is effecting for us an eternal weight of glory[1] that is incomparably greater" (2 Cor. 4:17).
- "So I may know him and the power of his resurrection and share in his sufferings, being conformed to his death, if by some means I may reach the resurrection from the dead" (Phil. 3:10–11).
- "If we endure, we'll also reign with him; if we deny him, he will also deny us" (2 Tim. 2:12).
- "Instead, to the extent that you're sharing Christ's sufferings, be glad, so you may celebrate with joy when his glory is revealed" (1 Pet. 4:13).

From the Vantage Point of Eternity

And I tell you that you're Peter ["Rocky"], and on this rock I will build my holy community, and the gates of death will not overcome it. (Matt. 16:18)

In the context of discussing his and his followers' martyrdom (Matt. 16:21, 24–26), Jesus promises that the gates of hades (a common term in the Old Testament and other ancient sources for the realm of the dead) will not prevail against Jesus's church (16:18). God's kingdom does not rise or fall on any one of us, and when we have served his purpose in our generation (Acts 13:36), his work will continue without our labors until his return. Death is not the end for us individually, and our individual deaths are not the end for his church, which will prevail.

Before famous Russian dissident Alexei Navalny died in government custody in February 2024, he authored an engaging memoir published in October of the same year. He earlier regarded the amusement of others when he would make the sign of the cross as "my own pared-down version of suffering for the faith," since it did not require martyrdom.[2] In time he contemplated the likelihood of dying in prison because of his political stand,[3] but the book concludes with the hope that comforted him: "Are you a disciple of the religion whose founder sacrificed himself for others, paying the price for their sins? Do you believe in the immortality of the soul . . . ? If you can honestly answer yes, what is there left for you to worry about?" He appeals then to the Sermon on the Mount, which he had been memorizing:[4] "Don't worry about the morrow. . . . My job is to seek the Kingdom of God and his righteousness, and leave" the rest to the Lord.[5] As the psalmist celebrated, "Even when I walk in the darkest valley, I won't be afraid of being harmed, because you're with me. Your rod and staff comfort me!" (Ps. 23:4).

After recounting the dangers she survived in Communist Romania, Virginia Prodan concludes, "God displayed his protection, timing, and grace. . . . It is easy to look back now and see it. But while it was happening, it took faith to step up and to go on."[6] We can often recognize his grace in hindsight in this life, and we will certainly see it in eternity. The final vantage point is God's eternal one, and it will put everything in the right perspective.

Suffering is temporary, but Scripture promises that the reward for the faithful is eternal. Recall again:

> The sufferings of the present time are not worthy to even be compared with the coming glory to be revealed in [or to] us. (Rom. 8:18)

> For our momentary minor affliction is effecting for us an eternal weight of glory that is incomparably greater, watching not visible matters but invisible ones; for the visible ones are transitory, but the invisible ones eternal. (2 Cor. 4:17–18)

> It will be well for anyone who endures testing, because after proving faithful in the test they will receive the award of life that God promised to those who love him. (James 1:12)

> Now may the God of all grace himself, who called you to his eternal glory in Christ, after you have suffered *for a little while*, restore, strengthen, fortify and establish you. (1 Pet. 5:10, emphasis mine)

After Hindu extremists beat Nepali pastor Salindra, he forgave them and exhorted the local Christians, "The life here [on earth] is very short," but "even if we have to die, we'll die [willingly] because we'll have a long life [in eternity with Christ]."[7]

This long-range perspective helps us to persevere during short-term trouble or confusion. The psalmist laments that the wicked prosper (Ps. 73:2–14, 21–22) until he considers the longer-range divine perspective (73:15–20, 23–28; 92:7–9). Elsewhere the psalmist feels forsaken (Ps. 77:1–10), but experiences consolation by considering the longer-range perspective of God's acts in history (77:5–6, 11–20).

A book should not be needed to encourage Christians that suffering is a normal part of the Christian life, but here is one just in case you need it.

We don't face suffering with resigned despair, but with trust in a God who delivers, one way (in this life) or another (in the coming life). Psalms even provide examples of what we might call "positive confessions" of faith (e.g., Ps. 44:5), though at the same time they are equally honest about feelings of abandonment (e.g., Ps. 44:9). Reaffirming our trust in God is good to counter our human pessimism with faith. But we confess our need (Ps. 3:2, 7a) as well as our confidence in the one who can meet it (3:3–6, 7b–8). We can take joyful refuge in the Lord (Ps. 5:11) even if we groan in distress (5:1).

The Book of Revelation: What the Spirit Is Saying to the Churches

> Whoever has an ear, let them hear what the Spirit is saying to the churches. (Rev. 2:7)

The book of Revelation describes itself as a prophecy (Rev. 1:3; 22:7, 10, 18–19). In this prophetic book, the Spirit spoke to each of the seven churches of Asia Minor (2:7, 11, 17, 29; 3:6, 13, 22).

Each Church Must Overcome

Some of the seven churches were being tempted to compromise with the values of the world (Rev. 2:14, 20). Others had lost their first love (2:4). Two churches faced outright persecution (2:10; 3:8–9), with another having lost a member to martyrdom (2:13). But whatever their specific trials, the Spirit was calling *each* of the churches to overcome (2:7, 11, 17, 26; 3:5, 12, 21).

Church	What or How to Overcome	Promise
Ephesus (2:1–7)	Loss of first love (2:4)	Tree of life in paradise (2:7)
Smyrna (2:8–11)	Be faithful to death (2:10)	Unhurt by the second death (2:11)
Pergamum (2:12–17)	Condoning false teaching allowing idolatrous practice and sex outside marriage (2:14)	Hidden manna and a new name inscribed on stone (2:17)
Thyatira (2:18–29)	Condoning false teaching allowing idolatrous practice and sex outside marriage (2:20); must persevere (2:25)	Authority over the nations plus the morning star (2:26–28)
Sardis (3:1–6)	Must awaken, hold fast, and repent (3:1–3)	White garments, name remains in book of life, name confessed in heaven (3:5)
Philadelphia (3:7–13)	Keep persevering (3:11)	Home in God's temple, identified by God and his holy city (3:12)
Laodicea (3:14–22)	Repent of self-sufficiency (3:17–19)	Enthroned with Christ (3:21)

Whether individually, as churches, or as the church in various regions, we each have our own tests. We don't get to choose our tests, saying, "I'd rather have *their* test" or "I'm so glad I don't have *their* test." But whatever our respective tests, all of us are called to overcome. We overcome by the blood of the Lamb, by our witness for Jesus, and by not shrinking even from death for his honor (Rev. 12:11). The Spirit specifically promises rest to those who die in the Lord (14:13). The Spirit inspires us to speak prophetically for the Lord (19:10), so that those who witness for Christ in Revelation are called his prophets (11:18; 16:6; 18:20, 24; 22:9); those who compromise his message, by contrast, are false prophets (2:20).

From the world's vantage point, this way of overcoming might look like evil has conquered us (Rev. 11:7; 13:7), but from God's true standpoint "we are more than conquerors" (Rom. 8:37 NIV). (The word translated "overcome" can mean "conquer" or "be victorious.") Just as Nebuchadnezzar expected everyone to bow down to his image or die (Dan. 3:1–6), so evil in the world demands conformity, bowing down to its image (Rev. 13.15). Similarly, unlike thousands around her, Korean Christian Ahn E. Sook refused to bow to Japanese shrines during World War II,[8] risking execution and later enduring six years in prison. There she led many others to Christ.[9] Turkish Christian Semse, widow of a martyr, understood this well: "We want to be faithful unto death. . . . We are not victims. . . . We are victorious in Jesus."[10]

The Beast and the Lamb, Babylon and New Jerusalem

From the world's vantage point, the beast is the conqueror, against which a lamb—especially a slain lamb—is helpless. But from the divine viewpoint— the true perspective—the Lamb by his very death conquered death and the beast (Rev. 5:5–6). We who stay true to Jesus are the ones who overcome (15:2; 21:7). Jesus teaches, "In this world you have trouble; but be courageous! I have vanquished the world" (John 16:33). Evil remains in the world, but we overcome because the one who is in us is greater than the one who is in the world (1 John 4:4; 5:4–5).

Studying Revelation, Romanian Christian Joseph Ton discovered "how God always conquers by a love that is self-giving and self-sacrificing. It was there that I understood God's method of sending His Lamb into the world, followed by many thousands of other lambs, to overcome the world by proclaiming the love of God and by dying for the sake of their proclamation."[11]

When Jesus addresses the seven churches of Asia Minor in Revelation, he reproves most of them for various failures. The only two churches he does not reprove at all are the suffering churches. To one, the church in Philadelphia, he promises,

> Because you have kept my message about endurance, I'll also keep you from the hour of testing. (Rev. 3:10)

The Greek wording might mean that Jesus would preserve them in the *midst* of testing rather than preventing them from going through it (compare the identical construction in John 17:15), but whatever the particulars, it sounds like things would get better for the church in Philadelphia. But the other suffering church was the one in Smyrna. To that church, Jesus urges,

> Don't fear the things you're about to suffer. . . . Be faithful to the point of death, and I'll give you the crown of life. (Rev. 2:10)

Whereas God rescued Peter, James died (Acts 12:2); whereas Corrie ten Boom survived Ravensbrück, Betsie died. The outcomes may differ in the short run; what matters eternally is that we overcome.

Two worlds vie for humanity's attention, and these worlds are in conflict. Revelation depicts the ultimate expression of this world as Babylon the prostitute (Rev. 17:5), but our hope is in the world to come, as new Jerusalem the bride (21:2). Only those with faith to await the future world resist the allure of the prostitute; but we who do so have the privilege of being Christ's bride. The "great city" Babylon is decked with gold and pearls (17:4), but the much greater new Jerusalem is built of gold, and its gates are pearls (21:18, 21). For those ready to trust God's message, the future is well worth our wait.

It's not true hope or expectation if we already see it, Paul explains; but if our hope, our expectation, is for what we can't yet see, then through endurance we eagerly await it (Rom. 8:24–25). Indeed, God's Spirit within us groans eagerly for that day when we shall see our Lord (8:23, 26). God's Spirit keeps us faithful.

Conclusion: Why We Suffer, Why We Endure

We experience suffering:

- sometimes because of our wrong choices (Proverbs)
- always because we live in a fallen world in the midst of birthing a new one (Rom. 8:18–23)
- because God sometimes corrects us through it (Heb. 12:5–11)

- because God conforms us to Christ's image through it (Rom. 8:28–30)
- so we can learn to comfort others (2 Cor. 1:4)
- so God can be glorified by our faithfulness (compare Job 1:8; Mark 15:39; Eph. 3:10; 1 Pet. 2:12)

In the face of suffering, we hold firm because:

- we have the privilege of sharing *Christ's* suffering (Phil. 3:10; 1 Pet. 4:13)
- testing produces character (Rom. 5:3–4; James 1:3–4)
- suffering conforms the faithful to Christ's image (Phil. 3:10)
- we will share Christ's vindication and glory (Rom. 8:17; 2 Tim. 2:11–12; compare Mark 10:37–38)
- the present suffering cannot compare with our future hope (Rom. 8:18; 2 Cor. 4:17; Rev. 21:1–7; compare Rom. 5:3–5)

This world's sufferings are birth pangs heralding the world to come. The biblical message is not that we can avoid all sufferings. The biblical message tells us rather that our sufferings cannot begin to compare with the reward that awaits us when we see Jesus. God's loving plan is better for us than sparing us from all suffering; it is conforming us to the image of his Son—the crucified and risen one.

APPENDIX

The following are just samples of helpful organizations, but I have drawn on their resources in writing this book and/or have designated royalties from this book or *Miracles Today* for them. Besides those officially listed below, others include Christian Solidarity International, Christian Solidarity Worldwide, and International Christian Concern.

Some Organizations Helping Persecuted Christians

Global Christian Relief: https://globalchristianrelief.org/
Open Doors USA: https://www.opendoorsus.org/en-US/
Voice of the Martyrs: https://www.persecution.com/

Some Other Christian Organizations Providing Help for People in Need

Compassion International: https://www.compassion.com/
Iris Mozambique: https://www.irisglobal.org/
SIM Medical Missions: https://www.simusa.org/skills-interests/health-care/
World Vision: https://www.worldvision.org/

NOTES

Introduction

1. "Poverty and Development."

2. For more detail on both our stories, see Keener and Keener, *Impossible Love*.

3. Voice of Martyrs, *Whom Shall I Fear?*

4. There is, for example, no discussion of biblical documents' dates or authenticity here, the focus being their canonical voice.

5. I mix and match some translations and offer some of my own. When I offer my own translation, I usually prefer simpler colloquial English (the receptor language), changing passive to active constructions and the like rather than echoing the Greek or Hebrew syntax.

6. See, e.g., Marshall, *Blood*; Marshall and Shea, *Silenced*; Shortt, *Christianophobia*, written by the *Times Literary Supplement* religion editor; Marshall, Gilbert, and Shea, *Persecuted*; Doyle, *Killing Christians*; "Eyewitnesses to Persecution." One could also multiply individual accounts of suffering for Christ, sometimes with favorable outcomes in this life; in Europe, see, e.g., Bałuczynski, *Afraid*; Bubik, *Bubik*; Vorm, *Lives*.

7. Lee, *Persecution*.

8. Ton, *Suffering*.

9. Ton, *Suffering*, xii.

10. Even when clearly suffering for Christ, victims can question how they might have avoided the suffering had they done something differently; note, e.g., the story of Atamurat in Voice of Martyrs, *I Am N*, 298–99.

11. See Hagin, *Healing Belongs to Us*, 11, 27; Hagin, *Key to Healing*, 13; Hagin, *What Faith Is*, 7; Duplantis, "Faith the Facts"; Copeland, "Enforce Word."

12. Pettis, "Faith Prevents."

13. God heeded Moses's prayer for Israel (Exod. 33:16–17) and would have heeded even Abraham's prayer for Sodom had it held just a few more righteous residents (Gen. 18:32). God's warnings are often conditional, so that he may relent about judgment if people repent (Jer. 18:7–8; Jon. 3:4–10). But sometimes God warns a prophet not to bother praying, because God won't listen—rebellion has gone too far (Jer. 7:16; 11:14; 14:11). Sometimes he warns that even the prayers of Noah, Daniel, and Job could save only themselves (Ezek. 14:14, 20). In the New Testament, too, intercession sometimes goes only so far (1 John 5:16).

14. Readers interested in my own view may find it in Keener, *Revelation*, passim; and Brown and Keener, *Not Afraid*.

15. Young, *Walking*, 131.

210

16. Young, *Walking*, 145.

17. During the Japanese occupation, Korean Christians sought to learn from the grace that God had given their tortured pastors (Kim, *If I Perish*, 53).

Chapter 1 Jesus Is Worth Everything

1. Whether the father is already dead or the son asks for a longer delay is debated; so also is whether he envisages the original funeral or secondary burial. The demand is more about the priority of following Jesus than about the urgency of following him, but Luke 9:61–62 supplements this account with another that does address urgency.

2. Bonhoeffer, *Cost of Discipleship*, 90.

3. Wurmbrand, *Tortured for Christ* (2023), 67; compare also 110–11; "Afterword," 161.

4. Wurmbrand, *Wife*, 226.

5. I develop these paragraphs from Keener, *Matthew*, 364–65.

6. Note the hardships that then follow obedience to each of these words from the Lord. Compare many other passages, possibly including Judg. 20:18.

7. Deere, *Voice*, 87.

8. See Iris, "Core Values." Much of the wording reflects 1 Cor. 1:27.

9. See, e.g., Yung, "Endued," 81; Young, "Miracles," 116.

10. Tan, "Secret Work," 98; Leung, "Conversion," 89, 106; Oblau, "Healing in China," 309; Aikman, *Jesus in Beijing*, 43.

11. Bays, "Revival in China," 173.

12. Robert, "Introduction," 15.

13. Wu, "Dora Yu," 98. Benjamin Franklin discovered that thirty thousand people could hear Whitefield at one time (Noll, *History*, 93).

14. See, e.g., Anderson, *Introduction to Pentecostalism*, 129; Shao, "Heritage," 96; Koch, *Revival in Indonesia*, 54–57, 60–62.

15. Brougham, "Chinese in Indonesia," 141.

16. Keener, *Miracles*, 1:308, following especially Sung, *Diaries*, 190–91, 221–25 (although some question the work's authenticity).

17. Uncommon though they are, some conferences do address this. Thus, for example, I participated in a conference of the Every Nation movement in Cape Town, South Africa, that included the voices of persecuted believers.

18. On some of these revival movements, see Shaw, *Global Awakening*, including 33–53 for the revival in Korea; Noll and Nystrom, *Witnesses*, 174–81.

19. See, e.g., Ojo, "Civil War Revival."

20. On this last point, compare Johnstone, *Operation World* (1993), 293; Johnstone and Mandryk, *Operation World* (2001), 339.

21. Personal correspondence, June 4, 2023.

22. See especially Park, *Hurt*.

23. Park, *Conflict*, 12–15.

24. Kim, *If I Perish*, 33–34. For many living in secret or in the mountains because they refused to worship at the shrines, see, e.g., 49, 52. Some detention areas were too crowded for everyone to be able to lie down (118).

25. Kim, *If I Perish*, 137, 161.

26. Kim, *If I Perish*, 222. Kim herself counted rotten apples a delicacy (226).

27. Kim, *If I Perish*, 161, 171.

28. Kim, *If I Perish*, 57.

29. Shortt, *Christianophobia*, 223.

30. Shortt, *Christianophobia*, 220.

31. See, e.g., Kim, *If I Perish*, 266.

32. Shortt, *Christianophobia*, 221.

33. Shortt, *Christianophobia*, 222.

34. Marshall, Gilbert, and Shea, *Persecuted*, 1. For recent suffering in North Korea, likely the world's most repressive state, see, e.g., Martin and Bach, *Crimson Crucible*.

Chapter 2 Apostles and Suffering

1. Mission is a central issue in Acts and was never meant to be (nor is it today) a Western monopoly; see, e.g., Keener and Keener, "Commission." For example, Brazil sends forty thousand missionaries, South Korea sends close to thirty-five thousand, and Nigeria sends twenty thousand (Zurlo, *Global Christianity*, 66, 218, 269).

2. Deere, *Still Surprised*, 100.

3. 1 Cor. 4:8–13; 2 Cor. 4:7–13; 6:4–10; 11:21–33; 12:7–10. I quote from Kolenda's unpublished paper researching apostolic ministry in the Bible, shared with me in July 2024.

4. The meaning of the passage is understandably debated; for my interpretation, see Keener, *Matthew*, 360–62; Keener, *Gospel of Matthew*, 604–6. Elsewhere in Matthew, disciples are Jesus's siblings (12:50; 28:10) who could be received with food and drink (10:8–13, 42); whoever received them would receive Jesus (10:40–42).

5. In the interview in Maudlin, "God's Smuggler" (quotation on 46).

6. For early Jewish and Christian opposition to *seeking* martyrdom, see Martyrdom of Polycarp 4.1; Talbert, *Mediterranean Milieu*, 112–15.

7. Compare Kim, *If I Perish*, 139: "The harsher my torture, the more the Lord would comfort me."

8. For details, see Fitzgerald, *Cracks*.

9. See discussion in Keener, *Galatians*, 212–13; Keener, *Galatians* (Cambridge), 120–21.

10. For missions history, see, e.g., Neill, *History of Missions*; Tucker, *Jerusalem to Irian Jaya*; for Francis Asbury and early Methodists, e.g., Wigger, *American Saint*.

11. Rich Stevenson, personal correspondence, July 6, 2024.

12. Carey apparently saw the disaster as judgment but started afresh more zealously (Tucker, *Jerusalem to Irian Jaya*, 120).

13. See, e.g., Anderson, *Golden Shore*; Hunt, *Bless God*.

14. See Taylor and Taylor, *Secret*; on the Boxer Rebellion, see 214.

15. For earlier groundbreaking ministry there, with accompanying signs, see, e.g., Anderson, *Pelendo*; Emmett, *Burton*.

16. See Hochschild, *King Leopold's Ghost*.

17. See Williams, *Black Americans and Evangelization*, 138–40; Phipps, *William Sheppard*.

18. See Kara, *Cobalt Red*.

19. Roseveare, "Counting the Cost," 37–38. The article reflects her message from Urbana '76; I heard her similar message at Urbana '87. See further, e.g., Lagerborg, *Though Lions Roar*; Benge and Benge, *Helen Roseveare*; Roseveare, *Living Sacrifice*.

20. They were close friends with the Congo missionaries who owned our home before we did, and thus appear in, e.g., Braun, *Here Am I*, 82; Braun, *On the Way*, 230, 255, and especially 213.

21. His work with MAF appears in Hege, *We Two Alone*, 187. Hege was wounded when her missionary colleague Irene Ferrel was killed.

22. Again see Braun, *Here Am I*, 143–44; Braun, *On the Way*, 81. They too invested in leadership training in a movement that continues to bear fruit globally, today through Evangelism Resources (https://www.evangelism-resources.org/).

23. Tucker, *Heaven*, 210.

24. Tucker, *Heaven*, 224.

25. Gohr, "Blood."

26. Recounted in Tari, *Mighty Wind*. On the revival, see the concise Wiyono, "Timor Revival."

27. On Pullinger's ministry among addicts and others, see Pullinger, *Chasing Dragon*.

28. I take much of the following summary from Iris, "Iris Story."

29. Baker and Baker, *Always Enough*, 50.

30. Baker and Baker, *Always Enough*, 52.

31. Baker and Baker, *Always Enough*, 85.

32. Baker and Baker, *Always Enough*, 84.

33. Baker and Baker, *Always Enough*, 137–58.

34. Before her passing, Sandy was able to publish some of their stories in Thomas, *Walls*.

35. Olson, *Bruchko*; Olson and Lund, *Bruchko and Miracle*.

36. Partee, *Adventure in Africa*; Stafford, "Sit Still."

37. Dan Taylor, August 15, 1990. I had learned even more from Everett and Esther Cook, church planters who earlier mentored me when they ran Springfield Victory Mission.

38. Silliman, "Missionaries Killed." Global Christian Relief documented over one hundred kidnappings targeting pastors or other Christians in 2024 (GCR Red List, 17).

39. Brown, *Authentic Fire*, 76.

40. Michael L. Brown, personal correspondence, May 16, 2024. The journal entry is from 2012.

41. Brown, *Authentic Fire*, 77.

42. For another case in India of carrying on a murdered husband's ministry, see Voice of Martyrs, *Hearts of Fire 2*, 238.

43. For other Christian widows forgiving their husbands' killers, see, e.g., Voice of Martyrs, *Hearts of Fire 2*, 55–56, 85–88, 301–5.

44. For cases of persecution, from which, however, the ministry teams were usually protected, see Tari, *Mighty Wind*, 162–64 (the martyr is on 164).

45. Interview, May 23, 2012; updated confirmation, personal correspondence, May 26, 2012; September 19, 2024.

46. Correspondence from a mutual friend of Neil and Priya, January 10, 2009. Religious disagreement is not the only cause for martyrdom in Sri Lanka; twenty years after starting a house church, Kalithas's ministry had so impacted the community that black-market traders, losing too much business, had him beaten so badly that he died two days later (Voice of Martyrs mailing, August 6, 2024).

47. Nettleton, *When Faith Is Forbidden*, 241–42. For four thousand Laotian Christians earlier forced to stop meeting, see News Briefs (1995).

48. Regarding Ahmed in Kashmir, in a 2024 Voice of Martyrs mailing.

49. Panahi, *Didn't Survive*. Some groups in Iran fare even worse than Christians; Baha'is "may be murdered with impunity" (Shortt, *Christianophobia*, 46); likewise, in Pakistan, "at least ninety-nine Ahmadis were killed in faith-based attacks during 2010" (Shortt, *Christianophobia*, 81). My friendship with Nabeel Qureshi (Qureshi, *Seeking Allah, Finding Jesus*) helped alert me to the marginalization Ahmadis endure from many other Muslims.

50. Voice of Martyrs update, June 1, 2024.

Chapter 3 Biblical Prophets and Suffering

1. Iriyah was the grandson of a certain Hananiah, maybe the false prophet Jeremiah earlier confronted; but then, Hananiah was a common name (e.g., 2 Chron. 26:11; Ezra 10:28; Neh. 3:8, 30; 7:2; Jer. 36:12; Dan. 1:6).

2. See, e.g., Christerson and Flory, *Rise of Network Christianity*, 127–29.

3. See, e.g., Cosmos, *Huguenot Prophecy*, 46, 51, 113.

4. For unfulfilled (at least in their lifetime) Camisard hopes, see, e.g., Cosmos, *Huguenot Prophecy*, 35, 48, 59, 69–70. More problematic, though understandable, were the calls to arms (Cosmos, *Huguenot Prophecy*, 85–105, especially 89–90, 96–97, 101) and especially to vengeance (Cosmos, *Huguenot Prophecy*, 101; compare 144). Obviously those who set deadlines for the Lord's return have brought disappointment, including in 1981 (Christerson and Flory, *Rise of*

Network Christianity, 127, cite the example of Chuck Smith's predictions) or 1988 (Whisenant, *Reasons*). Additionally, Kyle, *Last Days*, 120, notes some other failed predictions.

5. Voice of Martyrs, *Hearts of Fire 2*, 256–57. For her and her colleague's story in greater detail, see Rostampour and Amirizadeh, *Captive in Iran*.

6. Kim, *If I Perish*, 218.

7. Kim, *If I Perish*, 216.

8. I borrow most of the wording from Keener and Keener, *Impossible Love*, 123–24.

9. In other circles, denying God's power today is more popular (compare 2 Tim. 3:5).

10. Adapted from my blog post, Keener, "Against Grain."

11. This paragraph is especially from my blog post, Keener, "Call and Cost."

12. For complaints that God waits too long to punish the wicked, see, e.g., Pss. 10:1–2; 13:2; 35:16–17; 74:10; 94:3; Hab. 1:2–4. God may often delay to let the wicked destroy themselves (Pss. 5:10; 9:15; 35:8; 37:13–15; 81:12; 141:10; Rom. 1:24, 26, 28), but also to allow the opportunity for repentance (Ezek. 18:23; 2 Pet. 3:9).

13. I adapt this section from my blog post, Keener, "Prophets Wrong."

14. February 10, 1982. Keep in mind that in 1982 most of us did not yet use inclusive language, but the wording in those days was nevertheless meant to cover both genders.

15. See Edwards, "Distinguishing Marks," a nuanced work valuable today as well.

16. See, e.g., "Nutritional Crusade."

17. Compare discussion in Keener, "Political Prophecies"; Keener, "Trump Prophecies." Given the 2024 election outcome, many in 2020 may have indeed been hearing something, just without specificity concerning timing, which is also true in many biblical prophecies. (Whether you see that outcome as a blessing, a judgment, or a mixture of each may depend on your political proclivities.)

18. I describe some of this experience in Keener, *Gift and Giver*, 45–46; Keener and Keener, *Impossible Love*, 22–23.

19. See Keener, *Spirit Hermeneutics*.

20. Catholics and Orthodox have a slightly larger canon than Protestants, but we all agree on most of it. For more specifics, see varied discussions in, e.g., McDonald, *Canon*; Kruger, *Question of Canon*.

Chapter 4 "Ordinary" Christians and Suffering

1. One cannot plow a straight furrow when looking backward. Right after this, Jesus sends out laborers for his kingdom (Luke 10:1–2).

2. Nettleton, *When Faith Is Forbidden*, 71–72.

3. Ibraheem with Bach, *Shackled*, 153, 175, 207.

4. Compare Hagin, *Prayer Secrets*, 22: "The offering was about $20 short of what we had claimed. I suggested that we count it again, because the money had to be there, for we had claimed it. I told him . . . that if it were not there, then I would have to go to every church where I had preached and tell them that Jesus was a liar and that the Bible was not so. If it did not work, I wanted to throw it away. I am just that honest." What if the problem was not the Bible or the intensity of his faith, but his interpretation of the Bible? Despite the wording here, in practice Hagin would have found a different explanation rather than throwing out the Bible. Sometimes his expectation was not effective immediately (see, e.g., Hagin, *Prevailing Prayer to Peace*, 75).

5. Hagin, *What Faith Is*, 3–4, 6, 12, 18, 20, 30; Hagin, *Thresholds*, 11; Hagin, in *The Word of Faith* (March 1983), 3.

6. Lives of the Prophets 1:1 (Charlesworth, *OTP* 2:385/§24; Schermann, p. 75, line 1); Jerusalem Talmud tractate Sanhedrin 10:2, §6; Pesiqta Rabbati 4:3; Justin, *Dialogue with Trypho* 120; Martyrdom and Ascension of Isaiah 5:1–14; Urbach, *Sages*, 1:559. Compare the gentile story in Ovid, *Metamorphoses* 8.758–76; for sawing apart as a punishment, Suetonius, *Caligula*

27.3; Genesis Rabbah 65:22; possibly (though the consensus of translations is against it) 2 Sam. 12:31; 1 Chron. 20:3.

7. Ibraheem with Bach, *Shackled*, 209.

8. Some have even prayed for suffering to help them grow (Voice of Martyrs, *Hearts of Fire 2*, 291); but testing comes easily enough, and overconfidence (Mark 10:38–39; 14:31) can lead us to underestimate our frailty (14:50, 66–72). Compare again Matt. 6:13; Luke 11:4.

9. Athanasius, *Festal Letters* 10 (Bray, *Peter*, 71).

10. Hilary of Arles, *Commentary on 1 Peter* (Bray, *Peter*, 71–72).

11. Sanneh, *West African Christianity*, 36, 167, 181–83; Isichei, *Christianity in Africa*, 233; Noll, *History*, 341.

12. Marshall, Gilbert, and Shea, *Persecuted*, 5. For the Christian movement's origination in Asia, see, e.g., Keener, "Asia and Europe"; see also discussion in Keener, "Western Religion."

13. Marshall, Gilbert, and Shea, *Persecuted*, 16, although they offered this estimate before some newer restrictions in China.

14. Shortt, *Christianophobia*, 117. See further Boyd, *Bomb*; Sanusi, *Gloria*.

15. Shortt, *Christianophobia*, 51.

16. E.g., Iraq, in Shortt, *Christianophobia*, 37.

17. E.g., Turkey, especially before the Armenian genocide (compare, e.g., Shortt, *Christianophobia*, 87, especially 91, where they remained at 13 percent in the early twentieth century).

18. Regarding Axum, see, e.g., Rufinus, *Ecclesiastical History*, book 1; Isaac, *Ethiopian Church*, 20; Jones and Monroe, *History of Ethiopia*, 26–31; Isichei, *Christianity in Africa*, 18, 31.

19. Taylor and Taylor, *Secret*, 141–45.

20. Wurmbrand, *Tortured for Christ* (2023), 88, 90; see also Wurmbrand, *Wife*, 41, 62.

21. Wurmbrand, *Wife*, 185–87.

22. Voice of Martyrs, *Hearts of Fire 2*, 187–93. For other cases of slanderous misrepresentation, see, e.g., 204–5.

23. Shortt, *Christianophobia*, 13.

Chapter 5 Sharing with *Jesus* in Suffering

1. On the "one thing lacking," John Piper remarks, "*The love offering of Christ is to be presented in person . . . to the peoples for whom He died*" (Piper, "Missions When Dying Is Gain," as cited in Voice of Martyrs, *Hearts of Fire 2*, 292).

2. Ibraheem with Bach, *Shackled*, 186.

3. Voice of Martyrs, *Hearts of Fire 2*, 220.

4. Roseveare, "Counting the Cost," 38–39. Similar is the experience of Jon in Malaysia, who while being beaten experienced a vision of Jesus being beaten, and who celebrated suffering for Christ (Voice of Martyrs, *I Am N*, 118–19).

5. A plaque inscribed with Rev. 6:10–11 appears at the mass grave of 483 Nigerians killed by Islamic militants in 2020 (Weber, "Cheeks").

6. Here I condense and adapt my article, Keener, "Succeed at Suffering," with permission from George P. Wood. At its 2025 convention, the Evangelical Press Association awarded this article first place in the biblical exposition category.

7. E.g., Josephus, *Jewish War* 1.664, 668; *Jewish Antiquities* 17.188; 18.36, 122, 136; *The Life* 37, 65; Luke 3:19; 9:7; Acts 13:1.

8. Even in Mexico, 2024 saw "138 verified Christian disappearances" targeting Christians speaking against trafficking and the like (GCR Red List, 17, 26; compare Open Doors, "World Watch List 2025," 40–41).

9. Kempis, *Imitation of Christ*, 83 ("On the Few Lovers of the Cross of Jesus"), often cited (e.g., in "Line of Demarcation"; Alcorn, *All About Jesus*, 243).

Chapter 6 Learning from the Persecuted Church

1. Josephus, *Jewish Antiquities* 18.63–64, 117–19; 20.200–201; Tacitus, *Annals* 15.44; Pliny, *Epistles* 10.96; compare also the expulsion from Rome occasioned by Jewish debates about Christ in Suetonius, *Claudius* 25.4. Post–New Testament early Christian works also emphasize it (e.g., 1 Clement 5.4–7; Ignatius, passim; Martyrdom of Polycarp).

2. Wurmbrand, *Tortured for Christ* (2023), 51, 142; Wurmbrand, *Wife*, 296. Grounds for imprisonment were often fabricated (Wurmbrand, *Wife*, 309).

3. Wurmbrand, *Tortured for Christ* (2023), 35.

4. Wurmbrand, *Wife*, 123, 146, noting that this torture was often applied all night after a full day of labor.

5. Wurmbrand, *Wife*, 109.

6. Wurmbrand, *Wife*, 182, 199, 232.

7. Wurmbrand, *Wife*, 177–80.

8. Wurmbrand, *Tortured for Christ* (2023), 35.

9. Wurmbrand, *Tortured for Christ* (2023), 34.

10. Wurmbrand, *Wife*, 162.

11. Wurmbrand, *Wife*, 183.

12. Wurmbrand, *Wife*, 35.

13. Wurmbrand, *Wife*, 36.

14. Wurmbrand, *Wife*, 36.

15. Wurmbrand, *Tortured for Christ* (2023), 147. He also invites us to feel their pain (153). Apologetics that answered hostile propaganda was also a major part of witness (150). Compare partnership in Istrate, "Partnership."

16. Wurmbrand, *Tortured for Christ* (2023), "Afterword," 156.

17. Marshall, Gilbert, and Shea, *Persecuted*, 311.

18. Shortt, *Christianophobia*, ix. Specifically in the US, by contrast, anti-Jewish attacks outnumber anti-Muslim and anti-Christian attacks.

19. Open Doors, "World Watch List 2024"; compare also Langham's work in "Langham Trains Pastors."

20. Marshall, Gilbert, and Shea, *Persecuted*, 4.

21. See, e.g., Shortt, *Christianophobia*, 264, 270–71.

22. News briefs (2012), quoting Hillary Clinton.

23. GCR Red List, 10. Russian military operations have also severely damaged or destroyed 1,270 churches in Ukraine (GCR Red List, 24).

24. Global Christian Relief, "Persecution Trends."

25. GCR Red List, 12. Given the difficulties of documentation in some countries, actual figures may vary (see especially 31–32).

26. See Doyle, *Dreams*, 244–45.

27. Shortt, *Christianophobia*, 121.

28. Marshall, Gilbert, and Shea, *Persecuted*, 242, 286.

29. Cited in Global Christian Relief, "Persecution Reports: Nigeria."

30. Chandler, "Hundreds Killed."

31. Chimtom, "Christians Slaughtered."

32. GCR Red List, 8, with a figure of 9,814. Open Doors' "World Watch List 2025," 5, 44, using a different method regarding what counted as martyrdom, estimated a much lower 3,100.

33. Shortt, *Christianophobia*, 111, citing sixty thousand from a source already in 2008.

34. Voice of Martyrs, *I Am N*, 169.

35. Voice of Martyrs, *I Am N*, 170.

36. Compass Direct, July 11, 2006.

37. Weber, "Cheeks," who also notes that several days after the reporter visited, militants killed two hundred other people in the area.

38. Voice of the Martyrs mailing, January 1, 2025, 3.

39. Weber, "Cheeks," notes that all the families in one service in Abuja had been touched by the conflict.

40. Voice of Martyrs March 24, 2024, email.

41. Weber, "Cheeks." On another camp, see Nwachukwu, "Ripped Apart."

42. Weber, "Cheeks."

43. Similarly, several years ago Dachollom Datiri, president of the Church of Christ in Nations, an evangelical Nigerian denomination, noted that "more than 1,000 of his members in 50 communities have lost their homes and churches to Fulani attacks" (Weber, "Cheeks").

44. Global Christian Relief email, April 14, 2024; GCR Red List, 38.

45. Voice of Martyrs, *I Am N*, 244–45.

46. Voice of Martyrs, "Nigerian Christian"; also Voice of Martyrs, *I Am N*, 220–21.

47. Voice of Martyrs, *I Am N*, 65.

48. The same has been true in better-publicized cases elsewhere, such as Egypt (Shortt, *Christianophobia*, 24) and Nigeria (Shortt, *Christianophobia*, 119).

49. The attack also appears in Weber, "Cheeks." For a video report, see "Jos Suicide Bombing."

50. I discuss some of these matters in Keener, "Mayhem." For more recent coverage, see Weber, "Cheeks"; more briefly, Chandler, "Hundreds Killed"; Casper, "Christmas Massacres."

51. Kristof, *Chasing Hope*, 296–97. For more on Darfur, see Hagan and Rymond-Richmond, *Darfur*.

52. Shortt, *Christianophobia*, x, 147.

53. Shortt, *Christianophobia*, ix.

54. Weber, "Cheeks."

55. Parkinson and Hinshaw, *Bring Back Our Girls*, 55, 59–60. One Nigerian woman, Oby Ezekwesili, was raising significant awareness (62–63).

56. Parkinson and Hinshaw, *Bring Back Our Girls*, 138–39.

57. Parkinson and Hinshaw, *Bring Back Our Girls*, 1; they note especially a tweet from Hillary Clinton (Parkinson and Hinshaw, *Bring Back Our Girls*, 78–79).

58. Local Christians and Muslims in Chibok itself coexisted peacefully and even intermarried (Parkinson and Hinshaw, *Bring Back Our Girls*, 17).

59. Parkinson and Hinshaw, *Bring Back Our Girls*, 106–7.

60. Parkinson and Hinshaw, *Bring Back Our Girls*, 139.

61. Parkinson and Hinshaw, *Bring Back Our Girls*, 140.

62. Parkinson and Hinshaw, *Bring Back Our Girls*, 142.

63. Shortt, *Christianophobia*, 14, notes Egypt, where, conversely, Muslim converts to Christianity "have been arrested and sometimes tortured."

64. Parkinson and Hinshaw, *Bring Back Our Girls*, 270–74.

65. GCR Red List, 17. Kidnapping is a risk elsewhere as well; my wife and I barely evaded being kidnapped during a visit to Congo-Brazzaville in summer 2008.

66. Compare, e.g., the killing of church leaders at a Sunday evening prayer meeting in News Briefs (1992).

67. Weber, "Cheeks" (noting more than 1,300 murdered in the first half of 2018, in some 314 villages).

68. See Usry and Keener, *Black Man's Religion*, 89–90.

69. See, further, Turaki, "Legacy."

70. Although others' subsequent reports appear unaware of my own testimony, they have reported the presence of Arabic speakers in some other Islamist actions in Nigeria, as well as some Boko Haram soldiers being trained abroad (Shortt, *Christianophobia*, 122).

71. Also recounted in Keener, "Mayhem." This appears to be the same incident in Kaduna mentioned in Shortt, *Christianophobia*, 111. On Kaduna persecution, see further Ozovehe, "Impacts." Sunday Bobai Agang, who now has his PhD and leads a seminary, has become a

significant leader in reconciliation and has published many books, such as Agang, *Impact*; Agang, *Evil Strikes*; Agang, *Moral Values*; he edited *African Public Theology*.

72. Open Doors, "He Is Always with Us." Compare also Open Doors, "World Watch List 2025," 29.

73. Mandryk, *Operation World*, 177.

74. Johnstone and Mandryk, *Operation World* (2001), 552; Mandryk, *Operation World* (2010), 722. At one local university, militants slaughtered some five hundred Tutsis and their Hutu defenders (Ilibagiza, *Left to Tell*, 99).

75. McDade, "Cannot Burn Jesus."

76. GCR Red List, 9.

77. GCR Red List, 15.

78. Voice of Martyrs, *I Am N*, 159–60.

79. McDade, "Cannot Burn Jesus," also noting that beheading is a typical killing method for the group.

80. McDade, "Cannot Burn Jesus." That assailants are often themselves victims can further complicate the ethics of war, although necessity limits options. For a Portuguese BBC report noting beheadings, see https://www.bbc.com/portuguese/internacional-54906823 (accessed Feb. 3, 2025; cited in Iacomini, "Unrest").

81. Voice of the Martyrs update, May 23, 2024.

82. Voice of the Martyrs update, May 7, 2024.

83. Voice of the Martyrs update, May 21, 2024.

84. I take the quotation from "Prisoner's Song."

85. The song quoted above is also the title of her book: Berhane, *Song*. See also "Singer Released"; Scammel, "Helen Berhane."

86. Voice of Martyrs, *I Am N*, 2, 14–15.

87. Voice of the Martyrs, June 25, 2024.

88. See Ogilvie and Miller, *Refuge Denied*; Thomas and Witts, *Voyage of Damned*.

89. Estimated percentages vary widely, from 6 to 20 percent (Miller, "Evangelicals," 250).

90. Shortt, *Christianophobia*, 20.

91. Shortt, *Christianophobia*, 17.

92. Shortt, *Christianophobia*, 18.

93. Shortt, *Christianophobia*, 18.

94. Shortt, *Christianophobia*, 19.

95. Shortt, *Christianophobia*, 17. Influenced by Wahhabi ideology introduced from the 1970s onward, many Egyptian Muslims see Coptic Christians as inferior, immoral, idolatrous infidels (Shortt, *Christianophobia*, 3–4).

96. Shortt, *Christianophobia*, 104. More recently, nationalists have been systematically removing evidence of the historic Armenian presence.

97. Marshall, Gilbert and Shea, *Persecuted*, 130–33; Shortt, *Christianophobia*, 106. Compare also the long denials of some Japanese politicians regarding the genocidal rape of Nanjing (on which see Chang, "Rape of Nanking"; Chang, *Rape of Nanking*). Azerbaijan forced 120,001 Armenians to leave their homes in Nagorno-Karabakh in 2024 (GCR Red List, 14).

98. Hefley and Hefley, *Blood*, 303.

99. As noted in Shortt, *Christianophobia*, 11, "Islamist demagogues frequently use events thousands of miles away as a means of scapegoating their Christian neighbors"; e.g., a pope quoted out of context as linking Islam and violence led to Christians being murdered in Africa and Asia.

100. Marshall, Gilbert, and Shea, *Persecuted*, 287–88.

101. Shortt, *Christianophobia*, 64.

102. Shortt, *Christianophobia*, 66–67.

103. Shortt, *Christianophobia*, 76.

104. Shortt, *Christianophobia*, 77–78.

105. Shortt, *Christianophobia*, 256.

106. See Global Christian Relief update, May 30, 2024.

107. Voice of Martyrs, *I Am N*, 38–42.

108. Voice of Martyrs, *I Am N*, 128–29.

109. "Targets for Oppression." Nevertheless, this action contravenes Pakistan's Penal Code (364A; 365B). Muslim men can marry multiple wives.

110. Maust, *Peace*. See briefly Tapia, "Arrest."

111. "Terror."

112. Voice of Martyrs, *I Am N*, 230–33. Such violence was not new; for example, in 1996, as Muslim rioters were burning churches, they burned to death a Pentecostal pastor, along with "his wife, daughter, and niece" (Shortt, *Christianophobia*, 129).

113. Shortt, *Christianophobia*, 129.

114. Marshall, Gilbert, and Shea, *Persecuted*, 227.

115. Shortt, *Christianophobia*, 32.

116. Doyle, *Killing Christians*, 97.

117. Doyle, *Killing Christians*, 99.

118. Doyle, *Killing Christians*, 101.

119. Doyle, *Killing Christians*, 112, 118–19.

120. Doyle, *Killing Christians*, 131, 135–36.

121. Doyle, *Killing Christians*, 144–45.

122. Marshall, Gilbert, and Shea, *Persecuted*, 165–66, noting that the Saudi embassy distributed this fatwa in the US.

123. Marshall, Gilbert, and Shea, *Persecuted*, 192, on scores of Egyptian girls; I supplement this with oral reports from Nigeria.

124. Marshall, Gilbert, and Shea, *Persecuted*, 204–5, citing multiple instances in Pakistan.

125. Marshall, Gilbert, and Shea, *Persecuted*, 193–94.

126. Here I draw from many sources, including Shortt, *Christianophobia*, 154–55.

127. For regulations cutting off funding for Christians, see, e.g., Kaur, "Regulation." The Hindu nationalist government has cut off millions in funding that was helping the needy in India.

128. Global Christian Relief, "Persecution Trends."

129. See, e.g., "Rakbar Khan"; Human Rights Watch, "Cow Protection Groups"; "Fresh Fears"; Jain, "Cow Vigilantes."

130. E.g., "Revenge in Gujarat"; "Genocide in Gujarat."

131. See, e.g., Marshall, Gilbert, and Shea, *Persecuted*, 101–9.

132. Open Doors report, May 6, 2024.

133. Shortt, *Christianophobia*, 149.

134. Wunderink, "Worse."

135. Shortt, *Christianophobia*, 159.

136. Hart, "Believers Displaced." Violence has since recurred (Global Christian Relief, "New Conflict"). GCR Red List, 15, claims "over 60,000" displaced.

137. Limaye, "Torture"; see also Arya, "Manipur Women."

138. E.g., "Bombshell on Manipur Police."

139. For an example of someone murdering his estranged wife in church, see "Gunman Kills Wife."

140. Sarnoff and Hutchinson, "Miracle." An AK-47 jamming allowed Farid, a believer in Afghanistan, to escape unharmed (Voice of Martyrs, *I Am N*, 132–33).

141. Smith, "Parishioners."

142. Tammy shared the account with me on December 17, 1991. In my journal I wrote, "Tammy thinks that maybe Shonda heard and believed the gospel. . . . For Shonda, now, we can never make a difference. I look at my dissertation and wonder if I make any difference . . . so meaningless; a 14-year old girl who should be alive and shouldn't have had to have lived in terror was strangled by some drug dealer doing business."

143. Ibraheem with Bach, *Shackled*, 273.

144. Ibraheem with Bach, *Shackled*, 280. For her military analogy, compare 2 Tim. 2:3–4.

Chapter 7 In Sickness and in Health

1. Destiny Image, "Powerful Sermon"; see now also Johnson, *Sting*.

2. Jack Deere likewise mentions being sick at an entire conference on healing (Deere, *Still Surprised*, 118).

3. Hagin, *What Faith Is*, 12. He also admitted that people were healed without following his line of teaching, but he sometimes said that it was because they were spiritual babes and didn't know any better (e.g., Hagin, *Prayer Secrets*, 10).

4. Hagin, *What Faith Is*, 7.

5. Hagin even expected people to have the ability to decide when to die (Hagin, *Covenant*, chap. 5): "So don't stop at less than 70. If you are satisfied with 70, go on home. If you're not satisfied, go on up to 80. When you get there, if you're not satisfied, go on up to 90. If you get satisfied, then go on home." But compare Deut. 31:14; 1 Sam. 26:10; 1 Kings 2:1; 1 Chron. 17:11.

6. Quadratus fragment 2.

7. Deere, *Still Surprised*.

8. Deere, *Darkness*, 201–3.

9. Curtis, *Faith*, 11–12, 26–50; Kidd, "Healing," 165.

10. Curtis, *Faith*, 21.

11. Curtis, *Faith*, 41.

12. Curtis, *Faith*, 51–80.

13. Curtis, *Faith*, 1. Here I reuse my summary from Keener, *Miracles*, 1:391–92, 397–99.

14. Curtis, *Faith*, 4–5.

15. Curtis, *Faith*, 5. See also the early summary of her account in Gordon, "Ministry of Healing," 241–43.

16. Opp, *Lord for Body*, 46–47, 196; Curtis, *Faith*, 81–82, 96–97; Alexander, *Pentecostal Healing*, 24–27.

17. Opp, *Lord for Body*, 129; Baxter, *Healing*, 99–100, 128–30.

18. Curtis, *Faith*, 194.

19. Curtis, *Faith*, 194; Hudson, "British Pentecostals," 295; Anderson, "Signs and Blunders," 207.

20. Opp, *Lord for Body*, 103–11, 115.

21. Baer, "Empowered Bodies," 249.

22. Curtis, *Faith*, 88–90.

23. Curtis, *Faith*, 11, 88, 197, 199.

24. Curtis, *Faith*, 197–99.

25. Hudson, "British Pentecostals," 297.

26. See King, *Believer with Authority*; King, *Moving Mountains*.

27. Chin, "Blindsided," 62.

28. A songwriter, David composed the song "Dying," about his experience of facing the likelihood of death in his twenties (see https://www.youtube.com/watch?v=vfxsC6IiwNA, accessed April 30, 2025).

29. See, e.g., Koestler, "Kepler and Psychology"; Lindberg and Numbers, *Essays*; Brooke, *Science*; Barbour, *Religion and Science*, 24–29, 64–65; Brooke, *Reconstructing Nature*; Livingstone, Hart, and Noll, *Perspective*; Frankenberry, *Faith*; Lindberg, *Beginnings*; Numbers, *Galileo*; Hunter, *Boyle*; Peterson, *Flat Earth*. See concisely the articles in *Christian History* 76, no. 4 (2002).

30. For the charismatic figure, see Mandryk, *Operation World*, 269. Pew Research Center in 2018 estimated the Christian population at 95.8 percent (cited in US Department of State, "2018 Report").

31. I borrow many lines in this chapter, and especially this section, from Keener, *Miracles Today*, 217–21.

32. Taylor and Taylor, *Secret*, 118; more detail in Taylor and Taylor, *Early Years*.

33. Taylor and Taylor, *Secret*, 134–35, 167.

34. Taylor and Taylor, *Secret*, 173–75.

35. Taylor and Taylor, *Secret*, 182, 213.

36. Kenneth Copeland, "God's Faith" (an audio recording). Victor Paul Wierwille, founder of The Way International cult, used the same argument in *Studies*, 16.

37. White, *Faith Under Fire*, 64. Many Spirit-filled believers emphasize this character of the kingdom (see, e.g., Vineyard USA, "Core Beliefs").

38. Morphew, *Breakthrough*, 143 (as cited in Clark, "Inaugurated Kingdom," 25).

39. Baker and Baker, *Always Enough*, 171–72.

40. Roseveare, "Cost of Loving Jesus."

41. On Wilberforce, see, e.g., Tomkins, *Wilberforce;* Metaxas, *Grace;* compare Wolffe, *Expansion.*

42. See Voice of Martyrs, *Hearts of Fire 2*, 269–70, 274.

43. Voice of Martyrs, *Hearts of Fire*, 82 (Aida's full story is 77–107).

44. Despite limited biblical precedent in Mark 14:36 (compare 1:40), I don't think we need to preface all prayers with, "If it be your will . . ." God knows his will, and if something's not his will, he doesn't have to do it whether we concede that point or not! Jesus sometimes welcomes persistent faith that even tries to persuade him (e.g., Matt. 15:24–28).

Chapter 8 For Richer, for Poorer

1. It precedes those known as prosperity preachers; see Harrell, *All Things Are Possible*, 48–49, 105, 159, 200–201.

2. Hagin, *Midas Touch.*

3. Oliver, *Revivals*, 239, noting Hagin's criticism of gimmicks such as promises of specific material benefits for giving, or treating prosperity as an indication of spiritual maturity.

4. Blomberg, *Neither Poverty nor Riches*. My published review (Keener, review of Blomberg, *Neither Poverty nor Riches*) sounds less positive only because editing for space constraints deleted more of my favorable comments.

5. Hagin, *Godliness Is Profitable*, 15–16. Hagin's works went through many printings, and I am not sure whether pagination changed in any of these.

6. Hagin, *Godliness Is Profitable*, passim; Hagin, *Redeemed*, 1.

7. Hagin, *Ministry of a Prophet*, 24.

8. Hagin, *Ministry of a Prophet*, 9. His argument is that God didn't put them there for the devil's children; otherwise, he reasons, God "loves the Devil's children more than He does His children."

9. Hagin, *Authority*, 21–22.

10. Hagin, *Redeemed*, 1.

11. Hagin, *Redeemed*, 5–6.

12. The example of Abraham does illustrate that God can provide abundance; the example of Paul's ministry shows that God can also bless us whether we have little or much (Phil. 4:11–12).

13. Hagin, *Prayer Secrets*, 18; compare Matt. 5:45.

14. Hagin, *Prayer Secrets*, 19; compare *Turn Faith Loose*, 16. He uses Matt. 7:11, but what if the child in Matt. 7:10 had asked his wise father for a snake?

15. Hagin, *Prayer Secrets;* compare p. 20.

16. See Hagin, *Visions*, 126; Hagin, *Prayer Secrets*, 20; Capps, *Tongue*, 57; Copeland, *Laws*, 104.

17. Copeland, *Laws*, 53. He boasts that his children can believe God "for anything in the world and get it!" (*Laws*, 25).

18. Copeland, *Laws*, 103, emphasis his.

19. Capps, "Keys," no. 3 (audiotape).

20. Copeland, *Decision*, 5, noting that choosers are in God's class of being. Discussion of some prosperity teachers' affirmations of believers' divinity (Copeland, *Laws*, 15; Capps, "Keys," nos. 1–5 [audiotapes]; compare Hagin, *Authority*, 11–12; Hagin, *Zoe*, 36, 39–42; Hagin, *Name of Jesus*, 105–6) would take us too far afield, but it is particularly concerning.

21. Copeland, *Laws*, 73 (compare 70ff.).

22. Copeland, *Laws*, 63–66.

23. Copeland, *Laws*, 66, 87, 91; compare *Believer's Voice of Victory* 7 (4, April 1979).

24. Capps, *Tongue*, 81.

25. Copeland, *Laws*, 59.

26. Hagin, *Prevailing Prayer to Peace*, 85; compare Copeland, *Laws*, 13; Capps, *Tongue*, 83; Wierwille, *Studies*, 18. For earlier examples, see Harrell, *All Things Are Possible*, 229.

27. Fee, *Disease*, 4; see Deissmann, *Light*, 151, 194, 202–3; Kim, *Form and Structure*, 15–16, 25–34; Aune, *Environment*, 163; Stowers, *Letter Writing*, 74; Grant, *Gods*, 57. For health wishes, see, e.g., 2 Maccabees 11:28; 3 Maccabees 7:1–2; Letter of Aristeas 35; *Corpus Papyrorum Judaicarum* 1:244–45, §132; *Zenon Papyri* 59060.1; *Oxyrhynchus Papyri* 292; *Griechische Papyri zu Giessen* 17; 80.13; Cicero, *Epistulae ad familiares* 14.8.1; Diogenes Laertius 8.4.79.

28. Walker, "Where God Guides."

29. Hammond, "Heroes." The account about the crates comes especially from Irwin, "Daily Bread"; Irwin worked with Trasher before her death. Recently, see also Ma, "Gospel," 163–64.

30. See, e.g., Müller, *Autobiography*.

31. Uwimana, *From Red Earth*, 126.

32. Fodor, "Migrants."

33. Omer, "Global Water Crisis."

34. UNESCO, "Valuing Water Supply."

35. UNICEF, "Nearly Every Minute."

36. It has also occurred during times of intense revival and persecution (see, e.g., Kim, *If I Perish*, 52).

37. See, e.g., Exod. 22:25; 23:6, 11; Lev. 19:10; 23:22; 25:35; Deut. 15:7, 9, 11; 24:14; Pss. 12:5; 72:12–13; 112:9; 140:12; Prov. 14:21, 31; 17:5; 28:8; 31:9, 20; Isa. 3:14–15; 10:2; 11:4; 58:7; Jer. 5:28; 22:16; Ezek. 16:49; 5:12; Zech. 7:10; Mark 10:21; Luke 12:33; 14:13; Acts 4:34; Rom. 15:26; 2 Cor. 8:14; Gal. 2:10; for a fuller sampling, see Sider, *Cry Justice*.

38. On these figures, see, e.g., Galli, *Francis of Assisi*; Evans, *Wycliffe*.

39. Peter Riedeman, an Anabaptist (1506–1556), argued for communal sharing of goods (still practiced among Hutterites; McGee, "Possessions," 167–68; Williams, *Radical Reformation*, 232, 426–29), though among Anabaptists, only Hutterites practiced this literally (Finger, *Meals*, 21–22). For Moravians, see Williams, *Radical Reformation*, 429; compare 229–33.

40. Anderson, *Introduction to Pentecostalism*, 135; Zhaoming, "Chinese Denominations," 452–64; Yamamori and Chan, *Witnesses*, 54–62; Wesley, *Church*, 56. Starting in 1921, they predated Communism's ascendancy in China.

41. Jackson, *Quest*, 32; Di Sabatino, "Frisbee," 395–96.

42. The following several paragraphs follow Keener, *Matthew*, 150–51.

43. Jennings, *Good News to the Poor*, 157–79.

44. Jennings, *Good News to the Poor*, 36, 98–102.

45. Jennings, *Good News to the Poor*, 111–16.

46. Jennings, *Good News to the Poor*, 105.

47. The church or parachurch organizations today typically offer better distribution mechanisms than we often have individually (see Acts 4:34–35; 6:1–3; 11:29–30; 1 Cor. 16:1–4), and we also do well to support the ministry, including outreach (Luke 10:7; Rom. 15:24; 1 Cor. 9:3–14; Gal. 6:6; Phil. 4:14–16; 1 Tim. 5:17–18). Nevertheless, sacrificial ministry to the truly needy is essential (e.g., Luke 12:20–21, 33; 14:13, 21, 33; Acts 4:34; Rom. 15:26; Gal. 2:10), and the church

in Wesley's day invested more in buildings than in human need. In all cases, accountability is also essential (2 Cor. 8:19–21; today note, e.g., the Evangelical Council for Financial Accountability).

48. Jennings, *Good News to the Poor*, 133.

49. Though Anabaptist ethicist Ron Sider, a Yale PhD in Reformation history, was controversial in some circles, he and his wife, Arbutus, certainly lived according to the values they preached. I owe their friendship more than I could possibly repay; see Keener, "Fidelity"; and especially Keener, "Sider." What first drew me to Ron was his honesty about the values I was already discovering in Luke-Acts.

50. Sider, *Rich Christians*, 152.

51. Sider, *Rich Christians*, 152; compare Jennings, *Good News to the Poor*, 119–23.

52. Finney, *Lectures*, 53.

53. Finney, *Lectures*, 53.

54. Finney, *Lectures*, 127, emphasis his.

55. Apart from salt, the term most often refers to becoming foolish, a possible wordplay here. On proposed meanings for Jesus's salt image, see Keener, "Salting."

56. Hefley and Hefley, *Blood*, 63.

57. Fodor, "Migrants."

58. See UN Refugee Agency, "Key Figures." Official statistics distinguish refugees beyond their nation and those displaced within the nation, but national boundaries are often of less relevance than cultural ones to the displaced themselves.

59. Holmes, "Losing 25,000 to Hunger Every Day." The figures are thankfully down from an estimated 40,000 a day several decades ago.

60. World Health Organization, "Hunger Numbers 2022." For COVID's impact in the US, see also Martin, *Nailing It*, 18–21.

61. Agence France-Presse, "Wasted Meals."

62. Food Research and Action Center, "Hunger," noting this involved 44.2 million Americans.

63. World Health Organization, "Hunger Numbers 2024." The report adds the contrast that, by medical definitions, some 15.8 percent of the world's population in 2022 was obese. At least a significant proportion of these cases (there are genetic and other causes) stem from abuse of food.

64. Gray, *Lit Up with Love*, 100.

65. Schoch, "Half the Population."

66. Omer, "Global Water Crisis."

67. UNESCO, "Children"; Cankara, "244M Children."

68. Schoch, "Half the Population." In 2011, more than four billion people, 71 percent of the world's population, lived on less than $10 daily (Kochhar, "$10 per Day").

69. Pew Research Center, "World Population by Income."

70. UN Inter-Agency Group, "Levels and Trends."

71. World Health Organization, "Child Mortality."

72. United Nations, "Everyone Included."

73. Homeless No More, "Understanding Global Homelessness."

74. Soucy, Janes, and Hall, "State of Homelessness."

75. Samuel, "Global 1%."

76. The organization's name comes from Ps. 146:7; see Food for the Hungry, "Who We Are."

77. Ward, *Famines*, 5.

78. Ward, *Famines*, 29.

79. On the value of empathy, see, e.g., Martin, *Nailing It*, 27–32.

80. Although this figure is not exorbitant by industry standards, and some churches need such construction more than others, it becomes an issue when churches neglect more crucial needs. Compare Luther's fiftieth of his Ninety-Five Theses: "Christians are to be taught that if the pope knew the exactions of the indulgence preachers, he would rather that the basilica of St. Peter were burned to ashes than built up with the skin, flesh, and bones of his sheep." And

number 86: "Why does not the pope, whose wealth is today greater than the wealth of the richest Crassus, build this one basilica of St. Peter with his own money rather than with the money of poor believers?" (From https://www.luther.de/en/95thesen.html, accessed Sept. 21, 2024).

81. Buckingham, "Heroes," 24, 35.

82. Buckingham, "Spirit of World." On August 26, 1991, Jamie Buckingham kindly called me about my first book, not knowing beforehand that I was charismatic. His voice was prophetic, and I regret that, because of his passing later that year, we were not able to pursue discussions further.

83. I suspect that the immediate context of the word translated "greed" suggests an emphasis on sexual desire more than monetary desire, but the term itself can bear a broader meaning, and the principle probably still applies.

84. At the Assemblies of God Theological Seminary, one required course for my major was "Indigenous Church," using as textbooks Hodges, *Indigenous Church;* Williams, *Partnership*.

85. See Feeding America, "Hunger." Compare also Hales and Coleman-Jensen, "Food Insecurity"; Mumphrey and Rodgers, "Focus." Compare Marian Wright Edelman in Powery, "Mark," 140–41.

86. Bread for the World, "Hunger." The higher figure of 40 percent may be more current, at Humberstone, "Single Mothers."

Chapter 9 Examples of Other Kinds of Hardships

1. See http://en.wikipedia.org/wiki/Nuclear_close_calls (accessed Feb. 2, 2025).

2. See Nagai, *Bells of Nagasaki;* Glynn, *Song for Nagasaki;* also the concise documentary "What Happened in Nagasaki on That Fateful Day in 1945?," *The Incredible Journey* (posted Oct. 4, 2024; accessed Oct. 28, 2024, at https://www.youtube.com/watch?v=5MTussgT5lY&t=117s). Regarding the attack on Nagasaki, see, further, Kantowicz, *Rage*, 1:433–34.

3. Currently the world has more than 12,000 nuclear warheads, nearly one-third of which are active. This number is far below the 70,300 in 1986, but a full-scale nuclear war between, say, Russia and the US could lead to (according to one study) five billion deaths, especially from starvation in the aftermath, killing some 99 percent of the population in Europe, Russia, the US, and China (Xia, "Global Food Insecurity").

4. Siddique, Baqui, Eusof, and Zaman, "Floods in Bangladesh," 310.

5. "Agony Is a Way of Life."

6. "Bailing Out Bangladesh."

7. Thirty million in "Bangladesh: Water"; forty million in Cryderman, "Agencies." Arshad Mahmub with the New York Times News Service estimated twenty-five million ("Floods Rage in Bangladesh," 8).

8. Undated emergency mailing from Fred Cottriel, Secretary of Foreign Missions Relations.

9. Cryderman, "Agencies"; Reliefweb, "Bangladesh: Floods: Aug 1988."

10. Siddique, Baqui, Eusof, and Zaman, "Floods in Bangladesh."

11. Six thousand appears in Association for Diplomatic Studies, "Floods in Bangladesh." Perhaps calculating causes of death more widely, "Disaster Fatigue" suggests 125,000 dead as well as nine million homeless.

12. Onion, "Bangladesh Cyclone."

13. Grant, "Floods," 1.

14. Buerk, "Fight"; Reliefweb, "Bangladesh: Floods 2004."

15. Veer, "Climate Change."

16. Religious minorities also face pressure from Islamists in Bangladesh; see, e.g., Jain and Kair, "Advocate." Recently regarding persecution of Christians in Bangladesh, see Open Doors, "World Watch List 2025," 34–35.

17. Wurmbrand, *Tortured for Christ* (2023), 84.

18. This was the highest figure since 2007. Nearly 30 percent of the homeless lived in California. See US Department of Housing and Urban Development, "2023 Homelessness Report."

19. For one seminary's experience in Ukraine, see Syniy, *Serving God*. Along with North Korea, the military regime in Myanmar is among the world's most unjust governments.

20. Sept. 2024 mailing; see https://www.opendoorsus.org/en-US/persecution/persecution-trends/ (accessed Sept. 18, 2024); Open Doors, "World Watch List 2025," 44.

21. The video is currently available at Africa Ministry, "IDP Camp."

22. See, e.g., Anonymous, *Exploitation*; Paluku, *Coltan*.

23. See Chibelushi, "Raped"; Rajvanshi, "Raped."

24. See Lee, "Psalm 91."

25. Peterman, Palermo, and Bredenkamp, "Estimates."

26. Belz, "Crimes," 75–76, 80–81; see also Mukwege, *Power*.

27. Moszynski, "Died."

28. For the contrast and summary of the history, see Satyavrata, *Pentecostals and Poor*, 31–32, noting the 2010 Lausanne report of Antoine Rutayisire.

29. Uwimana, *From Red Earth*, 46.

30. Uwimana, *From Red Earth*, 1.

31. Uwimana, *From Red Earth*, 164.

32. E.g., Uwimana, *From Red Earth*, 40.

33. Uwimana, *From Red Earth*, 130.

34. Ilibagiza, *Left to Tell*, 87.

35. Uwimana, *From Red Earth*, 59. For plans to murder another ten thousand sheltered in a stadium, see 100–101.

36. Uwimana, *From Red Earth*, 61, 130.

37. Uwimana, *From Red Earth*, 184.

38. Uwimana, *From Red Earth*, 169.

39. Haugen, *Good News About Injustice*, 111. The killers were ordinary workers, college students, and others (Uwimana, *From Red Earth*, 76).

40. Uwimana, *From Red Earth*, 56–57.

41. Uwimana, *From Red Earth*, 66.

42. Uwimana, *From Red Earth*, 75.

43. Uwimana, *From Red Earth*, 82.

44. Uwimana, *From Red Earth*, 88.

45. Uwimana, *From Red Earth*, 112. In some cases, survivors' guilt led to suicide (140; compare 152).

46. Uwimana, *From Red Earth*, 84, 86, 122.

47. Uwimana, *From Red Earth*, 190.

48. Uwimana, *From Red Earth*, 131.

49. Uwimana, *From Red Earth*, 140.

50. Uwimana, *From Red Earth*, 132, 139. At the time, AIDS medication was difficult to obtain (141). Yet HIV victims found welcome in Christian community (167).

51. Uwimana, *From Red Earth*, 163.

52. Uwimana, *From Red Earth*, 121.

53. Uwimana, *From Red Earth*, 123–25.

54. Uwimana, *From Red Earth*, 125.

55. Uwimana, *From Red Earth*, 143.

56. See Uwimana, *From Red Earth*, 188.

57. Uwimana, *From Red Earth*, 145.

58. Uwimana, *From Red Earth*, 167–69.

59. Uwimana, *From Red Earth*, 193–98.

60. Ilibagiza, *Left to Tell*, 73–74. There were originally six but then two more fled there (108). For the three months, see, e.g., 126, 133 (compare 113).

61. Ilibagiza, *Left to Tell*, 76, 134.

62. Ilibagiza, *Left to Tell*, 113. The temperature is presumably an estimate, as it is doubtful that a thermometer was available in the cramped bathroom.

63. Ilibagiza, *Left to Tell*, 91–92, 130–31.

64. Friends and neighbors murdered Tutsis (Ilibagiza, *Left to Tell*, 77–78).

65. Ilibagiza, *Left to Tell*, 91–94, 107.

66. Ilibagiza, *Left to Tell*, 171.

67. On God's protection, see, e.g., Ilibagiza, *Left to Tell*, 177–78.

68. Ilibagiza, *Left to Tell*, 175.

69. Ilibagiza, *Left to Tell*, 144–46, 195. For the destruction of their home, 61–62. Only her brother Aimable, studying in Senegal, was spared (194, 205).

70. Uwimana, *From Red Earth*, 154.

71. Uwimana, *From Red Earth*, 127; compare 180–81.

72. Ilibagiza, *Left to Tell*, 104; Uwimana, *From Red Earth*, 126.

73. Ilibagiza, *Left to Tell*, 104. For the UN debate about whether to label the killings "genocide," see Uwimana, *From Red Earth*, 127.

74. See my protest, Keener, "Did Not Know."

75. See Wurmbrand, *Wife*.

76. See Keener, *Peter*, 178–92.

77. Compare slavery as the climax in the list of items involved in economic exploitation in Rev. 18:13; Bauckham, *Climax*, 352–66 (especially 365–66); Kraybill, *Cult*, 66–67 and passim.

78. See, e.g., Kara, *Sex Trafficking*; Kara, *Modern Slavery*; Bales, *Disposable People*; Stickle, Hickman, and White, *Human Trafficking*; Vanek, *Abolitionist*; particularly for South Asia, see Kara, *Bonded Labor*.

79. "Modern Day Slavery?" Much lower estimates are closer to twenty million; much depends on how one defines *slavery* (involuntary labor).

80. This includes some farm workers in the US ("Modern Day Slavery?") and a Haitian housekeeper in a Florida hotel with whom I spoke several years ago.

81. For Usry and Keener, *Black Man's Religion*, 94–98.

82. The newspaper was cited in *Mercy Magazine*, January 1994, p. 3. For exploitation of Haitians, see, e.g., Masland, "Slavery," 38–39.

83. Masland, "Slavery," 30. This is despite the *official* emancipation of slaves there on July 5, 1980 (Gordon, *Slavery*, x; compare Lewis, *Race and Slavery*, 79).

84. Masland, "Slavery," 32. Gordon, *Slavery*, x, places the estimate at two hundred thousand men, women, and children.

85. Masland, "Slavery," 32. On Arab beatings and brandings of African slaves in the Sudan, see Bhatia, "Booty," 40.

86. FitzPatrick, "Training Journalists."

87. Pierce, "Faith," the research including interviews with Abdul Momen, born in Bangladesh and now professor at Merrimack College in North Andover, Massachusetts, and Faith Willard, the Christian with whom he works.

88. "Slavery in Bangladesh."

89. Lewis, *Race and Slavery*, 79 (Yemen and then Saudi Arabia a few weeks later); Fogel and Engerman, *Time*, 13. For persecution of religious minorities there in the 1990s, see *Amnesty Action* (Fall 1993): 4; "Saudi Arabia—Religious Intolerance."

90. Gordon, *Slavery*, 233, also citing the assessment of journalist Eric Rouleau.

91. Domínguez, "Assessing," 91; Gordon, *Slavery*, 233. Mannix, *Black Cargoes*, 257, complained that "the great powers are too much concerned with oil diplomacy to investigate the situation."

92. Gordon, *Slavery*, 231; the quotation is excerpted from a letter by the French ambassador to Saudi Arabia, dated November 7, 1953.

93. See Lewis, *Religion and Society*, 210 (as cited in Ellis, *Malcolm*, 109–10); Lewis, *Race and Slavery*, 55; Gordon, *Slavery*, 32. Later American and Boer interpreters repurposed the myth for their own slave cultures (Peterson, *Ham and Japheth*, 141–58; Davidson, *Africa in History*, 228–29). These claims contradict the actual text of Genesis (Gen. 9:25).

94. "Captive Workers." In Roman and even many cases of US slavery, slaves were paid small bonuses or wages (in the US, Fogel and Engerman, *Time*, 148–49)—but it was slavery nonetheless.

95. "Slavery in Saudi Arabia."

96. "Sudan: Caught in Cycle," 1.

97. "Sudan: Caught in Cycle," 3; "Forgotten Slaves"; Masland, "Slavery," 32.

98. Bhatia, "Booty." For releasing his findings Mahmoud was rewarded with two years in a Sudanese jail.

99. Bhatia, "Booty," 40.

100. See "Sudan: Ravages," 6–9. Compare also "Civil War." For genocide in Darfur, a different region of Sudan, see Hagan and Rymond-Richmond, *Darfur*.

101. "Forgotten Slaves"; "Sudan: Ravages," 6–9; "Civil War"; Bhatia, "Booty"; Gordon, *Slavery*, xi. For past Muslim enslavement of Christians, see also Shortt, *Christianophobia*, 7. For more comment on slavery today, see Usry and Keener, *Black Man's Religion*, 94–98.

102. Ibraheem with Bach, *Shackled*, 160–61. For frequent abuse of women in traditional Muslim households, even further north in Egypt, see "Garbage to Child."

103. See, e.g., O., "Christianity and Slavery"; for video, see Global Christian Relief, "Modern Slavery." Some earlier estimated even twenty million in bondage (Masland, "Slavery," 37).

104. Echoing the Septuagint's Greek translation of Ezek. 27:13; see Bauckham, *Climax*, 370; especially now Vasser, "Bodies." For references on human "bodies" signifying slaves, see Deissmann, *Bible Studies*, 160.

105. Amoafo, *Stand Up*, 42.

106. Global Christian Relief, December 22, 2024.

107. See Kanana, *Once Was Dead*.

108. Voice of Martyrs, *Hearts of Fire*, 159–92. For an example in Pakistan of a brother killing his sister who converted to Christianity, see Sheikh, *Call Him Father*, 13. Interfering in an honor killing could also prove fatal (Sheikh, *Call Him Father*, 170).

109. Shortt, *Christianophobia*, 80.

110. Shortt, *Christianophobia*, 80–81.

111. Voice of Martyrs, *Hearts of Fire 2*, 221.

112. Doyle, *Killing Christians*, 87–92, especially 92.

113. Doyle, *Dreams*, 58.

114. Doyle, *Dreams*, 59–61.

115. Voice of Martyrs, *I Am N*, 17; compare a similar attempt on p. 178.

116. Voice of Martyrs, *I Am N*, 21.

117. Voice of Martyrs, *I Am N*, 59.

118. Voice of Martyrs, *I Am N*, 190–91 (quotation from 191). In Islamic contexts, baptism (as opposed to simply reading the Bible) marks a Muslim convert to Christianity as an apostate (Sheikh, *Call Him Father*, 67).

119. On grieving with hope, see Pipkin, *Changed*.

120. Wurmbrand, *Wife*, 28. Compare likewise 272: "If one can be proud of a son who dies for his country, how much more one could be proud of a son who was a martyr for Jesus Christ."

121. Wurmbrand, *Wife*, 308.

122. Wurmbrand, *Wife*, 263.

123. Wurmbrand, *Tortured for Christ* (2023), 92, 136. In one case, after imprisoning a pastor, they deported his children (Wurmbrand, *Wife*, 309).

124. Wurmbrand, *Tortured for Christ* (2023), 34.

125. Wurmbrand, *Tortured for Christ* (2023), 136.

126. See Wurmbrand, *Wife*, 188–91.

127. Voice of Martyrs, *I Am N*, 316.

128. Voice of the Martyrs, December 21, 2024. Police took six-year-old Hana herself into custody soon afterward, along with other children, for attending Sunday school.

129. GCR Red List, 9. Compare also comment in Open Doors, "World Watch List 2025," 43.

130. Voice of the Martyrs update, July 6, 2024.

131. Voice of the Martyrs update, September 3, 2024.

132. Open Doors, "Pain and Faith," 4.

133. "Returning to Tchabi," 4–5.

134. See Feb. 20, 2025, reports (accessed Feb. 22, 2025) in, e.g., CNN (https://www.youtube .com/watch?v=gzG5djfzaOs), CBN (https://www.youtube.com/watch?v=UL-r1GVCvRE), and Newsweek (https://www.newsweek.com/christians-beheaded-congo-drc-2033864).

135. Voice of the Martyrs update, May 13, 2025. Accessed May 14, 2025, at https://etools .vomusa.org/a/vombm/viewasweb/vom_bulk_email_202505_13_web.html.

136. Voice of Martyrs, *I Am N*, 120–21.

137. Voice of Martyrs, *Hearts of Fire*, 5–44.

138. Voice of the Martyrs update, September 3, 2022.

139. Voice of Martyrs, *I Am N*, 47.

140. Voice of Martyrs, *I Am N*, 67. The son of another convert experienced torture from jihadists and resented his father's controversial witness (202).

141. Shortt, *Christianophobia*, 49.

142. Voice of Martyrs, *I Am N*, 247–49.

143. See Doyle, *Killing Christians*, 1–17.

144. Doyle, *Killing Christians*, 8.

145. Doyle, *Killing Christians*, 6–13.

146. Doyle, *Killing Christians*, 15.

147. Global Christian Relief update (Oct. 25, 2024).

148. Voice of Martyrs, *I Am N*, 286–88.

149. Keener and Keener, *Impossible Love*; Usry and Keener, *Black Man's Religion*; Keener and Usry, *Faith*; and in various essays and articles, such as Keener, "Reconciliation."

150. George O. Wood, *Mountain Movers*, June 1994, 9.

151. Here I adapt some material from Keener, "Succeed at Suffering," with permission from George P. Wood, May 8, 2024.

152. For the Lord's sake, we please people to bless them (Rom. 15:2–3) and win them to Christ (1 Cor. 10:33), but that is in a secondary sense.

153. I give more detail about the tree, though not the prophecy, in Keener, *Miracles*, 2:854–55.

Chapter 10 Suffering in God's Will

1. Panahi, *Didn't Survive*, 67–69.

2. Panahi, *Didn't Survive*, 108–10.

3. Panahi, *Didn't Survive*, 277.

4. E.g., Wurmbrand, *Tortured for Christ* (2023), 45; Ilibagiza, *Left to Tell*, 91–94, 107; Uwimana, *From Red Earth*, 123–25, 145, 193–98; Voice of Martyrs, *Hearts of Fire 2*, 55–56, 85–88, 301–5; Voice of Martyrs, *I Am N*, 47, 220–21, 236–41, 244–45; Nettleton, *When Faith Is Forbidden*, 112.

5. Some early Greek manuscripts of Rom. 8:28 say simply that "all things work for good," but even there the assumption is that God causes this, not that it simply happens by accident.

6. Ward and Brownlee, *Rare Earth*, cited in D'Souza, "Earthquakes." Compare also D'Souza, *God Forsaken*, but with the qualifications in Groothuis, "Necessary Evil."

7. I address Paul's argument related to the corruption of human intellect in Keener, *Mind*, 1–29.

8. Johnston, "Betancourt."

9. Cagle, "Where Was God?," 12.

10. With ESV, NIV; also Rom. 9:17 (against the Septuagint); but some understand the phrase as "allowed to remain" (NASB, NRSV; compare Exod. 9:15–16).

11. See ten Boom, *Hiding Place*.

12. See discussion in Keener, *Mind*, 143–72.

13. Tertullian, *Apology* 50.13, in the late second century.

14. See examples in Galli, "Persecution"; Guthrie, "Other Side."

15. Taylor and Taylor, *Secret*, 214.

16. Colson, *Loving God*, 27–34.

17. "The Car or the Cross," *Mountain Movers*, March 1996, 14.

18. Doyle, *Killing Christians*, 192–95.

19. Voice of Martyrs, *I Am N*, 236–41.

20. Kim, *If I Perish*, 184.

21. Kim, *If I Perish*, 189.

22. Kim, *If I Perish*, 271.

23. "Blank Space."

24. Baker, *Keeping the Fire*, 83.

25. Wurmbrand, *Tortured for Christ* (2023), 45.

26. Wurmbrand, *Tortured for Christ* (2023), 73.

27. Tari, *Mighty Wind*, 164.

28. Mel Tari, personal correspondence, August 1, 2024.

29. Hattaway, *China's Martyrs*, 248.

30. Hefley and Hefley, *Blood*, 43–45. While Catholics lost fewer foreign missionaries, they lost 15 times as many Chinese Christians as did Protestants (36). For far more details, see Hattaway, *China's Martyrs*, 111–344.

31. Hefley and Hefley, *Blood*, 46.

32. Hefley and Hefley, *Blood*, 76.

33. Others also suffered. Some estimate that in the four years between 1958 and 1962, Mao's regime cost forty-five million lives (Shortt, *Christianophobia*, 191).

34. Shaw, *Global Awakening*, 190.

35. Dalton, "Return."

36. Richardson, *Lords of the Earth*, 361.

37. Elliot, *Gates of Splendor*; Saint, *End of the Spear*.

38. Doyle, *Killing Christians*, 53–54, 63, 69–70; compare 67.

39. Voice of Martyrs, *Hearts of Fire 2*, 197.

40. Nettleton, *When Faith Is Forbidden*, 24–25.

41. Johnstone and Mandryk, *Operation World* (2001), 470; Mandryk, *Operation World* (2010), 619.

42. Hefley and Hefley, *Blood*, 391–93.

43. Hefley and Hefley, *Blood*, 462–63.

44. On Luwum, see, e.g., Noll and Nystrom, *Witnesses*, 111–23, especially 121. For one vignette of suffering under Amin, see Amoafo, *Stand Up*, 41.

45. Moeller and Hegg, *Privilege of Persecution*, 58.

46. "Church Triumphant in Iran," 7. Voice of Martyrs, *I Am N*, 90–92, recounts the experience of Pastor Soodmand's son Ramtin, who later had to flee Iran. For the story of his daughter, see Voice of Martyrs, *Hearts of Fire 2*, 169–72.

47. Voice of Martyrs, *I Am N*, 36.

48. Voice of Martyrs, *I Am N*, 136–37.

49. From Iris, "Core Values."

50. Wholey, *Miracle of Change*, 158. This is quoted also in "Sun Creates a Desert."

51. Yancey, "Memories."

52. Bach, *Jesus in Iran*, 112. I also draw on other sources (e.g., Shortt, *Christianophobia*, 49–50). In October 1969, the Hovsepians lost their baby son, and US missionaries Mark and Gladys Bliss their only three children, in a car accident. The anguished but faithful prayer of the Blisses deeply impacted the church: "Lord, we plant three seeds for the sake of the Gospel in Iran" (Voice of Martyrs, "50 Years"). Hovsepian also praised God in the midst of that suffering (for further detail, see Gohr, "Week"; "Three Children").

53. "Superintendent Martyred."

54. "Tragedy Turns."

55. "Overcome Evil."

56. E.g., Doyle, *Killing Christians*, 165–66, focusing on the Muslim Brotherhood. See also Tulloch, "Feast," regarding the twenty-one Coptic Christians beheaded by Isis in February 2015 (earlier, see https://www.bbc.com/news/world-31481797, from Feb. 15, 2015).

57. Doyle, *Killing Christians*, 167–69 (quote from 168).

58. Doyle, *Killing Christians*, 170.

59. Voice of Martyrs, *I Am N*, 140–41.

60. Voice of Martyrs, *I Am N*, 106.

61. Compare, e.g., God comforting his people in Isa. 49:13; 51:3, 12; 52:9; 66:13; the mission of God's anointed in Isa. 61:2.

62. Sometimes that comfort is just silent presence with those who are grieving (Smith, "Discerning"); Job's friends were doing well (Job 2:13) until they opened their mouths (Job 4–25).

63. See more in Kopaska and Liston, *Afterburn*.

64. Yancey, "Saturday."

65. Williams, "Not Mine." Prof. Williams showed particularly great sensitivity and compassion during my crisis of abandonment narrated elsewhere in this book.

Chapter 11 Rejoicing in Suffering

1. Weber, "Cheeks." Usually simply called ECWA, the denomination originally meant Evangelical Church of West Africa.

2. Sometimes I could write, "Imitate me just as I imitate Christ" (1 Cor. 11:1), but I have not earned the right to say that here.

3. For the former, see, e.g., Young, *Walking*; for the latter, e.g., John, "Investigation."

4. See Iris, "Core Values."

5. Baker, *Keeping the Fire*, 101–2.

6. Chrysostom, *Homilies on the Epistles of Paul to the Corinthians* 23.4 (Bray, *Corinthians*, 95); compare Hilary of Arles, *Commentary on 1 Peter* 4:16 (Bray, *Peter*, 119).

7. Wurmbrand, *Tortured for Christ* (2023), 42. Compare Wurmbrand, *Wife*, 86, on nuns imprisoned with her, who explained why they could sing: "We are allowed to sing, and they are allowed to beat us."

8. Wurmbrand, *Tortured for Christ* (2023), 77, 96–97.

9. Wurmbrand, *Wife*, 273.

10. Wurmbrand, *Tortured for Christ* (2023), 128. Compare Acts 5:41.

11. Nettleton, *When Faith Is Forbidden*, 31.

12. Nettleton, *When Faith Is Forbidden*, 117.

13. Nettleton, *When Faith Is Forbidden*, 253–54.

14. Moeller and Hegg, *Privilege of Persecution*, 71–72. Earlier in Vietnam, when Communist soldiers heard a classroom discussing religion, they drove chopsticks into students' ears, causing permanent deafness, and removed the teacher's tongue (Shortt, *Christianophobia*, 207).

15. Nettleton, *When Faith Is Forbidden*, 143.

16. Voice of Martyrs, *Hearts of Fire 2*, 260. See further, Rostampour and Amirizadeh, *Captive in Iran*; Amirizadeh, *Love Journey*.

17. Kim, *If I Perish*, 53.

18. Nettleton, *When Faith Is Forbidden*, 164.

19. Quoted in Tracy, "Let My People Go."

20. Voice of Martyrs, *I Am N*, 65–67.

21. Shortt, *Christianophobia*, 121. For the beheading of other Nigerian Christians, see, e.g., Casper, "11 Christians Executed"; Casper, "Pastor."

22. Voice of the Martyrs update, September 3, 2022.

23. Doyle, *Killing Christians*, xii.

24. Voice of the Martyrs update, February 7, 2025.

25. Wu, "Price."

26. Voice of Martyrs, *Hearts of Fire*, 69. Her full story is on 45–76. On Bhutan, compare also Open Doors, "World Watch List 2025," 46.

27. Voice of Martyrs, *Hearts of Fire*, 72.

28. Voice of Martyrs, *Hearts of Fire*, 75.

29. Miller and Wood, "Dangerous Territory." Already in 2021 numbers were close to eight hundred thousand (McDade, "Cannot Burn Jesus").

30. Voice of Martyrs, "Lion's Den."

31. McDade, "Cannot Burn Jesus."

32. See my article on this subject, Keener, "Deserters."

33. One of the key points I learned from my limited time with the now late theologian Jürgen Moltmann (during "Expectation and Human Flourishing," a special symposium sponsored by the Yale Center for Faith and Culture, June 22–23, 2015) is that, in contrast to the English term *hope* in the sense of mere wishes, we have *expectation* that rests on Christ's accomplished victory in history and unfailing promise.

34. Compare Frankl, *Death-Camp*; Frankl, *Embracing Hope*.

35. See Tacitus, *Annals* 15.44.

36. Nettleton, *When Faith Is Forbidden*, 142–43 (quotation from 142).

37. Hefley and Hefley, *Blood*, 213.

38. See Wurmbrand, *Tortured for Christ*; briefly, Lear, "Heartbeat," 14. For Sabina's story, see "Sabina: A Witness of Christ's Love," 109–58 in Voice of Martyrs, *Hearts of Fire*, for standing in a cupboard, 134; for Richard's love for his informer, 156.

39. Prodan, *Saving My Assassin*, 304.

40. Prodan, *Saving My Assassin*, 298.

41. Yi, "My Declaration," 224.

42. Yingqiang, "Face Persecution," 230.

43. One widely circulating book in the charismatic movement at that time, the main thesis of which also positively influenced me, was by Methodist minister Merlin Carothers, *Prison to Praise*.

44. As rightly noted in Young, *Walking*, 6.

Chapter 12 Conclusion: Overcomers

1. Although writing in Greek, Paul knows that the Hebrew term that can be rendered "glory" also means "heaviness."

2. Navalny, *Patriot*, 408. He did it, he said, not from superstition but as a public way of confessing his faith.

3. Navalny, *Patriot*, 475–78, practiced the exercise of imagining and then accepting the worst-case scenario, before (on 478–79) also finding encouragement in his faith.

4. On memorizing it, see Navalny, *Patriot*, 409. Shortly thereafter he took encouragement from that being the same reading in church (410–11).

5. Navalny, *Patriot*, 479, also cited in GCR Red List, 23–24. Even if one does not believe in biblical accounts of prediluvian longevity or the parting of the sea, he urges, one can trust in Jesus (Navalny, *Patriot*, 479).

6. Prodan, *Saving My Assassin*, 298.

7. Nettleton, *When Faith Is Forbidden*, 112.

8. Kim, *If I Perish*, 14–16. Elsewhere in Korea, many others refused to bow and had to go into hiding to avoid arrest (Kim, *If I Perish*, 52). During a later threat (218), the repressive governors perished when their plane was shot down, ending the immediate threat (234–35). After the war, others revered their stance (257).

9. See Kim, *If I Perish*.

10. Voice of Martyrs, *Hearts of Fire 2*, 57.

11. Ton, *Suffering*, xi.

BIBLIOGRAPHY

Africa Ministry, "IDP Camp." Africa Ministry. "Kigonze IDP Camp." Accessed September 15, 2024. https://youtu.be/_rX4targgwc?si=qCDGhLGCyUmwJuNZ.

"Afterword." "Afterword: The Book That Shocked the World." In *Tortured for Christ*, by Richard Wurmbrand, 155–61. VOM Books, 2023.

Agang, *African Public Theology*. Agang, Sunday Bobai, ed. *African Public Theology*. HippoBooks, 2020.

Agang, *Evil Strikes*. Agang, Sunday Bobai. *When Evil Strikes: Faith and the Politics of Human Hostility*. Pickwick, 2016.

Agang, *Impact*. Agang, Sunday Bobai. *The Impact of Ethnic, Political, and Religious Violence on Northern Nigeria, and a Theological Reflection on Its Healing*. Langham, 2011.

Agang, *Moral Values*. Agang, Sunday Bobai. *Endangered Moral Values: Nigeria's Search for Love, Truth, Justice and Intimacy*. HippoBooks, 2022.

Agence France-Presse, "Wasted Meals." Agence France-Presse. "UN Says Households Wasted 1 Billion Meals a Day in 2022 as About 800 Million People Face Hunger." United Nations website. Accessed August 3, 2024. https://www.scmp.com/news/world/united-states-canada/article/3256974/un-says-households-wasted-1-billion-meals-day-2022-about-800-million-people-face-hunger.

"Agony Is a Way of Life." "In Bangladesh, Agony Is a Way of Life." *U.S. News & World Report*, June 1985, 12.

Aikman, *Jesus in Beijing*. Aikman, David. *Jesus in Beijing: How Christianity Is Transforming China and Changing the Global Balance of Power*. Regnery, 2003.

Alcorn, *All About Jesus*. Alcorn, Randy. *It's All About Jesus*. Harvest House, 2020.

Alexander, *Pentecostal Healing*. Alexander, Kimberly Ervin. *Pentecostal Healing: Models in Theology and Practice*. Journal of Pentecostal Theology Supplement Series. Deo Publishing, 2006.

Amirizadeh, *Love Journey*. Amirizadeh, Marziyeh. *A Love Journey with God: From Pain to Love, Captivity to Freedom, Iran to the US*. Atlanta, 2022.

233

Amoafo, *Stand Up*. Amoafo, Emmanuel Kwasi. *Stand Up for the Gospel: Getting the Church Back on Track*. Oasis, 2022.

Anderson, *Golden Shore*. Anderson, Courtney. *To the Golden Shore: The Life of Adoniram Judson*. Little, Brown, 1956. Reprint, Judson, 1987.

Anderson, *Introduction to Pentecostalism*. Anderson, Allan. *An Introduction to Pentecostalism: Global Charismatic Christianity*. Cambridge University Press, 2004.

Anderson, *Pelendo*. Anderson, Alpha E. *Pelendo: God's Prophet in the Congo*. Moody Press, 1964.

Anderson, "Signs and Blunders." Anderson, Allan. "Signs and Blunders: Pentecostal Mission Issues at 'Home and Abroad' in the Twentieth Century." *Journal of Asian Mission* 2, no. 2 (2000): 193–210.

Anonymous, *Exploitation*. Anonymous. *The Illegal Exploitation of Coltan in the Democratic Republic of Congo: Which Influences Have the Economic Interests of the High-Tech Industry on the Maintenance and Intensification of the Conflict in the Country?* GRIN Publishing, 2014.

Arya, "Manipur Women." Arya, Divya. "Manipur Women in Naked Assault Video 'Will Not Give Up.'" BBC News, November 9, 2023. Accessed May 19, 2024. https://www.bbc.com/news/world-asia-india-67291370.

Association for Diplomatic Studies, "Floods in Bangladesh." Association for Diplomatic Studies and Training. "Preventing and Controlling Floods in Bangladesh: Tackling an Age-Old Problem." Accessed August 4, 2024. https://adst.org/2018/07/preventing-and-controlling-floods-in-bangladesh-tackling-an-age-old-problem/.

Aune, *Environment*. Aune, David Edward. *The New Testament in Its Literary Environment*. Library of Early Christianity 8. Westminster, 1987.

Bach, *Jesus in Iran*. Bach, Eugene. *Jesus in Iran*. Back to Jerusalem, 2015.

Baer, "Empowered Bodies." Baer, Jonathan R. "Perfectly Empowered Bodies: Divine Healing in Modernizing America." PhD diss., Yale University, 2002.

"Bailing Out Bangladesh." "Bailing Out Bangladesh." *Newsweek*, August 28, 1989, 42.

Baker, *Keeping the Fire*. Baker, Rolland. *Keeping the Fire: Discovering the Heart of True Revival*. Chosen, 2016.

Baker and Baker, *Always Enough*. Baker, Rolland, and Heidi Baker. *Always Enough: God's Miraculous Provision Among the Poorest Children on Earth*. Chosen, 2003.

Bales, *Disposable People*. Bales, Kevin. *Disposable People: New Slavery in the Global Economy*. 3rd ed. University of California Press, 2012.

Bałuczynski, *Afraid*. Bałuczynski, Jozef. *Be Not Afraid: How One Polish Pastor Triumphed over Hitler, Stalin and Death Itself*. Xulon, 2015.

"Bangladesh: Water." "Bangladesh: The Water This Time." *Newsweek*, September 19, 1988, 32.

Barbour, *Religion and Science*. Barbour, Ian G. *Religion and Science: Historical and Contemporary Issues*. HarperSanFrancisco, 1997.

Bauckham, *Climax*. Bauckham, Richard. *The Climax of Prophecy: Studies on the Book of Revelation*. T&T Clark, 1993.

Baxter, *Healing*. Baxter, J. Sidlow. *Divine Healing of the Body*. Zondervan, 1979.

Bays, "Revival in China." Bays, Daniel H. "Christian Revival in China, 1900–1937." In *Modern Christian Revivals*, edited by Edith Blumhofer and Randall H. Balmer, 161–79. University of Illinois Press, 1993.

Belz, "Crimes." Belz, Mindy. "War Crimes and Restoration in Congo." *Christianity Today*, May 2025, 74–81.

Benge and Benge, *Helen Roseveare*. Benge, Janet, and Geoff Benge. *Helen Roseveare: Mama Luka*. YWAM, 2019.

Berhane, *Song*. Berhane, Helen. *Song of the Nightingale: One Woman's Dramatic Story of Faith and Persecution in Eritrea*. Authentic Publishers, 2009.

Bhatia, "Booty." Bhatia, Shyam. "A War's Human Booty." *World Press Review*, August 1995, 40. From London's *Observer*, April 9, 1995.

"Blank Space." "The Blank Space on the Green Card." *Mountain Movers*, September 1993, 10–11.

Blomberg, *Neither Poverty nor Riches*. Blomberg, Craig L. *Neither Poverty nor Riches: A Biblical Theology of Material Possessions*. Eerdmans, 1999.

"Bombshell on Manipur Police." "CBI Drops a Bombshell on Manipur Police Role in Gang Rape Incident: 'Left at Mob's Mercy.'" *Hindustan Times*, May 1, 2024. Video, accessed May 19, 2024. https://www.youtube.com/watch?v=QCdnLsXhiVs.

Bonhoeffer, *Cost of Discipleship*. Bonhoeffer, Dietrich. *The Cost of Discipleship*. Rev. ed. Macmillan, 1963.

Boyd, *Bomb*. Boyd, Andrew. *Neither Bomb nor Bullet: Benjamin Kwashi—the Archbishop They Just Couldn't Kill*. Monarch Books, 2019.

Braun, *Here Am I*. Braun, Willys K. *Here Am I: An Autobiography*. Evangelism Resources, 2003.

Braun, *On the Way*. Braun, Thelma M. *On the Way: Joyful Jottings from a Missionary's Pen*. Evangel Publishing, 2009.

Bray, *Corinthians*. Bray, Gerald, ed. *1–2 Corinthians*. Ancient Christian Commentary on Scripture: New Testament 7. InterVarsity, 1999.

Bray, *Peter*. Bray, Gerald, ed. *James, 1–2 Peter, 1–3 John, Jude*. Ancient Christian Commentary on Scripture: New Testament 11. InterVarsity, 2000.

Bread for the World, "Hunger." Bread for the World. "Hunger and Poverty in Female-Headed Households." Bread for the World Fact Sheet, May 2019. Accessed August 4, 2024. https://www.bread.org/sites/default/files/downloads/hunger-poverty -female-headed-households-may-2019.pdf.

Brooke, *Reconstructing Nature*. Brooke, John Hedley, with Geoffrey Cantor. *Reconstructing Nature: The Engagement of Science and Religion*. T&T Clark, 1998.

Brooke, *Science*. Brooke, John Hedley. *Science and Religion: Some Historical Perspectives*. Cambridge History of Science Series. Cambridge University Press, 1991.

Brougham, "Chinese in Indonesia." Brougham, David Royal. "The Training of the Chinese in Indonesia for the Ministry." MA thesis, Fuller Theological Seminary, 1970.

Brown, *Authentic Fire*. Brown, Michael L. *Authentic Fire: A Response to John Mac-Arthur's "Strange Fire."* Excel Publishers, 2013.

Brown and Keener, *Not Afraid*. Brown, Michael L., and Craig S. Keener. *Not Afraid of the Antichrist: Why We Don't Believe in a Pretribulation Rapture.* Chosen, 2019.

Bubik, *Bubik*. Bubik, Rudolf, with Jim Dunn. *Rudolf Bubik: Prisoner Cell 304.* Nottingham: Lifestream, 1993.

Buckingham, "Heroes." Buckingham, Jamie. "Heroes for Eternity: Giving to the Ones God Has Called." In *1994 Great Commission Handbook*. Berry, 1993. Reprinting the "The Last Word" column from *Charisma*, December 1992.

Buckingham, "Spirit of World." Buckingham, Jamie. "The Spirit of the World." *Charisma & Christian Life*, May 1988, 98.

Buerk, "Fight." Buerk, Roland. "Losing the Fight Against Nature." BBC News, July 31, 2004. http://news.bbc.co.uk/2/hi/programmes/from_our_own_correspondent /3939495.stm.

Cagle, "Where Was God?" Cagle, Judy. "Where Was God When They Hurt Us?" *Pentecostal Evangel*, May 24, 1987, 12–13.

Cankara, "244M Children." Cankara, Fatma. "244M Children Won't Start the New School Year." UNESCO, September 1, 2022. Accessed August 4, 2024. https://www .unesco.org/gem-report/en/articles/244m-children-wont-start-new-school-year.

Capps, "Keys." Capps, Charles. "Keys to Understanding the Bible." Charles Capps Ministries, 198-? Audiocassette.

Capps, *Tongue*. Capps, Charles. *The Tongue, a Creative Force.* Harrison House, 1976.

"Captive Workers." "Captive Workers." *World Press Review*, May 1991, 50, following Denis MacShane in *Hong Kong's Far Eastern Economic Review*.

Carothers, *Prison to Praise*. Carothers, Merlin. *Prison to Praise.* Logos International, 1974.

Casper, "11 Christians Executed." Casper, Jayson. "11 Nigerian Christians Executed in ISIS Christmas Video." *Christianity Today*, December 28, 2019. Accessed September 11, 2024. https://www.christianitytoday.com/2019/12/isis-nigeria-executes -christians-iswap-christmas-boko-haram/.

Casper, "Christmas Massacres." Casper, Jayson. "Christmas Massacres Challenge Secular Explanations of Nigeria Conflict." *Christianity Today*, December 29, 2023. https://www.christianitytoday.com/2023/12/nigeria-christmas-massacre-plateau -fulani-herders-farmers/.

Casper, "Pastor." Casper, Jayson. "Boko Haram Executes Pastor Who Turned Hostage Video into Testimony." *Christianity Today*, January 21, 2020. Accessed September 11, 2024. https://www.christianitytoday.com/2020/01/nigeria-boko-haram -kidnapped-pastor-hostage-video-testimony/.

Chandler, "Hundreds Killed." Chandler, Diana. "Hundreds of Nigerian Christians Killed in Recent Attacks." *Christianity Today*, June 22, 2023. https://www.christi anitytoday.com/2023/06/nigeria-christians-killed-persecution-churches-destroyed/.

Chang, "Rape of Nanking." Chang, Iris. "Exposing the Rape of Nanking." *Newsweek*, December 1, 1997, 55–57.

Chang, *Rape of Nanking*. Chang, Iris. *The Rape of Nanking: The Forgotten Holocaust of World War II.* Basic Books, 2011.

Charlesworth, *OTP*. Charlesworth, James. *The Old Testament Pseudepigrapha.* 2 vols. Doubleday, 1983–85.

Chibelushi, "Raped." Chibelushi, Wedaeli. "More Than 100 Women Raped and Burned Alive in DR Congo Jailbreak, UN Says." BBC News, February 5, 2025. Accessed February 5, 2025. https://www.bbc.com/news/articles/ckgyrxz4k6zo.

Chimtom, "Christians Slaughtered." Chimtom, Ngala Killian. "Nigerian Christians Slaughtered in Christmas Attacks." *Crux: Taking the Catholic Pulse*, December 28, 2023. https://cruxnow.com/church-in-africa/2023/12/nigerian-christians-slaughtered-in-christmas-attacks.

Chin, "Blindsided." Chin, Peter. "Blindsided by God." *Christianity Today*, July 2013, 60–62.

Christerson and Flory, *Rise of Network Christianity*. Christerson, Brad, and Richard Flory. *The Rise of Network Christianity: How Independent Leaders Are Changing the Religious Landscape.* Oxford University Press, 2017.

"Church Triumphant in Iran." "The Church Triumphant in Iran." *Mountain Movers*, May 1995, 6–8.

"Civil War." "Civil War Brings Suffering to Sudan: Militants Single Out Christians for Persecution." *Christianity Today*, May 17, 1993, 82.

Clark, "Inaugurated Kingdom." Clark, Randy. "The Inaugurated Kingdom of God—Now and Not Yet." In *The Kingdom Case Against Cessationism: Embracing the Power of the Kingdom*, edited by Robert W. Graves, 17–26. The Foundation for Pentecostal Scholarship, 2022.

Colson, *Loving God*. Colson, Charles. *Loving God.* Zondervan, 1987.

Copeland, *Decision*. Copeland, Kenneth. *The Decision Is Yours.* Kenneth Copeland Ministries, 1978.

Copeland, "Enforce Word." Kenneth Copeland Ministries. "Enforce God's Word and Be Healed." Video, accessed September 4, 2024. https://www.youtube.com/watch?v=7CVdTNae2sQ.

Copeland, *Laws*. Copeland, Kenneth. *The Laws of Prosperity.* Harrison House, 1974.

Cosmos, *Huguenot Prophecy*. Cosmos, Georgia. *Huguenot Prophecy and Clandestine Worship in the Eighteenth Century: "The Sacred Theatre of the Cévennes."* Ashgate, 2005.

Cryderman, "Agencies." Cryderman, Lyn. "Agencies Rush to Help Bangladesh Bail Out." *Christianity Today*, October 7, 1988, 36.

Curtis, *Faith*. Curtis, Heather D. *Faith in the Great Physician: Suffering and Divine Healing in American Culture, 1860–1900.* Johns Hopkins University Press, 2007.

Dalton, "Return." Dalton, Adele Flower. "Return to Gombari." *Mountain Movers*, March 1992, 27.

Davidson, *Africa in History*. Davidson, Basil. *Africa in History: Themes and Outlines.* Macmillan, 1968.

Deere, *Darkness*. Deere, Jack. *Even in Our Darkness: A Story of Beauty in a Broken Life*. Zondervan, 2018.

Deere, *Still Surprised*. Deere, Jack S. *Why I Am Still Surprised by the Power of the Spirit*. Zondervan Reflective, 2020.

Deere, *Voice*. Deere, Jack. *Surprised by the Voice of God: How God Speaks Today Through Prophecies, Dreams, and Visions*. Zondervan, 1996.

Deissmann, *Bible Studies*. Deissmann, G. Adolf. *Bible Studies*. Translated by A. Grieve. T&T Clark, 1923.

Deissmann, *Light*. Deissmann, G. Adolf. *Light from the Ancient East*. Baker Book House, 1978.

Destiny Image, "Powerful Sermon." "Bill Johnson Preaches a Powerful Sermon After Wife's Passing." *Destiny Image*, July 19, 2022. Accessed October 11, 2024. https://www.youtube.com/watch?v=USfftDqIx0Q (at 10.13–24).

Di Sabatino, "Frisbee." Di Sabatino, David. "Appendix 3: Lonnie Frisbee." In *The Quest for the Radical Middle: A History of the Vineyard*, by Bill Jackson, 392–407. Vineyard International, 1999.

"Disaster Fatigue." "Disaster Fatigue." *Newsweek*, May 13, 1991, 38.

Domínguez, "Assessing." Domínguez, Jorge I., Nigel S. Rodley, Bryce Wood, Richard Falk, and 1980s Project/Council on Foreign Relations. "Assessing Human Rights Conditions." In *Enhancing Global Human Rights*, 21–116. McGraw-Hill, 1979.

Doyle, *Dreams*. Doyle, Tom, with Greg Webster. *Dreams and Visions: Is Jesus Awakening the Muslim World?* Thomas Nelson, 2012.

Doyle, *Killing Christians*. Doyle, Tom, with Greg Webster. *Killing Christians: Living the Faith Where It's Not Safe to Believe*. Thomas Nelson, 2015.

D'Souza, "Earthquakes." D'Souza, Dinesh. "Why We Need Earthquakes." *Christianity Today*, May 2009, 58.

D'Souza, *God Forsaken*. D'Souza, Dinesh. *God Forsaken*. Tyndale, 2012.

Duplantis, "Faith the Facts." Jesse Duplantis Ministries. "Faith the Facts: Jesus Doesn't Heal Halfway." Video, accessed September 4, 2024. https://www.youtube.com/watch?v=y_VYWS4YG-0.

Edwards, "Distinguishing Marks." Edwards, Jonathan. "The Distinguishing Marks of a Work of the Spirit of God." In *The Works of Jonathan Edwards*, vol. 4, *The Great Awakening*. Edited by C. C. Goen. Yale University Press, 1972.

Elliot, *Gates of Splendor*. Elliot, Elisabeth. *Through Gates of Splendor*. Hendrickson, 2011.

Ellis, *Malcolm*. Ellis, Carl. *Malcolm: The Man Behind the X*. Accord Publications, 1993.

Emmett, *Burton*. Emmett, David Neil. *W. F. P. Burton (1886–1971): A Pentecostal Pioneer's Missional Vision for Congo*. Brill, 2020.

Evans, *Wycliffe*. Evans, G. R. *John Wycliffe: Myth and Reality*. IVP Academic, 2005.

"Eyewitnesses to Persecution." "Eyewitnesses to the Modern Age of Persecution." Theme issue, *Christian History* 109 (2014).

Fee, *Disease.* Fee, Gordon D. *The Disease of the Health and Wealth Gospels.* The Word for Today, 1979.

Feeding America, "Hunger." Feeding America. "Hunger in America." August 4, 2024. https://www.feedingamerica.org/hunger-in-america.

Finger, *Meals.* Finger, Reta Halteman. *Of Widows and Meals: Communal Meals in the Book of Acts.* Eerdmans, 2007.

Finney, *Lectures.* Finney, Charles. *Lectures on Revivals of Religion.* 6th ed. New York, 1835.

Fitzgerald, *Cracks.* Fitzgerald, John T. *Cracks in an Earthen Vessel: An Examination of the Catalogues of Hardships in the Corinthian Correspondence.* Society of Biblical Literature Dissertation Series 99. Scholars Press, 1988.

FitzPatrick, "Training Journalists." FitzPatrick, Terry. "Training Journalists and Activists in Mauritania to Promote Government Accountability and Social Inclusion." Free the Slaves website. Accessed September 15, 2024. https://freetheslaves .net/training-journalists-and-activists-in-mauritania-to-promote-government-acc ountability-and-social-inclusion/; also available at https://humantraffickingsearch .org/resource/training-journalists-and-activists-in-mauritania/.

"Floods Rage in Bangladesh." "Floods Rage on in Bangladesh." *Duke Chronicle,* September 6, 1988, 1, 8.

Fodor, "Migrants." Fodor, Chloë-Arizona. "Nearly Half the World's Migrants Are Christian." *Christianity Today,* August 21, 2024. Accessed September 7, 2024. https://www.christianitytoday.com/2024/08/christian-migrant-immigration-religi on-world-pew-research/.

Fogel and Engerman, *Time.* Fogel, Robert William, and Stanley L. Engerman. *Time on the Cross: The Economics of American Negro Slavery.* Little, Brown, 1974.

Food for the Hungry, "Who We Are." Food for the Hungry. "Who We Are." Accessed September 15, 2024. https://www.fh.org/about/.

Food Research and Action Center, "Hunger." Food Research and Action Center. "Hunger and Poverty in America." Accessed August 3, 2024. https://frac.org/hunger -poverty-america.

"Forgotten Slaves." "Forgotten Slaves." *World Press Review,* January 1991, 57.

Frankenberry, *Faith.* Frankenberry, Nancy K. *The Faith of Scientists in Their Words.* Princeton University Press, 2008.

Frankl, *Death-Camp.* Frankl, Viktor E. *From Death-Camp to Existentialism: A Psychiatrist's Path to a New Therapy.* Beacon Press, 1959.

Frankl, *Embracing Hope.* Frankl, Viktor E. *Embracing Hope: On Freedom, Responsibility and the Meaning of Life.* Beacon Press, 2024.

"Fresh Fears." "Deaths Raise Fresh Fears over Cow Vigilantism in India." BBC News, May 8, 2023. Accessed September 15, 2024. https://www.bbc.com/news/world-asia -india-65229522.

Galli, *Francis of Assisi.* Galli, Mark. *Francis of Assisi and His World.* InterVarsity, 2002.

Galli, "Persecution." Galli, Mark. "Sometimes Persecution Purifies, Unites, and Grows the Church. Sometimes It Doesn't." *Christianity Today*, May 19, 1997, 16–19.

"Garbage to Child." "From 'Garbage' to Child of God: Sarah in Egypt." Open Doors, August 7, 2024. Accessed August 22, 2024. https://www.opendoorsus.org/en-US /stories/from-garbage-child-of-God-Sarah-Egypt/.

GCR Red List. The 2025 Global Christian Relief Red List. Global Christian Relief, 2025.

"Genocide in Gujarat." "Genocide in Gujarat: Government and Police Complicity." Asian Human Rights Commission. Accessed July 31, 2024. http://www.human rights.asia/resources/journals-magazines/article2/focus-detention-and-imprison ment/genocide-in-gujarat-government-and-police-complicity/.

Global Christian Relief, "Modern Slavery." "Inside Modern Slavery: The Christian Brick Kiln Workers of Pakistan." Global Christian Relief, June 26, 2023. Video, accessed May 28, 2024. https://www.youtube.com/watch?v=oIrAS9i0Z7w.

Global Christian Relief, "New Conflict." "New Conflict Leaves 11 Dead, 60 Injured in Manipur, India." Global Christian Relief, October 25, 2024.

Global Christian Relief, "Persecution Reports: Nigeria." "Persecution Reports: Nigeria." Global Christian Relief. Accessed September 11, 2024. https://globalchris tianrelief.org/christian-persecution/countries/nigeria/.

Global Christian Relief, "Persecution Trends." "Persecution Trends to Watch in 2024: Examples of Christian Persecution Today." Global Christian Relief, January 12, 2024. https://globalchristianrelief.org/christian-persecution/stories/persecution -trends-to-watch-in-2024-10-significant-examples-of-christian-persecution-today/.

Glynn, *Song for Nagasaki*. Glynn, Paul. *A Song for Nagasaki: The Story of Takashi Nagai, Scientist, Convert, and Survivor of the Atomic Bomb*. Ignatius, 2009.

Gohr, "Blood." Gohr, Glenn. "How J. W. Tucker's Blood Became a Seed of the Assemblies of God in Congo." Flower Pentecostal Heritage Center, November 19, 2015. https://ifphc.wordpress.com/2015/11/19/how-j-w-tuckers-blood-became-a -seed-of-the-assemblies-of-god-in-congo/.

Gohr, "Week." Gohr, Glenn W. "This Week in AG History—March 1, 1970." AG News, February 28, 2019. Accessed September 15, 2024. https://news.ag.org/en /article-repository/news/2019/02/this-week-in-ag-history-march-1-1970.

Gordon, "Ministry of Healing." Gordon, A. J. "The Ministry of Healing." In *Healing: The Three Great Classics on Divine Healing*, edited by Jonathan L. Graf, 119–282. Christian Publications, 1992.

Gordon, *Slavery*. Gordon, Murray. *Slavery in the Arab World*. New Amsterdam Books, 1989.

Grant, "Floods." Grant, David L. "Floods of Apocalyptic Proportions Devastate India and Bangladesh." Assemblies of God mission mailing, September 1998, 1.

Grant, *Gods*. Grant, Robert M. *Gods and the One God*. Library of Early Christianity 1. Westminster, 1986.

Gray, *Lit Up with Love*. Gray, Derwin L. *Lit Up with Love: Becoming Good-News People to a Gospel-Starved World*. NavPress, 2025.

Groothuis, "Necessary Evil." Groothuis, Douglas. "Necessary Evil: Could God Have Created a World Without Suffering?" *Christianity Today*, March 2012, 37–40.

"Gunman Kills Wife." "Gunman Kills Wife at Church, Police Say." *USA Today*, November 24, 2008, 3A.

Guthrie, "Other Side." Guthrie, Stan. "The Other Side of Church Growth." Interview with Philip Jenkins. *Christianity Today*, March 2009, 52–54.

Hagan and Rymond-Richmond, *Darfur*. Hagan, John, and Wenona Rymond-Richmond. *Darfur and the Crime of Genocide*. Cambridge Studies in Law and Society. Cambridge University Press, 2008.

Hagin, *Authority*. Hagin, Kenneth E. *Authority of the Believer*. Faith Library, 1979.

Hagin, *Covenant*. Hagin, Kenneth E. *A Better Covenant*. Rhema, 1980.

Hagin, *Godliness Is Profitable*. Hagin, Kenneth E. *Godliness Is Profitable*. Kenneth Hagin Ministries, 1982.

Hagin, *Healing Belongs to Us*. Hagin, Kenneth E. *Healing Belongs to Us*. Kenneth Hagin, 1976.

Hagin, *Key to Healing*. Hagin, Kenneth E. *The Key to Scriptural Healing*. Kenneth E. Hagin Evangelistic Association, 1977.

Hagin, *Midas Touch*. Hagin, Kenneth E. *The Midas Touch: A Balanced Approach to Biblical Prosperity*. Faith Library, 2000.

Hagin, *Ministry of a Prophet*. Hagin, Kenneth E. *The Ministry of a Prophet*. Kenneth Hagin Ministries, 1965.

Hagin, *Name of Jesus*. Hagin, Kenneth E. *The Name of Jesus*. Kenneth Hagin Ministries, 1979.

Hagin, *Prayer Secrets*. Hagin, Kenneth E. *Prayer Secrets*. Kenneth Hagin, 1976.

Hagin, *Prevailing Prayer to Peace*. Hagin, Kenneth E. *Prevailing Prayer to Peace*. Faith Library, 1974.

Hagin, *Redeemed*. Hagin, Kenneth E. *Redeemed from Poverty, Sickness, and Spiritual Death*. Kenneth E. Hagin, 1974.

Hagin, *Thresholds*. Hagin, Kenneth E. *New Thresholds of Faith*. Faith Library, 1981.

Hagin, *Turn Faith Loose*. Hagin, Kenneth E. *How to Turn Your Faith Loose*. Kenneth Hagin, 1983.

Hagin, *Visions*. Hagin, Kenneth E. *I Believe in Visions*. Fleming H. Revell, 1972.

Hagin, *What Faith Is*. Hagin, Kenneth E. *What Faith Is*. Kenneth Hagin Ministries, 1978.

Hagin, *Zoe*. Hagin, Kenneth E. *Zoe: The God-Kind of Life*. Kenneth Hagin Ministries, 1981.

Hales and Coleman-Jensen, "Food Insecurity." Hales, Laura J., and Alisha Coleman-Jensen. "Food Insecurity for Households with Children Rose in 2020, Disrupting Decade-Long Decline." US Department of Agriculture, February 7, 2022. Accessed August 4, 2024. https://www.ers.usda.gov/amber-waves/2022/february/food-insecurity-for-households-with-children-rose-in-2020-disrupting-decade-long-decline/.

Hammond, "Heroes." Hammond, Leslie. "Heroes of the Faith: Lillian Trasher." Christians for Social Action website, May 17, 2015. Accessed June 4, 2024. https://christiansforsocialaction.org/resource/heroes-of-the-faith-lillian-trasher/.

Harrell, *All Things Are Possible.* Harrell, David Edwin, Jr. *All Things Are Possible: The Healing and Charismatic Revivals in Modern America.* Indiana University Press, 1975.

Hart, "Believers Displaced." Hart, Abigail. "Persecuted Indian Believers Displaced in Manipur." Global Christian Relief, January 2, 2024. Accessed May 19, 2024. https://globalchristianrelief.org/christian-persecution/stories/persecuted-indian-believers-displaced-in-manipur/.

Hattaway, *China's Martyrs.* Hattaway, Paul. *China's Book of Martyrs (AD 845–Present).* Vol. 1 of *Fire & Blood: The Church in China.* Piquant Editions, 2007.

Haugen, *Good News About Injustice.* Haugen, Gary. *Good News About Injustice.* InterVarsity, 1999.

Hefley and Hefley, *Blood.* Hefley, James, and Marti Hefley. *By Their Blood: Christian Martyrs of the Twentieth Century.* 2nd ed. Baker, 1996.

Hege, *We Two Alone.* Hege, Ruth. *We Two Alone: Attack and Rescue in the Congo.* Thomas Nelson, 1965.

Hochschild, *King Leopold's Ghost.* Hochschild, Adam. *King Leopold's Ghost: A Story of Greed, Terror, and Heroism in Colonial Africa.* Houghton Mifflin, 1998.

Hodges, *Indigenous Church.* Hodges, Melvin L. *The Indigenous Church.* Gospel Publishing House, 1976.

Holmes, "Losing 25,000 to Hunger Every Day." Holmes, John. "Losing 25,000 to Hunger Every Day." United Nations, April 1, 2008. Accessed August 3, 2024. https://www.un.org/en/chronicle/article/losing-25000-hunger-every-day.

Homeless No More, "Understanding Global Homelessness." "Understanding Global Homelessness: A Comprehensive Analysis." Homeless No More, March 18, 2024. Accessed August 4, 2024. https://homelessnomore.com/understanding-global-homelessness-a-comprehensive-analysis/.

Hudson, "British Pentecostals." Hudson, Neil. "Early British Pentecostals and Their Relationship to Health, Healing, and Medicine." *Asian Journal of Pentecostal Studies* 6, no. 2 (2003): 283–301.

Human Rights Watch, "Cow Protection Groups." Human Rights Watch. "India: Vigilante 'Cow Protection' Groups Attack Minorities." February 18, 2019. Accessed September 15, 2024. https://www.hrw.org/news/2019/02/19/india-vigilante-cow-protection-groups-attack-minorities.

Humberstone. "Single Mothers." Humberstone, Julie. "Single Mothers & Self-Reliance." *Marriott Alumni Magazine*, Fall 2007. Accessed August 4, 2024. https://marriott.byu.edu/magazine/faculty-research/single-mothers-self-reliance.

Hunt, *Bless God.* Hunt, Rosalie Hall. *Bless God and Take Courage: The Judson History and Legacy.* Judson, 2005.

Hunter, *Boyle*. Hunter, Michael C. W. *Boyle: Between God and Science*. Yale University Press, 2010.

Iacomini, "Unrest." Iacomini, Franco. "Missionaries Flee Mozambique's Election Unrest." *Christianity Today*, January 29, 2025. Accessed February 3, 2025. https://www.christianitytoday.com/2025/01/mozambique-violence-brazilian-missionaries/.

Ibraheem with Bach, *Shackled*. Ibraheem, Mariam, with Eugene Bach. *Shackled: One Woman's Dramatic Triumph over Persecution, Gender Abuse, and a Death Sentence*. Whitaker House, 2022.

Ilibagiza, *Left to Tell*. Ilibagiza, Immaculée, with Steve Erwin. *Left to Tell: Discovering God Amidst the Rwandan Holocaust*. Hay House, 2006.

Iris, "Core Values." "Iris' Core Values." Iris Global. Accessed June 6, 2024. https://www.irisglobal.org/about/core-values.

Iris, "Iris Story." "The Iris Story." Iris Global. Accessed May 26, 2024. https://www.irisglobal.org/about/the-iris-story.

Irwin, "Daily Bread." Irwin, David. "Their Daily Bread." *Mountain Movers*, January 1993, 10.

Isaac, *Ethiopian Church*. Isaac, Ephraim. *The Ethiopian Church*. Henry N. Sawyer Company, 1968.

Isichei, *Christianity in Africa*. Isichei, Elizabeth. *A History of Christianity in Africa from Antiquity to the Present*. Eerdmans, 1995.

Istrate, "Partnership." Istrate, Cristian E. "Initiating Partnership with the Persecuted Church." DMin diss., Asbury Theological Seminary, 2025.

Jackson, *Quest*. Jackson, Bill. *The Quest for the Radical Middle: A History of the Vineyard*. Vineyard International, 1999.

Jain, "Cow Vigilantes." Jain, Rupam. "India's Far-Right Cow Vigilantes Bolster Clout Before High-Stake Elections." Reuters, December 29, 2023. https://www.reuters.com/world/india/indias-far-right-cow-vigilantes-bolster-clout-before-high-stake-elections-2023-12-29/.

Jain and Kair, "Advocate." Jain, Rishabh, and Surinder Kaur. "Bangladeshi Christians and Hindus Advocate for a Secular Country." *Christianity Today*, September 6, 2024. Accessed September 6, 2024. https://www.christianitytoday.com/2024/09/bangladeshi-christians-hindus-advocate-secular-country/.

Jennings, *Good News to the Poor*. Jennings, Theodore W., Jr. *Good News to the Poor: John Wesley's Evangelical Economics*. Abingdon, 1990.

John, "Investigation." John, Uma. "An Investigation of Selected Imprecations in the Old Testament in Light of Recent Psychological Biblical Criticism." PhD diss., Asbury Theological Seminary, 2025.

Johnson, *Sting*. Johnson, Bill. *Removing the Sting of Death: Experience New Depths of God's Presence in Times of Pain, Grief, and Loss*. Destiny Image, 2025.

Johnston, "Betancourt." Johnston, Alan. "Betancourt Reflects on Captivity." BBC News, December 18, 2008. http://news.bbc.co.uk/2/hi/7789630.stm.

Johnstone, *Operation World* (1993). Johnstone, Patrick J. *Operation World*. Zondervan, 1993.

Johnstone and Mandryk, *Operation World*. Johnstone, Patrick, and Jason Mandryk. *Operation World*. 6th ed. Paternoster, 2001.

Jones and Monroe, *History of Ethiopia*. Jones, A. H. M., and Elizabeth Monroe. *A History of Ethiopia*. Clarendon, 1955.

"Jos Suicide Bombing." "Jos Suicide Bombing: 4 People Killed in a Blast at COCIN Church." YouTube video, accessed September 12, 2024. https://www.youtube.com/watch?v=lV4mJjCirmA.

Kanana, *Once Was Dead*. Kanana, Cedric. *I Once Was Dead: How God Rescued Me from Islam, Drugs, Witchcraft, and Even Death*. Oasis, 2022.

Kantowicz, *Rage*. Kantowicz, Edward R. *The Rage of Nations*. Vol. 1 of *The World in the 20th Century*. 2 vols. Eerdmans, 1999.

Kara, *Bonded Labor*. Kara, Siddharth. *Bonded Labor: Tackling the System of Slavery in South Asia*. Columbia University Press, 2012.

Kara, *Cobalt Red*. Kara, Siddharth. *Cobalt Red: How the Blood of the Congo Powers Our Lives*. St. Martin's Press, 2023.

Kara, *Modern Slavery*. Kara, Siddharth. *Modern Slavery: A Global Perspective*. Columbia University Press, 2017.

Kara, *Sex Trafficking*. Kara, Siddharth. *Sex Trafficking: Inside the Business of Modern Slavery*. 2nd ed. Columbia University Press, 2017.

Kaur, "Regulation." Kaur, Surinder. "The Regulation Suffocating Christian Ministries in India." *Christianity Today*, April 2, 2024. https://www.christianitytoday.com/2024/04/india-fcra-ngo-world-vision-foreign-funding-close/.

Keener, "Against Grain." Keener, Craig S. "Against the Grain—the Prophet Jeremiah." Bible Backgrounds website, February 10, 2020. https://craigkeener.com/against-the-grain-the-prophet-jeremiah/.

Keener, "Asia and Europe." Keener, Craig S. "Between Asia and Europe: Postcolonial Mission in Acts 16:8–10." *Asian Journal of Pentecostal Studies* 11, nos. 1–2 (2008): 3–14.

Keener, "Call and Cost." Keener, Craig S. "The Call and the Cost—Jeremiah 1:4–19." Bible Backgrounds website, June 15, 2020. https://craigkeener.com/the-call-and-the-cost-jeremiah-14-19/.

Keener, "Deserters." Keener, Craig S. "From Deserters to Defenders." *Christian History* 156 (forthcoming, 2025).

Keener, "Did Not Know." Keener, Craig S. "We Cannot Say We Did Not Know." *Prism* 11, no. 2 (2004): 14–15.

Keener, "Fidelity." Keener, Craig S. "Biblical Fidelity as an Evangelical Commitment." In *Following Jesus: Journeys in Radical Discipleship; Essays in Honor of Ronald J. Sider*, edited by Paul Alexander and Al Tizon, 29–41. Regnum Studies in Global Christianity. Regnum, 2013.

Keener, *Galatians*. Keener, Craig S. *Galatians: A Commentary*. Baker Academic, 2019.

Keener, *Galatians* (**Cambridge**). Keener, Craig S. *Galatians*. New Cambridge Bible Commentary. Cambridge University Press, 2018.

Keener, *Gift and Giver*. Keener, Craig S. *Gift and Giver: The Holy Spirit for Today*. Baker, 2001.

Keener, *Gospel of Matthew*. Keener, Craig S. *The Gospel of Matthew: A Socio-Rhetorical Commentary*. Eerdmans, 2009.

Keener, *Matthew*. Keener, Craig S. *Matthew*. IVP New Testament Commentary. InterVarsity, 1997.

Keener, "**Mayhem**." Keener, Craig S. "Mutual Mayhem: A Plea for Peace and Truth in the Madness of Nigeria." *Christianity Today*, November 2004, 60–64. Accessed September 13, 2024. https://www.christianitytoday.com/2004/11/mutual-mayhem/.

Keener, *Mind*. Keener, Craig S. *The Mind of the Spirit: Paul's Approach to Transformed Thinking*. Baker Academic, 2016.

Keener, *Miracles*. Keener, Craig S. *Miracles: The Credibility of the New Testament Accounts*. 2 vols. Baker Academic, 2011.

Keener, *Miracles Today*. Keener, Craig S. *Miracles Today: The Supernatural Work of God in the Modern World*. Baker Academic, 2021.

Keener, *Peter*. Keener, Craig S. *1 Peter: A Commentary*. Baker Academic, 2021.

Keener, "**Political Prophecies**." Keener, Craig S. "When Political Prophecies Don't Come to Pass." *Christianity Today*, November 11, 2020. https://www.christianitytoday.com/2020/11/political-prophecy-false-bible-scholar-trump-election/.

Keener, "**Prophets Wrong**." "When Most Prophets Are Wrong—1 Kings 22." Bible Backgrounds website, January 1, 2018. https://craigkeener.com/when-most-prophets-are-wrong-1-kings-22/.

Keener, "**Reconciliation**." Keener, Craig S. "The Gospel and Racial Reconciliation." In *The Gospel in Black and White: Theological Resources for Racial Reconciliation*, edited by Dennis L. Okholm, 117–30. InterVarsity, 1997.

Keener, *Revelation*. Keener, Craig S. *Revelation*. NIV Application Commentary. Zondervan, 2000.

Keener, review of Blomberg, *Neither Poverty nor Riches*. Keener, Craig S. Review of *Neither Poverty nor Riches*, by Craig Blomberg. *Prism* (Nov. 1999): 28–29.

Keener, "**Salting**." "Salting Everyone with Fire (Mark 9:49–50): Purification, Preservation or Punishment?" *Journal of Greco-Roman Christianity and Judaism* 21 (2024): 9–28.

Keener, "**Sider**." Keener, Craig S. "Ron Sider Was the Real Deal." *Christianity Today*, August 1, 2022. Accessed September 14, 2024. https://www.christianitytoday.com/2022/08/died-ron-sider-social-justice-real-deal/.

Keener, *Spirit Hermeneutics*. Keener, Craig S. *Spirit Hermeneutics: Reading Scripture in Light of Pentecost*. Eerdmans, 2016.

Keener, "**Succeed at Suffering**." Keener, Craig S. "How to Succeed at Suffering: Lessons from the Gospel of Mark." *Influence Magazine*, February 2024, 56–62. https://influencemagazine.com/en/Practice/How-to-Succeed-at-Suffering.

Keener, "Trump Prophecies." Keener, Craig S. "Failed Trump Prophecies Offer a Lesson in Humility." *Christianity Today*, January 20, 2021. https://www.christi anitytoday.com/2021/01/trump-prophets-apologize-election-prophecies-humility/.

Keener, "Western Religion." Keener, Craig S. "Christianity Is Not a Western Religion." YouTube, October 14, 2023. Accessed September 18, 2024. https://www.youtube .com/watch?v=v-F-h-8soyM.

Keener and Keener, "Commission." Keener, Craig S., and Médine Moussounga Keener. "Commission, Mission and Migration in Acts: A Response to Ekaputra Tupamahu." *Pneuma* 46, no. 2 (2024): 196–215.

Keener and Keener, *Impossible Love*. Keener, Craig S., and Médine Moussounga Keener. *Impossible Love: The True Story of an African Civil War, Miracles, and Love Against All Odds.* Chosen, 2016.

Keener and Usry, *Faith*. Keener, Craig S., and Glenn Usry. *Defending Black Faith.* InterVarsity, 1997.

Kempis, *Imitation of Christ*. Kempis, Thomas à. *The Imitation of Christ.* Translated by Leo Sherley-Price. Penguin, 1952.

Kidd, "Healing." Kidd, Thomas S. "The Healing of Mercy Wheeler: Illness and Miracles Among Early American Evangelicals." *William and Mary Quarterly* 63, no. 1 (2006): 149–70.

Kim, *Form and Structure*. Kim, Chan-Hie. *Form and Structure of the Familiar Greek Letter of Recommendation.* Society of Biblical Literature Dissertation Series 4. Society of Biblical Literature, 1972.

Kim, *If I Perish*. Kim, Esther Ahn. *If I Perish: Facing Imprisonment, Persecution, and Death, a Young Korean Christian Defies the Japanese Warlords.* 2nd ed. Moody, 2001.

King, *Believer with Authority*. King, Paul L. *A Believer with Authority: The Life and Message of John A. MacMillan.* Christian Publications, 2001.

King, *Moving Mountains*. King, Paul L. *Moving Mountains: Lessons in Bold Faith from Great Evangelical Leaders.* Chosen, 2004.

Koch, *Revival in Indonesia*. Koch, Kurt. *The Revival in Indonesia.* Evangelization Publishers; Kregel, 1970.

Kochhar, "$10 per Day." Kochhar, Rakesh. "Seven-in-Ten People Globally Live on $10 or Less per Day." Pew Research Center, September 23, 2015. Accessed August 4, 2024. https://www.pewresearch.org/short-reads/2015/09/23/seven-in-ten-people -globally-live-on-10-or-less-per-day/.

Koestler, "Kepler and Psychology." Koestler, Arthur. "Kepler and the Psychology of Discovery." In *The Logic of Personal Knowledge: Essays Presented to Michael Polanyi on His Seventieth Birthday 11 March 1961*, 49–57. Routledge & Kegan Paul, 1961.

Kopaska and Liston, *Afterburn*. Kopaska, Kc, and Carole Liston. *Afterburn: The Kc Kopaska Story: A Story of Tragedy, Redemption, and Transformation.* Westbow, 2011.

Kraybill, *Cult*. Kraybill, J. Nelson. *Imperial Cult and Commerce in John's Apocalypse.* Journal for the Study of the New Testament Supplement Series 132. Sheffield Academic, 1996.

Kristof, *Chasing Hope*. Kristof, Nicholas D. *Chasing Hope: A Reporter's Life*. Knopf, 2024.

Kruger, *Question of Canon*. Kruger, Michael J. *The Question of Canon: Challenging the Status Quo in the New Testament Debate*. IVP Academic, 2013.

Kyle, *Last Days*. Kyle, Richard G. *The Last Days Are Here Again: A History of the End Times*. Baker, 1998.

Lagerborg, *Though Lions Roar*. Lagerborg, Mary Beth. *Though Lions Roar: The Story of Helen Roseveare, Missionary Doctor to the Congo*. CLC, 1995.

"Langham Trains Pastors." "How Langham Trains Pastors Where Christians Face Persecution." Langham Partnership website. Accessed May 30, 2024. https://us.lan gham.org/news-and-updates/stories/langham-partnership-christian-persecution/.

Lear, "Heartbeat." Lear, Steven. "The 'Heartbeat' of Our Founder." *Voice of the Martyrs*. Special issue, 2008.

Lee, *Persecution*. Lee, Chee-Chiew. *When Christians Face Persecution: Theological Perspectives from the New Testament*. Apollos, 2022.

Lee, "Psalm 91." Lee, Morgan. "He Prayed Psalm 91 as Bullets Landed on His Roof." *Christianity Today*, February 4, 2025. Accessed February 8, 2025. https://www .christianitytoday.com/2025/02/congo-m23-goma-rwanda-rebel-group-pray/.

Leung, "Conversion." Leung, Philip Yuen-Sang. "Conversion, Commitment, and Culture: Christian Experience in China, 1949–99." In *Christianity Reborn: The Global Expansion of Evangelicalism in the Twentieth Century*, edited by Donald M. Lewis, 87–107. Eerdmans, 2004.

Lewis, *Race and Slavery*. Lewis, Bernard. *Race and Slavery in the Middle East: An Historical Enquiry*. Oxford University Press, 1990.

Lewis, *Religion and Society*. Lewis, Bernard, ed. *Religion and Society*. Vol. 2 of *Islam from the Prophet Mohammed to the Capture of Constantinople*. Oxford University Press, 1974.

Limaye, "Torture." Limaye, Yogita. "Torture, Rape, Killings in Manipur: An Indian State's Brutal Conflict." BBC News, September 19, 2023. Accessed May 19, 2024. https://www.bbc.com/news/world-asia-india-66844028.

Lindberg, *Beginnings*. Lindberg, David. *The Beginnings of Western Science: The European Scientific Tradition in Philosophical, Religious, and Institutional Context, Prehistory to A.D. 1450*. 2nd ed. University of Chicago Press, 2008.

Lindberg and Numbers, *Essays*. Lindberg, David, and Ronald Numbers, eds. *God and Nature: Historical Essays on the Encounter Between Christianity and Science*. University of California Press, 1986.

"Line of Demarcation." "Line of Demarcation." *Christianity Today*, April 9, 1990, 38.

Livingstone, Hart, and Noll, *Perspective*. Livingstone, David N., D. G. Hart, and Mark A. Noll, eds. *Evangelicals and Science in Historical Perspective*. Religion in America. Oxford University Press, 1999.

Ma, "Gospel." Ma, Julie. "The Pentecostal Gospel." In *Five Views on the Gospel*, edited by Michael F. Bird and Jason Maston, 157–75. Zondervan Academic, 2025.

Mandryk, *Operation World*. Mandryk, Jason. *Operation World*. 7th ed. Biblica, 2010.

Mannix, *Black Cargoes*. Mannix, Daniel P., with Malcolm Cowley. *Black Cargoes: A History of the Atlantic Slave Trade, 1518–1865*. Viking, 1962.

Marshall, *Blood*. Marshall, Paul A. *Their Blood Cries Out: The Worldwide Tragedy of Modern Christians Who Are Dying for Their Faith*. Word, 1997.

Marshall, Gilbert, and Shea, *Persecuted*. Marshall, Paul, Lela Gilbert, and Nina Shea. *Persecuted: The Global Assault on Christians*. Thomas Nelson, 2013.

Marshall and Shea, *Silenced*. Marshall, Paul, and Nina Shea. *Silenced: How Apostasy and Blasphemy Codes Are Choking Freedom Worldwide*. Oxford University Press, 2011.

Martin, *Nailing It*. Martin, Nicole Massie. *Nailing It: Why Successful Leadership Demands Suffering and Surrender*. IVP, 2025.

Martin and Bach, *Crimson Crucible*. Martin, Luther, and Eugene Bach. *Crimson Crucible: Underground Christians in North Korea*. Back to Jerusalem, 2013.

Masland, "Slavery." Masland, Tom, Rod Nordland, Melinda Liu, and Joseph Contreras. "Slavery." *Newsweek*, May 4, 1992, 30–39.

Maudlin, "God's Smuggler." Maudlin, Michael G. "God's Smuggler Confesses: Brother Andrew Wonders If American Christians Are Willing to Die for Anything, Even Their Faith." *Christianity Today*, December 11, 1995, 45–46.

Maust, *Peace*. Maust, John. *Peace and Hope in the Corner of the Dead*. Latin America Mission, 1987.

McDade, "Cannot Burn Jesus." McDade, Stefani. "'They Cannot Burn Jesus Out of Me': Mozambique Pastors Minister to Survivors of Violent Insurgency." *Christianity Today*, August 3, 2021. Accessed August 1, 2024. https://www.christian itytoday.com/news/2021/august/mozambique-insurgency-attacks-cabo-delgado -pastors-minister.html.

McDonald, *Canon*. McDonald, Lee Martin. *The Biblical Canon: Its Origin, Transmission, and Authority*. Hendrickson, 2007.

McGee, "Possessions." McGee, Daniel B. "Sharing Possessions: A Study in Biblical Ethics." In *With Steadfast Purpose: Essays on Acts in Honor of Henry Jackson Flanders, Jr.*, edited by Naymond H. Keathley, 163–78. Baylor University Press, 1990.

Metaxas, *Grace*. Metaxas, Eric. *Amazing Grace: William Wilberforce and the Heroic Campaign to End Slavery*. HarperSanFrancisco, 2007.

Miller, "Evangelicals." Miller, Duane Alexander. "Evangelicals in Northern Africa and Egypt." In *Evangelicals Around the World: A Global Handbook for the 21st Century*, edited by Brian C. Stiller et al., 248–54. Thomas Nelson, 2015.

Miller and Wood, "Dangerous Territory." Miller, Sarah, and Mark Wood. "Dangerous Territory: A Deepening Humanitarian Emergency in Northern Mozambique." Refugees International, June 28, 2024. Accessed August 4, 2024. https:// www.refugeesinternational.org/reports-briefs/dangerous-territory-a-deepening -humanitarian-emergency-in-northern-mozambique/.

"Modern Day Slavery?" "What Is Modern Day Slavery?" Voices 4 Freedom. Accessed September 15, 2024. https://www.voices4freedom.org/what-is-modern-day -slavery/.

Moeller and Hegg, *Privilege of Persecution*. Moeller, Carl A., and David W. Hegg with Craig Hodgkins. *The Privilege of Persecution (And Other Things the Global Church Knows That We Don't)*. Moody, 2011.

Morphew, *Breakthrough*. Morphew, Derek. *Breakthrough: Discovering the Kingdom*. 5th ed. Vineyard International Publishing, 2019.

Moszynski, "Died." Moszynski, Peter. "5.4 Million People Have Died in Democratic Republic of Congo Since 1998 Because of Conflict, Report Says." *British Medical Journal* (Clinical Research ed.) 336, no. 7638 (2008): 235.

Mukwege, *Power*. Mukwege, Denis. *The Power of Women: A Doctor's Journey of Hope and Healing*. Flatiron Books, 2022.

Müller, *Autobiography*. Müller, George. *The Autobiography of George Müller*. Published in various editions.

Mumphrey and Rodgers, "Focus." Mumphrey, Cheyanne, and Arleigh Rodgers. "'It's Hard to Focus': Schools Say American Kids Are Hungry." Associated Press, March 11, 2023. Accessed August 4, 2024. https://apnews.com/article/free-school-lunch -child-hunger-7d38b5a84e533129f507d76cc05c622f.

Nagai, *Bells of Nagasaki*. Nagai, Takashi. *The Bells of Nagasaki*. Translated by William Johnston. Kodansha, 1994.

Navalny, *Patriot*. Navalny, Alexei. *Patriot: A Memoir*. Knopf, 2024.

Neill, *History of Missions*. Neill, Stephen. *A History of Christian Missions*. Penguin, 1964.

Nettleton, *When Faith Is Forbidden*. Nettleton, Todd. *When Faith Is Forbidden: 40 Days on the Front Lines with Persecuted Christians*. Moody, 2021.

News Briefs (1992). News Briefs. *Christianity Today*, July 20, 1992, 49.

News Briefs (1995). News Briefs. *Christianity Today*, October 23, 1995, 88.

News Briefs (2012). News Briefs. *Christianity Today*, September 2012, 15.

Noll, *History*. Noll, Mark A. *A History of Christianity in the United States and Canada*. Eerdmans, 1992.

Noll and Nystrom, *Witnesses*. Noll, Mark A., and Carolyn Nystrom. *Clouds of Witnesses: Christian Voices from Africa and Asia*. InterVarsity, 2011.

Numbers, *Galileo*. Numbers, Ronald L., ed. *Galileo Goes to Jail and Other Myths About Science and Religion*. Harvard University Press, 2009.

"Nutritional Crusade." "Nutritional Crusade." Oberlin College and Conservatory website. Accessed June 3, 2024. https://isis2.cc.oberlin.edu/175/didyouknow -graham.html.

Nwachukwu, "Ripped Apart." Nwachukwu, Emmanuel. "Boko Haram Ripped Apart Her Life. A Decade Later, It's Still Torn." *Christianity Today*, May 8, 2025. Accessed May 10, 2025. https://www.christianitytoday.com/2025/05/christians-displaced -by-boko-haram-still-struggle-to-rebuild-lives/.

O., "Christianity and Slavery." O., Brian. "Christianity and Slavery: The Unheard Stories from Pakistan's Brick Kilns." Global Christian Relief, June 14, 2023. Accessed September 15, 2024. https://globalchristianrelief.org/christian-persecution /stories/persecuted-christians-the-unheard-stories-from-pakistans-brick-kilns/.

Oblau, "Healing in China." Oblau, Gotthard. "Divine Healing and the Growth of Practical Christianity in China." In *Global Pentecostal and Charismatic Healing*, edited by Candy Gunther Brown, 307–27. Oxford University Press, 2011.

Ogilvie and Miller, *Refuge Denied*. Ogilvie, Sarah A., and Scott Miller. *Refuge Denied: The St. Louis Passengers and the Holocaust*. University of Wisconsin Press, 2010.

Ojo, "Civil War Revival." Ojo, Matthews. "The Civil War Revival and Its Pentecostal Progeny (1976–2006)." *Pneuma* 31 (2009): 105–60.

Oliver, *Revivals*. Oliver, Jeff. *Worldwide Revivals and Renewal*. Vol. 1 of *Pentecost to the Present*. Bridge-Logos, 2017.

Olson, *Bruchko*. Olson, Bruce. *Bruchko*. Rev. ed. Creation House, 1995.

Olson and Lund, *Bruchko and Miracle*. Olson, Bruce, and James R. Lund. *Bruchko and the Motilone Miracle*. Creation House, 2006.

Omer, "Global Water Crisis." Omer, Sevil. "Global Water Crisis: Facts, FAQs, and How to Help." World Vision, March 6, 2024. Accessed August 4, 2024. https://www .worldvision.org/clean-water-news-stories/global-water-crisis-facts.

Onion, "Bangladesh Cyclone." Onion, Amanda, et al. "Bangladesh Cyclone: April 29, 1991." History, April 29, 2019. Accessed August 4, 2024. https://www.history.com /topics/natural-disasters-and-environment/bangladesh-cyclone-of-1991.

Open Doors, "He Is Always with Us." Open Doors. "He Is Always with Us." *Open Doors Newsletter*, September 2024, 1–2.

Open Doors, "Pain and Faith." Open Doors. "Pain and Faith in a Displacement Camp." *Open Doors Newsletter*, September 2024, 4.

Open Doors, "World Watch List 2024." "World Watch List 2024." Open Doors. Accessed September 15, 2024. https://www.opendoors.org/en-US/persecution/coun tries/.

Open Doors, "World Watch List 2025." "World Watch List 2025." Open Doors. Accessed January 15, 2025. https://www.opendoors.org/en-US/persecution/countries/.

Opp, *Lord for Body*. Opp, James. *The Lord for the Body: Religion, Medicine, and Protestant Faith Healing in Canada, 1880–1930*. McGill-Queen's University Press, 2005.

"Overcome Evil." "Overcome Evil with Good." *Mountain Movers*, May 1991, 6.

Ozovehe, "Impacts." Ozovehe, Samson. "The Impacts of the Persecution of Christians in Northern Nigeria on the Mission of the Church: A Case Study of Churches in Sabon Tasha, Chikun Local Government Area, Kaduna State." DMin diss., Asbury Theological Seminary, 2025.

Paluku, *Coltan*. Paluku, Jerome. *Is Coltan a Development Opportunity or a Curse? Perceptions of the Impacts of the Mineral Mining in Masisi Territory, Democratic Republic of Congo*. Éditions universitaires européennes, 2018.

Panahi, *Didn't Survive*. Panahi, Naghmeh Abedini. *I Didn't Survive: Emerging Whole After Deception, Persecution, and Hidden Abuse*. Whitaker House, 2023.

Park, *Conflict*. Park, Andrew Sung. *Racial Conflict and Healing: An Asian-American Theological Perspective*. Orbis Books, 1996.

Park, *Hurt*. Park, Andrew Sung. *From Hurt to Healing: A Theology of the Wounded*. Abingdon, 2004.

Parkinson and Hinshaw, *Bring Back Our Girls*. Parkinson, Joe, and Drew Hinshaw. *Bring Back Our Girls: The Untold Story of the Global Search for Nigeria's Missing Schoolgirls*. HarperCollins, 2021.

Partee, *Adventure in Africa*. Partee, Charles. *Adventure in Africa: The Story of Don McClure*. Zondervan, 1990.

Peterman, Palermo, and Bredenkamp, "Estimates." Peterman, Amber, Tia Palermo, and Caryn Bredenkamp. "Estimates and Determinants of Sexual Violence Against Women in the Democratic Republic of Congo." *American Journal of Public Health* 101, no. 6 (2011): 1060–67. Accessed February 7, 2025. https://pmc.ncbi.nlm.nih .gov/articles/PMC3093289/.

Peterson, *Flat Earth*. Peterson, Derrick. *Flat Earth and Fake Footnotes: The Strange Tale of How the Conflict of Science and Christianity Was Written into History*. Cascade, 2020.

Peterson, *Ham and Japheth*. Peterson, Thomas Virgil. *Ham and Japheth: The Mythic World of Whites in the Antebellum South*. Scarecrow, 1978.

Pettis, "Faith Prevents." Steve Pettis Ministries. "Faith Prevents Persecution Power." YouTube video, accessed September 4, 2024. https://www.youtube.com/watch?v =96q7LD9SL3U.

Pew Research Center, "World Population by Income." "World Population by Income." Pew Research Center, July 8, 2015. Accessed August 4, 2024. https://www .pewresearch.org/global-migration-and-demography/feature/global-population -by-income/.

Phipps, *William Sheppard*. Phipps, William E. *William Sheppard: Congo's African American Livingstone*. Geneva, 2002.

Pierce, "Faith." Pierce, Larry. "Where There's Faith, There's Hope for Boys." *Christianity Today*, September 13, 1993, 80.

Piper, "Missions When Dying Is Gain." Piper, John. "Doing Missions When Dying Is Gain." *Desiring God*, October 27, 1996. Accessed September 8, 2024. https:// www.desiringgod.org/messages/doing-missions-when-dying-is-gain.

Pipkin, *Changed*. Pipkin, Whitney K. *We Shall All Be Changed: How Facing Death with Loved Ones Transforms Us*. Moody, 2024.

"Poverty and Development." "Poverty and Transformational Development: It's Transforming Students, Too." World Vision, September 4, 2019. Accessed September 15, 2024. https://www.worldvision.org/ignite/2019/09/04/poverty-and-transforma tional-development-its-transforming-students-too/.

Powery, "Mark." Powery, Emerson B. "The Gospel of Mark." In *True to Our Native Land: An African American New Testament Commentary*, edited by Brian K. Blount, 121–57. Fortress, 2007.

"Prisoner's Song." "A Prisoner's Song." *Christian History* 109 (2014): 32.

Prodan, *Saving My Assassin*. Prodan, Virginia. *Saving My Assassin: A Memoir*. Tyndale, 2016.

Pullinger, *Chasing Dragon*. Jackie Pullinger, with Andrew Quicke. *Chasing the Dragon*. Hodder & Stoughton, 1980.

Qureshi, *Seeking Allah, Finding Jesus*. Qureshi, Nabeel. *Seeking Allah, Finding Jesus: A Devout Muslim Encounters Christianity*. Zondervan, 2014.

Rajvanshi, "Raped." Rajvanshi, Astha. "Over 150 Women Raped During Congo Prison Break, U.N. Says." NBC News, February 6, 2025. Accessed February 7, 2025. https://www.nbcnews.com/news/world/democratic-republic-of-congo-women-rape-prison-break-goma-m23-rebels-rcna190954.

"Rakbar Khan." "Rakbar Khan: Did Cow Vigilantes Lynch a Muslim Farmer?" BBC News, February 22, 2019. Accessed September 15, 2024. https://www.bbc.com/news/stories-47321871.

Reliefweb, "Bangladesh: Floods: Aug 1988." "Bangladesh—Floods Aug 1988 UNDRO Situation Reports 1–13." Reliefweb, August 30, 1988. Accessed August 4, 2024. https://reliefweb.int/report/bangladesh/bangladesh-floods-aug-1988-undro-situation-reports-1-13.

Reliefweb, "Bangladesh: Floods 2004." "Bangladesh: Monsoon Floods 2004." Reliefweb, October 6, 2004. Accessed August 4, 2024. https://reliefweb.int/report/bangladesh/bangladesh-monsoon-floods-2004-post-flood-needs-assessment-summary-report.

"Returning to Tchabi." "Returning to Tchabi." *Voice of the Martyrs*, September 2024, 4–7. https://vom.com.au/stories/returning-to-tchabi/.

"Revenge in Gujarat." "Taking Revenge in Gujarat." CNN, May 15, 2002. Accessed April 2, 2025. https://edition.cnn.com/2002/WORLD/asiapcf/south/05/15/tully.gujarat/index.html.

Richardson, *Lords of the Earth*. Richardson, Don. *Lords of the Earth*. Regal, 1977.

Robert, "Introduction." Robert, Dana L. "Introduction: Historical Themes and Current Issues." In *Gospel Bearers, Gender Barriers: Missionary Women in the Twentieth Century*, edited by Dana L. Robert, 1–28. Orbis Books, 2002.

Roseveare, "Cost of Loving Jesus." "The Cost of Loving Jesus." Interview with Helen Roseveare. *Christianity Today*, May 12, 1989, 45.

Roseveare, "Counting the Cost." Roseveare, Helen. "Counting the Cost: Loving the Lord with Heart, Soul and Strength." *World Christian*, November 1986, 36–39.

Roseveare, *Living Sacrifice*. Roseveare, Helen. *Living Sacrifice: Willing to Be Whittled as an Arrow*. Rev. ed. Christian Focus, 2007.

Rostampour and Amirizadeh, *Captive in Iran*. Rostampour, Maryam, and Marziyeh Amirizadeh. *Captive in Iran: A Remarkable True Story of Hope and Triumph amid the Horror of Tehran's Brutal Evin Prison*. 2nd ed. Tyndale Momentum, 2013.

Saint, *End of the Spear*. Saint, Steve. *End of the Spear*. Tyndale, 2005.

Samuel, "Global 1%." Samuel, Sigal. "Lots of Americans Are in the Global 1%. A Tenth of Their Income Could Transform the World." *Vox*, September 15, 2023. Accessed August 4, 2024. https://www.vox.com/future-perfect/2023/9/15/23874111 /charity-philanthropy-americans-global-rich.

Sanneh, *West African Christianity*. Sanneh, Lamin. *West African Christianity: The Religious Impact*. Orbis Books, 1983.

Sanusi, *Gloria!* Sanusi, Abidemi. *Gloria! The Archbishop's Wife*. Zondervan, 2014.

Sarnoff and Hutchinson, "Miracle." Sarnoff, Leah, and Bill Hutchinson. "'Miracle': Pastor Credits Divine Intervention After Man Pulls Gun on Him During Sermon." *ABC News*, May 6, 2024. Accessed May 19, 2024. https://abcnews.go.com/US/man -arrested-after-allegedly-attempting-shoot-pastor-sermon/story?id=109945890.

Satyavrata, *Pentecostals and Poor*. Satyavrata, Ivan. *Pentecostals and the Poor: Reflections from the India Context*. Baguio City, Philippines: APTS Press, 2017.

"Saudi Arabia—Religious Intolerance." "Saudi Arabia—Religious Intolerance: The Arrest, Detention and Torture of Christian Worshippers and Shi'a Muslims." Amnesty International, September 14, 1993. https://www.amnesty.org/en/documents /mde23/006/1993/en/.

Scammel, "Helen Berhane." Scammel, Rosie. "Helen Berhane, Eritrean Gospel Singer and Torture Survivor, Tells Story." *Christian Century*, February 17, 2016. Accessed May 16, 2024. https://www.christiancentury.org/article/2015-12/eritrean-gospel -singer-tortured-her-beliefs-tells-story.

Schoch, "Half the Population." Schoch, Marta, et al. "Half of the Global Population Lives on Less Than US$6.85 per Person per Day." World Bank Blogs, December 8, 2022. Accessed August 4, 2024. https://blogs.worldbank.org/en/developmenttalk /half-global-population-lives-less-us685-person-day.

Shao, "Heritage." Shao, Joseph Too. "Heritage of the Chinese-Filipino Protestant Churches." *Journal of Asian Mission* 1, no. 1 (1999): 93–99.

Shaw, *Global Awakening*. Shaw, Mark. *Global Awakening: How 20th-Century Revivals Triggered a Christian Revolution*. IVP Academic, 2010.

Sheikh, *Call Him Father*. Sheikh, Bilquis, with Richard H. Schneider. *I Dared to Call Him Father: The Miraculous Story of a Muslim Woman's Encounter with God*. Chosen, 2023.

Shortt, *Christianophobia*. Shortt, Rupert. *Christianophobia: A Faith Under Attack*. Eerdmans, 2012.

Siddique, Baqui, Eusof, and Zaman, "Floods in Bangladesh." Siddique, A. K., A. H. Baqui, A. Eusof, and K. Zaman. "1988 Floods in Bangladesh: Pattern of Illness and Causes of Death." *Journal of Diarroeal Disease Research* 9, no. 4 (December 1991): 310–14.

Sider, *Cry Justice*. Sider, Ronald J., ed. *Cry Justice: The Bible on Hunger and Poverty*. Paulist Press, Bread for the World, 1980.

Sider, *Rich Christians*. Sider, Ronald J. *Rich Christians in an Age of Hunger*. 3rd ed. Word, 1990.

Silliman, "Missionaries Killed." Silliman, Daniel. "American Missionaries Killed in Port-au-Prince." *Christianity Today*, May 24, 2024.

"Singer Released." "Eritrean Gospel Singer 'Released.'" BBC News, November 4, 2006. http://news.bbc.co.uk/2/hi/africa/6117496.stm.

"Slavery in Bangladesh." "Modern Slavery in Bangladesh." Walk Free website. Accessed September 15, 2024. https://cdn.walkfree.org/content/uploads/2023/11/141 30724/gsi-country-study-bangladesh.pdf.

"Slavery in Saudi Arabia." "Modern Slavery in Saudi Arabia." Walk Free website. Accessed September 15, 2024. https://www.walkfree.org/global-slavery-index/country -studies/saudi-arabia/.

Smith, "Discerning." Smith, James K. A. "Discerning What Power Is For." *Mockingbird*, Feb. 4, 2025. Accessed February 8, 2025. https://mbird.com/the-magazine /discerning-what-power-is-for/.

Smith, "Parishioners." Smith, Patrick. "Parishioners Stopped Teen with a Rifle from Entering Church with 60 Children Inside." NBC News, May 13, 2024. Accessed May 19, 2024. https://www.nbcnews.com/news/us-news/parishioners-louisiana -stopped-teen-rifle-church-childrens-mass-rcna151925.

Soucy, Janes, and Hall, "State of Homelessness." Soucy, Daniel, Makenna Janes, and Andrew Hall. "State of Homelessness: 2024 Edition." National Alliance to End Homelessness. Accessed September 15, 2024. https://endhomelessness.org/home lessness-in-america/homelessness-statistics/state-of-homelessness/.

Stafford, "Sit Still." Stafford, Tim. "The Man Who Couldn't Sit Still." *Christianity Today*, March 11, 1991, 49–50.

Stickle, Hickman, and White, *Human Trafficking*. Stickle, Wendy, Shelby Nichole Hickman, and Christine A. White. *Human Trafficking: A Comprehensive Exploration of Modern Day Slavery*. SAGE, 2019.

Stowers, *Letter Writing*. Stowers, Stanley K. *Letter Writing in Greco-Roman Antiquity*. Library of Early Christianity 5. Westminster, 1986.

"Sudan: Caught in Cycle." "Sudan: Caught in a Vicious Cycle of Human Rights Abuses, Poverty and Political Turmoil." *Amnesty Action*, Winter 1995, 1, 3.

"Sudan: Ravages." "Sudan—the Ravages of War: Political Killings and Humanitarian Disaster." Amnesty International, September 29, 1993. https://www.amnesty.org /en/documents/afr54/029/1993/en/.

"Sun Creates a Desert." "Sun Alone Creates a Desert." *Christianity Today*, May 19, 1997, 36.

Sung, *Diaries*. Sung, John (Song, Shang-chieh). *The Diaries of John Sung: An Autobiography*. Translated by Stephen L. Sheng. Published by Luke H. Sheng and Stephen L. Sheng, 1995.

"Superintendent Martyred." "Iranian Assemblies of God General Superintendent Martyred." *Mountain Movers*, May 1994, 14.

Syniy, *Serving God*. Syniy, Valentyn. *Serving God Under Siege: How War Transformed a Ukrainian Community*. Eerdmans, forthcoming.

Talbert, *Mediterranean Milieu*. Talbert, C. H. *Reading Luke-Acts in Its Mediterranean Milieu*. Supplements to Novum Testamentum 107. Brill, 2003.

Tan, "Secret Work." Tan, David. "The Secret Work of the Holy Spirit in China Through Madame Guyon." *Journal of Asian Mission* 4, no. 1 (2002): 97–110.

Tapia, "Arrest." Tapia, Andrés. "Arrest of Evangelical Spurs Political Awareness." *Christianity Today*, April 25, 1994, 46.

"Targets for Oppression." "Targets for Oppression." Global Christian Relief, July 21, 2024.

Tari, *Mighty Wind*. Tari, Mel, with Cliff Dudley. *Like a Mighty Wind*. Creation House, 1971.

Taylor and Taylor, *Early Years*. Taylor, Frederick Howard, and Mary Geraldine Taylor. *Hudson Taylor in Early Years: The Growth of a Soul*. Morgan & Scott, China Inland Mission, 1943.

Taylor and Taylor, *Secret*. Taylor, Howard, and Geraldine Taylor. *Hudson Taylor's Spiritual Secret*. Urbana ed. Moody, 1987.

ten Boom, *Hiding Place*. Ten Boom, Corrie, with Elizabeth and John Sherrill. *The Hiding Place*. Chosen, 1971.

"Terror." "Terror." *Mountain Movers*, May 1991, 10.

Thomas, *Walls*. Thomas, Sandy. *Beyond Jungle Walls: Bringing Hope to the Forgotten Congo*. 21st Century Press, 2005.

Thomas and Witts, *Voyage of Damned*. Thomas, Gordon, and Max Morgan Witts. *Voyage of the Damned: A Shocking True Story of Hope, Betrayal and Nazi Terror*. Open Road Integrated Media, 2014.

"Three Children." "Our Three Children Were Killed in a Car Accident." *Evangelicals Now*, September 17, 2012. Accessed September 15, 2024. https://evangelicalsnow .wordpress.com/2012/09/17/our-three-children-were-killed-in-a-car-accident/.

Tomkins, *Wilberforce*. Tomkins, Stephen. *William Wilberforce: A Biography*. Eerdmans, 2007.

Ton, *Suffering*. Ton, Josef. *Suffering, Martyrdom, and Rewards in Heaven*. Romanian Missionary Society, 2000.

Tracy, "Let My People Go." Tracy, Kate. "Let My People Go." *Christianity Today*, November 22, 2013, 21.

"Tragedy Turns." "Tragedy Often Turns People to God." *Pentecostal Evangel*, April 19, 1987, 25.

Tucker, *Heaven*. Tucker, Angeline. *He Is in Heaven*. McGraw-Hill, 1965.

Tucker, *Jerusalem to Irian Jaya*. Tucker, Ruth. *From Jerusalem to Irian Jaya: A Biographical History of Christian Missions*. Zondervan, 1983.

Tulloch, "Feast." Tulloch, Joseph. "Vatican Marks First Feast of Coptic Martyrs." *Vatican News*, February 2024. Accessed February 2, 2025. https://www.vaticannews.va/en/vatican-city/news/2024-02/vatican-coptic-martyrs-feast-first-ecumenical-prayer.html.

Turaki, "Legacy." Turaki, Yusufu. "The British Colonial Legacy in Northern Nigeria." PhD diss., Boston University, 1982.

UNESCO, "Children." "Out-of-School Children and Youth." UNESCO. Accessed September 15, 2024. https://uis.unesco.org/en/topic/out-school-children-and-youth.

UNESCO, "Valuing Water Supply." "Valuing Water Supply, Sanitation Services." UNESCO, September 19, 2024. Accessed February 15, 2025. https://www.unesco.org/reports/wwdr/2021/en/valuing-water-supply-sanitation-services.

UNICEF, "Nearly Every Minute." "Nearly Every Minute, a Child Under 5 Dies of Malaria." UNICEF, November 2024. Accessed February 15, 2025. https://data.unicef.org/topic/child-health/malaria/.

UN Inter-Agency Group, "Levels and Trends." "Levels and Trends in Child Mortality." 2023 report. United Nations Inter-Agency Group for Child Mortality Estimation, March 12, 2024. Accessed August 4, 2024. https://data.unicef.org/resources/levels-and-trends-in-child-mortality-2024/.

United Nations, "Everyone Included." "Everyone Included—How to End Homelessness." United Nations Department of Economic and Social Affairs. Accessed August 4, 2024. https://www.un.org/tr/desa/everyone-included-%E2%80%93-how-end-homelessness.

UN Refugee Agency, "Key Figures." UN Refugee Agency. "Key Facts and Figures." Accessed September 13, 2024. https://www.unhcr.org/us/.

Urbach, *Sages*. Urbach, Ephraim E. *The Sages: Their Concepts and Beliefs*. 2nd ed. Translated by Israel Abrahams. 2 vols. Magnes Press, The Hebrew University, 1979.

US Department of Housing and Urban Development, "2023 Homelessness Report." US Department of Housing and Urban Development. "The 2023 Annual Homelessness Assessment Report (AHAR) to Congress." Accessed September 15, 2024. https://www.huduser.gov/portal/sites/default/files/pdf/2023-AHAR-Part-1.pdf.

US Department of State, "2018 Report." US Department of State. "2018 Report on International Religious Freedom: Democratic Republic of Congo." Accessed September 19, 2024. https://www.state.gov/reports/2018-report-on-international-religious-freedom/democratic-republic-of-the-congo/.

Usry and Keener, *Black Man's Religion*. Usry, Glenn J., and Craig S. Keener. *Black Man's Religion: Can Christianity Be Afrocentric?* InterVarsity, 1996.

Uwimana, *From Red Earth*. Uwimana, Denise. *From Red Earth: A Rwandan Story of Healing and Forgiveness*. Plough, 2019.

Vanek, *Abolitionist*. Vanek, John, ed. *The Essential Abolitionist: What You Need to Know About Human Trafficking and Modern Slavery*. Rev. ed. Daliwal Press, 2020.

Vasser, "Bodies." Vasser, Murray. "Bodies and Souls: The Case for Reading Revelation 18.13 as a Critique of the Slave Trade." *New Testament Studies* 64, no. 3 (2018): 397–409.

Veer, "Climate Change." Veer, Amruta. "Climate Change Exposes Bangladesh to Greater Risk." Johns Hopkins School of Advanced International Studies, Bologna Institute for Policy Research. Accessed August 4, 2024. https://bipr.jhu.edu/Blog Articles/31-Climate-Change-Exposes-Bangladesh-to-Greater-Risk.cfm.

Vineyard USA, "Core Beliefs." "Core Values and Beliefs." Vineyard USA. Accessed September 15, 2024. https://vineyardusa.org/about/core-values-beliefs/.

Voice of Martyrs, "50 Years." "Iran: 50 Years Since Seeds for the Gospel Were Planted." Voice of the Martyrs, November 21, 2019. Accessed September 15, 2024. https://www.icommittopray.com/request/1953/gladys-bliss/.

Voice of Martyrs, *Hearts of Fire.* Voice of the Martyrs. *Hearts of Fire: Eight Women in the Underground Church and Their Stories of Costly Faith.* VOM Books, 2015.

Voice of Martyrs, *Hearts of Fire 2.* Voice of the Martyrs. *Hearts of Fire 2: Twelve Inspiring Stories of Costly Faith from Today's Persecuted Christians.* VOM Books, 2023.

Voice of Martyrs, *I Am N.* Voice of the Martyrs with Mikal Keefer. *I Am N: Inspiring Stories of Christians Facing Islamic Extremists.* Rev. ed. Edited by Sheryl Martin Hash. VOM Books, 2024.

Voice of Martyrs, "Lion's Den." "Mozambique: In the Lion's Den." Voice of the Martyrs, March 3, 2023. https://vom.com.au/stories/mozambique-in-the-lions-den/.

Voice of Martyrs, "Nigerian Christian." "Nigerian Christian Shot in Face by Boko Haram, Survives Attack." Voice of the Martyrs, December 22, 2021. Accessed May 14, 2024. https://www.persecution.com/stories/nigerian-christian-shot-by -boko-haram/.

Voice of Martyrs, *Whom Shall I Fear?* Voice of the Martyrs with Mikal Keefer. *Whom Shall I Fear? 366 Scriptures for Following Christ and Facing Persecution.* Edited by Ethel Gould. VOM Books, 2023.

Vorm, *Lives.* Vorm, Dan. *If I Had Two Lives: The Extraordinary Life and Faith of Costas Macris.* Clovercroft, 2017.

Walker, "Where God Guides." Walker, Louise Jeter. "Where God Guides, He Provides." *Mountain Movers*, September 1992, 31.

Ward, *Famines.* Ward, Larry. *And There Will Be Famines.* Regal Books, G/L Publications, 1973.

Ward and Brownlee, *Rare Earth.* Ward, Peter D., and Donald Brownlee. *Rare Earth: Why Complex Life Is Uncommon in the Universe.* Copernicus, 2000.

Weber, "Cheeks." Weber, Jeremy. "No Cheeks Left to Turn: The Double Persecution of Africa's Largest Church." *Christianity Today*, October 19, 2018. Accessed September 11, 2024. https://www.christianitytoday.com/2018/10/nigeria-fulani-boko -haram-no-cheeks-left-to-turn/.

Wesley, *Church.* Wesley, Luke. *The Church in China: Persecuted, Pentecostal, and Powerful.* AJPS Books, 2004.

Whisenant, *Reasons*. Whisenant, Edgar. *88 Reasons Why the Rapture Could Be in 1988*. World Bible Society, 1988.

White, *Faith Under Fire*. White, Andrew. *Faith Under Fire: What the Middle East Conflict Has Taught Me About God*. Monarch, 2011.

Wholey, *Miracle of Change*. Wholey, Dennis. *The Miracle of Change: The Path to Self-Discovery and Spiritual Growth*. Simon & Schuster, 1998.

Wierwille, *Studies*. Wierwille, Victor Paul. *Studies in Human Suffering*. American Christian Press, 1971.

Wigger, *American Saint*. Wigger, John. *American Saint: Francis Asbury and the Methodists*. Oxford University Press, 2009.

Williams, *Black Americans and Evangelization*. Williams, Walter L. *Black Americans and the Evangelization of Africa, 1877–1900*. University of Wisconsin Press, 1982.

Williams, "Not Mine." Williams, Morris. "Not Mine, but Thine." *Pentecostal Evangel*, April 19, 1987, 22.

Williams, *Partnership*. Williams, Morris O. *Partnership in Mission: A Study of Theology and Method in Mission*. Morris Williams, 1986.

Williams, *Radical Reformation*. Williams, George Huntston. *The Radical Reformation*. Westminster, 1962.

Wiyono, "Timor Revival." Wiyono, Gani. "Timor Revival: A Historical Study of the Great Twentieth-Century Revival in Indonesia." *Asian Journal of Pentecostal Studies* 4, no. 2 (2001): 269–93.

Wolffe, *Expansion*. Wolffe, John. *The Expansion of Evangelicalism: The Age of Wilberforce, More, Chalmers, and Finney*. InterVarsity, 2007.

World Health Organization, "Child Mortality." "Child Mortality (Under 5 Years)." World Health Organization, January 28, 2022. https://www.who.int/news-room /fact-sheets/detail/levels-and-trends-in-child-under-5-mortality-in-2020.

World Health Organization, "Hunger Numbers 2022." "UN Report: Global Hunger Numbers Rose to as Many as 828 Million in 2021." World Health Organization, July 6, 2022. Accessed August 3, 2024. https://www.who.int/news/item/06-07-2022 -un-report--global-hunger-numbers-rose-to-as-many-as-828-million-in-2021.

World Health Organization, "Hunger Numbers 2024." "Hunger Numbers Stubbornly High for Three Consecutive Years as Global Crises Deepen: UN Report." World Health Organization, July 24, 2024. Accessed August 4, 2024. https://www.who .int/news/item/24-07-2024-hunger-numbers-stubbornly-high-for-three-consecutive -years-as-global-crises-deepen--un-report.

Wu, "Dora Yu." Wu, Silas H. L. "Dora Yu (1873–1931): Foremost Female Evangelist in Twentieth-Century Chinese Revivalism." In *Gospel Bearers, Gender Barriers: Missionary Women in the Twentieth Century*, edited by Dana L. Robert, 85–98. Orbis Books, 2002.

Wu, "Price." Wu, C. J. Interview with John Sanqiang Cao. "'I Knew I Would Pay a Price for My Faith': China Releases Missionary After Seven Years." *Christianity*

Today, May 10, 2024. https://www.christianitytoday.com/2024/05/john-cao-prison -china-missionary-myanmar-faith/.

Wunderink, "Worse." Wunderink, Susan. "Worse Than Ever." *Christianity Today*, November 2008, 15–16.

Wurmbrand, *Tortured for Christ*. Wurmbrand, Richard. *Tortured for Christ*. 50th anniv. ed. David C. Cook, 2017.

Wurmbrand, *Tortured for Christ* (2023). Wurmbrand, Richard. *Tortured for Christ*. VOM Books, 2023.

Wurmbrand, *Wife*. Wurmbrand, Sabina. *The Pastor's Wife*. VOM Books, 2023 (orig. 1970).

Xia, "Global Food Insecurity." Xia, Lili, et al. "Global Food Insecurity and Famine from Reduced Crop, Marine Fishery and Livestock Production due to Climate Disruption from Nuclear War Soot Injection." *Nature Food* 3, no. 8 (2022): 586–96.

Yamamori and Chan, *Witnesses*. Yamamori, Tetsunao, and Kim-kwong Chan. *Witnesses to Power: Stories of God's Quiet Work in a Changing China*. Paternoster, 2000.

Yancey, "Memories." Yancey, Philip. "Happy Memories of Bad Times." *Christianity Today*, March 8, 1993, 88.

Yancey, "Saturday." Yancey, Philip. "Saturday Seven Days a Week." *Christianity Today*, March 19, 1988, 64.

Yi, "My Declaration." Yi, Wang. "My Declaration of Faithful Disobedience." In *Faithful Disobedience: Writings on Church and State from a Chinese House Church Movement*, edited by Hannah Nation and J. D. Tseng, 221–27. IVP (also Center for House Church Theology from Urban China), 2022.

Yingqiang, "Face Persecution." Yingqiang, Li. "How Should the Church Face Persecution?" In *Faithful Disobedience: Writings on Church and State from a Chinese House Church Movement*, edited by Hannah Nation and J. D. Tseng, 228–30. IVP (also Center for House Church Theology from Urban China), 2022.

Young, "Miracles." Young, William. "Miracles in Church History." *Churchman* 102, no. 2 (1988): 102–21.

Young, *Walking*. Young, May. *Walking with God Through the Valley: Recovering the Purpose of Biblical Lament*. IVP Academic, 2025.

Yung, "Endued." Yung, Hwa. "Endued with Power: The Pentecostal-Charismatic Renewal and the Asian Church in the Twenty-First Century." *Asian Journal of Pentecostal Studies* 6, no. 1 (2003): 63–82.

Zhaoming, "Chinese Denominations." Zhaoming, Deng. "Indigenous Chinese Pentecostal Denominations." In *Asian and Pentecostal: The Charismatic Face of Christianity in Asia*, edited by Allan Anderson and Edmond Tang, 437–66. Regnum Studies in Mission. Regnum, 2005.

Zurlo, *Global Christianity*. Zurlo, Gina A. *Global Christianity: A Guide to the World's Largest Religion from Afghanistan to Zimbabwe*. Zondervan Academic, 2022.

INDEX OF SCRIPTURE AND OTHER ANCIENT WRITINGS

"I cannot recommend this book highly enough. Everybody should read it, whether Christian or non-Christian, whether charismatic or non-charismatic. It shook me, showing me not only how little I know but also how little I have suffered. This book shows how any measure of suffering for Jesus is worth all the pain. Craig Keener is a scholar's scholar but writes with the kind of simplicity and urgency that will grip you no end. No one will be the same after reading this book."

—**Dr. R. T. Kendall**, former Senior Minister,
Westminster Chapel (1977–2002)

"*Suffering: Its Meaning for the Spirit-Filled Life* is a wonderful resource that teaches us how to endure trial, persecution, and suffering. It is packed full of insights from Scripture along with difficult but profound stories of those who have given their lives for the sake of the gospel. I'm so thankful for the sanctified brilliance of Craig Keener, on display once again in this most valuable book. May we all be filled with courage and give Jesus our absolute yes—no matter what."

—**Bill Johnson**, senior leader, Bethel Church, Redding, California; author of
Removing the Sting of Death and *God Is Good*

"The subject of suffering needs to be studied, taught, and kept on the front burner of our faith. Many have lost their way from God for want of biblical teaching on the subject. This book is a significant contribution in this area. After comprehensive discussions on the teachings of Jesus relating to suffering and persecution, the author gives well-documented and sometimes graphic descriptions of the torture and killing of thousands of Christians from around the world. Many of these examples have never been reported by the Western press or admitted to by Western governments. All, however, bear witness to my own long-standing maxim: We have a gospel worth living for and a gospel worth dying for."

—**Most Rev. Dr. Benjamin A. Kwashi**, former archbishop of the
Ecclesiastical Province of Jos in the Anglican Church of Nigeria

"Craig Keener is one of the kindest and humblest men I've ever met, who just so happens to be a brilliant Bible scholar. His wisdom is riddled with Jesus-shaped compassion, which makes him a trustworthy shepherd to follow into the sober subject matter of suffering. His exegesis of Scripture and the experiences he relates from the milieu of human hardship prove that getting the life we hoped for is not a sustainable source of peace, contentment, and joy. Instead, our Savior's presence in those moments we *didn't hope for* is what gives us peace beyond our understanding, contentment in the midst of chaos, and joy even when our eyes are wet with tears. This book is a necessary treasure."

—**Lisa Harper**, author, Bible teacher, and host of the
Back Porch Theology podcast

"Dr. Keener describes how those who have come before us answered the call to follow Christ—regardless of the obstacles and hardship—and how their lives beckon us to imitate their faith. In *Suffering: Its Meaning for the Spirit-Filled Life*, we are given the courage to not shrink back in fear but to boldly advance the kingdom of God with a fresh faith that rejoices in the privilege of suffering for the sake of the name of Jesus."

—**Rice Broocks**, cofounder, Every Nation Churches and Ministries

"Craig Keener's new book, *Suffering*, is a much-needed addition to the Pentecostal and Charismatic movement in the world. It is biblical, historical, and full of contemporary examples of Christian suffering. I highly recommend it for pastors, denominational leaders, and apostolic overseers. I recommend it for any Christian seeking a solid biblical theology that reflects the now and the not yet of the biblical understanding of the kingdom of God. The book is written to appeal to both the popular audience and the academic audience, though it is written with intentionality so as not to discourage non-academics."

—**Randy Clark**, overseer of the Apostolic Network of Global Awakening;
president, Global Awakening Theological Seminary